Tolley's Data Protection Handbook

by

Susan Singleton
Singletons
www.singlelaw.com

Tolley
LexisNexis™

Members of the LexisNexis Group worldwide

United Kingdom	Butterworths Tolley, a Division of Reed Elsevier (UK) Ltd, 2 Addiscombe Road, CROYDON CR9 5AF
Argentina	Abeledo Perrot, Jurisprudencia Argentina and Depalma, BUENOS AIRES
Australia	Butterworths, a Division of Reed International Books Australia Pty Ltd, CHATSWOOD, New South Wales
Austria	ARD Betriebsdienst and Verlag Orac, VIENNA
Canada	Butterworths Canada Ltd, MARKHAM, Ontario
Chile	Publitecsa and Conosur Ltda, SANTIAGO DE CHILE
Czech Republic	Orac sro, PRAGUE
France	Editions du Juris-Classeur SA, PARIS
Hong Kong	Butterworths Asia (Hong Kong), HONG KONG
Hungary	Hvg Orac, BUDAPEST
India	Butterworths India, NEW DELHI
Ireland	Butterworths (Ireland) Ltd, DUBLIN
Italy	Giuffré, Milan
Malaysia	Malayan Law Journal Sdn Bhd, KUALA LUMPUR
New Zealand	Butterworths of New Zealand, WELLINGTON
Poland	Wydawnictwa Prawnicze PWN, WARSAW
Singapore	Butterworths Asia, SINGAPORE
South Africa	Butterworths Publishers (Pty) Ltd, DURBAN
Switzerland	Stämpfli Verlag AG, BERNE
USA	LexisNexis, DAYTON, Ohio

A CIP Catalogue record for this book is available from the British Library.

ISBN 0 75451 242 8

Typeset by Columns Design Ltd, Reading, England
Printed and bound in Great Britain by The Cromwell Press, Trowbridge, Wiltshire

Visit Butterworths LexisNexis *direct* at www.butterworths.com

To my children, Rachel, Rebecca, Ben, Sam and Jo,
whose use and abuse of the Internet
has thrown up many an interesting data protection problem.

Introduction

Data protection legislation is relevant to most UK businesses and institutions. One of the greatest advantages of the PC and the Internet is the ease of access to, and ability to use, personal data in all its forms. However, many are concerned about the use of their data. This A–Z Handbook aims to provide practical advice to UK businesses and institutions on compliance with UK data protection legislation, principally in the *Data Protection Act 1998*. The Act came into force on 1 March 2000 and has given a right of subject access to all manual data since the first transitional period expired on 24 October 2001. It is therefore a very timely moment in which to publish the first edition of this annually updated book.

Individuals have widely different views on privacy issues. The legislation tries to achieve a fair compromise between freedom of expression and rights of privacy. An important practical consideration is ease of access to information. Often information has been available publicly for years, but has been difficult to access. Allowing access over the Internet means that in practice availability is hugely eased. Data protection implications then arise.

In advising clients in my commercial law practice, the greatest wisdom one gains, after nearly 20 years in the City and running one's own practice, is not knowledge of the law (which should be taken as read), but the ability to advise commercially and provide practical solutions – pragmatism and risk analysis. Applying this to the data protection area is particularly difficult. Those seeking to advise corporate directors of the seriousness with which data protection should be taken are not helped by the few prosecutions and low level of fines. However, there are certainly investigations each year, and a number of cases are settled without enforcement proceedings being launched. Consequently, for some businesses which handle large amounts of data, or in bigger companies with a high profile, complete compliance must be the aim.

Clearly it is necessary to notify (register) where personal data is held, and there are criminal penalties and fines for breach, but ensuring basic compliance should not be complicated or expensive for most companies. They need to understand that the legislation is in places overly complicated; no one knows with certainty what all its provisions mean and they should put such reasonable resources as they have into compliance without worrying unnecessarily over this legislative area. Breach of data protection legislation is not a major concern or risk area for most businesses. However a public breach, a security glitch, a difficult customer making public complaints, can result in appalling and very damaging publicity for bigger companies, so where possible procedures should be put in place to minimise the risk of such problems arising.

Increasingly in my practice jurisdictional issues are to the fore. For example the data may be in the US. It is used in the UK at a call centre, processed cheaply in India or the client runs an Internet betting operation in an offshore tax haven and ships personal data around. The EU/US Safe Harbor Agreement has not at the date of writing been adopted with much enthusiasm – only a handful of companies have taken part. As with many areas of E-commerce law, what is really needed is international harmonisation.

Now that the 1998 Act is in place a period of relative calm may ensue in the relevant legislative arena. However, those involved with financial services will need to take note of new EU legislative changes in the data protection area, and at the time of writing the Commissioner has still not finalised her important Code of Practice for employer and employees, after a draft in 2000 was heavily criticised. Finally, case law under the 1998 Act is needed to aid those interpreting what at times seem very unclear provisions in certain important areas. Details of the Robertson v Wakefield City Council decision (November 2001) were becoming available as the book went to press. It was a decision applying human rights legislation to an individual's right to register to vote without his details being used for commercial purposes once his name has appeared on the electoral roll and which also held that the 1998 Act did not properly implement the Data Protection Directive. It followed closely on the heels of the decision in Baker (October 2001) holding blanket exemption on the grounds of national security did not necessarily apply.

For human resources managers, data protection officers and similar staff, the day-to-day issues of data protection are more mundane. This book seeks to provide practical advice on the major topics in an accessible A–Z format. As it will be updated annually, readers are invited to e-mail suggestions for improvements to me at the address below.

Susan Singleton
Singletons
The Ridge
South View Road
Pinner
Middlesex
HA5 3YD
Tel: 020 8866 1934
Fax: 020 8429 9212
E-mail: susan@singlelaw.com
www.singlelaw.com
21 November 2001

Contents

1 – Automated Decision-taking

At a glance **1.1**

- ✓ Decisions made about individuals, particularly employees, by automated means can lead to injustices. The *Data Protection Act 1998* (*DPA 1998*) includes protection where 'automated decision-taking' takes place.
- ✓ Individuals may, by written notice, require a data controller to ensure that no decision which significantly affects them is taken based solely on the processing by automatic means of their personal data (*DPA 1998, s 12*).
- ✓ Upon request, an individual has a right to be told the 'logic' behind a decision taken by these means (*DPA 1998, s 7*).
- ✓ Where a decision is taken about an individual based on automated means, and the individual has not served such a notice, then the data controller must notify the individual that such a decision has been taken as soon as is reasonably practicable.

Introduction **1.2**

Section 12 of *DPA 1998* gives examples of personal data processing which may significantly affect the individual, where processing by automated means is the sole way of evaluating a data subject as to their:

- performance at work;
- creditworthiness;
- reliability; and
- conduct.

Normally, appraisal of an individual will be based on non-automated means. For example, checking the speed with which supermarket checkout employees scan goods is usually done by automated means, whereas assessing that person on whether they have a good manner with customers and wear appropriate clothes to work is not. Assessing workers simply by checking whether they have clocked into work on time is automated means, whereas using other factors alone or in conjunction with this factor would be outside the scope of *section 12* of *DPA 1998*. The provisions of *section 12* are based on *Article 15* of the *Data Protection Directive (95/46/EC)* which *DPA 1998* implements.

Example: Shortlisting for a job 1.3

The shortlisting of those applying for a job based only on the evaluation of an applicant's attributes by automated means must safeguard applicants' interests. This will be the case if an applicant is rejected or treated in a way that is significantly different from other applicants solely as a result of an automated process. According to the Information Commissioner (previously known as the Data Protection Commissioner) (see CHAPTER 3 COMMISSIONER/REGISTRAR) it will not be the case if the automated process merely provides information (for example a score resulting from a psychometric test that is just one of a range of factors taken into account in a human decision). However, any automated system must process information about individuals fairly. In the Draft Code of Practice on the Use of Personal Data in Employer/Employee Relationships the Commissioner suggests the following standards.

Standards

- Ensure that shortlisting is carried out in a way which produces results that are objective, consistent and fair to applicants (implying the drawing up and use of criteria for assessing applications) (Principle 1).
- Only use an automated system in shortlisting if the system can be demonstrated to produce results that are objective, consistent and fair to applicants (Principle 1).
- Where an automated system using some form of evaluation is used as the sole basis for a decision to reject an applicant, inform the applicant that an automated system has been used, give the applicant an opportunity to make representations, and consider these representations before a final decision is reached (Principle 6).

Data subject notice 1.4

Individuals are allowed, within 21 days of receipt of the data controller's notice, to serve a 'data subject notice' requiring the data controller to reconsider the decision taken or to take a new decision. Within 21 days of receipt of a data subject notice the data controller must give the individual a written notice specifying the steps they intend to take to comply with the data subject notice.

Exempt decisions 1.5

Certain decisions are excluded from these provisions (*DPA 1998, ss 12(5)–(7)*). These can be set out in an order of the Secretary of State (none have been drafted at the time of writing).

An exempt decision can also occur where a decision is made during steps taken when considering to enter into a contract with the data subject, either with a view to entering such a contract, in the course of performing such a contract, or where authorised or required to do so under an enactment.

However, the contracts and other exemptions above will not apply unless the effect of the decision is to grant a request of the data subject, or steps have been taken to safeguard the legitimate interests of the data subject, for example by letting them make representations.

Exemption conditions 1.6

The conditions for exemption are:

(*a*) the decision must be taken in the course of steps taken:

- (i) for the purpose of considering whether to enter into a contract with the data subject,
- (ii) with a view to entering into such a contract, or
- (iii) in the course of performing such a contract; or

(*b*) the decision must be authorised or required by or under any enactment.

In addition, either:

- the effect of the decision must be to grant a request of the data subject; or
- steps must have been taken to safeguard the legitimate interests of the data subject (for example, by allowing them to make representations).

Examples of exemptions 1.7

The relationship between employees and employers is contractual, and automated decision-taking in that area is likely to be an exempt decision as long as an unsuccessful employee or potential employee has a right of appeal or a right to make representations in some other effective way. The following examples are given by the Commissioner in the Draft Code of Practice on the Use of Personal Data in Employer/Employee Relationships.

(*a*) An employer places the educational qualifications of job applicants into categories and then enters these into a computer system which produces a score for each applicant. Only those applicants with a score of 25 or over are shortlisted. This is an automated decision but, provided safeguards are in place for those not shortlisted, it is an exempt decision as it is taken for the purpose of considering whether to enter into a contract of employment with the applicant. Safeguards would be notifying applicants that an automated process is to be or has been used, giving them an opportunity to state why they should be considered separately and, if the case is valid, doing so.

(*b*) An employer produces a bulletin on its pension scheme with background information for those approaching retirement age. The system is programmed to send the bulletin to all those employees who are likely to receive a pension of more than £10,000 per year and are aged over 60. The decision on who receives the bulletin and who does not falls outside the specific requirements on automated decision-taking because although it is automated, it only affects the provision of background information and not benefits. It does not significantly affect employees.

(*c*) An employer has a system that scans application forms. The employer asks applicants on the form what the minimum starting salary is they would accept. The system automatically rejects those applicants that put more than £50,000 per year. The decision falls outside the specific provisions on automated decision taking because it is not based on an evaluation of matters relating to the individual of the type referred to in *DPA 1998*.

Positive decisions in respect of an application for a product or services are an example of one category of exempt decision. A lender operating a credit scoring system will fall within the exemption in many cases and be allowed to take a decision on that basis. The application has been made at the data subject's request.

In their documentation data controllers may want to add that they use automated processing to decide whether to enter into a contract with an individual.

Court orders 1.8

A court, on application by the data subject, and where the person taking the decision ('the responsible person') has not complied with the requirements, can order the responsible person to reconsider their decision. No such order will affect the rights of any person other than the data subject and the responsible person.

An application for a *DPA 1998, section 12* order may be made where the data controller has failed to notify the data subject that the decision was taken by automated means, or where the individual was not given 21 days to give notice to require the data controller to reconsider the decision or reach a different decision.

Generally, individuals are entitled to claim compensation from data controllers where *DPA 1998* has been contravened and the individual has suffered damage or damage and distress.

'Logic' 1.9

Section 7 of *DPA 1998* provides that where an individual's personal data will be processed by automatic means in order to evaluate matters relating to him or her (such as performance at work, creditworthiness, reliability or conduct), and this will constitute or be likely to constitute the sole basis for any decision which significantly affects that person, they are entitled to be informed by the data controller 'of the logic involved in that decision-taking'.

This means that when individuals make subject access requests they are entitled to be told of the logic involved in any automated decision-making that comes within the scope of these provisions and affects or is likely to affect them. An employer need not provide the information in response to a broader subject access request unless it is referred to in the request. If it is the subject of a separate request, a separate fee can be charged. An employer is not required to provide information in response that constitutes a trade secret.

The use of the word 'logic' is unusual in a statute, as it is not defined. Presumably it can be interpreted as meaning 'reasons'. Under *section 7(2)* of *DPA 1998,* however, there is no need to provide this information unless the individual has made a request in writing and paid the relevant fee. Regulations may also deal with this area but have not yet been drafted.

Regulation 3 of the *Data Protection (Subject Access) (Fees and Miscellaneous Provisions) Regulations 2000* (*SI 2000/191*) provides that the maximum such fee is £10.

The Commissioner says:

> 'Neither the term "logic" nor the term "trade secret" is defined. The Commissioner takes the view that an employer is required to provide an explanation that enables the individual to understand the sorts of factors taken into account in the discussion and the way in which they are evaluated and translated into the decision. However, the employer is not required to give matters such as the precise weighting given to each factor which either the system supplier or the employer would reasonably want to keep secret from a competitor on the basis that it provides it with a significant competitive advantage.'

In respect of this right to information the Commissioner proposes the following standard.

Standards 1.10

- Ensure that on request, promptly, and in any event within 40 days, employees are provided with a statement of how any automated decision-making process to which they are subject works. Include sufficient explanation for them to understand the range of factors taken into account and the way they are assessed without revealing 'trade secrets' of those who design or supply the systems (Principle 6).

  (Draft Code of Practice on the Use of Personal Data in Employer/ Employee Relationships, 2000 version.)

Action list 1.11

Businesses need to ensure the following in all areas of their business.

(*a*) Whether they do assess people by automated means only. In many cases such means are just one of a number of factors therefore *section 12* of *DPA 1998* will not apply.

(*b*) Whether they notify individuals in accordance with *section 12* of *DPA 1998* if they do assess by automated means.

(*c*) Keep a register of decisions made by automated means. This will allow individuals who have objected to these means to be noted.

(*d*) Ensure individuals are given the right to object as required by the legislation. A system should be set up to handle *section 12* notices which can operate across the whole business.

(*e*) Keep a register of individuals' applications for such decisions to be reconsidered.

(*f*) Change terms and conditions of contract with customers etc. so that sufficient protection is included to ensure, where possible, the decision becomes an exempt decision.

(*g*) Check whether an exemption might apply, e.g. someone may be assessed by automated means in order to decide whether to hire them as an employee. This may be exempt under *section 12(4)* of *DPA 1998* due to the provisions of *section 12(6)* and *(7)* of *DPA 1998*.

2 – CCTV

At a glance 2.1

- ✓ Closed circuit television often involves recordings of individuals and their movements. These are 'personal data' (*Data Protection Directive (95/46/EC), Article 14*).
- ✓ The Information Commissioner has issued a Code of Practice on CCTV (July 2000) which sets out what those operating CCTV systems must do to ensure compliance with the *Data Protection Act 1998* (*DPA 1998*), including in many cases putting up warning notices to tell people they are being recorded.
- ✓ Employers should also pay regard to the CCTV sections of the Draft Code of Practice on the Use of Personal Data in Employer/Employee Relationships when it is finalised.

Recording and use of personal data 2.2

Closed circuit television (CCTV) involves the recording and use of personal data about individuals. CCTV pictures of individuals are defined as 'personal data' under *DPA 1998*. *Article 14* of the *Data Protection Directive* (*95/46/EC*) provides that the Directive applies to 'the techniques used to capture, transmit, record, store or communicate sound and image data relating to natural persons'.

Therefore, those using CCTV (such as employers and those with business premises who record customers and others inside and outside those premises) need to ensure they comply with *DPA 1998* in their use of such systems. It is important that individuals are told they are being recorded by displaying a notice in the shop, office or other premises as necessary.

Code of Practice 2.3

The Information Commissioner's Code of Practice on CCTV (July 2000), made under *section 51(3)(b)* of *DPA 1998*, gives guidance on how to ensure compliance with *DPA 1998* with respect to such systems. Ideally, those charged with ensuring legal compliance in this area should read and follow the detailed guidance. The Code of Practice is not intended to apply to 'targeted and intrusive surveillance activities' covered by the provisions of the *Regulation of Investigatory Powers Act 2000*, meaning the use of surveillance techniques by employers to monitor their employees' compliance with their contracts of employment. This will be covered by the Draft Code of Practice on the Use of Personal Data in Employer/Employee Relationships considered at 2.4 below. The Code of Practice on CCTV does not cover security equipment installed in homes for security purposes or use of cameras for journalism or media purposes.

Advice to employers 2.4

The Draft Code of Practice on the Use of Personal Data in Employer/Employee Relationships, due to be finalised in 2001/2002, provides guidance on both video and audio monitoring of employees. The Information Commissioner believes that continuous monitoring by either video or audio equipment is 'particularly intrusive for employees'. Employers should not, therefore, routinely engage in this practice unless there are particular safety or security risks that cannot be properly addressed in less intrusive ways.

> 'Covert monitoring will only be justified in specific cases where openness would prejudice the prevention or detection of crime or the apprehension of offenders.'

The Information Commissioner has proposed draft standards (set out at 2.5 below) in this area in the Draft Code of Practice on the Use of Personal Data in Employer/Employee Relationships.

Standards – video and audio monitoring 2.5

- In assessing whether the adverse impact of video or audio monitoring is out of proportion to the benefits, bear in mind that such routine monitoring is only likely to be justified where there are particular safety or security risks that cannot be adequately addressed in other less intrusive ways (Principle 1).
- In this assessment treat video and audio capability separately. Cases where both video and audio monitoring are justified are likely to be extremely rare (Principles 1 and 2).
- Ensure that if people other than employees, such as visitors, are likely to be caught by video or audio monitoring they are

made aware that it is in operation and the purposes for which the information will be used (Principle 1).

- Do not install covert video or audio monitoring unless the standards set out in section 6.2 [a reference to an earlier paragraph in the draft Guidance] are met. Even then, do not install it in locations where individuals have a reasonable expectation of privacy, for example in cloakrooms, vehicles, or to monitor individuals in their private offices. If monitoring in such locations is justified, the police should be involved (Principle 1).

Sample form – CCTV requests 2.6

Employers should ensure that whenever someone asks to view CCTV pictures they keep a record of the request and who has obtained the data. This record might be kept along the following lines.

Name of person requesting the footage:
Address:
Tel:
Fax:
E-mail:
Identification obtained from person named above to verify identity:
Legal basis on which information released:
Reason for request:
Manner in which footage was viewed and if tapes returned:

The Commissioner says that recorded images should not be made widely available, for example routinely making them available to the media or putting them on the Internet. There may be a case to disguise or blur some pictures.

Code of Practice 2.7

The draft advice to employers at 2.5 above is short. For more thorough guidance on CCTV under *DPA 1998*, the general guidance in this area in the first Code of Practice on CCTV issued by the Information

Commissioner should be considered.(A copy of the Code of Practice appears in APPENDIX 1.)

Initial assessment 2.8

The Commissioner advises that before CCTV or similar equipment is used it should be established who will be responsible for it, whether it is appropriate to use it at all and the reasons for doing so. Ideally the assessment process should be documented, including reasons behind any decisions made. The appointment of the data controller, indicating that they will be holding personal data, should be registered with the Information Commissioner. The purposes for which the equipment should be used should also be covered. Ideally security and disclosure policies should also be documented.

Siting cameras 2.9

The way in which images are captured must comply with the First Data Protection Principle. The equipment should only monitor those areas intended to be monitored, although sometimes it is difficult not to record adjoining areas. In the Code of Practice on CCTV the Information Commissioner refers to recording back gardens of neighbouring premises and states that neighbours should be consulted in advance.

In addition, operators of the equipment should not be able to alter the areas covered to examine other areas.

Examples 2.10

The following are examples of common situations that can occur due to the placement of CCTV cameras.

Sunbathing 2.11

The Commissioner states that 'individuals sunbathing in their back gardens may have a greater expectation of privacy than individuals mowing the lawn of their front garden'.

ATMs 2.12

In some cases it may be appropriate for the equipment 'to be used to protect the safety of individuals when using ATMs, but images of PIN numbers, balance enquiries etc. should not be captured'.

Signs used **2.13**

Importantly, signs should be placed so that the public are aware that they are entering a CCTV zone, in order to comply with the First Principle. A sign at the entrance to a building society office may only need to be A4 size as it would be at eye level for all those entering the building. However, in car parks the size should be larger, such as A3, in order for them to be viewed by someone from their car.

Information on the sign **2.14**

The following information should be included on the sign:

- identity of person responsible for the scheme;
- purpose of the scheme; and
- details of whom to contact.

Recommended wording **2.15**

The Information Commissioner's recommended wording for the notice (where no image of a camera appears on the sign) is:

> 'Images are being monitored for the purposes of crime prevention and public safety. This scheme is controlled by the Greentown Safety Partnership. For further information contact 01234 567 890'.

Where there is an image of a camera on the sign the following wording is recommended:

> 'This scheme is controlled by the Greentown Safety Partnership. For further information contact 01234 567 890'.

Ocassionally, there may be exceptional and limited cases where the use of signs is not appropriate. For example, where specific criminal activity has been identified, surveillance is needed to obtain evidence and signs would prejudice the success of the operation. Even in such a case, the surveillance must not take place over a longer period than is necessary to obtain the evidence. The Code of Practice on CCTV, Part II, section 3(e) sets out when the requirement for signs may be set aside. *Section 29(1)* of *DPA 1998* allows the processing of data to prevent crime to be excluded from the First Principle and this might be used in such cases where no sign appears.

Quality of images 2.16

The Information Commissioner gives guidance in the Code of Practice on CCTV on the need to ensure that the quality of the images is accurate, and that good quality tapes are used etc. If the system is to detect crime, obviously faces should be identifiable. If the system is in place to monitor traffic flow, for example, then cameras should not capture details of the drivers of vehicles. Sometimes an automatic facial recognition system is used to match images captured against a database of images. To ensure compliance with the Third and Fourth Data Protection Principles the sets of images must be clear enough to ensure an accurate match. In poorly lit areas infra red equipment may need to be installed.

Ideally a maintenance log of the system should be kept.

Processing the images 2.17

The images must not be kept for longer than is necessary. In an example given by the Commissioner in the guidance, a publican may only need to keep recorded images for seven days (as they will generally be aware, should a brawl occur in their public house, as soon as the fight has started). Images of town centres and streets may not need to be kept for longer than 31 days, unless required as evidence in court proceedings. Images at ATMs may need to be kept for three months to resolve customer disputes about cash withdrawls. This period is based on the length of time it takes individuals to receive bank statements, states the Commissioner.

If images are kept for evidential purposes then they should be securely stored.

Access to and disclosure of images to third parties 2.18

The Commissioner proposes standards in the Code of Practice on CCTV relating to third party access to, and disclosure of, images. Only those staff who need access to achieve the purpose for which the footage was obtained should have access, and access should be documented to ensure compliance with the Seventh Data Protection Principle.

Access by data subjects 2.19

Those filmed may wish to view themselves and can make a subject access request in that regard under *section 8* of *DPA 1998*. The Commissioner recommends the following.

'Data subjects should be provided with a standard subject access request form which:

(1) indicates the information required in order to locate the images requested;

(For example: an individual may have to provide dates and times of when they visited the premises of the user of the equipment.)

(2) indicates the information required in order to identify the person making the request;

(For example: if the individual making the request is unknown to the user of the equipment, a photograph of the individual may be requested in order to locate the correct image.)

(3) indicates the fee that will be charged for carrying out the search for the images requested – a maximum of £10 may be charged for the search;

(4) asks whether the individual would be satisfied with merely viewing the images recorded;

(5) indicates that the response will be provided promptly and in any event within 40 days of receiving the required fee and information; and

(6) explains the rights provided by *DPA 1998*.'

Individuals could be given a leaflet which describes the images being recorded. It may be necessary to hire an editing company to edit the tape to provide the relevant extract. If this is done then contract guarantees about confidentiality will need to be included as provided in the Code of Practice on CCTV.

It is important to ensure that images of other people are not disclosed in responding to a subject access request. The Code of Practice on CCTV, Part II, section 4 deals with this. If the individual will not be able to identify the other individual from the information given then it can be provided. It may also be provided where the other individual has consented, or it is reasonable in all the circumstances to comply with a request without the consent of the other person. Under *section 29* of *DPA 1998* (the 'criminal exemption') it may be reasonable to refuse a subject access request for footage where the information is held for the prevention or detection of crime or apprehension or prosecution of offenders.

Further information 2.20

The British Standards Institute's *BS 7958: 1991 – Closed Circuit Television (CCTV) – Management and Operation – Code of Practice* provides guidance on issues of security, tape management etc. and is referred to in the Information Commissioner's guidance on CCTV.

The Information Commissioner's Code of Practice For Users of CCTV under *DPA 1998* is under 'Codes of Practice' on the Data Protection website (www.dataprotection.gov.uk) and is reproduced in APPENDIX 1.

3 – Codes of Practice

At a glance 3.1

- ✓ Under *section 51* of the *Data Protection Act 1998* (*DPA 1998*), the Commissioner is charged with issuing codes of good practice to be followed by data controllers.
- ✓ A Code of Practice on CCTV has been issued and draft codes proposed in areas such as employer/employee relationships.
- ✓ In addition, the Commissioner comments on proposed general legislation which may have data protection implications.
- ✓ Three Codes of Practice have been proposed under the *Regulation of Investigatory Powers Act 2000.*
- ✓ The Commissioner, under *section 51(4)* of *DPA 1998* has a duty to encourage trade associations to bring out their own codes and to comment thereon.
- ✓ Codes in the financial services sector, on direct marketing, factors, fire officers, the Church of England, the Office of National Statistics and the General Medical Council have been issued.

Introduction 3.2

The Information Commissioner has a duty under *section 51* of *DPA 1998* to promote the following of good practice by data controllers. *Section 51(2)* of *DPA 1998* provides that she may arrange the dissemination of information as appears expedient to give information:

> '…to the public about the operation of [the Act], about good practice and about other matters within the scope of [her] functions under [the] Act, and may give advice to any person as to any of those matters'.

In her First Annual Report (June 2001) the Commissioner wrote:

> 'Codes of Practice do not add to the regulatory burden, nor go beyond the requirements of the law already in place. Their aim is further to explain the interpretation which this Office (as regulator) is taking of the requirements of *DPA 1998*'.

Good practice 3.3

When new legislation is proposed the Commissioner will often comment on any adverse data protection implications. The Commissioner's general duty is to encourage good practice.

Definition of good practice 3.4

The Codes of Practice should set out good practice. *Section 51(9)* of *DPA 1998* defines good practice as:

> '…such practice in the processing of personal data as appears to the Commissioner to be desirable having regard to the interests of data subjects and others, and includes (but is not limited to) compliance with the requirements of this Act'.

Factors in encouraging good practice 3.5

In considering the encouragement of good practice, the following factors are relevant.

- ***Transparency***: that except in cases where it would be 'prejudicial to the prevention and detection of crime or the collection of taxes, data subjects should be fully informed of the uses to which their personal data may be put'.
- ***Fairness***: that personal data should be processed in a way which is fair to data subjects. The Commissioner states that 'although fairness may be difficult to define in precise terms, clearly it is a concept which embraces the notion of equity and is opposed to action which is discriminatory'.
- ***Purpose limitation***: having collected information for specified purposes, that information should not be used or disclosed for other purposes (once again except in cases where there is prejudice to the prevention and detection of crime or the collection of taxes).
- ***Security***: ensuring that data are stored in a manner appropriate to the sensitivity of those data and are not disclosed to others.

Commenting on proposed legislation 3.6

Set out below are four recent examples of the Commissioner commenting on or criticising proposed legislation. This is likely to be more common than the issuing of formal Codes of Practice.

(*a*) The draft *Nursing and Midwifery Order 2001* envisaged a public register of nurses and midwives including their home addresses, which the Commissioner said would not be compliant with *DPA 1998*.

(*b*) *Social Security Fraud Act 2001* (*SSFA 2001*) – here the Commissioner considered that the objectives of the Department of Social Security could be achieved by less intrusive means than were set out in the Social Security Fraud Bill. The Act provides that where benefit fraud is suspected, investigating officers can ask organisations to provide them with any information for the purpose of the prevention and detection of crime (under the exemption to data protection legislation set out in *DPA 1998, s 29*). However, they cannot compel organisations to provide information under the exemption.

In the explanatory notes to *SSFA 2001* the Department of Trade and Industry states that 'Many organisations are bound by a duty of confidentiality to their customers and are therefore uncertain whether they should provide information on this basis. Consequently, investigating officers obtain very little information in this way.' The Commissioner reports in her First Annual Report (June 2001) that she was pleased to see the Government take account of these comments by way of amendment before the Bill became enacted.

(*c*) *Criminal Justice and Police Act 2001* (*CJPA 2001*)– here, as with *SSFA 2001*, the Commissioner commented on the proposed legislation. *Section 51* of *CJPA 2001* gives powers to seize equipment such as personal computers which might contain personal data and *section 82* of *CJPA 2001* provides restrictions on the use and destruction of fingerprints and samples which may have data protection implications.

(*d*) Before the enactment of the *Health and Social Care Act 2001* (*HSCA 2001*), it was subject to criticism and comment by the Commissioner. *Section 60* of *HSCA 2001* concerns the control of patient information. It enables the Secretary of State to require or permit patient information to be shared for medical purposes where he considers that this is in the interests of improving patient care or in the public interest.

In May 2001 the Commissioner issued Draft Guidance on the Use and Disclosure of Medical Data.

The issuing of Codes of Practice 3.7

Where the Commissioner thinks it appropriate or the Secretary of State directs by order, the Commissioner shall prepare Codes of Practice for guidance as to good practice and disseminate them to those people she considers appropriate.

It is such Codes, enacted under *section 51(3)* of *DPA 1998,* which are considered in this chapter. The Codes should be produced 'after such consultation with trade associations, data subjects or persons representing data subjects' as the Commissioner deems appropriate. There are also duties on the Commissioner in *section 51(6)* of *DPA 1998* to disseminate information about EU decisions.

If the Secretary of State has ordered the production of the Code, which is unlikely to occur often, then the Code of Practice resulting from that exercise must under *section 52(3)* of *DPA 1998* be laid before each House of Parliament.

Codes have long been issued in the data protection field, including under the *Data Protection Act 1984* (*DPA 1984*).

The usefulness of Codes of Practice 3.8

In her invitation to tender document (August 2001) the Commissioner implicitly recognises the fact that Codes of Practice can entrench 'one time interpretation', by suggesting that Part II of the Draft Code of Practice on the Use of Personal Data in Employer/Employee Relationships should perhaps exist as a web-based reference document only and be updated regularly as and when the Commissioner's interpretation of the law develops. This would accommodate the problem of changes in interpretation.

Invitation to tender 3.9

A lot of work goes into producing a Code of Practice so it is not surprising that not many have been issued. On the second proposed code (the first was the Code of Practice on CCTV) the Commissioner, having produced a draft which was much criticised, put out an invitation to tender for help in finalising the code (the Draft Code of Practice on the Use of Personal Data in Employer/Employee Relationships).

Trade associations 3.10

Trade associations are defined in *section 51(9)* of *DPA 1998* as 'includes any body representing data controllers'.

Practical advice 3.11

Codes of Practice should be contrasted with the guidance which the Commissioner issues in a number of areas which is not subject to the provisions of *section 51* of *DPA 1998*. However, for practical purposes the effect is the same – businesses and others are provided with advice on how the Commissioner views particular areas or practices under *DPA 1998* and can act accordingly.

In either case the Commissioner may be wrong in her interpretation of the law and the Codes could be legally challenged in appropriate cases. However, the cautious data controller will seek to operate in accordance with all relevant codes and guidance.

Issued Codes of Practice 3.12

The Commissioner has so far proposed two Codes of Practice: the Code of Practice on CCTV and the Draft Code of Practice on the Use of Personal Data in Employer/Employee Relationships.

Code of Practice on CCTV 3.13

The Code of Practice on CCTV was the first Code of Practice to be issued by the Commissioner under *DPA 1998*. It was issued in July 2000 after a consultation related to CCTV (see CHAPTER 2 CCTV).

Draft Code on the Use of Personal Data in Employer/Employee Relationships 3.14

In late 2000 the Commissioner issued a Draft Code on the Use of Personal Data in Employer/Employee Relationships. This was heavily criticised by employers in many areas and, illustrating how important the consultation process is, the Commissioner has agreed to make major revisions before the Code is finally released in 2001/2002. In response to criticism of the Code the put out an invitation to tender for assistance with this (see 3.9 above).

The Commissioner said:

> 'Many of the responses suggested that the draft code was over long, unduly complex and difficult to follow. The Commissioner now wishes to engage expert assistance to help her present the final version of the code in a way that makes it as accessible as possible to the target audience of human resources practitioners'.

Codes of Practice must be workable. The invitation document in relation to the Draft Code of Practice on the Use of Personal Data in Employer/Employee Relationships shows the Commissioner's thinking on this. The aim for the revised code will be:

> 'to take the data protection standards the Commissioner considers appropriate and present them in a way that makes them as clear, concise, practical and useful as possible to human resources practitioners. The real test is will the Code succeed in encouraging human resources practitioners to put its standards into practice?'

With this Code, the initial document was thought to be too long and it is likely to be divided into sections such as:

- recruitment and selection;
- management of employment records;
- monitoring at work; and
- medical testing (including drug testing, genetic testing etc.).

Its main target is human resources practitioners in larger businesses and will be supplemented with additional material to support the Code, for example guidance leaflets for small businesses, employees etc. Interestingly, the Commissioner also suggested that research might be commissioned into how other Codes of Practice in areas other than data protection operate in practice.

Structure of codes 3.15

Codes of Practice under *DPA 1998* have so far always included recommended standards (some of which are quoted from in this book). Of those standards parts are obligatory, with compliance being necessary to comply with *DPA 1998*, and other parts are voluntary, but it would be good or best practice to follow them.

Regulation of Investigatory Powers Act 2000 3.16

Under the *Regulation of Investigatory Powers Act 2000* (*RIPA 2000*) Codes of Practice are also issued. These were considered under the topic 'Confidentiality and Security' and at the time of writing were all still draft codes.

- Draft Code of Practice on Accessing Communications Data (see www.homeoffice.gov.uk/ripa/consultintro.htm).

- Draft Code of Practice on the Use of Covert Human Intelligence Sources (see www.homeoffice.gov.uk/ripa/covhis.htm).
- Draft Code of Practice on Covert Surveillance (see www.homeoffice.gov.uk/ripa/covsurv.htm).

Industry guides 3.17

Various guides and codes of practice are produced by industry, and details of some of these are given at 3.18–3.21 below.

A duty to consider codes of trade associations 3.18

Section 51(4) of *DPA 1998* provides that the Commissioner shall encourage trade associations to prepare and disseminate codes of practice to their members. If a trade association submits a code to the Commissioner for consideration, then the Commissioner has a duty to consider that and consult with data subjects and those who represent them, and then to notify the trade association of whether, in the opinion of the Commissioner, the code does promote the following of good practice.

Under *section 51(8)* of *DPA 1998* the Commissioner is allowed to charge for services such as approving trade associations' codes, although it is thought she has not done so to date.

Financial services 3.19

In September 2000 the main trade associations in the financial services sector published guidance on the Act entitled *The New Data Protection Act 2000: A Practitioner's Handbook*. Each chapter includes practical examples for banks and other financial institutions. Appended to the book are many examples and practical advice (see CHAPTER 22 FINANCIAL SERVICES). Copies can be ordered from the British Bankers' Association website at www.bba.org.uk under Publications.

Direct marketing 3.20

In August 2000 the Direct Marketing Association (DMA)'s Colin Fricker, produced a *Guide to the Data Protection Act 1998 – For Direct Marketing*.

Other industry guides 3.21

In her First Annual Report (June 2001) the Commissioner mentions the financial services and direct marketing guidelines mentioned at 3.19 and 3.20 above, as well as having commented on guidance produced by:

- the Factors and Discounters Association;
- the Chief and Chief Fire Officers Association;
- the Church of England;
- the Office of National Statistics; and
- the General Medical Council.

EU Codes of Practice and Standards 3.22

The Information Commissioner supports European Union Codes of Practice. The Federation of European Direct Marketing Associations (FEDMA) have produced a Code of Practice relating to direct marketing under the *Data Protection Directive (95/46/EC)*, and the International Commerce Exchange (ICX) has prepared a comprehensive code for EU based multi-nationals who wish to follow one system of good practice throughout their international operations, the Commissioner reports in her First Annual Report.

OECD Privacy Statement Generator for websites 3.23

In 2000 the Organisation for Economic Co-operation and Development (OECD) Privacy Statement Generator for websites was adopted, and can be found at http://cs3-hq.oecd.org/scripts/pwv3/pwhome.htm.

Summary 3.24

Codes of Practice are rarely likely to be issued. The Code of Practice on CCTV is useful and detailed (see CHAPTER 2 CCTV). The Draft Code of Practice on the Use of Personal Data in Employer/Employee Relationships has had a tortuous start and is not likely to be issued until 2002. It is not clear if any other codes are proposed. Given that the Commissioner has had to put out to tender improvement of the Draft Employer/Employee Code, it is unlikely a large number of other codes will be issued. More informal guidance is likely to be the path taken in many areas, which can then be more quickly amended as case law and good practice develop.

All Codes of Practice are under Codes of Practice on the Commissioner's website at www.dataprotection.gov.uk.

4 – Commissioner

At a glance 4.1

- ✓ The Information Commissioner is an independent public official who reports to Parliament.
- ✓ The role of Information Commissioner involves duties under both the *Data Protection Act 1998* (*DPA 1998*) and the *Freedom of Information Act 2000* (*FIA 2000*).
- ✓ Under *section 59* of *DPA 1998* the Commissioner is restricted from disclosing certain information.

Introduction 4.2

The current Information Commissioner is Mrs Elizabeth France. Under the *Data Protection Act 1984* (*DPA 1984*) the Commissioner was called the 'Registrar' and then renamed 'Data Protection Commissioner'. *FIA 2000* led to a new title and responsibilities for the Commissioner on 30 January 2001, when the post was renamed the 'Information Commissioner', and given a dual role under both that legislation and *DPA 1998*.

Role of the Commissioner 4.3

The role of the Commissioner is self-described thus:

> 'The Commissioner is an independent supervisory authority and has an international role as well as a national one. In the UK the Commissioner has a range of duties including the promotion of good information handling and the encouragement of codes of practice for data controllers, that is, anyone who decides how and why personal data, (information about identifiable, living individuals) are processed.'

Under *section 6(2)* of *DPA 1998* the Commissioner is an independent person appointed by the Queen. He or she reports to Parliament directly. The duties of the Commissioner include:

- the promotion of the following of good practice by data controllers and, in particular, compliance with *DPA 1998*;

- the dissemination of information on *DPA 1998*; and
- encouraging the development of Codes of Practice to show good practice under *DPA 1998*.

Section 6 of *DPA 1998* sets out these provisions. There are more detailed provisions in *Schedule 5* to *DPA 1998*. In legal terms, the Information Commissioner is a 'corporation sole'. The Commissioner and her officers and staff are not servants or agents of the Crown. This chapter examines the Commissioner's main duties, responsibilities and powers under first *DPA 1998* and then under *FIA 2000*.

Requests for assessment and workload 4.4

The Commissioner deals with requests for assessment made under *section 42* of *DPA 1998*, which can be made by someone affected by the processing of personal data. A request for assessment is not strictly called a 'complaint' under *DPA 1998*.

The Commissioner has a duty to make an assessment where such a request is made, except where she has not been given sufficient information to be satisfied as to:

(*a*) the identity of the person making the request; or

(*b*) the ability to identify the processing concerned.

Most of the requests for assessment are made by individuals who believe their data has not been properly processed under *DPA 1998*. The Commissioner has powers to make assessments in relation to businesses and their compliance with the Act.

Dealing with a request 4.5

In deciding how to deal with a request, the Commissioner takes account of a variety of factors, such as whether the issue raised is a 'matter of substance'; whether the complainant has shown undue delay in making the request; and whether there is a right of subject access in respect of the personal data concerned. The Commissioner's threshold criteria for determining when to handle a request for assessment are whether:

- the request is made by or on behalf of a person who is, or who believes themselves to be, directly affected by the processing in question;
- the Commissioner is satisfied as to the identify of the person making the request;

- the Commissioner can identify the processing in question; and
- the processing is of personal data.

The person who made the request should be told by the Commissioner whether an assessment has been made as a result, and of any views formed or action taken by the Commissioner in consequence.

In a 'considerable number of cases', insufficient information is given to make an assessment (see the Commissioner's First Annual Report (June 2001)). In those cases written advice is given and the Commissioner treats them as 'enquiries'. In the period to 31 March 2001 the Commissioner's office dealt with 8,875 requests for assessment and enquiries, which included 1,721 complaints about breaches of telecommunications regulations (unsolicited faxes etc.). In 27.4 per cent of cases in that period advice was given; in 3.9 per cent a request for assessment was declined; and in 4 per cent the requirements for assessment were not met. 55,500 telephone enquiries were received by the Information Line (working out to be 9.12 enquiries per line per hour). These represent 35 per cent of calls received by the office overall.

Factors to consider 4.6

In making assessments, the Commissioner can make either a verified or unverified assessment. In deciding which of the following factors are taken into account, as described in the Commissioner's First Annual Report, the Commissioner decides

> 'whether:
>
> - the request raises, on the basis of the impact on the person making the request or on whose behalf the request is made and the wider impact, what we consider to be a matter of substance;
> - the request is made without undue delay;
> - the request is from a person who is entitled to make a subject access request in respect of the personal data in question;
> - an assessment has previously been carried out in respect of the processing in question;
> - the matters to which the request relates are being or could better be dealt with by another body or alternative mechanism;
> - the matters to which the request relates have already been resolved;

- the issues raised by the request are fundamentally about data protection (rather than data protection being merely incidental to the main issues); and
- an investigation by the Commissioner is likely to require resources disproportionate to the value of the assessment'.

Education 4.7

A principal duty of the Commissioner is to educate people about the legislation concerning data protection. To that end, an important part of her role and that of her staff is the issuing of Codes of Practice (see CHAPTER 3 CODES OF PRACTICE), guidance, telephone advice, and attending workshops and issuing leaflets to ensure as many people as possible are aware of *DPA 1998* and its provisions. For example, in August 2000 the Commissioner implemented a national television advertising campaign. Education packs for schools are also prepared. Further details on the Commissioner's role in this area are included in Chapter 4 of the First Annual Report.

Inspection visits and search warrants 4.8

As well as handling complaints and assessments, the Commissioner organises inspection visits. There were 715 such visits to premises in the year to 31 March 2001 in the course of investigations into criminal breaches of *DPA 1998*. No notice search warrants were obtained in relation to nine premises in the same period.

Departments 4.9

The Commissioner's office is divided into different departments although this is not laid down by statute and may change from time to time. The Commissioner has an Investigations Department and also a Legal Department. The Legal Department considers whether prosecutions should be brought amongst other matters and in the year to 31 March 2001, out of 129 cases submitted to the department, 23 were put before the courts and 21 resulted in convictions.

Cautions 4.10

The Commissioner's current policy is to administer 'cautions' rather than prosecuting offenders. In the year to 31 March 2001 cautions were administered in six cases of unregistered data users, four cases of unlawfully procuring information, and two cases of employees of a data user using data for an unregistered purpose.

Enforcement and information notices 4.11

When the Commissioner decides to prosecute, an 'enforcement notice' is served, often preceded by a 'preliminary enforcement notice'. Where the Commissioner simply wants information, an 'information notice' is served. In 2000/01 four enforcement notices and five preliminary enforcement notices were served. No information notices were served. CHAPTER 17 ENFORCEMENT, REMEDIES AND POWERS provides further information regarding the Commissioner's powers. In brief, the Commissioner can serve enforcement notices on those who are contravening the legislation.

Holding of office 4.12

The Commissioner holds office for up to five years at a time, with a maximum of 15 years' service. Should the Commissioner reach 65 years of age while in office, he or she must leave office on completion of the year of service during which the birthday occurs. A reappointment for a third term is not allowed unless by reason of special circumstances. The role is a paid role with a salary and pension, the details of which are set out in *paragraph 3* of *Schedule 5* to *DPA 1998*. *DPA 1998* provides for the appointment of a Deputy Commissioner and another member of staff.

Freedom of information role 4.13

The Information Commissioner's role was created with effect from 30 January 2001 when the then Data Protection Commissioner took on responsibility for *FIA 2000*. *FIA 2000* must be implemented in full by 30 November 2005.

The Commissioner issues guidance on *FIA 2000*. Both her roles cover aspects of information policy and the Government has said that 'joint responsibility will allow the Information Commissioner to provide an integrated and coherent approach to information handling and will provide a single point of contact for public authorities and the public.' (*FIA 2000 Overview, June 2001*).

In relation to freedom of information the Commissioner has the following duties.

- Approve/revoke publication schemes.
- Promote the following of good practice.
- Promote public authorities' compliance with *FIA 2000*.
- Disseminate information and give advice about *FIA 2000*.

- With consent, assess whether a public authority is following good practice.
- Report annually to Parliament.

FIA 2000 allows the Commissioner to charge for certain services.

Where a breach of *FIA 2000* occurs, for example where an individual has requested information of a public body and the information has been refused or the individual has received no reply, then they can apply to the Information Commissioner for a decision as to whether the request has been addressed in accordance with *FIA 2000*. The Information Commissioner may then serve a decision notice on the public authority and the applicant stating what must be done to comply. The duties of the Commissioner also include the service of information or enforcement notices on public authorities. Notices can be issued requiring information to be disclosed in the public interest. However, a Cabinet Minister can override such notice (an executive override) and there is no appeal procedure following such a ministerial certificate. This illustrates a limitation on the powers of the Commissioner in the *FIA 2000* field. At the date of writing it is not yet known how often the executive override will be exercised.

Where the Commissioner serves a notice, the other party may appeal to the Information Tribunal.

The new role 4.14

The new Information Commissioner position created from 30 January 2001 was not just a renaming of the Data Protection Commissioner. The Commissioner describes it as a 'new organisation' which expects to double in size by 2005 when *FIA 2000* is fully in force. The Commissioner's role is therefore likely to broaden and change as *FIA 2000* comes fully into force. New premises and staff will be sought and internal procedures will be formalised. Legislative change may also occur.

The Commissioner and disclosure 4.15

Section 59 of *DPA 1998* provides that the Commissioner, members of her staff and agents of the Commissioner must not disclose information which has been obtained by the Commissioner under *DPA 1998*, relates to an identified or identifiable individual or business, and is not available to or has never been available to the public from other sources, unless the disclosure is made with lawful authority.

'Lawful authority' is defined in *section 59(2)* of *DPA 1998* as being applicable in cases where:

- a disclosure is made with the consent of the individual or business;
- information was provided for the purpose of its being made available to the public;
- the disclosure is made to discharge functions under *DPA 1998* or *FIA 2000* or an EU obligation;
- the disclosure is made for the purposes of proceedings (whether criminal or civil); or
- having regard to the rights and freedoms or legitimate interests of any person, the disclosure is necessary in the public interest.

The Commissioner says in her First Annual Report that *section 59* of *DPA 1998* 'imposes inappropriate restrictions on [her] ability to disclose information about [her office's] activities'. Such a restriction may not be compatible with the Data Protection Office's own duties to disclose information under *FIA 2000*.

If a member of the Commissioner's staff or the Commissioner breaches *section 59* of *DPA 1998* they commit an offence.

Transparency consultation paper 4.16

The Commissioner wishes to establish a policy on the extent and manner in which information coming into her office in connection with her data protection functions should be published. A consultation paper was published setting out the legislative background and some policy considerations in 2001. As seen at 4.14 above, *section 59* of *DPA 1998* imposed a criminal sanction on the Commissioner, her staff or agents if they disclose information obtained in the course of their duties otherwise than in accordance with the rules laid out in that section of *DPA 1998*.

To date, the Commissioner has been open about her office's activities, while protecting the privacy of complainants. The office issues guidance, annual reports, codes of practice, press releases and other publications. *Section 1* of *FIA 2000* provides that:

> 'Any person making a request for information to a public authority is entitled:
>
> (*a*) to be informed … whether it holds information … ;and
>
> (*b*) … to have that information communicated to him.'

There are certain types of information which the Commissioner believes should be kept confidential, such as information about complainants, details of informants, details of those who complain under 'whistleblowing' legislation (the *Public Interest Disclosure Act 1998*), evidence obtained from third parties in the course of investigation, and information such as trade secrets entrusted in confidence. The Commissioner feels a certain balance must be achieved. Restrictions under *section 59* of *DPA 1998* only apply to information:

- obtained for statutory functions;
- relating to an identifiable individual or business; and
- not previously available to the public from other sources.

Where the restrictions in *section 59* of *DPA 1998* apply, there is a list of circumstances in which information can be disclosed. The Commissioner states that three useful rules permitting disclosure might apply in particular cases, as set out below.

(*a*) Where the individual or business has consented.

(*b*) Where the information was provided with the object of being disclosed under *DPA 1998*.

(*c*) Where the disclosure is for the purposes of any civil or criminal legal proceedings.

It should be clear from the circumstances where one of these three rules applies. A typical case of information being provided for disclosure under *DPA 1998* would be notification particulars which are to be included on the Register of Companies. The two other rules permitting disclosure of restricted information are more general. They can provide further bases for the Data Protection Office giving out information. They are:

- where the disclosure is for the purposes of and is necessary for the discharge of statutory functions or a community obligation; or
- where the disclosure is, having regard to the rights and freedoms or legitimate interests of any person, necessary in the public interest.

The consultation paper stated that the Commissioner has come to the conclusion that the best way of reconciling the tension between the various legislative provisions and policy issues would be to 'adopt formally a policy about the information which she considers expedient to disseminate to the public thereby crystallising her duty to disseminate that information under *section 51(2)* of *DPA 1998*. Information published under that duty would seem to be disclosed with lawful authority by virtue of *section 59(2)(c)(i)* of *DPA 1998*.'

Contacting the Commissioner 4.17

The contact details of the Commissioner and her office are as follows:

Information Line Tel: 01625 545 745	E-mail: mail@dataprotection.gov.uk
To notify Tel: 01625 545 745	E-mail: mail@notification.demon.co.uk
Switchboard: 01625 545 700 Fax: 01625 524 510 DX 20819 Wilmslow	

5 – Compensation, Damages and Prevention of Processing

At a glance 5.1

- ✓ Those suffering damage through a breach of the *Data Protection Act 1998* (*DPA 1998*) can recover damages (*DPA 1998, s 13*).
- ✓ In limited cases compensation for distress, where no damage is also suffered, may be available.
- ✓ Under *section 10* of *DPA 1998* there is also a right to prevent processing which causes damage or distress.

Introduction 5.2

The *Data Protection Act (DPA) 1998* provides redress for those who have suffered through a breach of the legislation.

The provisions do not seem to have been widely used, although a threat to seek such redress may in practice lead to a payment which would of course not then be recorded in any court decision.

This section looks at the right to recover compensation under *section 13* of *DPA 1998* and also the right for data subjects to sue to prevent processing which causes them damage or distress under *section 10* of *DPA 1998*.

Compensation 5.3

Under *section 13* of *DPA 1998* individuals have the right to sue for the damage they have suffered if the requirements of *DPA 1998* have not been met by a data controller. The individual must have suffered 'damage' by reason of any contravention by a data controller of any *DPA 1998* requirement. The compensation is paid by the data controller for that damage. Under *section 13* compensation is also available for 'distress'.

Where distress rather than damage is caused then compensation is only paid where:

(*a*) the individual also suffers damage by reason of the contravention (in other words the claim is for both damages and distress and both claims are valid); or

(*b*) the contravention relates to the processing of personal data for the special purposes.

Section 3 of *DPA 1998* defines 'the special purposes' as being journalism, artistic and literary purposes. Therefore if a tabloid newspaper publishes details of a confidential extra-marital affair of a individual, and the individual suffers distress but no provable economic damage then the individual can sue for damages. However, if the same facts were published, but by the disgruntled wife pasting notices on trees and lamp posts on the road where the man lives (which is not journalism or literary or artistic publication) then the husband can sue the wife for the distress, even if no damage is shown.

Right to prevent processing 5.4

Section 10 of *DPA 1998* contains a right for data subjects to prevent the processing of any data which will cause them damage or distress. Individuals can exercise this right at any time by notice in writing to the data controller.

The data subject notice 5.5

A data subject notice is given to stop someone processing data or to prevent them beginning to do so. The notice is for them to stop or cease for a specific purpose, or in a certain manner. It must relate to data being used or processed in relation to which the complainant is the data subject. The right set out by *section 10* of *DPA 1998* cannot be used by someone where the processing of data relates to someone else. The period of notice to be given in such a case should be that which is 'reasonable in the circumstances'.

Section 10 of *DPA 1998* applies where, with reference to the data subject:

(*a*) the processing of those data or their processing for that purpose or in that manner is causing or is likely to cause substantial damage or substantial distress to him or to another, and

(*b*) that damage or distress is or would be unwarranted.

As can be seen above, if the processing of data about a person causes distress to someone else then *section 10* of *DPA 1998* can be invoked. Thus, processing data about someone's husband may distress the wife and in such a case the husband could complain, even if he were not personally distressed or damaged.

When section 10 does not apply **5.6**

Section 10 of *DPA 1998* does not apply where the conditions in *paragraphs 1–4* of *Schedule 2* to *DPA 1998*, are met. These are the conditions relevant to the First Data Protection Principle (data processing). *Section 10* of *DPA 1998* does not apply:

(*a*) where the data subject consents;

(*b*) where the processing is necessary to perform a contract to which the data subject of a party or to take steps at the request of the data subject with a view to entering into a contract;

(*c*) if the processing is necessary for compliance with a legal obligation, other than an obligation imposed by contract; and

(*d*) if the processing is necessary to protect the vital interests of the data subject.

In addition, *section 10* of *DPA 1998* will not be applicable where the Secretary of State so orders.

Once a notice is received from a data subject under *section 10* of *DPA 1998* the data controller has 21 days from receipt of the data subject notice to return a notice to the data subject stating that the controller has complied with the notice or intends to do so. Otherwise, a statement must be issued detailing reasons for regarding the notice of the data subject as unjustified and how, if at all, the data controller intends to comply with part of it.

If the controller refuses thus to comply, a court – on application of the data subject – may order the data controller to take such steps to comply with the notice or part of it as the court thinks fit (*DPA 1998, section 10(4)*). No data subject can be obliged to serve a data subject notice nor will they lose rights if they do so. A failure by a data subject to exercise its rights above does not affect any other right under *DPA 1998* by virtue of *section 10(5)*. Indeed, in many cases the data subject will choose to make an application for assessment (complaint) to the Information Commissioner rather than suing for damages. Suing for damages, given the small loss the data subject has probably suffered (at least in financial terms), is rarely likely to be worthwhile because of the costs of litigation.

Telecommunications law and damages 5.7

There are also rights to claim damages for breach of the *Telecommunications (Data Protection and Privacy) Regulations 1999* (*SI 1999/2093*), for example where loss is suffered through the sending of an unsolicited fax in breach of those regulations.

Summary 5.8

There have not been any publicised cases where individuals have sued to recover damages. However, in practice many individuals write to those who have caused them damage or distress themselves, and through their solicitors, both to require that such processing be stopped and to recover damages. Frequently a small sum is offered in settlement and that is the end of the matter. No litigation results.

6 – Confidentiality and Data Security: Seventh Principle

At a glance 6.1

- ✓ The Seventh Data Protection Principle requires that personal data be kept safe and secure.
- ✓ Security should also extend to e-mails and companies must set up appropriate security procedures. In some cases encryption will be necessary.
- ✓ Draft Codes of Practice under the *Regulation of Investigatory Powers Act 2000* on Accessing Communications Data, on the Use of Covert Human Intelligence Sources and on Covert Surveillance have been issued and should be considered in this field.
- ✓ Security and data protection issues arising from the use of CCTV are addressed in the Code of Practice on CCTV (see CHAPTER 2 CCTV).

Appropriate measures 6.2

The Seventh Data Protection Principle states that appropriate technical and organisational measures must be taken against unauthorised or unlawful processing of personal data and against accidental loss or destruction of, or damage to personal data (*Data Protection Act 1998 (DPA 1998), Sch 1, Part I, para 7*).

Data controllers handling personal data need to ensure they take appropriate security measures to protect that data. The Seventh Principle, like all the principles, applies whether or not the data controller has notified their holding of data. The nature of the data determines to some extent the precautions which must be taken in relation to it. Sensitive data, as defined in *DPA 1998* (such as data about race), needs to be treated even more carefully than other data.

Levels of security 6.3

Relevant factors to the levels of security provided include:

- the state of technological development; and
- the cost of implementing a measure.

These factors are mentioned in the Seventh Data Protection Principle. One example might be a newsagent whose computer screen can be seen by customers. Customers therefore have access to the personal data of those who have paid for their newspapers and their addresses. The Commissioner has held in one instance that this breached *DPA 1998*. Criminals could in such a case see whose newspapers had been cancelled for holidays. If the screen is turned to the counter the breach of the Act is removed.

The level of security must be appropriate to:

(*a*) the harm that might result from such unauthorised or unlawful processing or accidental loss, destruction or damage; and

(*b*) the nature of the data to be protected.

British Standard *BS7799* is helpful for companies assessing whether their security precautions are adequate. The Information Commissioner in her Draft Code of Practice on the Use of Personal Data in Employer/Employee Relationships recommends compliance with *BS7799*.

Practical guidance 6.4

The Seventh Principle refers to appropriate measures being taken to protect data. The following practical guidance is given by the Commissioner in the draft Code.

> 'The holding of inaccurate data will be unlawful processing in that it contravenes the requirements of the *Data Protection Act 1998*. An employer should have in place technical and organisational measures to protect against inaccuracy. Technical measures might include a system that has accuracy and consistency checks built into the software. Organisational measures might include requiring employees to confirm the accuracy of the information held about them from time to time.'

Employees 6.5

The data controller must take reasonable steps to ensure the reliability of any employees who have access to the personal data (*DPA 1998, Sch 1, Part II, para 10*). The Act does not specify what those steps should be. Under the *Data Protection Act 1984* (*DPA 1984*) there was an identical provision, and the Registrar recommended asking the following questions.

- Is proper weight given to the discretion and integrity of staff when they are considered for employment in or promotion/a move to an area where they have access to personal data?
- Are staff aware of their responsibilities? (A compliance or education programme on the Act will help with this.)
- Do disciplinary rules and procedures take account of the Act's requirements and are they enforced?
- If the employee is found to be unreliable, is his access to personal data immediately withdrawn?

Example **6.6**

A case study given in the Commissioner's First Annual Report (June 2001) describes an example of a breach of the Seventh Principle. A council employee sent to the Data Protection Office a large amount of employee personnel information found in a black bin liner in a skip at the council depot where he was employed. He said the manager of the depot disposed of the personnel files of employees working at the depot by placing them in black bin liners and from there into skips to be transported to a public refuse tip, and that he had found two additional bags which contained similar information.

The documents which had been retrieved contained a large amount of personal data about the employees and their relatives, including details of:

- their pay;
- their relatives;
- applications for leave; and
- medical information about sick leave.

Most of the documents retrieved were copies of manual documents which did not then fall within the scope of *DPA 1998*. The Commissioner said:

> 'However, there was one document, a sickness record relating to the complainant, which appeared to have been computer-generated. On this basis we notified the council concerned that we had formed the view that

there had been a contravention of the Seventh Data Protection Principle in this case.'

The council's response was to explain that although systems and procedures were in place at the depot these had not been strictly followed. The result of the case was that all depots were issued with shredders and the management was reminded of the procedures. All employees then received data protection awareness training, and data protection liaison officers throughout the council were told of the incident and asked to apply the lessons learned in their own areas.

E-mails **6.7**

The use of e-mail can cause security problems. In her Draft Code of Practice on the Use of Personal Data in Employer/Employee Relationships the Information Commissioner says that an employer who allows the transmission of confidential employee information by e-mail without taking proper security measures will breach the Seventh Principle. Some companies use encryption to protect e-mail in transit but it can still then be vulnerable at either end. Employers need to be aware that even deleting a confidential e-mail does not mean it is irretrievable. Indeed, the Commissioner's guidance on subject access rights under *section 7* of *DPA 1998* and e-mails includes a section on possible obligations upon employers to retrieve deleted e-mails in response to a subject access request.

Encryption **6.8**

Encryption is one method of security which can be used to protect e-mails, although it can cause problems when it concentrates too much power in the hands of the employee who has the encryption key. The *Regulation of Investigatory Powers Act 2000* (*RIPA 2000*) was heavily criticised during its passage through Parliament because it permits the police to require an employee to hand over an encryption key without telling the employer they have done so, and indeed makes it an offence for the employee to inform their employer of this. *Section 49(2)* of *RIPA 2000* sets out the principal provision requiring an individual to hand over a key.

Under *section 53* of *RIPA 2000*, a person to whom a *section 49* notice has been given is guilty of an offence if he 'knowingly fails, in accordance with the notice, to make the disclosure required by virtue of the giving of the notice'. A jail sentence of up to two years and/or a fine can be imposed on an individual who does not comply.

Section 54 of *RIPA 2000* is called 'tipping off', and states that where the notice served said 'to keep secret the giving of the notice, its contents and the things done in pursuance of it', and the individual does not do this, they can be jailed for up to five years and/or fined.
There are defences under *section 54* where:

(*a*) the disclosure was effected entirely by the operation of software designed to indicate when a key to protected information has ceased to be secure; and

(*b*) that person could not reasonably have been expected to take steps, after being given the notice or (as the case may be) becoming aware of it or of its contents, to prevent the disclosure.

Under *section 54(6)* of *DPA 1998* there are also certain defences involving disclosures to legal advisers, or where the disclosure was to the Interception of Communications Commissioner, the Intelligence Services Commissioner or any Surveillance Commissioner or Assistant Surveillance Commissioner.

Draft Codes of Practice 6.9

At the time of writing there are three Codes of Practice, all still in draft form, made under *RIPA 2000*. They all contain sections relevant to data protection and security, and in essence require the authorities to comply with *DPA 1998* in carrying out their duties.

Draft Code of Practice on Accessing Communications Data 6.10

In November 2001, the Home Office finished its consultation on a Code of Practice under *RIPA 2000* – the Draft Code of Practice on Accessing Communications Data (see www.homeoffice.gov.uk/ripa/consultintro.htm). Under that Code the following 'relevant public authorities' would be permitted under *RIPA 2000* to grant authorisations or serve notices to require access to communications data:

- a police force (as defined in *section 81(1)* of *DPA 1998*);
- the National Criminal Intelligence Service;
- the National Crime Squad;
- HM Customs and Excise;
- the Inland Revenue;
- the Security Service;

- the Secret Intelligence Service; and
- the Government Communications Headquarters.

Communications data does not include information in e-mails or about access to websites as it is not related to the content of the communications.

Under the Draft Code the data could be accessed for the following purposes:

- in the interests of national security;
- for the purpose of preventing or detecting crime or of preventing disorder;
- in the interests of the economic well-being of the United Kingdom (see para 4.2 in the Draft Code);
- in the interests of public safety;
- for the purpose of protecting public health;
- for the purpose of assessing or collecting any tax, duty, levy or other imposition, contribution or charge payable to a government department; or
- for the purpose, in an emergency, of preventing death or injury or any damage to a person's physical or mental health, or of mitigating any injury or damage to a person's physical or mental health.

The Draft Code provides that:

> 'Communications data, and all copies, extracts and summaries of it, must be handled and stored securely. In addition, the requirements of the *Data Protection Act 1998* and its Data Protection Principles should be adhered to'.

RIPA 2000 provides for an Interception of Communications Commissioner who provides independent oversight of the use of the powers contained within *Part I* of *RIPA 2000*.

Draft Code of Practice on the Use of Covert Human Intelligence Sources **6.11**

RIPA 2000 deals with other aspects of interception too, and a Draft Code of Practice on the Use of Covert Human Intelligence Sources has been issued, in part covering security issues (see 6.12 below).

Retention and destruction of the product and records of the use of a source **6.12**

> 3.16 Authorising officers are reminded of the guidance in paragraph 2.25 [of the Code] relating to the retention and destruction of confidential material. To the extent that such material has not been destroyed, the following guidance may be relevant.
>
> 3.17 Subject to 3.18 [of the Code], all records should be retained for a minimum of one year to ensure that they are available for inspection by a Commissioner. Thereafter material must not be destroyed, save with the authority of the authorising officer. It is essential that this responsibility should be managed at a senior level in the relevant organisation and that officers are clearly identified and are held accountable for carrying out this function.
>
> 3.18 Records must be capable of being retrieved at a central point within each public authority.
>
> 3.19 Where there is reasonable belief that material relating to any activity by a source could be relevant to pending or future criminal or civil proceedings, it should be retained in accordance with established disclosure requirements. In the cases of the law enforcement agencies (not including the Service Police), particular attention is drawn to the requirements of the Code of Practice issued under the *Criminal Procedure and Investigations Act 1996*. This requires that material should be retained if it forms part of the unused prosecution material gained in the course of a criminal investigation, or which may be relevant to an investigation.
>
> 3.20 Authorising officers must also ensure compliance with data protection requirements and, where appropriate, with any relevant code of practice on data protection.
>
> *Draft Code of Practice on the Use of Covert Human Intelligence Sources*

Draft Code of Practice on Covert Surveillance **6.13**

Under *RIPA 2000* there is also a Draft Code of Practice on Covert Surveillance (see www.homeoffice.gov.uk/ripa/covsurv.htm). As regards the Police (including Service Police), the National Criminal Intelligence Service, the National Crime Squad and HM Customs & Excise it says:

> '2.17 Authorising officers must ensure compliance with the appropriate data protection requirements and any relevant codes of practice produced by individual authorities in the

handling and storage of material. Where material is obtained by surveillance, which is wholly unrelated to a criminal or other investigation or to any person who is the subject of the investigation, and there is no reason to believe it will be relevant to future civil or criminal proceedings, it should be destroyed immediately. Consideration of whether or not unrelated material should be destroyed is the responsibility of the senior authorising officer.

2.18 There is nothing in *RIPA 2000* that prevents material obtained through the proper use of the authorisation procedures from being used in other investigations. However, the use outside the public authority which authorised the surveillance, or the courts, of any material obtained by means of covert surveillance and, other than in pursuance of the grounds on which it was obtained, should be authorised only in the most exceptional circumstances.'

Faxes 6.14

Security issues relating to fax machines should also be considered by readers. Sometimes a confidential fax is sent to a machine where many people can pick it up and read the contents, and sometimes faxes are misdirected by using the wrong number. All these activities could amount to breach of the Seventh Principle.

Standards 6.15

- Apply proper security standards, such as those identified in *BS7799*, that take account of the risks of unauthorised access to or accidental loss or destruction of or damage to employment records (Principle 7).
- Institute a system of access controls and passwords that ensure staff access to employment records is strictly on a 'need to know' basis (Principle 7).
- Keep a log of non-routine access to employment records and, as far as possible, use systems that record an audit trail of all access to computerised records whether routine or not (Principle 7).
- Take steps to ensure the reliability of staff who have access to employee records (Principle 7).
- Treat accessing, disclosing or otherwise using employee records without authority as a serious disciplinary offence.

Make staff aware of this and also that such conduct may constitute a criminal offence (Principle 7; *DPA 1998, s 55*).

- Pay particular attention to the risks of transmitting confidential employee information by e-mail or fax by:
  - only transmitting information between locations if a secure network or comparable arrangements are in place or if, in the case of e-mail, encryption is used;
  - ensure that all copies of e-mails and fax messages received by managers are held securely;
  - provide a means by which managers can effectively expunge e-mails they receive or send from the system and make them responsible for doing so;
  - draw the attention of all employees to the risks of sending confidential, personal information by e-mail or fax; and
  - ensure that the information systems security policy properly addresses the risk of transmitting employee information by e-mail (Principle 7).

Data processors and security 6.16

Where a data processor is given the job of processing data on behalf of a data subject, then the data controller must do the following (*DPA 1998, Sch 1, Part II, para 11*):

(*a*) choose a data processor providing sufficient guarantees in respect of the technical and organisational security measures governing the processing to be carried out; and

(*b*) take reasonable steps to ensure compliance with those measures.

Where processing is carried out by a data processor the Seventh Principle will not be complied with unless:

(i) the processing is carried out under a contract in writing and under which the data processor is to act only on instructions from the data controller; and

(ii) the contract requires the data processor to comply with obligations equivalent to those imposed on a data controller by the Seventh Principle.

These obligations on data processors require the data controller to be very careful when choosing a data processor.

CCTV 6.17

The Commissioner's Code of Practice on CCTV (see CHAPTER 2 CCTV) (www.dataprotection.gov.uk/cctvcop.htm) gives guidance on how to ensure compliance, *inter alia*, with the Seventh Principle with respect to such systems. It includes ensuring that all requests for access to CCTV pictures are recorded and details kept of who has obtained the data. Consideration should be given to the harm which might result from the disclosure of the data. The nature of the data should also be considered. The more sensitive the data the more security measures are required.

Sensitive personal data 6.18

Some data is classed as 'sensitive personal data' under *section 2* of *DPA 1998* (see CHAPTER 43 SENSITIVE PERSONAL DATA). The conditions for processing such data are contained in *Schedule 3* to *DPA 1998*. There is a requirement that such data is only processed with the explicit consent of the data subject or other conditions are met. Data controllers have to be particularly careful to preserve confidentiality of sensitive personal data.

Confidentiality and the Commissioner 6.19

Section 59 of *DPA 1998* imposes strict duties on the Commissioner and her staff to keep information confidential. In 2001 she issued a consultation document on transparency (see 4.16) suggesting important changes in this area. *Section 59* can hamper her work. Details of this can be found in CHAPTER 3 COMMISSIONER/REGISTRAR.

Further information 6.20

For information on the *RIPA 2000* Codes of Practice see the following pages on the Home Office website.

Draft Code Of Practice on Accessing Communications Data	www.homeoffice.gov.uk/ripa/consultintro.htm
Draft Code Of Practice on the Use of Covert Human Intelligence Sources	www.homeoffice.gov.uk/ripa/covhis.htm)
Draft Code of Practice on	www.homeoffice.gov.uk/ripa/covsurv.htm)

7 – Credit References and Access to Credit Files

At a glance 7.1

- ✓ Legal liability can attach to the giving of references.
- ✓ The *Consumer Credit Act 1974* (*CCA 1974*) was amended by the *Data Protection Act 1998* (*DPA 1998*) such that individuals could make credit access requests only under the 1998 Act and not under *section 159* of *CCA 1974*. There is a seven day response period for credit requests under *section* 7 of *DPA 1998*.
- ✓ The use of third party data in the consumer lending process needs particular care. The Commissioner has issued guidance in this area including Model Letters for credit reference agencies and others.

Introduction 7.2

Few businesses will offer credit to new customers without a credit reference. As most customers want to operate on credit terms, credit references are a very important area both in the UK and abroad. Where an adequate reference cannot be obtained, businesses have to deal on a 'cash up front basis', which is not conducive to good cash flow and unacceptable for many businesses. The data protection implications of credit references are important because often the information contained in the reference is 'personal data' under *DPA 1998*, and compliance with the Act is therefore necessary. This section examines credit references under *DPA 1998* and also access to credit files generally. Reference in that respect should be made also to CHAPTER 43 SUBJECT ACCESS REQUESTS.

Reluctance to give references 7.3

Clearly, simply stating that 'XYZ plc' is good for £10,000 credit is not a statement containing any personal data at all, so the starting point for businesses is to ascertain the extent to which the references they may give or need will contain any personal data, and thus whether *DPA 1998* is relevant or not. However, even if the Act is not applicable, companies are increasingly showing reluctance to give references for other legal reasons. Normally there is no fee for the giving of such a reference, and if the consequence is to expose the person giving the reference to possible legal liability then it may be simpler to refuse to give references at all.

Legal liability 7.4

Some companies already have such a policy in relation to employee references. Rarely is there a contractual or other legal obligation to give a reference, although these issues should always be considered. When an employee is dismissed it may well be the term of a settlement agreement that a reference will or will not be given. In such a case the provisions of the contract should be followed. The other areas of legal liability might include liability in tort for negligent misstatement or liability for defamation if the statement is defamatory.

Disclosure 7.5

Under the *Data Protection Act 1984* (*DPA 1984*) credit references could not be disclosed to data subjects under subject access rights. *DPA 1998* reversed that, leading to many companies ceasing to provide such references (they are not happy that those about whom they write will see what they have written). Under consumer credit legislation, credit reference agencies do not have to disclose the names of referees.

Overlap with the Consumer Credit Act 1974 7.6

Section 62 of *DPA 1998* made some substantial changes to *CCA 1974*. In particular, individuals (but not those trading in partnership) lost their right of subject access under *section 158* of *CCA 1974*, and instead have subject access rights under *section 7* of *DPA 1998* (but with an enhanced seven day response period). Individuals in partnerships, however, have rights to see data held about them under both *DPA 1998* and *CCA 1974*.

However, the right of individuals/data subjects under *section 159* of *CCA 1974* was not modified or removed by *DPA 1998* and remains. This section grants the right to give notice to a credit reference agency for the removal or amendment of an entry where the individual considers the entry to be both incorrect, and to cause prejudice if it is not corrected.

When an individual makes a request under *section 7* of *DPA 1998*, and is also entitled to information under *section 159* of *CCA 1974*, then under *section 9(3)* of *DPA 1998* the individual should be provided with the information. The data controller cannot simply say that the *section* 7 request is requested and that *section 159* of *CCA 1974* must be used. Each year around one million references are made for access to information credit reference files.

Proposed changes to consumer credit law 7.7

In July 2001 the Government proposed major changes to *CCA 1974*, although not specifically in any area which affects data protection. The Department of Trade and Industry consultation document, *Tackling loan sharks and more: Consultation document on modernising the Consumer Credit Act 1974*, arose from its Task Force on over-indebtedness which was set up in October 2000 (see www.dti.gov.uk/consultations). The changes are likely to result in:

- greater information being given to those seeking credit;
- a rise in the £25,000 limit above which certain protection does not arise; and
- the enabling of online credit agreements, which should save costs.

Use of third party data in the consumer lending process 7.8

Historically, it was in accordance with the Data Protection Tribunals and Enforcement Notices agreed between the Credit Reference Agencies and the Data Protection Registrar in April 1992 that information on individuals other than a credit applicant could be included under two conditions:

- where the third party has resided concurrently with the credit applicant; and
- where it was reasonably believed that the third party has been living as a member of the same family as the applicant in a single household.

The credit industry application for change 7.9

In November 2000 the credit industry submitted an application to the Information Commissioner to allow the use of 'third party data' in the consumer lending process. The proposals were in response to concerns that the industry's current use of 'third party data' was becoming increasingly contentious. The result of a detailed review, the proposals would give the individual reassurance that their own information will not be seen or used inappropriately in connection with credit applications. The Commissioner in her press release at the time said:

> 'For example, no longer will a parent's credit information be seen by their children when a copy of a credit file is requested. But, at the same time, the individual will be protected from over-commitment and fraud by enabling the credit industry to continue to use aspects of "third party data".'

Proposed changes 7.10

The changes will be as follows.

- There will no longer be an assumption made that there is a financial connection simply on the basis of a shared surname and address – parents and children are no longer automatically assumed to be formally connected.
- When customers request a copy of their credit file, the process will be amended so that an individual will only see their own credit data and not that of any financially connected 'third party'.
- Individuals will be able to opt-out of the automatic use of their financial partner's data enabling them, on occasion, to be assessed in their own right.
- An 'alert process' using household data will be created, providing lenders with the ability to detect fraud. Consideration is also being given to the use of this system as a means of assessing over-commitment within a financial unit.

At the time of writing these changes have not yet been put into force.

Credit reference agencies as data controllers 7.11

In January 2001 the Information Commissioner issued guidance on the definition of 'data controller' under *DPA 1998*. She said that the credit reference agency and agency customers/subscribers are data controllers as they both decide why and how they process personal data.

In respect of the credit reference agency, its tasks, amongst other things, include obtaining, recording, holding, organising, adapting, altering and disclosing personal data. The agency customer/subscriber consults, obtains or retrieves personal data disclosed to it by the agency before using such data; for example, to inform a decision on whether to supply a customer. It is the ability to decide these things that makes them data controllers.

Information for data subjects 7.12

The Commissioner produces a leaflet 'No Credit?' (August 2001) (available by calling 0870 442 1211 or online at www.dataprotection.gov.uk) which explains how data subjects can ascertain what information is held about them on their credit file. It is the lender rather than the credit reference agency who informs the data subject about why they might have been refused credit on a particular occasion.

Common complaints 7.13

The most common complaints to the Commissioner about credit reference files relate to:

- the amount of data which appears in the file, and in particular the fact that there may be information about a person other than the applicant for credit;
- the accuracy of one or more of the entries which appear on the file; and
- the length of time for which a record continues to appear on a file.

Others of less creditworthiness 7.14

There have been a number of well-publicised cases where individuals have been unable to obtain credit because others of less creditworthiness live with them or have lived at the same address. The Commissioner says the following in her guidance.

> 'The circumstances in which information about another person may appear on your credit reference file are set out in an Enforcement Notice which resulted from a decision of the Data Protection Tribunal. The rules are complex, and the following is a summary of them:
>
> - the agencies must not supply information about anyone who has not lived at the same address at the same time as you;
> - the agencies can provide information where the name is the same or similar and the address is the same as yours;
> - the agencies can provide information about someone of a different name where the agency knows beforehand that it applies to you;
> - the agencies can provide information about other people as long as those others have the same surname as you and they have been living, at either your present or last address, at the

same time as you (it is this provision which enables the agencies to include information about family members at the same address on your credit file);

- the agencies can provide information about people with different surnames from you where they already have information from which it is reasonable for them to believe that these other people are or have been living as a member of your family in a single household (at either your present or last address); and
- the agencies must not supply information about any other person (even those indicated above) if the agency has information from which it is reasonable to believe that either that person is not you or that there is no financial connection between you and that person.'

Allowable information 7.15

Agencies are only allowed to give information about:

- the data subject;
- people with the same name, or a very similar name, living at the address;
- other family members living in the household;
- people with the same name, or a very similar name, who have, in the past, lived with the data subject at his or her current or last address; and
- other people who have, in the past, lived with the data subject as part of the family at the current or last address.

Agencies must not report financial information about other people if:

- they have not lived at the data subject's current or last address as a member of the family at the same time as the data subject;
- the agencies have information which makes it reasonable to believe that the data subject has no financial connection with them.

However, agencies can supply the names of other people, whether or not they are members of the family, who are or have been listed on the electoral roll at the data subject's addresses.

When individuals make access requests relating to their financial standing they are assumed to be limited to that area unless the request says otherwise.

Disassociation 7.16

Individuals can apply to be 'disassociated' from someone who lives at their address, but not from information on the electoral role. This information can continue to be associated with the complainant even if they object.

Model letters 7.17

Credit reference agencies 7.18

The Commissioner suggests the following wording for data subjects wanting to find out which credit reference agencies have been used.

123 Any Street
Anytown, A45 6EC
21 March 200–

Dear Loan Company

Data Protection Act 1998

Please tell me the name and address of any credit reference agency which you have asked to give information about me. I expect a reply within seven working days of your getting this letter.

Yours faithfully

Adam Neil Other

Disassociation 7.19

For disassociation the Commissioner suggests the following text.

123 Any Street
Anytown, A45 6EC
10 June 200–

Dear Credit Reference Agency

Your reference 123456–7890

Thank you for sending me my file. The information on it about John James Other relates to my adult son. He has now left home and I no longer have any financial connection with him. Please 'disassociate' us, so that financial information about him no longer appears on my file, and information about me does not appear on his.

Yours faithfully

Adam Neil Other

Inaccurate data **7.20**

One of the major credit complaints is about the lack of accuracy of the data. There is a right to have inaccurate data 'rectified'. The agencies obtain data from the electoral role and from bodies such as Registry Trust Limited (who keep the Registry of County Court Judgments) and financial institutions. The agencies will often offer to add a 'Notice of Correction' to the data subject's file. This is a statement of up to 200 words written by the individual saying why the information is not correct or is misleading. An example of such a notice is given at 7.21 below.

Sample wording for data correction **7.21**

The Commissioner suggests the following sample wording for having the data corrected.

> 123 Any Street
> Anytown, A45 6EC
> 18 June 200–
>
> Dear Credit Reference Agency
>
> Your Reference 123456–7890
>
> Thank you for sending me my credit reference file.
>
> I no longer owe any money to Anytown Lending Company Limited. The file shows that I did get into arrears on my loan and they recorded a default. I have now paid this off. I enclose a letter from the company which confirms this. I expect a reply within 28 days of your getting this letter. Please make it clear that the debt has been cleared.
>
> Yours faithfully
>
> Adam Neil Other

Sample wording for notices of correction **7.22**

Under *CCA 1974* the agency has to notify the data subject within 28 days as to whether the data has been corrected as specified in 7.20 above. Further model wording from the Commissioner is given below for notices of correction.

123 Any Street
Anytown, A45 6EC
10 August 200–

Dear Credit Reference Agency

Your Reference 123456–7890

Thank you for your letter of 15 July 200–.

I note that you will not remove the entry from my file. Please add the following notice of correction to my file.

NOTICE OF CORRECTION

I, Mr Adam Neil Other, of 123 Any Street, Anytown, A45 6EC would like it to be known that the judgment recorded against me for £200 relates to a bill which I could not pay because I was made redundant in 1996. I paid the bill in full after I got a job in 1997. I would ask anyone searching this file to take these facts into account.

I look forward to receiving confirmation from you within 28 days of receiving this letter that you have added this notice of correction to my file.

Yours faithfully

Adam Neil Other

Writing to the Commissioner 7.23

If correspondence such as that at 7.21 and 7.22 above does not result in a correction or notice, the Commissioner recommends that data subjects write to her along the following lines. In addition, there are rights under *DPA 1998* to have an assessment made as to whether or not the companies are complying with *DPA 1998*.

123 Any Street
Anytown, A45 6EC
23 September 200–

Dear Information Commissioner

I am writing under *section 159(5)* of the *Consumer Credit Act 1974*.

I got my file (reference number 123456–7890) from (the name of the credit reference agency) and asked them to change an entry about (details of the entry: county court judgment/ sheriff court decree/bankruptcy etc). Because they would not remove this from my file, I sent the agency a notice of correction to add to my file explaining the situation. It is now more than 28 days since I wrote and they have not told me whether they have put the notice on the file.

I believe that if the notice of correction is not added to my file, it will not be clear why this situation happened and as a result I may be refused credit. Please can you contact the agency and resolve the matter. I enclose copies of all my letters to the agency and copies of the letters to and from the court.

Yours faithfully

Adam Neil Other

Breaches by credit grantors 7.24

The Commissioner says:

> 'We cannot accept that a failure of a credit grantor to produce a copy of the signed credit agreement is, on its own, evidence that your debt does not exist and therefore should not appear on your credit file. If the credit grantor can supply some other evidence of the agreement and you have no evidence to contradict this then it is likely to be proper for the debt to continue to appear.'

Nor is she likely to accept that the failure of a credit grantor to produce evidence of notification to the data subject of the purposes for which the data will be collected is a reason for requiring the deletion of the data.

Duration 7.25

The Fifth Data Protection Principle requires that personal data are held no longer than is necessary. The Commissioner says that

> 'In general, credit reference agencies retain records for six years for the use of credit grantors in deciding whether or not to grant you credit. Records of bankruptcies are held for six years after the date of bankruptcy, records of County Court Judgments are held for six years from the date of the judgment, whether or not they are subsequently satisfied. Account records are held for six years from the date of the last entry on that record. In the Commissioner's view, it is not inappropriate for both a default and a subsequent judgment or bankruptcy to appear on a credit file.'

Finally, those suffering through inaccurate credit data as in any other area, may be able to claim compensation (see CHAPTER 5 COMPENSATION/DAMAGES).

Access to credit files for data subjects 7.26

Individual data subjects' access rights under *section* 7 of *DPA 1998* differ for credit files – the period for production is seven days.

The Commissioner's Questions and Answers contain the following guidance on access to credit files.

> '**Q. How can I obtain a copy of my credit file?**
>
> **A.** Credit grantors exchange information with each other about their customers. They also have access to the electoral roll and to publicly available financial information, which will have a bearing on an individual's credit worthiness, including County Court Judgments and Scottish decrees. This information is held by credit reference agencies. In order to get a copy of the information which relates to your financial standing (i.e. your credit file), you should write to the two main credit reference agencies. These are:
>
> - Equifax plc, Credit File Advice Service, PO Box 3001, Glasgow, G81 2DT; and
> - Experian Ltd, Consumer Help Service, PO Box 8000, Nottingham, NG1 5GX.
>
> You should send a fee of £2.00 and provide your full name and address, including postcode, and any other addresses you have lived at during the last 6 years and details of any other names you have used or been known by in that time. Unless the agencies require any further information to locate your file, they have 7 working days from the receipt of your letter in which to provide you with a copy of your file. For further information look at the paper *'No Credit'* @ www. dataprotection.gov.uk *under Guidance & other publications/sub heading your rights.*'

Transitional provisions 7.27

Complicated transitional provisions apply in this area – see *Schedule 8* to *DPA 1998*.

8 – Crime

At a glance 8.1

- ✓ Breach of the *Data Protection Act 1998* (*DPA 1998*) may involve the commission of a criminal offence under the Act.
- ✓ Proceedings are initiated by the Information Commissioner's Office which also operates a Police Working Party.
- ✓ Under *section 61* of *DPA 1998*, offences committed under the Act with the consent or connivance of a director or similar officer will result in liability on that individual.
- ✓ Examples of breach are listed in the Commissioner's First Annual Report (June 2001) and include the offences of unlawful disclosure, unlawful use and unlawful procurement.
- ✓ A new Criminal Records Bureau is being established to which employers will have access to check what general criminal offences their staff or proposed staff may have committed.
- ✓ The Council of Europe is developing a Cybercrime Convention.
- ✓ The *Computer Misuse Act 1990* makes computer hacking a criminal offence. Hacking can be used to access personal data.
- ✓ Criminal offences can also be committed in relation to computer software, and organisations such as BSA and FAST will investigate and/or civil or criminal proceedings may follow.

Introduction 8.2

Data protection can often become a criminal issue. The methods used to obtain the data may be criminal. Investigators may have broken into an office or hacked into a computer in breach of the *Computer Misuse Act 1990*. CHAPTER 32 OFFENCES looks in detail at the criminal offences created by *DPA 1998*.

Statistics 8.3

In 2000/2001 there were 21 criminal convictions for breach of *DPA 1998*:

- 13 were for being an unregistered data user;
- 4 were for unlawfully procuring information;
- 3 were offences of employees of data users 'disclosing data'; and
- 1 was an employee of a data user using data for an unregistered purpose.

12 cases resulted in cautions.

New media and telecoms 8.4

The fast development of communications such as mobile phones and the Internet has been used by criminals. There is a conflict between privacy and law enforcement. Law enforcement agencies want access to communications which may contain personal data. The *Regulation of Investigatory Powers Act 2000* contains important provisions about when the police and others can access e-mails and monitor telephone calls and Internet use etc. (See CHAPTER 3 CODES OF PRACTICE for details about codes issued in this area relating to surveillance; also CHAPTER 38 RECORDING TELEPHONE CALLS AND E-MAILS.)

The Commissioner, in her First Annual Report (June 2001), writes that in some cases new media provides new opportunities for surveillance: 'one example is the use of the increasingly precise location data generated by mobile phones to track individuals' movements'. She writes that the use of such data where it is a key element in addressing specific criminal activity will be justified, provided that proper controls are in place. The Commissioner recommends a proportionate response.

Personal data as a business 8.5

Some individuals make a business of obtaining personal data and pass it on to clients for a fee. The Commissioner in August 2000 set up a joint initiative with the then Department of Social Security, the Inland Revenue and the Commissioner's Office to stop such people. A number of organisations were reported to be subject to 'close scrutiny' when the Commissioner published her Annual Report in June 2001.

Commencement of criminal proceedings 8.6

In England and Wales, proceedings for a criminal offence under *DPA 1998* are commenced only by the Commissioner or by or with the consent of the Director of Public Prosecutions. Scotland has a different legal regime and there the Procurator Fiscal brings the proceedings. In

Northern Ireland, proceedings are started by the Commissioner or by or with the consent of the Director of Public Prosecutions for Northern Ireland. *Section 60* of *DPA 1998* contains these provisions. It also sets out the penalties of fines or prison sentences.

The Commissioner operates an EU Data Protection Commissioners' Police Working Party amongst other working groups. Criminal activities in relation to data are closely followed by both the Commissioner and police forces.

Liability of directors etc. 8.7

Body corporate 8.8

If an offence is committed under *DPA 1998* by a body corporate and it is proved to have been committed

> '...with the consent or connivance of or to be attributable to any neglect on the part of any director, manager, secretary or similar officer of the body corporate or any person who was purporting to act in any such capacity, he as well as the body corporate shall be guilty of that offence and be liable to be proceeded against and punished accordingly.'

(DPA 1998, s 61(1))

Shareholders 8.9

If the shareholders of a company manage its affairs then *section 61(1)* of *DPA 1998* (see 8.8 above) also applies to any acts or defaults of a member of the company or shareholder. This is unusual as normally shareholders do not carry the same type of legal liability as directors. In 2001 the Government announced a sweeping review of company law which will lead to the duties of directors being codified for the first time in a statute, as well as other changes. The Company Law Review report was published in July 2001 (see www.dti.gov.uk/cld/review.htm) and draft legislation is currently awaited. This will include obligations in relation to data protection as well as other areas. *Section 61(3)* of *DPA 1998* also contains provisions about Scottish partnerships.

Examples 8.10

The Commissioner's First Annual Report (June 2001) gives examples of convictions for offences under *DPA 1998* including the following.

Unlawful disclosure 8.11

A telecoms employee passed information on to a friend about a female customer's telephone account in order to assist that friend with a domestic situation. He was convicted of the unlawful disclosure of data.

Unlawful use 8.12

A man left one employer to set up on his own, taking data on his computer with him. He was convicted of having unlawfully used the data for his own purposes. His new company was also prosecuted for failing to notify.

Unlawful procurement – bank 8.13

A lady who worked at a bank used the bank's online credit checking facilities to do a credit search which had nothing to do with her work and which related to her domestic situation. She was convicted of unlawfully procuring information from the credit reference agency.

Unlawful procurement – DVLA 8.14

In two cases, convictions were secured for obtaining information from the Driving and Vehicle Licensing Agency (DVLA) by deception about registered keepers of cars. The prosecutions were for unlawfully procuring information from the DVLA.

Victim support 8.15

An individual was the victim of a crime. Acting under good motives, the police passed his details to a third party which provides counselling services to victims, but did so without the consent of the individual. The police force accepted this was an error after the individual complained and agreed to ensure that they would review procedures to ensure victims' wishes were respected.

Prosecutions 8.16

Below is a list from the Commissioner's First Annual Report (June 2001) of prosecutions from 1 April 2000 to 31 March 2001 which resulted in convictions. The Report also gives the hearing date, court and result (all guilty), and the costs ordered to be paid in addition to the sentences below. These costs are up to £1,000 in addition to the fines below. No one was sent to prison.

Offence (section of DPA 1998)	Sentence (£)
5(1)	100
5(1)	200
5(1)	250
5(1)	450
5(1)	750
5(1)	800
5(1)	1,000
5(1)	1,000
5(1)	2,000
5(1)	3,000
5(1)	Absolute Discharge
5(1)	Conditional Discharge 12 months
5(2)(b)	250
5(2)(d)(3) x 3	1,400
5(6)	200
5(6)	250
5(6)	Conditional Discharge 12 months
5(6)	Conditional Discharge 2 years

Criminal Records Bureau 8.17

In late 2001 the new Criminal Records Bureau will begin issuing 'disclosures' – criminal conviction certificates based on information on the Police National Computer. Many employers will take these disclosures into account when recruiting new staff.

Cybercrime 8.18

The Council of Europe is developing a Cybercrime Convention, which at the date of writing has not yet been agreed. This would to some extent harmonise the laws in this area internationally. The UK Information Commissioner has concerns that the retention of traffic data beyond that needed for technical and commercial reasons, as provided in the current draft, would be a breach of the right to private life in *Article 8* of the *European Convention on Human Rights*, and indeed now the *Human Rights Act 1998* in the UK.

Computer Misuse Act 1990 — 8.19

The *Computer Misuse Act 1990* makes it a criminal offence to gain unauthorised access to computer systems, and separately makes it a further offence to modify material having gained such access. There are few prosecutions, although a special department of police forces around the country handles this area – the Computer Crimes Unit. Many employers do not want to draw public attention to problems with their own security, so offences are covered up or not much reported. Even when prosecutions are brought before local courts the penalties are often weak. A UK man was arrested in August 2001 on charges that he created and released the W32-Leave worm, a virus-like program that was designed to let hackers take control of home computers. The man was charged under the *Computer Misuse Act 1990*, and if he is convicted could be jailed for up to five years.

Such hacking will usually involve access to personal data, for example someone may obtain details of the credit card and spending habits of a famous person through hacking. The data which is then accessed will be personal data under *DPA 1998*. Other countries have similar hacking legislation, so a hacker who has been hacking in many nations may find him or herself prosecuted in a number of different locations. The US Department of Justice is active in the computer crime area and has a cybercrime website at www.cybercrime.gov/.

Copyright, Designs and Patents Act 1988 — 8.20

Crimes in this field can also be committed under the *Copyright, Designs and Patents Act 1988*, although sentences can be light. Some computer software owners will seek to have a criminal prosecution brought against a computer software pirate or counterfeiter as a threat of a jail sentence can be more of a deterrent to some individuals than a large damages claim or the seizure of the infringing programs.

FAST and BSA — 8.21

Bodies such as the Federation Against Software Theft (FAST) (www.fast.org.uk) and the Business Software Alliance (BSA) (www.bsa.org/uk) will obtain court orders on behalf of their members to seize infringing products. However, this is in relation to copyright infringement, not a breach of data protection legislation. They also help companies ensure that all software used within the business is properly licensed and run a telephone line for infringements to be reported, with rewards of thousands of pounds paid to those tipping off the organisation about infringement of copyright where this leads to a successful prosecution.

Pirated software 8.22

Businesses buying software online need to ensure it is not pirated. The BSA estimates that more than 90 per cent of the software sold on auction sites is pirated. The BSA runs an Online Investigative Unit which recently looked at counterfeit software on Internet auction sites in the US and Europe. Its investigation called 'Operation Bidder Beware', found sales of pirated or counterfeit software from vendors in the UK, Germany and the US. Each of the 13 defendants caught in the US faces damages of up to $150,000 per work infringed.

Further information 8.23

In addition to this chapter, see CHAPTER 3 CODES OF PRACTICE, CHAPTER 32 OFFENCES and CHAPTER 38 RECORDING TELEPHONE CALLS AND E-MAILS.

Federation Against Software Theft (FAST)
Clivemont House
54 Clivemont Road
Maidenhead
Berkshire
SL6 7BZ
Tel: 01628 622 121
Fax: 01628 760 355
E-mail: fast@fast.org.uk
Website: www.fast.org.uk

Business Software Alliance (BSA)
79 Knightsbridge
London
SW1X 7RB
Tel: 0800 510 510
Website: www.bsa.org/uk

US Department of Justice Computer Crime
Website: www.cybercrime.gov/

9 – Data Controller

At a glance 9.1

- ✓ The data controller is the principal entity charged with compliance with the *Data Protection Act 1998* (*DPA 1998*) as regards personal data which it processes.
- ✓ There will often be more than one data controller for particular data.
- ✓ The Commissioner has issued useful guidance on this definition.
- ✓ Anonymisation of data can be a sensible procedure, however it will not necessarily render such data outside the scope of *DPA 1998*.

Introduction 9.2

'Who is the data controller?' is one of the most common questions asked of IT lawyers by their clients. This chapter seeks to provide some guidance on this topic. In 2001 the Information Commissioner issued some useful guidance on definitions under *DPA 1998* including the definition of a data controller, set out at 9.3 below and examined in this chapter. Data controllers may be companies, partnerships or individuals who control the use of personal data. Under the *Data Protection Act 1984* (*DPA 1984*) they were called a 'data user'. Data controller is the equivalent term under *DPA 1998*.

Definition of a data controller 9.3

A data controller is a person who either alone, jointly or in common with other persons 'determines' the purposes for which and the manner in which any personal data are processed or are to be processed (*DPA 1998, s 1(1)*). Where personal data is processed because of an enactment which requires such processing, then the data controller is the person on whom the obligation to process the data is imposed by the enactment (*DPA 1998, s 1(4)*).

Alone or jointly 9.4

A data controller will be covered by *DPA 1998* whether they act alone or jointly with others. There may therefore be two or more data controllers in relation to any piece of personal data. All data controllers would have to notify their holding of data and follow *DPA 1998*. Where data is controlled in 'common', those so holding it will all be data controllers. This may be the case where data controllers share a pool of personal data and each process it independently of each other.

Commissioner's advice on the interpretation of the expression 'data controller' 9.5

In January 2001 the Data Protection Commissioner issued guidance on the interpretation of the definition 'data controller' and 'personal data' (see 9.14 below). The former is considered below.

The Commissioner draws attention to *section 4(4)* of *DPA 1998* which provides that:

> '…it shall be the duty of a data controller to comply with the Data Protection Principles in relation to all personal data with respect to which he is the data controller.'

Jurisdictional issues 9.6

DPA 1998 only applies where the data controller is established in the UK and the data are processed in the context of that establishment or the controller uses equipment in the UK for processing the data 'otherwise than for the purposes of transit through the UK' (*DPA 1998, s 5(1)(b)*). 'Transit' means transient passing of the data such as where data is sent by e-mail and passes, often unnoticed, across servers in several states before ending up at the recipient.

Who is established in the UK? 9.7

If a data controller based abroad sends data to the UK and uses equipment in the UK to process the data then *DPA 1998* applies. *Section 5(3)* of *DPA 1998* deals with who is established in the UK. The following are so classified:

(*a*) individuals ordinarily resident in the UK;

(*b*) companies registered in the UK;

(*c*) partnerships or other unincorporated associations formed under the law of any part of the UK;

(*d*) anyone else not within (*a*)–(*c*) who maintains in the UK an office, branch or agency through which they carry on any activity or who maintains in the UK a regular practice.

Nominated representatives 9.8

Where a data controller is not established in the UK or any other state of the European Economic Area, but they use equipment to process data in the UK, then they must nominate a representative established in the UK (*DPA 1998, s 5(2)*). Few other sections of *DPA 1998* refer to such a representative. *DPA 1998, Sch 1, Part II, para 3*, which sets out the information which should be given to data subjects to ensure their data is fairly processed, includes a requirement that if there is a nominated representative under the Act then the identity of the representative must be given, along with the other information which has to be provided such as the identity of the data controller and the purpose for which the data is processed.

Consequences of being a data controller 9.9

Data controllers are the bodies or individuals who have the principal duties to comply with *DPA 1998*. They must accede to requests for subject access and must follow the Eight Data Protection Principles.

Group companies and data controllers 9.10

The controller is the person who determines the purposes for which and the manner in which the data is processed. A data controller must be a legal person, so it could be one subsidiary company, rather than the parent company. It is likely that for many corporate groups most if not all the group companies will have to notify (register).

Delegation 9.11

The data controller, or data controllers, must decide the purposes for which personal data are, or will be processed and the way in which personal data are, or will be, processed. The Commissioner recognises, however, that a person may decide the purposes for which personal data are to be processed, but may delegate responsibility for the way in which those data are to be processed to another person. She advised:

> 'In such a situation, the person determining the purposes will be the data controller because the Commissioner takes the view that when a person determines the purposes for which personal data are to be processed, a decision as to the

> manner in which those data are to be processed is inherent in that decision. The Commissioner's view is that the determination of the purpose for which personal data are to be processed is paramount in deciding whether or not a person is a data controller.'

Joint controllers 9.12

In deciding the purposes for which data are processed, it does not have to be exclusively processed by one data controller. There may be joint control of the data. 'Jointly' covers where the determination is exercised by acting together equally. 'Determination in common' is where data controllers share a pool of personal data, each processing independently of the other.

The Commissioner's advice is as follows.

> 'It is likely to be the case that data users under the previous data protection regime are data controllers under the new regime. However, it is important to appreciate the difference between the two definitions as it is quite possible that persons who were not data users under the 1984 Act will be data controllers under the Act. It is also possible that persons who carried on a computer bureau, as defined in the 1984 Act, and who were not also data users may find that they fall within the definition of data controller in the Act rather than the definition of "data processor".'

Example 9.13

A good illustration of the difference between the concepts of data user and data controller is in the context of credit reference agency data. Credit reference agencies were data users under *DPA 1984* and are data controllers under *DPA 1998*. The agency customers or subscribers who had access to credit reference agency data by way of a remote terminal, on a read-only basis, were not considered to be data users under *DPA 1984*. This was because they had no control of the content of the agency data and therefore fell outside the definition of data user.

Under *DPA 1998*, the Commissioner's view is that the credit reference agency and agency customers/subscribers are data controllers. This is because they each decide why and how they process personal data. Remember that the concept of 'processing' is very wide. The word can be used to encompass all manner of activities and operations that a particular data controller may want to perform on the personal data in question.

In respect of the credit reference agency, it, amongst other things, obtains, records, holds, organises, adapts, alters and discloses personal data. The agency customer or subscriber consults, obtains or retrieves personal data disclosed to it by the agency before using such data, for example, to inform a decision on whether to supply a customer. It is the ability to decide these things that makes them data controllers.

There will be many other examples of people, businesses and organisations who were not subject to *DPA 1984* but who are subject to *DPA 1998* because of the fact that they are now data controllers.

Personal data 9.14

The question of what constitutes personal data is also addressed in detail by the Commissioner. She suggests certain questions in assessing any particular case, and these are set out at 9.15–9.20 below.

What determines whether data relate to an individual? 9.15

Whether data relates to an individual is a question of fact. One issue is whether a data controller can form a connection between the data and the individual. Data do not have to relate solely to one individual and the same data may relate to two or more people and still be personal data about each of them; for example, joint tenants of a property, holders of a joint bank account or even individuals who use the same telephone or e-mail address. Information may relate to an individual in a business capacity and not just to their private life. Information about the business of a sole trader will amount to personal data as information about the business will be about the sole trader. Information about an individual in a partnership will be personal data if it relates to a specific partner. This will be more likely in a small partnership.

Although *DPA 1998* refers to individuals and not other legal entities such as limited companies, there will be situations where information about a limited company or other legal entity amounts to personal data because it relates to a specific individual, for example, the performance of a department. According to the Commissioner information relating solely to the legal entity will not be personal data.

Does the Act only relate to living individuals? 9.16

Yes. *DPA 1998* is only concerned with living individuals and so if the subject of the information is dead, then the information cannot be personal data.

The individual must be capable of being identified. How does the Commissioner approach this issue? 9.17

The individual must be capable of being identified from data in the possession of the data controller, or from those data and other information in the possession of, or likely to come into the possession of, the data controller. The issue of information likely to come into the data controller's possession has always puzzled the writer. A data controller could always promise to itself never to let certain information come into its possession and thus could avoid the information being personal data. The writer has had at least one client in this class.

The Commissioner recognises that an individual may be 'identified' without necessarily knowing the name and address of that particular individual. The Commissioner's view is that it is sufficient if the data are capable of being processed by the data controller to enable the data controller to distinguish the data subject from any other individual. This would be the case if a data subject could be treated differently from other individuals.

Examples of this are as follows.

- The capture of an image of an individual by a CCTV camera may be done in such a way that distinguishable features of that individual are processed and identified from the captured images. This will amount to personal data.
- In the context of the Internet, many e-mail addresses are personal data where the e-mail address clearly identifies a particular individual, for example the address elizabethfrance@dataprotection.gov.uk.

In the majority of cases the ability to 'identify' an individual will be achieved by knowing the name and address of an individual, or by the data controller being in possession of some other information. The definition also allows for an individual to be identified from data together with information 'likely to come into the possession of' the data controller. It will be for a data controller to satisfy himself whether it is likely that such information will come into his possession to render data personal data. This will depend largely on the nature of the processing undertaken by a data controller, the Commissioner says.

This issue is clearly relevant in the context of personal data which a data controller wishes to keep anonymous (see 9.21 below).

Example 9.18

> The following example is given by the Commissioner.
>
> If information about a particular web user is built up over a period of time, perhaps through the use of tracking technology, with the intention that it may later be linked to a name and address, then that information is personal data. Information may be compiled about a particular web user, but there might not be any intention of linking it to a name and address or e-mail address. There might merely be an intention to target that particular user with advertising, or to offer discounts when they re-visit a particular website, on the basis of the profile built up, without any ability to locate that user in the physical world. The Commissioner takes the view that such information is, nevertheless, personal data. In the context of the online world the information that identifies an individual is that which uniquely locates him in that world, by distinguishing him from others.

CCTV images 9.19

Another way in which information may come into the possession of a data controller is in relation to an image captured on CCTV. This might produce an image which is not of a distinguishable individual, but the actual identity of that individual may become apparent from other information likely to come into the possession of the data controller.

What is meant by the expression 'possession' in this context? 9.20

The concept of possession is very wide. In the Commissioner's view possession does not necessarily mean that the identifying data are in the physical control of the data controller, or likely to come under his physical control. A data controller enters into a contract with a data processor for the processing of personal data. The arrangement is that the data processor may receive some of the identifying data from a third party and some from the data controller. The data are processed in accordance with the terms of the contract. The data controller determines the purposes for which and the manner in which the personal data are to be processed by the data processor but may not have sight of all or any of the information which identifies a living individual. The data controller would, however, be deemed to be in possession of those data. The data controller could not argue in such a situation that the identifying data are not in his 'possession' and absolve himself of his responsibilities as data controller.

Can personal data be made anonymous? 9.21

The issue of information in the possession of, or likely to come into the possession of, a data controller has an impact on a data controller who seeks to make anonymous the personal data he is processing by stripping those data of all personal identifiers.

The Commissioner says:

> 'The fact that personal data may be anonymised is referred to in *Directive 95/46/EC* (the "Directive"), at Recital 26, and in the matter of *R v The Department of Health ex parte Source Informatics Limited [2000] 1 All ER 786*. In that case it was acknowledged by the Court of Appeal that the Directive does not apply to anonymised data. In anonymising personal data the data controller will be processing such data and, in respect of such processing, will still need to comply with the provisions of the Act.'

The Commissioner recognises that the aim of anonymisation is to provide better data protection. However, some people use it to avoid the onerous obligations of *DPA 1998*. The Commissioner thinks it is a good thing but very hard to achieve. The fact that the data controller is in possession of this data set which, if linked to the data which have been stripped of all personal identifiers, will enable a living individual to be identified, means that all the data, including the data stripped of personal identifiers, remain personal data in the hands of that data controller and cannot be said to have been anonymised. The fact that the data controller may have no intention of linking these two data sets is immaterial.

A data controller who destroys the original data set retaining only the information which has been stripped of all personal identifiers and who assesses that it is not likely that information will come into his possession to enable him to reconstitute the data, ceases to be a data controller in respect of the retained data.

Whether or not data which have been stripped of all personal identifiers are personal data in the hands of a person to whom they are disclosed, will depend upon that person being in possession of, or likely to come into the possession of, other information which would enable that person to identify a living individual.

It should be noted that the *disclosure* of personal data by a data controller amounts to processing under *DPA 1998*.

For example, the obtaining of clinical information linked to a National Health Service number by a person having access to the National Health Service Central Register will amount to processing of personal data by that person, because that person will have access to information enabling him to identify the individuals concerned.

It will be a duty upon someone processing data to take measures to ensure that the data cannot be reconstituted to become personal data and to be prepared to justify any decision made on processing of the data.

In the case of data collected by the Office of National Statistics, where there is a disclosure of samples of anonymised data, it is conceivable that a combination of information in a particular geographic area may be unique to an individual or family who could therefore be identifiable from that information. In recognition of this fact, disclosures of information are done in such a way that any obvious identifiers are removed and the data presented so as to avoid particular individuals being distinguished.

If data have been stripped of all personal identifiers such that the data controller is no longer able to single out an individual and treat that individual differently, the data cease to be personal data. Whether this has been achieved may be open to challenge. Data controllers may therefore be required to justify the grounds for their view that the data are no longer personal data. When a subject access request is received, a data controller must be able to identify the data relating to the data subject making the request, to enable him to provide information specific to that data subject. In making a subject access request, a data subject might provide the data controller with sufficient information to enable his data to be distinguished from data relating to other individuals, in a situation where the data controller would not otherwise be able to do so from the information in his possession, which he may have stripped of all personal identifiers. In this case the data relating to the individual making the request become personal data, but the information provided by the data subject does not render the other data being held personal data unless the data controller believes that it is likely that information will come into his possession to render the other data personal data.

If there are any doubts as to whether data are personal data, the Commissioner's advice would be to treat the data as personal data, having particular regard to whether those data are sensitive personal data. In respect of such data, if a subject access request is received and the data controller cannot satisfy himself as to the identity of the person making the subject access request, or as to his ability to locate the information to which the subject access request relates because the data have been stripped of identifiers, then the data controller would not be obliged to comply with that subject access request, advising the data subject accordingly.

What about expressions of opinion or intention? 9.22

The definition of personal data contained in *DPA 1998* now expressly includes any indication of the intentions of the data controller or any other person in respect of an individual. This aspect of the definition was not included in the definition of 'personal data' in *DPA 1984*. The consequence of this may mean, for example, that an employer who processes appraisals of employees would have to disclose not only his opinions of the employees, but also any intention to offer or decline promotion on the basis of those opinions subject to any exemption available at any particular time.

General 9.23

To date, there have been no cases reported addressing the question of these definitions in order to provide judicial guidance as to their meaning.

10 – Data Processor and Processing

At a glance 10.1

- ✓ Data processors process personal data on behalf of data controllers.
- ✓ The data controller is responsible for ensuring that the data processor acts properly in relation to the data (*Data Protection Act 1998 (DPA 1998), Sch 1, Part II, paras 11, 12*).
- ✓ The data processor does not need to notify their holding of personal data although many data processors are also data controllers.
- ✓ Example letter from data controller to data processor.

Introduction 10.2

DPA 1998 contains special provisions in relation to those who process data. Processing includes most uses of data. Anyone who processes personal data on behalf of a data controller is called a 'data processor'. A data controller will have a higher duty of care where they have someone else process data on their behalf than would otherwise be the case.

A major change from the *Data Protection Act 1984* (*DPA 1984*) is that now a data processor does not have to notify their holding of personal data nor comply with the Data Protection Principles. *DPA 1998* requires that the data controller must impose a control on the data processor by contract terms to ensure the 1998 Act is followed. However, many data processors are also data controllers so the relaxation in the rules for data processors contained in *DPA 1998* has not had a major impact. *DPA 1998, Sch 1, Part II, paras 11* and *12* contain provisions relating to data processors – see 10.6 below.

What is processing? 10.3

Processing means obtaining, recording or holding the information or data, or carrying out any operation or set of operations on the information or data.

This might include things such as:

(*a*) organisation, adaptation or alteration of the information or data;

(*b*) retrieval, consultation or use of the information or data;

(*c*) disclosure of the information or data by transmission, dissemination or otherwise making it available;

(*d*) alignment, combination, blocking, erasure or destruction of the information or data.

(DPA 1998, s 1(1))

In most instances of data use processing is involved because of the width of the definition above. The definition of processing is much broader than under *DPA 1984*.

The Commissioner in her Introduction to *DPA 1998* writes:

> 'It is a compendious definition and it is difficult to envisage any action involving data which does not amount to processing within this definition. It is important for data controllers to bear in mind the extension of the concept of processing in the Act and not assume any similarity with the term as used in the 1984 Act'.

Processing by reference to data subject 10.4

Processing otherwise than in relation to the data subject is now also covered by *DPA 1998* although transitional provisions apply. *DPA 1984* did not include this. As of 24 October 2001 (the end of the first transitional period under *DPA 1998*), eligible automated data which are processed by reference to the data subject are exempt from the requirement in the First Data Protection Principle for one or more of the conditions for processing to be complied with, and such data *not* processed by reference to the data subject are exempt from:

- the First Data Protection Principle, except paragraphs 2 and 3 of the Fair Processing Code (which requires data controllers to tell data subjects about certain matters);
- the Second, Third, Fourth and Fifth Principles; and
- the rectification, blocking, erasure and destruction provisions.

The *Guide to the Data Protection Act 1998 for Direct Marketing* by Colin Fricker (2000) describes the position under *DPA 1984* which meant that those processing a direct marketing database of businesses with 'names of key office holders such as sales directors would not normally fall within the scope of "processing" – and would therefore normally fall outside the scope of the Act – if the names of the sales directors were added to enhance the likelihood of targeting an offer of a business product or service to a personal who had the relevant internal responsibilities but where the actual name or personal characteristics of the sales director were of no consequence per se.'

Some may think removing contact names from a database will remove the application of *DPA 1998*. If living individuals are able to be identified from the data when added to other information in the possession of or likely to come into the possession of the data controller then *DPA 1998* will apply.

> 'So, processing leading to mail addressed to "The Prime Minister" or "The Chairman, XYZ Bank" is likely to fall within the Act as the identity of such persons should be known, or become known, as a matter of course.'
>
> *Colin Fricker, Guide to the Data Protection Act 1998 for Direct Marketing (2000, DMA)*

Processor 10.5

DPA 1998 defines a data processor as, in relation to personal data:

> 'any person (other than an employee of the data controller) who processes the data on behalf of the data controller'

(DPA 1998, s 1(1))

Companies have to act through their employees and their use of the data on behalf of the employer does not make the employee a data processor, as some business people erroneously believe. However, a third party company or independent contractor processing data for their customer will be a data processor.

A data processor is the equivalent of a computer bureau under *DPA 1984*. In her January 2001 guidance on certain definitions under *DPA 1998* (see CHAPTER 9 DATA CONTROLLER) the Commissioner wrote:

> 'It is also possible that persons who carried on a computer bureau, as defined in the 1984 Act, and who were not also data users may find that they fall within the definition of data controller in the Act rather than the definition of "data processor".'

Whether that is the case in a particular instance will depend on the particular circumstances as seen above. The term 'data processor' catches more businesses than the old computer bureau definition. It will apply, for example, to market researchers who collect data for a data controller and also disposal contractors.

Schedule 1, Part II – the Seventh Principle and data processors 10.6

DPA 1998, Sch 1, Part II, paras 11 and *12* state that where processing is carried out by a data processor on behalf of a data controller then the data controller must, in order to comply with the Seventh Principle (security – see CHAPTER 6 CONFIDENTIALITY AND DATA SECURITY: SEVENTH PRINCIPLE),

> '(*a*) choose a data processor providing sufficient guarantees in respect of the technical and organisational security measures governing the processing to be carried out, and
>
> (*b*) take reasonable steps to ensure compliance with those measures.'

Such processing by a data processor will not, on the part of the data controller, comply with the Seventh Principle unless the processing is carried out under a contract which is made or evidenced in writing (which presumably even since the advent of the *Electronic Communications Act 2000* would not include being made by e-mail, although a prosecution on that basis would be unlikely in practice to be brought if clear e-mailed terms had been agreed), and under which the data processor is to act only on instructions from the data controller. The contract must require the data processor to comply with obligations equivalent to those imposed on a data controller by the Seventh Principle.

In practice this means that those using data processors need to ensure written contracts are in place, otherwise the data controller may breach the Seventh Principle.

Heather Rowe of Lovells in her book *Data Protection Act 1998: A Practical Guide* (Tolley) suggests the following practical steps which data controllers should take.

- Users should check their standard forms for appointment of third parties to process their data and ensure that appropriate references to the Seventh Principle are incorporated as well as including references to the appropriate level of control of the data by the data controller.
- Users should ask themselves who is a data processor. Is it the person who processes a company's payroll (almost certainly yes), but what about the person who shreds confidential paperwork. Could that be personal data?
- Users should also consider, when appointing a new processor, incorporating detailed questionnaires in tender documents, say, requiring the prospective processor to describe its security measures so that they can be carefully assessed.
- The Commissioner has suggested that data controllers should review that their existing security measures are appropriate for the types of data they are processing. She has suggested that reference to the British Standards Institute Standard BS 7799 may help data controllers assess the adequacy of their current data protection regime.
- New contracts must contain an ongoing right of audit/inspection of the processor's security procedures

(Heather Rowe, Lovells, Data Protection Act 1998: A Practical Guide (Tolley))

The following sample letter from a data controller to a data processor is also suggested by the same source.

An example of a draft letter from a data controller to a data processor

[appropriate officer to Data Processor]

[address of Data Processor]

[For the attention of: [appropriate representative of Data Processor]]
Dear [Sir] [ ]

Processing contract between [Data Processor] and [Data Controller]

We refer to the processing contract between us dated [ ] ('the Contract') under which you have undertaken to provide certain processing services ('Services') on our behalf.

On 1 March 2000 the Data Protection Act 1998 ('the Act') became law. Under that Act, by virtue of the Seventh Data Protection

Principle contained in Schedule 1 of the Act, "data controllers" (in the case of our relationship with you, that will be [full name],) are obliged to impose certain obligations of security in relation to personal data upon their 'data processors' which, in the context of the Contract, is you.

Since it is our legal requirement to include such a provision in our Contract, we would be grateful if you would undertake to us as set out below. [In consideration of that undertaking, we would be prepared to contemplate continuing future relationships with you.] If you are unable to give such an undertaking, then we may [be forced to seek services elsewhere in the future] [will not renew the Contract] [on expiry of the Contract] since, if we are unable to obtain appropriate assurances from you, we will be in breach of our legal obligations under the Act.

The assurance that we seek from you is that you undertake to us to comply with the obligations of a 'data controller' under the provisions of the Seventh Data Protection Principle, as set out in Schedule I, Part II of the Act as regards any personal data you process in providing the Services. In addition, you:

(*a*) Warrant and undertake that you have and will have at all times during the term of the Contract appropriate technical and organisational measures in place acceptable to us to protect any personal data accessed or processed by you against unauthorised or unlawful processing of personal data and against accidental loss or destruction of, or damage to, personal data held or processed by you [(such measures as at the date of this letter being described in the attached Annex)] and that you have taken all reasonable steps to ensure the reliability of any of your staff which will have access to personal data processed as part of the Services;

(*b*) Undertake that you will act only on our instructions in relation to the processing of any personal data provided to you by us, [or] on our behalf, [or] by our employees [or former employees];

(c) Undertake [to provide the Services at least to the level of security set out in the Annex to this Letter and] to allow us (or our representative) access to any relevant premises owned or controlled by you on reasonable notice to inspect your procedures described at (a) above and will, on our request from time to time, prepare a report for us as to your then current technical and organisational measures used to protect any such personal data.

[(d) Undertake to consider all [reasonable] suggestions which we may put to you to ensure that the level of protection you provide for personal data is in accordance with this Letter and to make changes suggested unless you can prove to our reasonable satisfaction that they are not necessary to ensure ongoing compliance with your warranty and undertaking at (a) above.]

Breach of any of the above warranties or undertakings will entitle us to terminate the Contract forthwith.

Any terms defined in the Act will have the same meaning in this letter.

Please indicate your agreement to the provisions set out above by signing and returning the attached copy of this letter.

Yours faithfully,

....

For and on behalf of [Data Controller]

....

Accepted and Agreed
[Data Processor]

....

Annex
The Current Security Procedures

(Source: Heather Rowe, Lovells, Data Protection Act 1998: A Practical Guide (Tolley).)

Processing sensitive personal data 10.7

The processing of sensitive personal data (see CHAPTER 42 SENSITIVE PERSONAL DATA) is addressed in the *Data Protection (Processing of Sensitive Personal Data) Order 2000* (*SI 2000/417*).

Summary 10.8

Most uses of data amount to processing under the definitions in *DPA 1998.* The important practical point to note from this section is that if a data processor is used to process the data the data controller must impose contractual provisions as stipulated in *DPA 1998* on the data processor as described above.

11 – Data Subject

At a glance 11.1

- ✓ A data subject is an individual under the *Data Protection Act 1998* (*DPA 1998*) whose personal data is controlled by a data controller (*DPA 1998, s1(1)*).
- ✓ Data subjects must be living individuals. Limited companies cannot be data subjects.
- ✓ *DPA 1998* applies to data controllers established in the UK even if they process data relating to those living abroad.
- ✓ Consideration should be given to when data can be made anonymous, such that it then comes outside the scope of protection under *DPA 1998*. Guidance from the Information Commissioner is available in this area.

Introduction 11.2

Those about whom data is held are known as data subjects under the *Data Protection Act 1984* (*DPA 1984*). *Section 1(1)* of *DPA 1998* defines this as 'an individual who is the subject of personal data'. There is no definition of data subject in the *EU Data Protection Directive* (*95/46/EC*).

- The data subject is required to be a living individual.
- A limited company cannot be classified as a data subject.
- A partnership is a group of living individuals. Individual partners would be data subjects as would members of a limited liability partnership under the *Limited Liability Partnerships Act 2000*.
- Animals cannot be data subjects. The position on unborn children is not clear.

The definition of data subject is identical to that under *DPA 1984*.

Living individuals 11.3

The use of the word 'living' in the legislation has led to some concern about whether the law could apply to those who had been living but have then died. However that appears not to be the case.

> 'In fact, a literal interpretation of the Directive might arguably have applied the definition to individuals who had died, but the Home Office have interpreted this sensibly.'

(Heather Rowe, Data Protection Act 1998 – A Practical Guide (Tolley 2000))

> 'Does the Act only relate to living individuals?
>
> Yes. The Act is only concerned with living individuals and so if the subject of the information is dead, then the information cannot be personal data.'

(Guidance on Personal Data , Information Commissioner)

Given the Commissioner's view above, it seems reasonable for data controllers to assume that *DPA 1998* will not apply to personal data they hold about people who have died.

Personal data **11.4**

Data controllers assessing what constitutes personal data should consider the guidance which the Commissioner has issued on the subject. For that purpose, the individual must be capable of being identified from data in the possession of the data controller, or from those data and other information in the possession of, or likely to come into the possession of, the data controller.

> 'The Commissioner recognises that an individual may be "identified" without necessarily knowing the name and address of that particular individual. The Commissioner's view is that it is sufficient if the data are capable of being processed by the data controller to enable the data controller to distinguish the data subject from any other individual. This would be the case if a data subject could be treated differently from other individuals.'

The data subject **11.5**

In most cases there is not much doubt about who a data subject is. Sometimes personal data will contain information about several data subjects, and then the issue arises of ensuring that where a subject access request is received, information about one data subject is not disclosed to the other without consent, but the identity of the data subject themselves is largely clear.

By way of example, Susan Singleton is a data subject. Her sole legal practice, Singletons, operates as a sole trader. Singletons is the trading name and is not a data subject. The publisher of this book, Reed Elsevier (UK) Limited, is a limited company registered at Companies

House. The company cannot be a data subject as it is not a living individual.

Age and data subjects 11.6

Individuals of any age can make a subject access request and this includes children. In her guidance *Subject access to social services records* (November 2000) (accessible under Guidance on the Commissioner's website), the Commissioner says that:

> 'Subject access requests may be made by the individuals to whom the data relate irrespective of age or any other criteria. A data subject can make a request through agents such as a solicitor or advice worker, although they may be asked for evidence that they are acting on behalf of the data subject. In cases where data subjects are incapable of understanding or exercising their rights, for instance because they are too young or suffer from a severe mental handicap, then subject access requests may be made by parents or other persons who are legally able to act on behalf of the data subjects. In many cases a Social Services Department may choose to disclose information about a client who is incapable of exercising his or her rights to a parent or other third party. However, it cannot be compelled to make the disclosure if the third party does not act on behalf of the data subject in law.'

In her February 2001 Advice Sheet on the Disclosure of Examination Results by Schools to the Media, the Commissioner comments on the issue of children giving consent. The rights which *DPA 1998* gives data subjects are not affected by their ages, she says. The Commissioner generally advises that providing people are able to understand their rights then it is they and not their parents or guardians who should be informed of the uses and disclosures of data, and who have the right to object to processing. In most cases, therefore, it is sufficient to provide information in advance notifying pupils that their examination results will be published. In a small number of cases, it may be that pupils are not capable of understanding their rights or of understanding the consequences of publication. In these cases, schools should provide the relevant information to parents or guardians.

For example, a premature baby born at 21 weeks gestation, and arguably damaged during its delivery by the doctors, where litigation may result, could therefore make a subject access request. Presumably despite its birth below the normal lawful age for abortion in the UK the fact it has 'lived' will make it a living individual entitled to exercise a request under *DPA 1998* through the agency of its parents or solicitors. Whereas, had the child died before birth, it may not be a 'living individual' and thus could not make a request whether through an agent or not. However the Act does not state at what point life begins so the issue is not free of doubt.

Territorial application 11.7

DPA 1998 protects personal data relating to British citizens and foreigners, protecting those living abroad as much as those living in the UK. *Section 5* of *DPA 1998* provides that the Act applies to data controllers who are established in the UK and the data is processed in the context of their establishment, or they are established elsewhere but they use equipment in the UK to process data in the UK.

A UK business processing data about customers in Japan, for example, deals with 'data subjects' even if all those people are Japanese residents who have never been to the UK.

International co-operation 11.8

The *Data Protection (International Co-operation) Order 2000* (*SI 2000/190*) gives the Commissioner powers to enforce *DPA 1998* over data controllers who are processing their data in the UK, but to whom the Act does not apply because of *section 5* of *DPA 1998*, and where they are processing data within the scope of the functions of a supervisory authority in another member state. Upon the request of that authority the Commissioner can then act. The Commissioner sends the authority details of the action she has taken as she thinks fit.

Similarly the Commissioner may request a supervisory authority in another EEA state to exercise its functions under *Article 28(3)* of the *EU Data Protection Directive (95/46/EC)* in relation that processing.

Anonymising data 11.9

Data will not fall within *DPA 1998* if it does not relate to a data subject. Some data controllers will seek to strip data of all personal identifiers.

The *Data Protection Directive* (*95/46/EC*) refers to the anonymising of data as did the case *R v The Department of Health ex parte Source Informatics Limited [2000] 1 All ER 786.* There the court held that the Directive does not apply to anonymised data. The Commissioner's view in guidance on the definition of 'personal data' is that it is hard to anonymise data but that it is laudable, where possible, to strip data of information 'relating to a data subject, which is not necessary for the particular processing being undertaken...This does not amount to anonymisation but is in line with the requirements of the Data Protection Principles.'

Normally where anonymisation is sought the data controller still keeps the original data out of which the personal identifiers have been stripped. The Commissioner says in her guidance:

> 'The fact that the data controller is in possession of this data set which, if linked to the data which have been stripped of all personal identifiers, will enable a living individual to be identified, means that all the data, including the data stripped of personal identifiers, remain personal data in the hands of that data controller and cannot be said to have been anonymised. The fact that the data controller may have no intention of linking these two data sets is immaterial.'

However, if a data controller destroys the original data set and only keeps the information which has been stripped of all personal identifiers, and assesses that it is not likely that information will come into his possession to enable him to reconstitute the data will then cease to be a data controller for that data which is kept.

Commissioner's examples **11.10**

The obtaining of clinical information linked to a National Health Service number by a person having access to the National Health Service Central Register will amount to processing of personal data by that person, because that person will have access to information enabling him to identify the individuals concerned.

The person processing the data should take the steps needed to ensure that the data cannot be reconstituted so as to become personal data. They must also be prepared to 'justify any decision they make with regard to the processing of the data'.

In the case of data collected by the Office of National Statistics, where there is a disclosure of samples of anonymised data, it is conceivable that a combination of information in a particular geographic area may be unique to an individual or family who could therefore be identifiable from that information. In recognition of this fact, disclosures of information are done in such a way that any obvious identifiers are removed and the data presented so as to avoid particular individuals being distinguished.

> 'If data have been stripped of all personal identifiers such that the data controller is no longer able to single out an

individual and treat that individual differently, the data cease to be personal data. Whether this has been achieved may be open to challenge. Data controllers may therefore be required to justify the grounds for their view that the data are no longer personal data.'

Identifying the data subject 11.9

Normally there is little doubt, in relation to data which is not anonymised, as to whether or not it is data about a 'data subject' or not. Another issue however is ensuring that the individual data subject is who they say they are. Reference should be made here to CHAPTER 6 CONFIDENTIALITY AND DATA SECURITY: THE SEVENTH PRINCIPLE in this respect.

Those making subject access requests must provide the data controller with enough information to enable the data to be distinguished from data relating to other individuals. If the data controller, as seen above, has stripped the data of personal identifiers he may then find it hard to determine whose data is whose. If this stripping exercise, undertaken with laudable objectives, has not so fully anonymised the data that it is not 'personal data' at all (which the Commissioner believes will rarely be achieved) then the subject access request must still be complied with. The data relating to the individual making the request may become personal data but the information provided by the data subject does not, the Commissioner believes, 'render the other data being held personal data unless the data controller believes that it is likely that information will come into his possession to render the other data personal data'.

> 'If there are any doubts as to whether data are personal data the Commissioner's advice would be to treat the data as personal data, having particular regard to whether those data are sensitive personal data. In respect of such data, if a subject access request is received and the data controller cannot satisfy himself as to the identity of the person making the subject access request, or as to his ability to locate the information to which the subject access request relates because the data have been stripped of identifiers, then the data controller would not be obliged to comply with that subject access request, advising the data subject accordingly.'

(Information Commissioner – Guidance on Definition of Personal Data)

12 – Direct Mail

At a glance 12.1

- ✓ The direct mail industry makes much use of personal data and thus is subject to the *Data Protection Act 1998* (*DPA 1998*).
- ✓ Under *section 11* of *DPA 1998* individuals have a right to object to their personal data being used for the purposes of direct marketing.
- ✓ The Mailing Preference Service is a voluntary service in which companies can participate. Participants will check whether individuals have opted out of direct mail before marketing to them by post.

Introduction 12.2

The direct mail industry makes major use of personal data and must fully comply with *DPA 1998*. CHAPTER 13 DIRECT MARKETING looks at general direct marketing issues under the Act and the various preference schemes available where individuals can register so as not to receive certain unsolicited communications in various areas. This topic examines specifically 'direct mail' sent by post.

Most direct mail is addressed to individuals and thus uses personal data under *DPA 1998*. (See CHAPTER 35 PERSONAL DATA.) However, the legislation will not apply in most cases. In particular, the Mail Preference Service described at 12.9 below will not apply where:

- mailings are anonymously addressed, such as to 'the householder';
- without a name but simply stating the postal address; or
- leaflets are delivered by hand to the door without any recipient's name appearing on them,

because those mailings do not include personal data in most cases.

Rights to object to direct mail 12.3

Under *section 11* of *DPA 1998* individuals have a right to object to their personal data being used for the purposes of direct marketing. *Section 11* is closely allied to *section 10* of *DPA 1998* which gives the right to prevent processing which is likely to cause damage or distress.

Section 11 provides:

> '(1) An individual is entitled at any time by notice in writing to a data controller to require the data controller at the end of such period as is reasonable in the circumstances to cease, or not to begin, processing for the purposes of direct marketing personal data in respect of which he is the data subject.
>
> (2) If the court is satisfied, on the application of any person who has given a notice under subsection (1), that the data controller has failed to comply with the notice, the court may order him to take such steps for complying with the notice as the court thinks fit.'

Under this section direct marketing means 'the communication (by whatever means) of any advertising or marketing material which is directed to particular individuals' (*DPA 1998, s 11(3)*).

The application of this is wider than simply in relation to direct mail and is concerned with other forms of direct marketing as well.

Section 11 of *DPA 1998* implements *Article 14* of the *Data Protection Directive* (*95/46/EC*) which requires every state in the EU to allow data subjects rights to object on request and free of charge to processing of their personal data for direct marketing purposes. The *Direct Marketing Association (DMA) Guide to the Data Protection Act 1998 for Direct Marketing* points out that *DPA 1998* does not include a provision in the directive that member states must make individuals aware of their rights in this area and that under EU law, in the event of a conflict between national and EU law, EU law will prevail. Anyone who suffers loss because the UK has not implemented an EU directive properly can sue the Government for damages, but may only act as if the directive were in force against a state entity.

It is probably the role of the Information Commissioner to make individuals aware of this right rather than the data controller. Does the data controller have to put on all its marketing material when it gathers personal data that individuals have a right of opt-out in this way?

Example: Wording of opt-out provision and response 12.4

The DMA suggests some wording in its guide (see 12.7 below). One suggestion made is to add a phrase such as:

> 'We may wish to send you promotional material about our other products/services.'

This might be appropriate in an off the page advertisement where the data would not be passed on or shared with anyone else. Then additional words could be added:

> 'If you don't want us to do this please let us know by writing to the above address.'

or

> 'If you would prefer us not to do this please tick this box when sending in your order'.

Dealing with suppression requests 12.5

When a business receives a written notification under *section 11* of *DPA 1998* the Information Commissioner recommends as follows:

> **'Dealing with direct marketing suppression requests**
>
> The *Data Protection Act 1998* gives individuals the right not to have their personal data processed for direct marketing purposes. When collecting data, for example from customers, you should give them the opportunity to let you know whether or not they wish to receive marketing material from you. If they do not, you must ensure that you can suppress their details on any mailing lists you use. If you intend to pass personal data to other companies for direct marketing purposes, again you must first check with the individuals concerned if they are happy for you to do this. This should be done when you first collect the data, perhaps on an application form. You must not pass on the details of anyone who says that they object to their details being used in this way. If you have not previously sent out marketing material or passed on details to third parties for marketing, you should obtain the consent of existing customers before beginning to process their data for either of those purposes.'

Direct mail issues 12.6

There are no special rules in relation to the dispatch of mail by post rather than by other means (see CHAPTER 13 DIRECT MARKETING). However, the preference scheme described below is specific to the use of postal services.

DPA 1998 and direct mail – a guide 12.7

A Guide to the Data Protection Act 1998 for Direct Marketing is published by the DMA written by Colin Fricker, former DMA Director of Legal and Regulatory Affairs.

Specific explanation, interpretation and guidance is given in the Guide in relation to:

- increased controls over data processing;
- the new express provision that gives individuals a right to opt-out of receiving a company's own future direct marketing approaches;
- the type of information that must be provided to the data subject;
- what opt-outs are necessary and the wording to be used in different circumstances;
- the restrictions on the transfer of data to countries outside the European Economic Area; and
- the increased rights of data subjects and the notification process.

The Mailing Preference Service 12.8

The Mailing Preference Service (sometimes known as MPS) was set up as and remains a non-profit organisation. It is a member of the Committee of Advertising Practice and enables individuals to register so as not to receive unsolicited post/mail from companies which participate in the voluntary scheme. The scheme does not remove the rights under *section 10* of *DPA 1998* which state that every data subject has to notify the data controller individually that they do not want to receive unsolicited mail.

The direct mail industry funds the Mailing Preference Service. It pays a levy whenever a particular volume mailing service of Consignia (Post Office) is used.

What the Mailing Preference Service does **12.9**

The MPS will remove a name from mailing lists or have it added to many lists, as it works both ways around. Individual data subjects can register on the following link www.mpsonline.org.uk/MpsR/html/Register.asp and use forms which appears there for completion.

Points to note **12.10**

The MPS says:

'• Your name will remain on file for five years. If you want to continue receiving the service beyond this date, you will need to apply again.

- If you are currently receiving mailings with an incorrect version of your name and address, you will need to contact the mailer directly to correct this information.
- You will still receive mailings from companies with whom you have done business in the past, as well as from some small local companies. If you wish to stop these mailings you should contact the companies directly.
- Allow at least three months for mail to start to decrease.
- Unaddressed material is not covered by MPS.
- Please remember to let us know of any change of address.'

The Information Commissioner describes the scheme thus:

> 'When you provide your surname and address to the MPS they will place the information on their consumer file which is then made available to those members of the direct marketing industry who subscribe to the MPS scheme. They undertake to ensure that the mailing lists they use and supply are "cleaned" of any names and addresses which appear on the MPS file, the result being that you should not, in future, receive their mailings.
>
> Membership of the MPS scheme by direct marketers is not a specific requirement of the Data Protection Act 1998. However the Data Protection Commissioner strongly supports the scheme. In some circumstances she can insist that direct marketers who do not currently subscribe to the scheme, do so in future. Furthermore, several direct marketing

industry codes of practice specify that direct marketers should clean their lists against the MPS file. This means there is substantial voluntary adherence to the scheme.

You can register your details with the MPS free of charge and your registration will be effective for five years. However, the MPS can only assist in respect of mailings, which are personally addressed. It is unable to assist with mailings, which are unaddressed, or those, which are addressed to "the occupier". It is also unlikely to prevent the mail you may receive from organisations you have done business with – you should write to those organisations directly and request that they exclude you from their marketing lists.'

Further information 12.11

See also CHAPTER 13 DIRECT MARKETING, CHAPTER 31 MARKETING and CHAPTER 33 OPT- IN AND OPT-OUT.

The Direct Marketing Association (UK) Ltd's Guide to the Data Protection Act 1998 for Direct Marketing The Guide costs £75 (members) and £150 (non-members).	www.dma.org.uk

Mailing Preference Service FREEPOST 22 London W1E 7EZ Tel: 020 7766 4410.

13 – Direct Marketing

At a glance 13.1

- ✓ Direct marketing normally involves processing of personal data.
- ✓ Under *section 11* of the *Data Protection Act 1998 (DPA 1998)* individuals can object to their personal data being processed for such purposes.
- ✓ Mailing preference schemes of various types exist to enable individuals to object to direct marketing.
- ✓ Special rules apply to direct marketing by fax, based on the *EU Telecommunications Directive*.

Introduction 13.2

Direct marketing takes many forms, from unsolicited e-mails (spam) to telephone calls. This section examines direct marketing in general. For further information on direct mail, see CHAPTER 12 DIRECT MAIL.

Various preference schemes are available under which individuals can register to object to direct marketing and *section 11* of the *DPA 1998* enables individuals to notify individual data controllers that they do not want their personal data processed for direct marketing purposes.

Notice to data controllers 13.3

Under *section 11* of *DPA 1998*, notice must be given in writing to a data controller to cease – or not to begin – processing personal data relating to the individual for direct marketing purposes. Individuals can apply to the court for an order to that effect if the data controller does not comply with the notice.

Direct Marketing Authority 13.4

In May 1997, the Direct Marketing Association (DMA) Board approved proposals to reform the governance of the direct marketing industry by bringing the then disparate direct marketing self-regulatory services together under one administration by creating a new body, the Direct

Marketing Authority, to act as the final arbiter on complaints referred to it by the DMA governance secretariat. It is the Authority, not the Association, which runs the various preference schemes.

The Direct Marketing Authority operates preference schemes such as the Mailing Preference Service (MPS) (see 13.7 below), Telephone Preference Service (TPS) (see 13.8 below), and the Fax Preference Service (FPS) (see 13.9 below). It also runs the Direct Mail Accreditation and Recognition Centre (DMARC), List and Data Suppliers Group (LADS) and the List Warranty Register (LWR).

It complements the work of the Advertising Standards Authority, which administers the general advertising code (BSCAP). The Direct Marketing Authority has a quasi-judicial function and considers complaints arising from the other self-regulatory bodies. It ensures all DMA members stick to the DMA Code of Practice. It does this, in particular, by considering complaints made against member organisations by consumers. It can issue a private or public admonition to the member concerned, and it may also suspend or expel a company from membership of the Association. Its powers extend to cover breaches of the TPS, FPS and MPS licences and of DMARC accredited suppliers' terms and conditions whether committed by DMA members or by non-DMA members.

The Direct Marketing Association 13.5

The Direct Marketing Association (www.dma.org.uk) requires its members to adhere to codes of practice in this field. It is a trade organisation for those involved in direct marketing in the UK. It is also a member of the International Federation of Direct Marketing Associations (IFDMA) and FEDMA (Federation of European Direct Marketing).

Preference schemes 13.6

Various preference schemes are operated, in most cases on a self-regulated basis, by the Direct Marketing Authority. They enable individuals to register so that they do not receive certain forms of direct marketing materials.

Mailing Preference Service 13.7

Individuals and businesses can register so as not to receive unsolicited mail under the Mailing Preference Scheme. It is not compulsory for companies to join. For further information on the service see CHAPTER 12 DIRECT MAIL.

Telephone Preference Service 13.8

Similarly, the Telephone Preference Service only applies to those companies which have voluntarily chosen to be a member of the scheme. The TPS can be contacted by telephoning 020 7766 4420. Further details are available on the Direct Marketing Association website at www.dma.org.uk.

Fax Preference Scheme 13.9

The Fax Preference Scheme is slightly different from those mentioned above. It was set up under the *Directive on the Processing of Personal Data and the Protection of Privacy in the Telecommunications Sector* (*97/66/EC*) and is of universal application. It allows those businesses who object to unsolicited faxes to register, and those sending unsolicited faxes must check first before sending the fax.

For individuals, the *Telecommunications (Data Protection and Privacy) Regulations 1999* (*SI 1999/2093*) implement the Directive in the UK and give all individuals including sole traders and partners (no matter how large the partnership) the right not to receive unsolicited faxes unless they have consented, whether they have registered or not. It is unlawful under those Regulations to send an unsolicited fax to an individual without his or her consent.

The FPS can be contacted by telephoning 020 7766 4422. Information relating to regulations in the area of direct marketing by fax is given later in this section.

E-mail preference 13.10

Junk e-mail or 'spam' is a major data protection problem for many individuals and businesses. The Direct Marketing Association has set up an e-mail preference service which currently operates on a voluntary basis. The preference service (e-MPS) is described as 'a suppression file only and it is not released to marketers or any other third parties who may wish to send commercial messages.'

According to the organisers, those using the e-MPS service send their e-mail address lists electronically to e-MPS at a nominal charge per annum. All e-mail addresses registered with e-MPS are removed from the service user's lists, thus being 'cleaned' and then returned electronically to the marketer.

Under *DPA 1998* those who wish to send data to be cleaned against the e-MPS file can do so only if they have a processing contract with the US DMA. (See CHAPTER 20 EXPORT OF DATA.)

Unsolicited faxes – the legislation 13.11

Data protection legislation concerning mailings by fax are dealt with, at least in part, by the *Telecommunications Directive* (*97/66/EC*). This was implemented in the UK and is now covered by the *Telecommunications (Data Protection and Privacy) Regulations 1999* (*SI 1999/2093*).

Unsolicited communications on lines of individual or corporate subscribers 13.12

Section 23 of *DPA 1998* applies to the use of publicly available telecommunications services for the unsolicited communication of material, for direct marketing purposes, by means of fax both for companies and individuals. It says that no one should send an unsolicited fax where the called line is that of a subscriber who has previously notified the caller that such unsolicited communications as are so mentioned should not be sent on that line. The communication of material mentioned above is not to be treated as unsolicited where the called line is that of a subscriber who has notified the caller that 'he does not for the time being object to such communications as are so mentioned being sent by, or at the instigation of, the caller in question on that line'. A record is kept of those who have so objected, to which businesses can have access on payment of fees (the fax preference services has been delegated this role).

Communications on lines of subscribers who are individuals. 13.13

Special rules apply under the *Telecommunications (Data Protection and Privacy) Regulations 1999* (*SI 1999/2093*). *Regulation 24* sets out the rules in relation to those who are individuals. This includes businesses which are sole traders, such as the writer's solicitor's firm and even large firms of accountants who are not incorporated with hundreds of partners. It states:

> 'A person shall not use, or instigate the use of, publicly available telecommunications services, and a subscriber to such services shall not permit his line to be used, as mentioned in paragraph (1), except where the called line is that of a subscriber who has previously notified the caller that he consents for the time being to such communications as are there mentioned being sent by, or at the instigation of, the caller in question on that line.'

This makes the sending of an unsolicited fax to an individual unlawful. In practice many such faxes are still sent.

Unsolicited calls for direct marketing purposes on lines of subscribers who are individuals. 13.14

Regulation 25 of the *Telecommunications Regulations* (*SI 1999/2093*) prohibits unsolicited sales calls where:

(i) the called line is that of a subscriber who has previously notified the caller that such unsolicited calls as are there mentioned should not for the time being be made on that line, or

(ii) the number allocated to a subscriber in respect of the called line is one listed in the record kept under paragraph (4) (the section under which a central register is kept – telephone preference).

A call on a subscriber's line shall not be treated as an unsolicited call if that subscriber has notified the caller that he does not object to calls being made by, or at the instigation of, the caller in question for direct marketing purposes on that line.

Example: Second Telecom Case 13.15

In the cases *Second Telecom Limited v The Data Protection Commissioner* and *Top 20 Limited v The Data Protection Commissioner*, the fax preference rules were the subject of legal action when two companies – Second Telecom Ltd and Top 20 Ltd – appealed against May 2000 enforcement notices which had been issued against them by the Information Commissioner. However, they agreed to comply on the following terms:

> 'That the Caller, Second Telecom Limited and/or Top 20 Limited, shall within the period of thirty days from the date of this Notice have taken such steps as are necessary to ensure compliance with *Regulation 23* of the *Telecommunications (Data Protection and Privacy) Regulations 1999* (the "Regulations"), namely:
>
> (*a*) The Caller shall not use, or instigate the use of, publicly available telecommunications services for the unsolicited communication of material, for direct marketing purposes, by means of facsimile transmission, where the called line is that of a subscriber who has previously notified the Caller that such unsolicited communications as are so mentioned should not be sent on that line;
>
> (*b*) The Caller shall not use, or instigate the use of, publicly available telecommunications services for the

unsolicited communication of material, for direct marketing purposes, by means of facsimile transmission, where the called line is one that is subject to this paragraph (b). A called line shall be subject to this paragraph (b) at the expiration of seven working days of any notice in writing from the Commissioner to the Caller that the line in question is the subject of a complaint alleging a breach by the Caller of paragraph (a) above of this Notice; and

(*c*) The Caller shall not use, or instigate the use of, publicly available telecommunications services for the unsolicited communication of material, for direct marketing purposes, by means of facsimile transmission, where the number allocated to a subscriber in respect of the called line is one listed in the record kept under regulation 23(4) of the Regulations except when that number was not so listed at any time within the 28 days preceding that on which the call is made.'

Background

The Commissioner had received numerous complaints about the companies and served an enforcement notice which contained, *inter alia*, the following information:

'In view of the matters referred to above, the Commissioner hereby gives notice that in exercise of her powers under *section 40* of the *1998 Act* (as extended and modified by *regulation 36* of, and *Schedule 4* to, the Regulations) she requires that the Caller, Top 20 Limited, shall take such steps as are necessary to ensure compliance with the Relevant Requirement, namely:

(i) Within 28 days of the date of this Notice the Caller shall screen its entire database against an independent database which satisfies the criteria set out below so as to identify those lines on the Caller's database which are listed as lines of residential subscribers on the said independent database (the "screening exercise").

Criteria for independent database:

(*a*) the database is a comprehensive database of UK publicly listed telephone/fax numbers;

(*b*) the database was last updated no earlier than seven days before the screening exercise; and

(*c*) where the database consists of both residential and business listings, it is possible to distinguish residential listings on the database.

(ii) Within seven working days of the screening exercise the Caller shall notify the Commissioner, in writing, of the completion of the screening exercise, and of the date that it was carried out.

(iii) The Caller shall conduct further screening exercises of its entire database ("subsequent screening") at intervals no greater than 90 days commencing from the date of completion of the screening exercise conducted under (i) above. Subsequent screenings shall be conducted as in (i) above.

(iv) Within seven working days of each subsequent screening the Caller shall notify the Commissioner in writing of the completion of each subsequent screening, and the date that the subsequent screening in question was carried out.

(v) Before adding any number/line to its database the Caller shall screen such a number/line ("additional screening"). Additional screening shall be conducted as in (i) above.

(vi) The Caller shall, after seven working days following any screening, not use, or instigate the use of, publicly available telecommunications services for the communication of material, for direct marketing purposes, where the called line is one that has been identified as a residential line either as a result of the screening exercise, any subsequent screening, any additional screening, or otherwise, and is that of a subscriber who is an individual who has not previously notified the Caller that he consents for the time being to such communications being sent by, or at the instigation of, the Caller on that line.

(vii) For evidential purposes the Caller shall compile and maintain a historical record of notifications of consent it has received and shall make such record available to the Commissioner at any time, upon request, within seven working days of such request.

(viii) For the purposes of the Relevant Requirement the Caller may only rely upon consent which is a freely given specific and informed indication of his or her wishes by which the subscriber in question signifies his or her agreement for the time being to such communications as are referred to in paragraph (vi) above being sent by, or at the instigation of, the Caller on the line in question.'

Details of the decision are under the 'Guidance' section (under 'Tribunal Decisions') on the Information Commissioner's website (www.dataprotection.gov.uk).

Further information 13.16

The DMA has four offices. These are in London, Edinburgh, Leeds and Bristol.

DMA (UK)
Haymarket House
1 Oxendon Street
London
SW1Y 4EE
Tel: 020 77321 2525
Fax: 020 7321 0191
E-mail: dma@dma.org.uk

DMA North
8th Floor
29 Wellington Street
Leeds
Yorkshire
LS1 10
Tel: 0113 244 7103
Fax: 0113 244 7224
E-mail: sharon@dma.org.uk

DMA West
University of the West of England
Dupont Bristol Centre
Cold Harbour Lane
Bristol
BS16 1OD
Tel: 0117 976 2599
Fax: 0117 976 3839
E-mail: anna@uwe.ac.uk

DMA Scotland
41 Comely Bank
Edinburgh
EH4 1AF
Tel: 0131 315 4422
Fax: 0131 315 4433
E-mail: joscobie@dma.org.uk

The DMA has available a range of publications on its website (www.dma.org.uk) including:

- An Introduction to Direct Marketing
- Best Practice Guidelines for Fax Marketing
- 10 Best Practice Guidelines for List Suppliers
- DMA Guide to the List Industry
- DMA Guide to Renting Business Lists
- DMA Guide to Renting Consumer Lists
- DMA Broadcast Guidelines
- DMA Best Practice Guidelines for Responsible Sampling
- DMA Best Practice Guidelines for Catalogue and Home Shopping
- Labour and Direct Marketing Guidelines
- NVQs and SVQs in Direct Marketing and Telesales
- Suggested Terms and Conditions for Contract of Agreement between Client and Agency
- The Advertisers' Perspective on Address Management

The publications are free of charge. For copies contact Patricia Burrows at the DMA. E-mail: patricia@dma.org.uk. Tel: 020 7766 4445.

14 – Distance Selling Regulations

At a glance 14.1

- ✓ The *EU Distance Selling Directive (97/7/EC)* was implemented in the UK by the *Consumer Protection (Distance Selling) Regulations 2000* (*SI 2000/2334*).
- ✓ These Regulations set out certain information which must be given to consumers purchasing most goods or services at a 'distance', such as in response to unsolicited mail or telephone calls, or via a website. This has a major impact on wording to be used in connection with direct marketing. Sample wording is provided.
- ✓ The Regulations give individuals the right to cancel contracts made by these means within a statutory withdrawal period.
- ✓ Major changes are made in the area of inertia selling, which concerns unsolicited goods and services.
- ✓ A separate draft EU Directive is proposed for distance selling and financial services.

Introduction 14.2

Directive 97/7/EC on distance selling contracts contains provisions relating to unsolicited e-mails which are very relevant in the data protection area. The UK implemented the Directive with the *Consumer Protection (Distance Selling) Regulations 2000* (*SI 2000/2334*). The Regulations have been in force since 31 October 2000.

The Regulations apply to contracts made at a distance via the following mediums:

(*a*) unaddressed printed matter;

(*b*) addressed printed matter;

(*c*) letters;

(*d*) press advertising with order form;

(*e*) catalogue;

(*f*) telephone with human intervention;

(*g*) telephone without human intervention (e.g. automatic calling machine, audiotext);

(*h*) radio;

(*j*) videophone (telephone with screen);

(*k*) videotext (microcomputer and television screen) with keyboard or touch screen;

(*l*) e-mail;

(*m*) facsimile machine (fax); and

(*n*) television (teleshopping).

The Regulations are not principally a data protection measure, although they are very relevant for those involved with direct marketing.

Example: Application of the Regulations 14.3

Questions to determine whether the *Consumer Protection (Distance Selling) Regulations 2000 (SI 2000/2334)* apply.

(*a*) Does our business supply goods or services to consumers directly rather than just to other businesses?

If no, then the regulations do not apply.

If yes then:

(*b*) Does our business supply to consumers by distance methods?

If yes, the regulations apply.

Distance methods are defined below, but are essentially most selling methods which are not face to face. E-commerce, telesales and mail order come within the Regulations.

Timing 14.4

A distance contract is one where the consumer and supplier do not have face-to-face contact up to and including the moment when the contract is concluded. The *EU Distance Selling Directive (97/7/EC)* covers the sale of goods or services concluded via e-commerce as well as other means of distance selling such as mail order and telephone sales, and fax.

The *Consumer Protection (Distance Selling) Regulations 2000* (*SI 2000/2334*) include certain key features set out below.

- The consumer must be given clear information about the goods or services offered.
- After making a purchase, the consumer must be sent confirmation.
- The consumer has a cooling-off period of seven working days.
- Local Trading Standards Departments and the Office of Fair Trading receive new powers.

The Regulations do not apply to all distance contracts, the most important exception being for financial services. A separate proposed Directive on the distance marketing of financial services is currently being debated.

Distance contract 14.5

The list of means of distance communications covered by the *EU Distance Selling Directive* (*97/7/EC*) (see 14.2 above) includes direct mail and e-mail. The *Consumer Protection (Distance Selling) Regulations 2000* (*SI 2000/2334*) only apply to organised distance selling contracts. If the business does not normally sell to consumers in response to telephone calls then the Regulations do not apply. The DTI state the following on this point in their guide to the *Distance Selling Regulations* (see 14.2 above):

> 'If, for example, you do not usually sell goods or services by distance, but you agree to do so in response to a one-off request from a consumer over the phone, you do not need to comply with the Regulations. However if your business regularly handles 'one-off' requests from consumers and is organised so that it can deal with such requests (i.e. there is for example a mail order facility) you do need to ensure that you fulfil the Regulations.'

(Para 3.9, The Consumer Protection (Distance Selling) Regulations 2000: A Guide for Business).

The definition in the Regulations states:

> '"Distance contract" means any contract concerning goods or services concluded between a supplier and a consumer under an organised distance sales or service provision scheme run by the supplier who, for the purpose of the contract, makes exclusive use of one or more means of distance communication up to and including the moment at which the contract is concluded'.

The Regulations apply where there are exclusive use of distance communications. The DTI states this means that the consumer has no face-to-face meeting with an employee, representative of the business, or someone acting on the business' behalf up to and including the time the consumer confirms the order.

Exclusions 14.6

Exclusions include any contract:

(*a*) for the sale or other disposition of an interest in land except for a rental agreement;

(*b*) for the construction of a building where the contract also provides for a sale or other disposition of an interest in land on which the building is constructed, except for a rental agreement;

(*c*) relating to financial services, a non-exhaustive list of which is contained in *Schedule 2* of the Regulations and includes:

- (i) investment services;
- (ii) insurance and reinsurance operations;
- (iii) banking services; and
- (iv) services relating to dealings in futures or options;

(*d*) concluded by means of an automated vending machine or automated commercial premises;

(*e*) concluded with a telecommunications operator through the use of a public pay-phone; and

(*f*) concluded at an auction (including Internet auctions).

The major provisions of the *EU Distance Selling Directive* (*97/7/EC*) (relating to compulsory information to be given to consumers and the right to cancel a contract) do not apply to contracts for the provision of accommodation, transport, catering or leisure services, where the supplier undertakes – when the contract is concluded – to provide these services on a specific date or within a specific period.

Application to home supermarket shopping? 14.7

The DTI, in its guide for business, suggests the following in relation to supermarket deliveries:

> 'This exception (from information and cancellation provisions) will not generally apply to the growing market for home deliveries by supermarkets. Such deliveries are normally

ordered specifically on each occasion by telephone, on the Internet or by fax. The consumer must be informed of the price and delivery arrangements etc. in accordance with *Regulation* 7 at the time he places the order and receive a written confirmation of the order, at the latest at the time of delivery. There is, however, a specific exception to the right to cancel in respect of the supply of perishable goods'.

Premium-rate telephone services 14.8

With regard to premium-rate telephone services, consumers must be given prior information such as the cost of using the service before they are charged. In paragraph 5.6 of their guide for business, the DTI indicates that the business may provide the information required before the contract is made. The business does not need to provide written confirmation of the service but must ensure the consumer is able to obtain the postal address of the supplier's place of business in order to know where to send consumer complaints if necessary. Premium-rate websites must provide the information clearly before the charge is applied, for example at a point prior to the consumer switching to the premium rate service.

Prior information right 14.9

Those involved with direct marketing should note in particular the compulsory information which must be given to consumers. The Regulations give the consumer the right to receive clear information about the goods or services before deciding to purchase. This is called the prior information right.

Regulation 7 of the *Consumer Protection (Distance Selling) Regulations 2000* (*SI 2000/2334*) states that this must be provided in good time prior to the conclusion of the contract. The supplier must:

(*a*) provide to the consumer the following information:

- (i) the identity of the supplier and – where the contract requires payment in advance – the supplier's address;
- (ii) a description of the main characteristics of the goods or services;
- (iii) the price of the goods or services including all taxes;
- (iv) delivery costs where appropriate;
- (v) the arrangements for payment, delivery or performance (if no specified delivery date is given then this must be within 30 days of the order);

(vi) the existence of a right of cancellation except in the cases referred to in *Regulation 13*;

(vii) the cost of using the means of distance communication where it is calculated other than at the basic rate, for example premium rate telephone charges;

(viii) the period for which the offer or the price remains valid; and

(ix) where appropriate, in the case of contracts for the supply of goods or services to be performed permanently or recurrently, the minimum duration of the contract;

(*b*) inform the consumer if he proposes, in the event of the goods or services ordered by the consumer being unavailable, to provide substitute goods or services (as the case may be) of equivalent quality and price; and

(*c*) inform the consumer that the cost of returning any such substitute goods to the supplier in the event of cancellation by the consumer would be met by the supplier.

The supplier must ensure that the information required above is provided in a clear and comprehensible manner appropriate to the means of distance communication used, with 'due regard in particular to the principles of good faith in commercial transactions and the principles governing the protection of those who are unable to give their consent such as minors'.

The supplier must ensure that 'his commercial purpose is made clear when providing the information'. In the case of a telephone communication, the identity of the supplier and the commercial purpose of the call shall be made clear at the beginning of the conversation with the consumer.

Confirmation of the prior information in writing or by e-mail 14.10

Confirmation of the prior information in writing or in another appropriate durable medium, e.g. fax or e-mail must be given. The *EU Distance Selling Directive* (*97/7/EC*) on which the *Consumer Protection (Distance Selling) Regulations 2000* (*SI 2000/2334*) are based requires that the consumer be given information in writing or another 'durable medium that is available and accessible to him'. It does not say what this means so the DTI take the view that e-mail is a durable medium in the sense that it is open to the consumer to retain the information. Giving the details verbally is not, however, enough.

The written confirmation must give details of:

- the prior information (see above);
- how to exercise the right to cancel and if the consumer is responsible for return of the goods;
- any guarantees and after sales services; and
- how to end any open-ended service contract, such as gas, telephone, cable or satellite TV, etc.

The information must be provided at the latest by the time the goods are delivered, or in the case of services, before or at any early state during performance of the contract. However, for Internet selling it makes more sense to give the information both on the website before purchase and in the confirmation e-mail on receipt and acceptance of order.

Cooling off 14.11

A 'cooling off' period is given of seven working days from the day after delivery of the goods, in which the consumer can withdraw from the contract, unless extended by an additional three months because notice of the period was not given to the consumer at the relevant time (see 14.12 below). The DTI states:

> 'If the contract is made on Monday, Tuesday will be the first working day of the cooling off period and the seventh working day will be Wednesday of the following week (unless there are any public holidays during this period). If the sale is agreed on Thursday the seventh working day will fall on Monday in the second week following the sale to allow for the two intervening weekends'.

The statutory right of withdrawal below does not apply for:

(*a*) the supply of services if the supplier has complied with *Regulation 8(3)* and performance of the contract has begun with the consumer's agreement before the end of the cancellation period applicable under *Regulation 12*;

(*b*) the supply of goods or services the price of which is dependent on fluctuations in the financial market which cannot be controlled by the supplier;

(*c*) the supply of goods made to the consumer's specifications or clearly personalised, or which by reason of their nature cannot be returned or are liable to deteriorate or expire rapidly;

(*d*) the supply of audio or video recordings or computer software if they are unsealed by the consumer;

(*e*) the supply of newspapers, periodicals or magazines; or

(*f*) for gaming, betting or lottery services.

Cooling off extension 14.12

The cooling off period extends for an extra three calendar months where the supplier has not given notice of the seven day period to the customer. This point illustrates the importance for businesses in amending their terms and conditions to cover these rights, so that the legal position can to some extent be ameliorated. *Regulation 11(3)* of the *Consumer Protection (Distance Selling) Regulations 2000* (*SI 2000/2334*) state:

> 'Where a supplier who has not complied with *regulation 8* (information requirements) provides to the consumer the information referred to in *regulation 8(2)*, and does so in writing or in another durable medium available and accessible to the consumer, within the period of three months beginning with the day after the day on which the consumer receives the goods, the cancellation period ends on the expiry of the period of seven working days beginning with the day after the day on which the consumer receives the information'.

Where the supplier never supplied the information requirement then 'the cancellation period ends on the expiry of the period of three months and seven working days beginning with the day after the day on which the consumer receives the goods' (i.e. three months and seven working days).

Often delivery is contracted to be to a third party. In such a case this is treated as if the consumer had received the goods on the day on which they were received by the third party (*Regulation 11(5)*).

The DTI point out that the cooling off period is to give the consumer the chance he or she would have had in a conventional shop to 'examine the goods or to reflect on the nature of the service before deciding to buy'.

The effect of a notice of cancellation is that the contract shall be treated as if it had not been made. For contracts for the supply of goods the cancellation period ends on the expiry of the period of seven working days beginning with the day after the day on which the consumer receives the goods.

Paragraph (d) in 14.11 above is causing some lawyers problems. It is obviously logical that goods of which the consumer could avail themselves, use/read etc and then conveniently return cancelling the contract should be excluded from the cancellation right. It is a shame that not all computer software is excluded – only that which is 'unsealed'. Unsealed is not defined. This can create problems if, for example, a company supplies software to consumers online who have first given a credit card number. In such cases, the services are provided within the cancellation period, and there is nothing to 'unseal' except on a very broad and purposive interpretation of the provision which perhaps in practice is the best one to take, unless and until it is challenged. It would be advisable to include the relevant wording to ensure the cancellation period is seven (not 30) days. It may also be possible to argue that software is the provision of services, rather than supply of goods (assuming it falls into either category at all which, following the decision in *St Albans v ICL (CA) [1996] 4 All ER 481* it does not) including the provisions set out in *Regulation 8(3)* (see below). *Regulation 8(3)* states:

> 'Subject to *regulation 9*, prior to the conclusion of a contract for the supply of services, the supplier shall inform the consumer in writing or in another durable medium which is available and accessible to the consumer that, unless the parties agree otherwise, he will not be able to cancel the contract under *regulation 10* once the performance of the services has begun with his agreement.

Suppliers of services such as solicitors and accountants who provide chargeable advice to clients by telephone, e-mail or fax (and thus form a contract at a distance) may be caught by the Regulations (but only as regards 'consumer' clients such as those wanting wills to be written or personal tax advice or a divorce, etc.) It seems that even in such cases the right to cancel may apply. Could this be the case if the services are provided within the seven day cancellation period? Unless the service provider gives notice under *Regulation 8(3)*, the customer could theoretically cancel after receipt of the advice, possibly even after having signed a valid will, for example, provided under such advice within the seven days, the will, presumably, remaining valid. In most cases, therefore, providers are advised to include a new condition in their contracts.

Unless agreed otherwise with the supplier, there is a right to receive goods or services within 30 days. This accords with the period which is usual in the mail order industry in any event.

Example: Wording of condition 14.13

A sample of suitable wording is provided below:

> 'For consumer customers where we carry out work for you, you have a right to withdraw your instructions, without any charge, by giving us a notice in writing or by e-mail at any time within seven working days from instructing us. This does not apply if we start work within this period and you do hereby consent to our starting work right away.

Books 14.14

Another problem that could arise with the *Consumer Protection (Distance Selling) Regulations 2000* (*SI 2000/2334*) is that although there is an exclusion from cancellation for magazines (which obviously is necessary to stop people buying the magazine reading it and sending it back) there is, illogically, no such exclusion for books. Internet booksellers who often despatch books the day after ordering must be encountering significant problems with the Regulations.

Examples: Online supplier's right to cancel 14.15

Example 1

'You may normally cancel your purchase (where we have accepted your order and delivered the product) if you notify us within the 14 days following the day the product was delivered.You can do this by:

- returning the product to one of our shops (take the card you used to buy it with you and the receipt); or
- notifying us by telephone on ____________; or
- notifying us by letter or e-mail at ____________.

You may only return your product if it is complete, unused and in good condition with the box, packaging and accessories with which it came. Recorded tapes, compact discs, DVDs, software and minidiscs must be sealed. Free gifts sent with the product must be returned too.

We cannot refund your money when:

- you cannot provide proof of purchase, or
- when there is a service contract with the product (such as on a mobile telephone) which has already started.

If you do not return the goods in person, you will receive the refund in 30 days of notifying us of your cancellation.'

The terms should also deal with the consumer's rights if there are defects and/or manufacturers' warranties.

Example 2
'You have the right to cancel your contract with us at any time during the period which commences on the day the contract comes into existence and ends on the expiry of seven working days after the date of delivery of the products.

If the goods are to be rejected in the time limit set out above, you must comply with the returns procedure set out below. In that case we will accept any returned goods if the return is complete and with a valid proof of purchase and, in the case of an order which you wish to cancel, if the return is in unused and re-saleable condition.

You can contact us at the address or telephone number set out at the end of these terms with details of your original order number and receipt and we will arrange to collect the return. Subject to the terms provided below, your credit or debit card will then be debited with the cost of return delivery charge being £___ per return.

You will then receive e-mail notice that your return is registered with our carrier who will collect the goods within ______ working days of your contacting us as provided above.

If you prefer, you can return the goods to one of our stores with details of your order number, receipt and card details.

You will receive a full refund of the purchase price and the delivery charge to be credited to your card. Faulty products have to be returned before the refund will be made.

If there is a defect or discrepancy in the order then you will not have to pay the return delivery charge mentioned above. When the return arrives at our office it will be considered by us and if the goods are found to be defective or there was a discrepancy the return delivery charge will be credited to your card.'

Example: Companies with more than one type of product 14.16

This example would be appropriate for a company which supplies some products that include contracts which can be cancelled and others which cannot (see final clause):

> 'If you do not wish to buy the goods you have received then you can return them as new within 14 days either for a refund or replacement. We can arrange to collect the goods from you by telephoning ______________________ or take them to the post office obtaining a certificate of posting as your proof of the return. The return is free of charge by either means.
>
> If you do not return the goods in the same condition in which you received them, and not within 14 days, then we reserve the right to charge you for the goods.
>
> Your right of return does not apply to food hampers, wines, spirits, personalised merchandise and certain electrical goods and other items where indicated in the product description.'

Cold calling 14.17

When a supplier 'cold calls' someone at home confusion can often arise over what is on offer and who is behind the call. The DTI hope the *Consumer Protection (Distance Selling) Regulations 2000* (*SI 2000/2334*) will prevent this. Under these Regulations suppliers who cold call consumers at home must identify clearly the company they represent and the commercial purpose of their call at the beginning of the conversation.

How to send the cancellation notice 14.18

The consumer must send the cancellation notice in writing only (including by fax or e-mail). The notice is given to the supplier or the person whom the supplier has nominated for this purpose.

Goods returned damaged 14.19

Consumers who use or damage the goods are not entitled to exercise the cancellation right. This is a very important point in practice.

However, if the goods are defective then under sale of goods law the consumer may be allowed to reject them or sue for breach of contract. From January 2002, when the UK implements the *EU Consumer Guarantees Directive* (*99/44/EC*), there will be additional rights to reject goods which do not 'conform to the contract' within stipulated 6 and 18 month periods.

Goods and services – mobile phones 14.20

The cancellation period differs between goods and services as seen above. The DTI in *The Consumer Protection (Distance Selling) Regulations 2000: A Guide for Business* refers to mobile contracts where a phone is sold, but a service contract is undertaken with the customer. The DTI believes that *Directive 97/7/EC* does not deal with this kind of circumstance, stating that: 'if the hardware is given away or sold at a significantly discounted price the contract could be treated as one for service provision, and cancellation would mean the phone must be returned too. So the cooling off period would run for seven working days from the date of the contract. If the phone is sold at full price with limited additional elements then probably the cancellation period for goods would apply, so that it ends seven working days after delivery of the phone'.

Refunds 14.21

Whilst in some industries, such as the clothing industry, it is common (provided the goods are undamaged) to let the consumer return them for various reasons, there has until now been no right for the consumer to return even undamaged goods. If the goods are defective that is a different matter. Rights of rejection exist under the *Sale of Goods Act 1979* as amended by the *Sale and Supply of Goods Act 1994* and are included in many consumer contracts. Leaving that aside, the law now allows returns.

In the past, many clothing suppliers have allowed exchanges or credit notes but have not given monetary refunds unless the law requires it, for example if the goods are defective. This practice has worked well, but has been altered by the Regulations. If the consumer cancels the contract all money paid has to be returned within 30 days of the date the notice of cancellation is given. Usually this means crediting the payment or credit card. Goods purchased by distance methods are rarely paid for in cash, although sometimes they are paid by cheque.

One of the DTI's frequently asked questions in its Guide to the Regulations is whether a refund must be paid for a gift wrapping service for goods ordered. The answer is no because the service has already been carried out so cannot be cancelled, but normal delivery costs must be refunded where a consumer has paid for those separately.

Recovering the goods 14.22

Ownership in the goods reverts to the seller when the consumer exercises the right to cancel. The consumer has to take reasonable care of the goods even after giving the cancellation notice. The goods should be returned as new.

Nevertheless, the supplier is obliged to collect the goods unless the contract says otherwise. The consumer simply has to make them available for collection. The supplier cannot force the consumer to return the goods unless the contract terms say so. Suppliers, therefore, would be well advised to include such a term in their contracts – stating that the consumer must return the goods, making it much less likely that the cancellation right will be exercised.

The supplier has to notify the consumer within 21 days when the supplier will collect the goods, and if this is not done then the consumer does not have to look after them with reasonable care anymore, although the consumer must still be given a refund by the supplier in such a case.

If the consumer has been told in the contract – and written confirmation is provided – that they have to return the goods, then the consumer has to take care of them for up to six months and indefinitely if the supplier serves a notice requiring them to be handed over. If a consumer does undertake due care in looking after the goods the supplier can claim any resulting loss in value. In practice, if the goods are destroyed this might be the whole value of the goods. It is unlikely that a supplier in such a case offset the refund of the price against this, due to the length of time involved. The refund will have to have been made before the consumer has returned the goods.

Delivery dates 14.23

Most mail order companies are already subject to specific legislation which requires them to deliver in 30 days or else tell consumers this will not be the case. The Regulations do the same thing across all distance selling sectors. Goods must be delivered or services provided within 30 days from the date when the order was placed and if the deadline cannot be met then the consumer must be told before the period expires and must refund money paid in a further 30 days unless the consumer agrees to accept substitute goods or services or to propose a revised delivery date. If the consumer does not agree the later delivery date, which he or she may well not do, e.g. if the goods were for a birthday etc, then the contract is cancelled and the consumer is paid his or her money back.

Changes to unsolicited goods law 14.24

The Regulations also make changes to the *Unsolicited Goods and Services Act 1971 (UGSA 1971)* . The Act is amended slightly by the Regulations, but only in relation to goods sent from 31 October 2000 (see *Regulation 22(4)*).

The Act makes it an offence to demand payment for goods known to be unsolicited. The person receiving the goods does not have to pay for or return goods if they do not want them. Until October 2000 the law contained particular periods after which the goods could be kept by the recipient. *Article 9* of the *EC Distance Selling Directive (97/7/EC)* bans the supply of unsolicited goods and services where supply involves a demand for payment (free samples etc. are unaffected).

The Regulations provide that in the case of unsolicited goods, (i.e. those where the recipient has no reasonable cause to believe that they were sent with a view to being acquired for the purposes of a business and where the recipient has not agreed to acquire or return them) the recipient may, as between himself and the sender, 'use, deal with or dispose of the goods as if they were an unconditional gift to him...The rights of the sender to the goods are extinguished.'

The *Distance Selling Directive (97/7/EC)* also exempts the consumer from the 'provision of any consideration' in cases of unsolicited supply. In this context, the DTI said in a 1999 consultation that it considered that this means the consumer is under no obligation to enable the supplier to retrieve the goods and services but can treat them as his or her own property from the time of receipt. The Regulations now provide for this.

The reference for the consultation paper is URN 99/1257 and it is on the Internet at www.dti.gov.uk/cacp/ca/goodserv.htm.

The DTI advises that anyone who receives a demand for payment for unsolicited goods should report the matter to their local Trading Standards department.

What are unsolicited goods? 14.25

Inertia selling is defined in the Regulations as to be where:

- unsolicited goods are sent to a person ('the recipient') with a view to his/her acquiring them;

- the recipient has no reasonable cause to believe that they were sent with a view to their being acquired for the purposes of a business; and
- the recipient has neither agreed to acquire nor agreed to return them.

Regulation 24 states:

> 'A person who, not having reasonable cause to believe there is a right to payment, in the course of any business makes a demand for payment, or asserts a present or prospective right to payment, for what he knows are:
>
> - unsolicited goods sent to another person with a view to his acquiring them for purposes other than those of his business; or
> - unsolicited services supplied to another person for purposes other than those of his business;
>
> is guilty of an offence and liable, on summary conviction, to a fine not exceeding level 4 on the standard scale.'

The regulations also prohibit in such cases the demanding of payment, the threatening of legal proceedings, the placing of an individual on a list of defaulters, or the invoking debt collection procedures.

Action for companies 14.26

- Check if the Regulations apply to the particular business.
- Are the goods or services excluded?
- Are the sales to consumers rather than businesses?
- Assuming the Regulations apply check that the correct information is given to consumers.
- Check compliance with other requirements such as 30 day delivery dates.
- Ensure the right to cancel is implemented.
- Take legal advice in cases of doubt.

Future legislation 14.27

In its guide to the Regulations the DTI list future legislation relevant in this field, the status of which is included at the time of publication:

- E-commerce Directive – due to come into force in 2001.
- Draft Directive on distance marketing of financial services – currently being negotiated.
- Draft Directive on general product safety – currently being negotiated to amend existing such directives.
- Directive on consumer credit – currently under review.
- Brussels convention on jurisdiction – (*Regulation 44/2001/EC* on jurisdiction has now been adopted).
- Worldwide agreement on jurisdiction – currently under discussion in the Hague Conference on private international law.

Distance selling and financial services 14.28

On 27 September 2001 political agreement was reached on the 'Selling of financial services by mail, telephone and the Internet' in the EU Council. Described as 'common rules for selling contracts for credit cards, investment funds, pension plans, etc. to consumers by phone, fax or Internet', the Commission described its main features as:

(*a*) the prohibition of abusive marketing practices seeking to oblige consumers to buy a service they have not solicited ("inertia selling");

(*b*) rules to restrict other practices such as unsolicited phone calls and e-mails ("cold calling" and "spamming");

(*c*) an obligation to provide consumers with comprehensive information before a contract is concluded; and

(*d*) a consumer right to withdraw from the contract during a cool-off period – except in cases where there is a risk of speculation.

The next stage is for the Council to adopt its common position on the proposed Directive (due late 2001) and then proceed to final adoption once the European Parliament has finished its second reading on the proposal.

'Distance marketing' means selling by telephone, fax, proprietary computer networks and the Internet. A Directive regulating the distance selling of (all other) goods and services was adopted in 1997 and entered into force in 2000 (see 14.20–14.27 above where this is considered in detail). Financial services were excluded from the scope of the 1997 Directive. The *Distance Selling Directive (97/7/EC)* will prohibit 'inertia selling', which involves sending unsolicited financial products or services to a consumer and charging the consumer for their use.

'Cold faxing', or unsolicited communication about such products and services by fax is also to be prohibited.

The legislation gives EU Member States two optional ways of treating 'spamming' (unsolicited communication by e-mail) and 'cold calling' (the same practice by telephone). The Commission says 'Under the first option ('opt-in') cold calling and spamming are prohibited unless the consumer has expressly consented; under the second option ('opt-out') this is prohibited only if the consumer has signalled his/her objection, e.g. by entering his/her name in a registry set up for this purpose.' (See CHAPTER 33 OPT-IN AND OPT-OUT.)

Sellers of financial services and products will also be obliged to provide consumers with a comprehensive package of information before an eventual contract is concluded. This package should include the identity, and contact details of the supplier, the price and payment arrangements, contractual rights and obligations as well as information about the performance of the service offered. Information on the technical quality and nature of the financial service must also be provided in accordance with the rules of the Directives on credit, insurance and investment services or with relevant national rules for services not currently subject to Community legislation.

Cancellation of financial services distance contracts 14.29

The *Directive* will also give consumers the right to cancel a contract within 14 days after signing, extended in the case of life insurance and pension plans to 30 days. This right will however not apply to financial services that may be subject to price speculation, such as sales of foreign currency and securities. The Commission says that Member States may also exclude mortgage or property credit from this right of withdrawal from a contract. In addition, in the event of fraudulent use of payment cards or other non-cash means of payment consumers will be able to cancel transactions and be entitled to reimbursement of any sums charged.

Reference should also be made to the Commission Communication on E-Commerce and Financial Services (COM (2001) 66 final) The Directive is to be adopted by the Council once the European Parliament has concluded its second reading in the framework of the so-called 'co-decision procedure'.

Further information 14.30

A DTI introductory guide for business and set of FAQs for business are available on the DTI website (www.dti.gov.uk/CACP/ca/dsdbulletin.htm).

As stated above, a copy of the *Consumer Protection (Distance Selling) Regulations 2000* (*SI 2000/2334)* is also on the website of the Stationery Office (www.hmso.gov.uk).

Copies of the introductory leaflet for business entitled *Home Shopping: New Rights for Consumers* can be obtained by telephoning the DTI Order Line on 020 7215 6024. It can also be found on the DTI website at www.dti.gov.uk/cacp/ca/dsdbulletin.htm.

A 1999 consultation document on unsolicited goods laws is available from the DTI's website at www.dti.gov.uk/cacp/ca/goodserv.htm.

The DTI has also published a detailed booklet, entitled *The Consumer Protection (Distance Selling) Regulations 2000 : A Guide for Business* (October 2000). This is also available from the DTI's Publications department by telephoning the Order Line above.

15 – E-mails

At a glance 15.1

- ✓ Marketing by e-mail is covered by the *Data Protection Act 1998* (*DPA 1998*).
- ✓ New rules take effect in January 2002 when the *Electronic Commerce Directive* comes into force in the UK.
- ✓ The European Commission has proposed a new directive relating to electronic commerce and privacy which may or may not include a ban on unsolicited e-mails.
- ✓ Information in e-mails may be 'personal data' and may need to be considered in dealing with a subject access request. Detailed guidance is available from the Commissioner.

Introduction 15.2

DPA 1998 applies to personal data in most forms, including that contained in e-mails. This section considers two different subjects:

(*a*) sending unsolicited e-mails; and

(*b*) subject access rights and information in e-mails.

Data controllers therefore need to ensure that their data protection policies and processes allow for this and that staff are told how to handle e-mails in this context. This chapter examines the law on the use of e-mail for marketing purposes and the sending of unsolicited e-mails. In general in the UK there is no ban on such marketing, but that is not the case across the EU, and a proposed new *EU Data Protection/Communications Directive* may alter the position. The chapter also looks at the guidance given by the Information Commissioner on e-mails and subject access rights under *DPA 1998*.

Distance Selling Directive 15.3

Article 10.2 of the *EU Distance Selling Directive* (*97/7/EC*) provides that methods of distance selling other than faxes and automated calling machines may only be used where there is no clear objection from the consumer. However, the UK regulations implementing that Directive did not contain that provision. The means of communication concerned include e-mail, as well as telephone and mail delivered by post. Options include an opt-in or an opt-out system (see CHAPTER 33 OPT-IN AND OPT-OUT). Reference should also be made to the proposed *Distance Selling of Financial Services Directive*. (See CHAPTER 14 DISTANCE SELLING REGULATIONS.)

The Directive covers unsolicited e-mails sent by businesses to consumers for the purposes of distance selling contracts under the Directive. Business to business e-mails are not covered, nor does the Directive cover all contracts. Financial service contracts are excluded and will be covered under a separate directive.

The Directive defines a consumer as 'any natural person who, in contracts covered by this Directive, is acting for purposes which are outside his trade, business or profession'. The type of e-mail will determine whether the recipient has been sent it in the capacity of a consumer. An e-mail sent to someone at work about a business conference is clearly a business e-mail. One sent to them about family holidays at a resort would not be.

Codes for e-commerce 15.4

The Government is working with the Alliance for Electronic Business (AEB) and the Consumers' Association, in consultation with the Office of Fair Trading, to develop:

- additional core principles to meet consumer concerns about e-commerce which will be developed further by the AEB and other bodies that issue e-commerce codes, including how consumers can avoid unsolicited e-mail;
- a new body, with the title of TrustUK, to accredit e-commerce codes that also accord with the core principles for codes described above;
- a 'hallmark' that accredited codes may use on their websites or incorporate into their logos;
- the use of existing links to establish international complaints handling networks;
- a way to market the e-commerce hallmark internationally;
- work with the European Commission to encourage the development of an EU wide code; and

- work with the Organisation for Economic Co-operation and Development on its guidelines for consumer protection in e-commerce.

This aims to ensure the Government's intent that the UK provides the best environment in the world for electronic trading, as well as reducing the problems for consumers of unsolicited bulk e-mails.

Electronic Commerce Directive and Information Society Services Regulations 2001 15.5

The *EU Electronic Commerce Directive* (*2000/31/EC*) on certain legal aspects of information society services, in particular electronic commerce, in the Internal Market (OJ L178/1 17.7.2000) will introduce some changes in this area considered in detail below. It is neutral on opt-in or opt-out as regards unsolicited e-mails. Where Member States permit unsolicited e-mails, *Article 6* of the *Electronic Commerce Directive* requires them to ensure that service providers established on their territory make unsolicited e-mail clearly identifiable as such as soon as it shows up in the recipient's in-tray, in recognition of the additional communication costs of the recipient and the need to promote responsible filtering initiatives by industry.

Other states' rules 15.6

The Department of Trade and Industry (DTI) say that a number of Member States (for example Austria, Italy, Germany and Sweden) either have or are likely to implement the e-mail provision of the *Distance Selling Directive* by opt-in, although others, such as Belgium, have gone for opt-out. In August 2001 the UK issued a consultation paper on implementation of the *Electronic Commerce Directive* by the *Information Society Services Regulations 2001* due to be brought into force in January 2002.

Article 2(f) of the *Electronic Commerce Directive* defines 'commercial communications' (such as advertising and direct marketing). *Article 6* makes these communications subject to certain transparency requirements to ensure consumer confidence and fair trading.

The DTI in their August 2001 consultation document on the Directive state that 'In order to allow individuals to deal more easily with unwanted intrusion, *Article 7* requires commercial communications by e-mail to be clearly identifiable and senders to consult and respect opt-out registers'. *Article 8* of the *Electronic Commerce Directive* deals with regulated professions and requires them to respect certain rules of professional ethics in their use of commercial communications; these should be reflected in codes of conduct to be drawn up by professional associations.

In most EU Member States there is no obligation to indicate on a website that commercial communication is involved or to indicate on whose behalf it appears. The Directive requires the provider of the commercial communication to give contact details to assist the consumer in lodging and resolving complaints or securing enforcement by the authorities.

Unsolicited commercial communications under the Directive 15.7

The DTI says that

> 'Some commercial communication practices can be seen as intrusive and undermine the confident use of the Internet by consumers. The undisciplined sending of bulk e-mails can also impair the functioning of networks. Responsible and disciplined unsolicited advertising, respecting rules on the processing of the personal data of the target, is legitimate and well established in most forms of communication (e.g. mail or telephone), subject to safeguards in law and self-regulatory practice. In the case of online advertising, the Directive depends on empowering the recipient and on industry codes of conduct as the first lines of defence against these risks'.

The four new rules 15.8

The Directive, when implemented in January 2002, will bring in four new rules which complement the *Data Protection Directive* (*95/46/EC*), the *Distance Selling Directive* (*97/7/EC*) and the *Telecoms Data Protection Directive* (*97/66/EC*).

- *Article 5* requires all providers of information society services (including advertisers) to give at least their name, geographic address, e-mail contact details and the particulars of any supervisory authority to which they belong so that recipients of unwanted e-mails can readily take action to avoid receiving such communications in future.

- *Article 6* requires all commercial communications, solicited or unsolicited, to be identifiable as such and also requires the senders to identify clearly the natural or legal person on whose behalf the e-mail was sent.

- *Article 7* provides that unsolicited commercial communications must be clearly identifiable as such, as soon as they are received so that individuals or their Internet access service providers can delete them (or use filtering software to block or delete) without the need to read them.

- *Article 7* also requires Member States to ensure that senders of unsolicited commercial communications consult regularly and respect opt-out registers through which individuals can indicate that they do not want to receive such communications.

The Information Commissioner will enforce these powers with regard to the fair processing of data and industry codes of conduct (as envisaged in *Article 16* of the *Electronic Commerce Directive*). The powers are designed to provide a high level of legislative and self-regulatory safeguards against unwanted e-mail.

Opt-out registers – legal obligation to consult 15.9

The Directive requires Member States to provide for senders of unsolicited commercial communications to 'consult regularly and respect the opt-out registers in which natural persons not wishing to receive such commercial communications can register themselves'. Member States need to provide for this whether or not they effectively ban such communications by:

- having national opt-in arrangements;
- maintaining national opt-out systems; or
- having no national systems at all.

The Directive is careful to avoid specifying that opt-out should necessarily be operated on a national basis since this may not be the most effective way of dealing with cross-border communications in a global market.

Application of national rules to cross-border unsolicited e-mail 15.10

The exclusion of the 'permissibility of unsolicited e-mail' from country of origin supervision in the Annex to the Directive indicates that Member States may continue to choose to apply their own national controls, for example by enforcing an opt-in system. *Article 21(2)* of the *Electronic Commerce Directive* provides for possible proposals in 2003 on 'the possibility of applying the internal market principles to unsolicited commercial communications by electronic mail' in the light of legal, technical and economic developments.

Unsolicited commercial communications in the UK under the Electronic Commerce Directive 15.11

The European Commission has proposed a *Communications Data Protection Directive* (see 15.14 below). As it currently stands this would provide for an opt-in of e-mails only being sent to those who have expressly chosen to receive them, a reversal of the currently perceived position under English law.

The DTI states:

> 'The UK's position has been that harmonised opt-in is a disproportionate response to the perceived problems of unsolicited commercial communications and that Member States should continue to be able to choose their approach at least until the outcome of that review. In the meantime, mail and e-mail addresses would, in many cases, be covered by data-protection legislation, enabling the Information Commissioner to take action on behalf of the individual.'

Main bodies involved **15.12**

The DTI usefully lists the bodies involved in the UK with unsolicited e-mails in the Consultation Document on Implementation of the E-Commerce Directive (10 August 2001) (see www.dti.gov.uk/cii/ecommerce/europeanpolicy/ecommerce_directive.shtml).

- **The Information Commissioner**

  Where a data controller processes personal data in the form of e-mail addresses subject to *DPA 1998* and continues to send unsolicited commercial communications to those individuals who have expressly advised the company concerned that they do not wish to receive such communications or have registered free with the e-mail preference scheme (e-MPS) or another opt-out scheme, the Commissioner would take the view that this would involve unfair processing. The Commissioner has not received a significant number of complaints about this but could issue an Enforcement Notice (the breach of which would render the company liable for criminal prosecution and a fine of up to £5,000 in a magistrates court for each breach) where it seemed the only way to ensure compliance in the face of persistent transgression. Sending unsolicited commercial communications has a low marginal cost, and there is an absence of public directories from which e-mail addresses could, in the absence of any indication to the contrary, be collected fairly in the first place (unlike, for example, telephone or fax). Given that e-mail addresses often constitute personal data because they contain an individual's name, those capturing individuals' addresses should ensure that those individuals have an appreciation of any further use that might be made of the data.

The Information Commissioner also takes the view that direct marketing includes the promotion of an organisation's aims and ideals and that, therefore, e-mails canvassing for political or charitable purposes are direct marketing communications.

- **Direct Marketing Association (DMA)**

  Until now, promotion of the e-MPS has largely been online, but the DMA is considering ways to make the service more widely known, including the supply of information to citizens' advice bureaux, trading standards offices and direct-marketing companies for use by their customer services departments.

  The DMA's online code for e-commerce stipulates that members must use the e-MPS and not send e-mail communications to individuals who have registered an objection to receiving such communications. In respect of this code, the DMA has obtained approval from TrustUK, a non-profit organisation run by the Alliance for Electronic Business (which includes the Confederation of British Industry, the Computing Software and Services Association, the DMA, e centre^{UK} and the Federation of the Electronics Industry) and the Consumers' Association.

- **Advertising Standards Authority (ASA)**

  Advertising and sales promotion in the non-broadcasting media in the UK is subject to a self-regulatory system of control overseen by the ASA. The ASA is an independent body, and the High Court has rejected an application for judicial review of its adjudication on the British Code of Advertising and Sales Promotion (the code of conduct drawn up by the advertising industry's Committee of Advertising Practice by which all advertisers agree to abide). The Codes effectively require companies involved in direct sales promotion to use their own, the e-MPS or another more appropriate preference service in respect of unsolicited e-mail.

- **Internet Service Providers Association (ISPA)**

  ISPA represents some 90 per cent of the UK dial-up market for Internet access. It is currently preparing information for its website on how individuals can deal with unwanted e-mails and is also encouraging ISPA members to provide information to their users if they do not already do so. Many Internet service providers (ISPs) already provide this information on their websites and in customer 'starter' packs. ISPs' customer services assist any individual reporting unsolicited commercial communications so far as they are able. ISPs' contract terms and conditions require all customers to comply with UK legislation. In addition, ISPs'

Acceptable Use Policies form the basis for ISPs to manage between themselves the optimum functioning of their networks by setting out clear prohibitions against potentially disruptive unsolicited e-mails sent in bulk. Therefore, ISPA and its members have a number of avenues to reduce the incidence of unwanted unsolicited commercial communications through contractual relations, codes of conduct and peer pressure on ISPs that allow their subscribers to send such communications.

- **The e-MPS**

  The e-MPS is a global service hosted in the United States and supported by the DMA worldwide. It allows individuals to enter their details free on a register if they do not wish to receive unsolicited commercial communications and direct marketers to clean their names or e-mail addresses from lists of targets for a nominal charge, currently $100 per year (see www.e-mps.org).

Approach to the Regulations 15.13

The Government intends to follow the detail of *Articles 6* and *7(1)* of the *Electronic Commerce Directive* closely. It will not embellish what the Directive says.

In its August 2001 consultation it asks the following question for consultees.

4.1	To receivers of unsolicited commercial communications: what is your experience of using voluntary opt-out schemes?
4.2	How could the functioning and advertising of this system be improved?
4.3	Have such schemes cut down on the amount of e-mail that you receive?

Reference should be made here to the general rules on opt-in and opt-out under *DPA 1998* (see CHAPTER 33 OPT-IN AND OPT-OUT).

Proposed Communications Data Protection Directive 15.14

The European Commission has proposed a directive on the processing of personal data and protection of privacy in the electronic communications sector (Com(2000)385). However, at the date of writing EU Member States cannot agree whether it would provide for opting-in or opting-out for unsolicited e-mail mailings. At its plenary session on 6 September 2001, Parliament remitted the draft Directive back to that Committee.

As can be seen above, in practice there are likely to be changes in this area and those involved with direct marketing by e-mail need to consider these and any future rules carefully.

Data protection and access to information in e-mails 15.15

Data subjects under *section* 7 of *DPA 1998* have a right of access to much of the data held about them. (On this topic generally see CHAPTER 43 SUBJECT ACCESS REQUESTS.) The Information Commissioner under *section 42* of *DPA 1998* has a duty to examine forms of processing and offer guidance. She has now issued such guidance in relation to access to personal data held in e-mails, and this guidance is summarised below. Importantly, data controllers do need to consider *section* 7 in relation to information in e-mails; they can require data subjects who are exercising their rights to help identify the information required, and in extreme cases the controller may have to retrieve information in a deleted e-mail (this is technically possible).

An organisation which operates an e-mail system falls within the definition of a data controller if the e-mails processed or stored within its system identify living individuals and either:

(*a*) are held in automated form in live, archive or back-up systems, or have been 'deleted' from the live system but are still capable of recovery; or

(*b*) are stored, as print outs, in relevant filing systems (that is non-automated or 'manual' systems, organised according to criteria relating to individuals and allowing ready access to specific pieces of information).

In some cases data controllers may be able to take advantage of the transitional provisions contained in *DPA 1998*. In brief, transitional relief may be claimed if the processing of personal data was already underway immediately before 24 October 1998.

Some protection by the transitional relief provisions expired on 23 October 2001.

Making assessments **15.16**

In making an assessment of an alleged failure by a data controller to give access to personal data held in e-mails, the Commissioner will consider a number of questions including the following.

> '(*a*) Has the data subject provided sufficient information to the data controller to enable him to locate the data in question?
>
> (*b*) Do the e-mails exist?
>
> (*c*) Do they contain personal data covered by the Act?
>
> (*d*) Do they contain personal data relating to third parties and, if so, should this information be withheld or disclosed?
>
> (*e*) What information (other than a copy of the personal data) should be provided in response to a subject access request?
>
> (*f*) If access has not been granted, should enforcement action be taken?'

Each of these questions is considered in turn in the guidance from the Commissioner as set out below.

Information needed to find the data **15.17**

Sometimes data subjects are trying to be difficult and they ask for all data held about them. *Section 7(3)* of *DPA 1998* states that:

> 'Where a data controller–
>
> (a) reasonably requires further information in order to satisfy himself as to the identity of the person making a request under this section and to locate the information which that person seeks …
>
> the data controller is not obliged to comply with the request unless he is supplied with that further information.'

In most cases an open-ended request will not satisfy this provision.

Information which may assist the data controller might include:

(*a*) the fact that the data may be held in the form of e-mails;

(*b*) the names of the authors and recipients of the messages;

(*c*) the subjects of the e-mails;

(*d*) the dates or range of dates upon which the messages have been sent;

(*e*) whether it is believed that e-mails are held as 'live' data or in archived or back-up form; and (*f*) any other information which may assist the data controller in locating the data.

In making an assessment, the Commissioner has to take a view on whether the data subject has failed to provide information that the data controller reasonably needs to narrow down the search. If so, then it is likely to be concluded that there has been no breach of *DPA 1998*. By contrast, where a data controller appears to be making demands for information which the data subject cannot reasonably be expected to give and where it appears that a copy of at least some of the personal data requested could be provided, then it is likely to be judged that there has been a breach, the Commissioner says.

Does the e-mail exist? **15.18**

Sometimes the individual data subject states that there is information they have not been given but they know it is there. Where the evidence submitted by the data subject showing that the e-mails in question exist or existed in the past is inconclusive, the Commissioner must form a judgement based not only on the information supplied but also upon other similar cases, particularly ones involving the same data controller.

If the Commissioner is satisfied that the e-mails are likely to exist, 'then the alleged failure to respond to the access request will generally be put to the data controller for comment. E-mails may be held locally, for instance on a stand-alone PC, and not be immediately accessible by data protection officers/systems administrators. In putting the concerns of data subjects to data controllers, therefore, the Commissioner will seek to ascertain that a proper search has been carried out for the e-mails in question.'

Do the e-mails contain personal data covered by the Act? **15.19**

This is an interesting question and the Commission says there are a number of different aspects to this question. In particular, it will be important to determine whether the transitional provisions are relevant and whether the e-mails are held in the form of 'live' data or otherwise, for instance as back-up or archive data.

E-mails are caught if they contain information about identifiable living individuals unless they have been printed off, deleted and stored in manual filing systems falling outside the scope of *DPA 1998* (for instance references to an individual in the e-mailed minutes of a meeting which have been printed off and stored on the 'Meetings File'). In all other cases with the implementation of *DPA 1998*, the e-mails will be caught because of the ending of provisions contained in the *Data Protection Act 1984* (*DPA 1984*), in particular:

- the text preparation exception which took outside the scope of *DPA 1984* the processing of personal data for the sole purpose of the preparation of the text of a document;
- the exemption relating to back-up data; and
- the part of the definition of 'processing' which specified that in order to process personal data, processing must take place 'by reference to the data subject'.

Even though data may have been 'deleted' from the live system, the e-mails will be caught if they can be recovered by, say, the systems administrator before their final destruction.

'A "deleted" e-mail may still constitute personal data if it can be retrieved, albeit with some difficulty, by the data controller', the Commissioner says. Some e-mails contain personal data but fall outside the scope of *DPA 1998* since those data are not processed by reference to the data subject. An example may be a reference to an individual in the minutes of a meeting which are kept as a record of the meeting. This is an example given by the Commissioner. Others will clearly fall within the scope of the Act, for instance where the name of the data subject appears in the title of the e-mail or she/he is the sender or recipient. Other cases will be less clear cut.

However, the Data Protection Tribunal decision in the Equifax enforcement case *Equifax Europe Ltd v Data Protection Registrar (June 1991)* helps, the Commissioner says. This suggests that if an e-mail is stored because it contains information about an individual and may be accessed to discover information about an individual then processing takes place by reference to the data subject regardless of how the search is carried out.

Third party data and human rights 15.20

E-mails often contain personal data about third parties. In responding to subject access requests, therefore, controllers will need to have regard to the tests set out in *section 7(4)–(6)* of *DPA 1998*. In making assessments, the Commissioner will seek to assure herself that the tests have been properly applied as they would whenever a record contains information relating to a third party.

In addition, the Commissioner will consider the effect of *Article 8* of the *European Convention on Human Rights*. This specifies that:

> 'Everyone has the right to respect for his private and family life, his home and his correspondence.'

and:

> 'There shall be no interference by a public authority with the exercise of this right except such as in accordance with the law and is necessary in a democratic society in the interests of national security … or for the protection of the rights and freedoms of others.'

On an area where there has been a lot of recent publicity, the Commissioner writes:

> 'If an e-mail was written in a private rather than an official capacity, then it is likely that only exceptional circumstances will justify disclosure of third party information without the consent of the individual concerned. Cases which involve possible breaches of Article 8 provisions will be considered on their individual merits.'

Other section 7 rights **15.21**

Section 7 of *DPA 1998* is the section which gives individuals the right of access to their data. It also contains a number of rights in addition to the right to be given a copy of personal data. In particular individuals have the right to be informed whether they are the subject of personal data being processed by the controller and, if so, to be given a description of:

(*a*) the personal data in question;

(*b*) the purposes of the processing;

(*c*) the recipients or classes of recipients; and

(*d*) the sources of the personal data (if known to the controller).

It can be hard for the controller to reconstitute data which has been deleted from a live system in order to provide a copy. However, it may still be able to provide some of this information. In particular, it may be helpful to explain that the purposes of the processing are to erase the data and that only in exceptional circumstances would those data be reconstituted and used for other purposes (for instance as evidence in serious criminal cases or as evidence in industrial tribunals).

Good practice tip **15.22**

> 'As a matter of good practice controllers should develop clear policies as to the circumstances under which they would reconstitute "deleted" data before they are faced with subject access requests.'
>
> *Information Commissioner Guidance on Data Protection Act and E-mails*

The Commissioner's enforcement policy **15.23**

The following is the Information Commissioner's policy on enforcement.

Unless the personal data contained in e-mails are covered by the transitional provisions in *DPA 1998*, in principle data subjects have a right of access and the Commissioner has the power to take enforcement action in the event of non-compliance. Notices are not served automatically, however, and in deciding whether it is proper in particular cases to serve a notice, the Commissioner will take a number of factors into account.

She will consider first whether the data controller has been given sufficient evidence to locate the data. If transitional relief is available to the data controller, exempting back-up data and processing which does not take place by reference to the data subject, this question may be relatively simple. If the Commissioner considers that the controller can locate the data but has not provided a copy to the data subject then she will be more inclined to recommend enforcement.

If transitional relief is not available and the Act extends to data not held on 'live systems', then the data subject may have had to provide more information to enable the data controller to locate the data. Data held other than on 'live systems' may include back-up data and data which have been 'deleted' but not yet finally erased.

In practice, however, the Commissioner might exercise her discretion and not seek to enforce a data subject's rights if she is satisfied that to give access would involve disproportionate effort on the part of the controller. In forming a judgement as to whether the effort involved would be disproportionate, she will consider the following.

- What is the nature of the data and the likely effect on the individual if the data are or are not retrieved? The more serious, the more likely it will be that the Commissioner will take action.
- What is the controller's policy in relation to archive or other 'non-live' data? If it is to retrieve data only in exceptional circumstances (for example serious criminal allegations) then it may be dispro-

portionate to have to retrieve data in response to a request from a data subject who only wants a copy out of interest. In attempting to determine what a data controller's policy is, the Commissioner may request sight of policy documents and/or an account of the practices followed by the controller in the past.

- How hard would it be for the controller to retrieve the data? Is it possible to retrieve small amounts of data or is it necessary to reconstitute large computer archives? How much will it cost?
- In the case of back-up data is there any evidence to suppose that this version differs materially from that held on the live system?

Summary 15.24

The Commissioner's approach is that where e-mails are held on live systems and can be located, she will seek to enforce subject access if this has been denied. Where data are held elsewhere, the Commissioner will weigh the interests of the data subject against the effort that the controller would have to take to recover the data and in many instances may be likely to decide not to take action.

The decision not to take action does not imply that a complaint will not be assessed nor does it deny the individual the right to seek access through the courts.

Further information 15.25

See also CHAPTER 29 INTERNET, CHAPTER 34 OPT-IN AND OPT-OUT and CHAPTER 44 SUBJECT ACCESS REQUESTS, and the Commissioner's guidance on the Internet on her website.

The Information Commissioner

The Office of the Information Commissioner
Wycliffe House
Water Lane
Wilmslow
Cheshire
SK9 5AF
Tel: 01625 545 700
Fax: 01625 524510
E-mail: mail@dataprotection.gov.uk
Website: www.dataprotection.gov.uk

Useful Internet addresses

Consultation Document on the Implementation of the E-Commerce Directive (August 2001)	www.dti.gov.uk/cii/ecommerce/europeanpolicy/ecommerce_directive.shtml
International/US e-mail preference scheme	www.e-mps.orgDirectives

Directives

Proposal for a Directive of the European Parliament and of the Council concerning the processing of personal data and the protection of privacy in the electronic communications sector (COM (2000) 385)
Directive 95/46/EC of the European Parliament and of the Council of 24 October 1995 on the protection of individuals with regard to the processing of personal data and on the free movement of such data (OJ L 281, 23.11.1995, p 31)
Directive 97/7/EC of the European Parliament and of the Council of 24 May 1997 on the protection of consumers in respect of distance contracts (OJ L 1444, 4.6.1997 p 19)
Directive 97/66/EC of the European Parliament and of the Council of 15 December 1997 concerning the processing of personal data and the protection of privacy in the telecommunications sector (OJ L 24, 30.1.98, p 1)
Directive 2000/31/EC of the European Parliament and of the Council of 8 June 2000 on certain legal aspects of information society services, in particular electronic commerce, in the Internal Market (Directive on electronic commerce) (OJ L 178/1, 17.7.2000, p 1)

16 – Employment

At a glance 16.1

- ✓ Employers handle lots of personal data and the Information Commissioner has issued a Draft Code of Practice on the Use of Personal Data in Employer/Employee Relationships.
- ✓ In September 2001 the European Commission issued a working paper on the processing of personal data in the employment context.
- ✓ There is a staff administration exemption from the *Data Protection Act 1998* (*DPA 1998*) under the *Data Protection (Notification and Notification Fees) Regulations 2000* (*SI 2000/188*) which may keep some employers outside of the obligation to notify under *DPA 1998*.
- ✓ An exemption under *Schedule 7* to *DPA 1998* exists for certain confidential employment references, providing exemption from the subject access provisions in *section* 7 of *DPA 1998*.
- ✓ Those exporting from the European Economic Area (EEA) personal data of employees should obtain their consent and comply with the Eighth Data Protection Principle.
- ✓ Under *section 61* of *DPA 1998* directors can be personally liable for certain offences under the Act.
- ✓ Under *para 10* of *Schedule 1* to *DPA 1998* employers must take proper steps to ensure their employees who will have access to personal data are suitable.

Introduction 16.2

Employers handle large amounts of personal data. Most need to have notified their holding of data with the Information Commissioner. This chapter examines the principal ways in which *DPA 1998* will apply to employers and their employees. Credit reference issues in this context are dealt with in CHAPTER 6 CREDIT REFERENCES and are not therefore included here. On 13 September 2001 the European Commission issued Opinion 8/2001 'on the processing of personal data in the employment context' (5062/01/EN/Final WP 48). In order to contribute to the uniform application of the national measures adopted under the *Data Protection Directive* (*95/46/EC*), the Working Party has set up a subgroup to examine this question and has adopted an extensive document (see 16.55 below).

The Information Commissioner issued in late 2000 a Draft Code of Practice on the Use of Personal Data in Employer/Employee Relationships. At the time of writing, this has not yet been finalised and is likely to be issued in stages in 2002. However, the draft guidance provides some useful pointers, some of which are examined in this chapter.

The Draft Code of Practice is in two parts: Part I sets out the standards which must be met if the Code is to be complied with. Part II sets out the interpretation of *DPA 1998* on which the standards are based.

In the first section there are two types of standard. They both reflect the Commissioner's view of the requirements of 'good practice'. Those that the Commissioner considers to be necessary for compliance with *DPA 1998* are in plain text. After each such standard a reference is given to the section of the Act on which the standard is based. In most cases this is one of the Data Protection Principles.

Where the standard appears in italics it is one of the Commissioner's recommendations for good practice that goes beyond a requirement of *DPA 1998*. Such standards may not be directly enforceable as a breach of the Data Protection Principles.

The Commissioner's draft Employer/Employee Code of Practice considered in this chapter is based on the original draft issued by the Commissioner. At the time of writing the following timetable for finalisation of this important measure was proposed.

Human Resources Code of Practice Provisional Timetable

The Code of Practice will appear as follows in four sections.

- Recruitment and selection – published by 30 November 2001.
- General records maintenance – end of December 2001.
- Monitoring – January 2002.
- Testing – March/April 2002.

Note: Readers are advised to check the final version of the Code rather than simply relying on the draft described in this chapter, although the basic principles and standards are unlikely to radically change from those described herein.

Manual records 16.3

DPA 1998, covers some manual records as well as computer records. The Commissioner says in the Code that it is likely that many employment records, because of their structured nature, will come within the scope of the Act even if they are paper-based, but some will not. This is discussed in more detail in Part II of the Draft Code of Practice. However, to keep things simple the Code does not make a distinction.

Importance of the Code 16.4

The Commissioner will take into account the extent to which an employer has complied with the Code when determining whether there has been a breach of the Principles and, if there has, whether formal action is appropriate.

Areas covered 16.5

Part I: Standards covers

- managing data protection;
- recruitment;
- employment records;
- access and disclosure;
- contract and agency staff;
- employee monitoring (this includes monitoring e-mail and Internet use);
- medical testing;
- discipline and dismissal; and
- retention of records/former employees.

Part II deals with *DPA 1998* and includes the following:

- definitions;
- principles;
- individual rights;
- exemptions;
- *DPA 1998, section 55*; and
- *DPA 1998, section 56*.

Releasing third party information 16.6

There is also a procedure suggested in an appendix to the Code for the release of third party information in response to a subject access request (see 16.50 below).

General issues under DPA 1998 16.7

There are some types of personal data where it does not matter too much if the data is incorrect. In an employment record, for example, the name of the employee's wife is not particularly material, although even that may become important if death benefits have to be paid. Those who have bought a car from a supplier may move house. It is not important if their new address is not changed and the personal data record is not up-to-date. However, with disciplinary matters in employment accuracy is very important indeed and it is likely that employees will increasingly use failure to comply with data protection obligations against employers in unfair dismissal cases.

Within many companies it is most frequently the human resources department which has to address data protection legal issues, and often the data protection manager within an organisation is involved in the personnel side of the company.

Staff administration exemption 16.8

The schedule to the *Data Protection (Notification and Notification Fees) Regulations 2000* (*SI 2000/188*) includes an exemption for staff administration. This is an exemption from the requirement of the employer to notify (register) under *DPA 1998*. However, most employers will find they have to register because of some other use of data within their business as a whole.

The exemption is from the requirement to notify, not from compliance with all the principles of *DPA 1998* in relation to that data. So, for example, it will still be necessary to comply with the Eight Data

Protection Principles, such as keeping data safe and secure and up-to-date. The staff administration exemption is for processing:

(*a*) for the purposes of appointments or removals, pay, discipline, superannuation, work management or other personnel matters in relation to the staff of the data controller;

(*b*) of personal data in respect of which the data subject is:

- (i) a past, existing or prospective member of staff, or
- (ii) any person the processing of whose personal data is necessary for the exempt purposes;

(*c*) personal data which is the name, address and other identifiers of the data subject or information about qualifications, work experience or pay or other matters, the processing of which is necessary for exempt purposes;

(*d*) which does not involve disclosure of the personal data to any third party other than with the data subject's consent or where necessary to make the disclosure for the exempt purposes; and

(*e*) does not involve keeping the personal data after the relationship between the data controller and the staff member ends, unless and for as long as is necessary for the exempt purposes.

Note that these requirements must all be met before this provision applies.

Staff 16.9

The *Data Protection (Notification and Notification Fees) Regulations 2000* (*SI 2000/188*) define staff as including employees or office holders, workers under *section 296* of the *Trade Union and Labour Relations (Consolidation) Act 1992*, people working under any contract for services and volunteers.

Third party 16.10

The exemption only applies where there is no disclosure to a third party except with the data subject's consent or where this is necessary for the exempt purposes.

However, in her Notification Handbook the Commissioner states the limitations of this exemption.

> '**Your data subjects are restricted to** any person the processing of whose personal data is necessary for staff administration.

> **Your data classes are restricted to** data which are necessary for staff administration.
>
> **Your disclosures other than those made with the consent of the data subject are restricted to** those third parties which are necessary for staff administration.
>
> **Retention of the data:** The personal data are not kept after the relationship between you and the data subjects ends, unless and for so long as it is necessary to do so for staff administration.'

Notwithstanding these limitations, some companies will be able to rely on this exemption and may not even have to be registered under *DPA 1998*. However, if a business should have registered or notified and has not, it is still legally obliged to comply with the principles of the Act, including the right of subject access in *section* 7 of *DPA 1998*.

Confidential employment references 16.11

Paragraph 1 of *Schedule* 7 to *DPA 1998* provides that references given in confidence by the data controller are exempt, but only from the subject access provisions in *section* 7 of *DPA 1998*. They are not exempt from all the other provisions of the Act. The reference must relate to education, training or employment, or prospective such matters of the data subject, the appointment or prospective appointment of the data subject to any office, or the provision or prospective provision by the data subject of any service. The last category is not an employment one.

Note that this provision only applies to confidential references. In addition, it only applies to references given by the data controller. If the data controller has on its file, after checking an employee's past employment history, references written by a former employer, the employee can obtain those from the new employer under *section* 7 of *DPA 1998*. The Commissioner's Introduction to *DPA 1998* (accessible at www.dataprotection.gov.uk), page 25 says that 'the exemption is not available for such references when they are received by the data controller'.

Credit references are considered in CHAPTER 6 CREDIT REFERENCES.

There are special exemptions from *DPA 1998* for Crown Employment, judicial appointments and the armed forces which are not addressed here.

In her draft Code of Practice the Information Commissioner says the following on references.

'There is a special exemption from the right of access to a confidential reference in the hands of the person who gave it. However, good data protection practice is to be as open as possible with employees about information which relates to them. They should be able to challenge information that they consider to be wrong or misleading particularly when, as in the case of a reference, inaccurate information may have an adverse impact on them. When a confidential reference is in the hands of the recipient there is no blanket exemption from the right of access, although the recipient is entitled to take steps to protect the identity of third parties such as the author of the reference.

Standards: References

- Allow access by employees to confidential references written about them. Only withhold information that if given to the employee would be likely to:
  - result in harm to the author of the reference or some other person;
  - reveal information provided by a person other than a supervisor or manager of the employee who would not have expected it to be revealed.
- Allow access to references received in so far as the identity of a third party, such as the author of the reference, is not revealed (Principle 6).
- In deciding whether to release third party information, follow the process set out in *Appendix 1.* Bear in mind that the release of information that identifies the author of a reference in his/her business capacity rather than in a private capacity is less likely to intrude on his/her private life (Principle 6).
- Do not provide confidential references on employees unless you are sure they have given their consent to your disclosure either directly to you or to a third party you can trust (Principles 1 and 7).'

Export of data and employees 16.12

One area which employers have to watch carefully is sending personal data about employees abroad. The Eighth Data Protection Principle prohibits export to countries outside the EEA except where there is adequate protection. If the employee consents to the export then it is allowed. A clause should therefore be considered in employment contracts, in contracts with employment agencies and on application forms for jobs.

Data export by employers is addressed in the Draft Code. Often employers will send employee details abroad. The Information Commissioner suggests the following standards.

Standards: Data export 16.13

- Do not transfer employee data to countries outside the EEA unless:
  - the destination country has been designated as providing adequate protection by the European Commission,
  - the destination country is the USA and the recipient has signed up to the 'safe harbor' (sic) principles,
  - the employee has been told about the intended transfer and has agreed to it,
  - the transfer is to an organisation that acts only as a processor, the processor is reliable, the country in which it is located is stable and the required controller-processor contract is in place (see Section 3.5), or
  - steps have been taken to ensure that taking account of all the circumstances of the transfer and the Data Protection Commissioner's guidance on international transfers, adequate protection is provided in other ways (Principle 8).
- Ensure employees are made aware of any transfers of their personal data outside the EEA (Principle 1).

Liability of directors 16.14

An officer of a company proven to have committed a breach of *DPA 1998* through his or her neglect or with their consent is guilty of an offence under *section 61* of *DPA 1998*. This applies to directors, managers, secretaries or similar officers or anyone acting in their capacity.

Checking up on employees 16.15

The data controller must take reasonable steps to ensure the reliability of any employees of his who have access to the personal data (*DPA 1998,*

Sch 1, Part II, para 10). *DPA 1998* does not say what those steps should be. Under the *Data Protection Act 1984* (*DPA 1984*), which included an identical such provision, the following questions were recommended to be asked, in guidance of the Registrar.

- Is proper weight given to the discretion and integrity of staff when they are considered for employment or promotion or a move to an area where they have access to personal data?
- Are staff aware of their responsibilities? (A compliance or education programme on the Act will help with this)
- Do disciplinary rules and procedures take account of the Act's requirements and are they enforced?
- If the employee is found to be unreliable, is his access to personal data immediately withdrawn?

Recruitment 16.16

Individuals send confidential data, sometimes comprising sensitive personal data to prospective employers. In her Draft Code of Practice the Information Commissioner suggests the following standards to be used in the recruitment phase.

Standards: Recruitment 16.17

- Inform individuals responding to job advertisements who they are providing their information to and how this will be used if it is not obvious (Principle 1).
- Where responses are simply to obtain details of how to apply, explain any uses that go beyond dispatching and keeping a short term record of the dispatch of these details (Principle 1).
- Provide any explanation that is needed in the advertisement or at the start of the telephone call if telephone responses are sought (Principle 1).
- If the employer is not identified in the advertisement, ensure the recruitment agency is identified and that no personal data are passed from the agency to the employer (Principle 1).

Review/Appraisal 16.18

The Information Commissioner's Draft Code of Practice says that any system of staff review or appraisal is likely to involve the collection and recording of personal information. It is beyond the scope of the Code to set detailed standards for the proper conduct of review or appraisal systems. Information recorded should be relevant in that it supports or will inform employment decisions and should not be misleading. All readers should ensure their systems follow the provisions below. Only the last provision in italics is regarded by the Commissioner as 'voluntary'. The principles mentioned are those in *DPA 1998*.

Standards: Review/Appraisal 16.19

- Operate review/appraisal systems in accordance with accepted good practice to ensure personal information is obtained and used fairly and lawfully (Principle 1).
- Limit the recording of information to that needed to support recent or future employment decisions (Principle 3).
- Ensure that the record identifies the source of any comments, that opinions are not presented as facts, that the information recorded is correct and not misleading and that if the employee has challenged the accuracy this is recorded (Principles 3 and 4).
- Show employees all information recorded in the review/appraisal system about them. Provide a facility whereby they can record their own observations as part of the record. Ensure these observations are taken into account whenever the record is consulted.

Many employees prepare comments as part of an appraisal system about the members of staff for which they are responsible very quickly, often fitting it around other work they have to do, which they see as more important. It is not surprising that often the record is inaccurate. In extreme cases employees may even be muddled with other employees with serious consequences. The standards above are designed to ensure that it is clear whether something is a statement or an opinion, to ensure the information is obtained fairly and lawfully (the individual should normally have given consent to the processing of the data under *DPA 1998*) and to ensure that more information than is actually needed is not gathered.

The last suggested standard is just a recommendation – that employees should see all the information recorded about them in the review.

Employers do not have to do this. Most allow the employee to put in their own comments on their appraisal too and as can be seen from the above this is also recommended by the Commissioner in the Draft Code.

Discipline and dismissal 16.20

Many of the issues that arise in disciplinary proceedings are addressed in other parts of the Code, such as the point that the accuracy of personal information is crucial if it is to form the basis of disciplinary action. Readers should, where time allows, read the Code in its entirety. The security of unsubstantiated allegations, for example, of sexual harassment, is crucial because of the prejudice that can be caused even if the allegations prove to be unfounded. There are, however, some particular issues that are specific to discipline and dismissal. The following standards are suggested by the Commissioner.

Standards: Discipline and dismissal 16.21

- Ensure that when employment is terminated both you and the employee are clear about the basis of the termination and that this is accurately recorded. Breaches of *DPA 1998* arise where an employee has been allowed to resign but because he/she has been left with little choice the employer has recorded 'dismissed'. Such cases must be recorded as resignations, although further details may be added to ensure the record is adequate (Principle 4).

- Disciplinary procedures generally provide for warnings to 'expire' after a set period of time. Ensure the procedure clarifies what is meant by 'expire'. Is the warning removed from the record or is it simply disregarded in determining a future disciplinary penalty? Have in place arrangements (e.g. a diary system) to ensure that the procedure is put into practice and that where the procedure provides for warnings to be removed or deleted this is actually achieved (Principle 5).

Comments 16.22

The first of these standards is an important practical point. Many employers like to avoid a 'nasty' situation by giving the employee the chance to resign. This may then present matters to the world putting the employee in a better light than is the true case. However, the employee is unlikely to complain about this from a data protection point of view as the misdescription is to his or her advantage. The Commissioner turns this round and says that if the employer does not describe the situation in such as a case as 'resignation' then the record will be wrong. If the employee is in fact dismissed and does not put in his or her resignation then clearly the record can and should show dismissal. Make sure that procedures for employees who resign because of pressure put on them by the employer are described as 'resignations'. The Code does say that further details can be recorded to ensure the data is accurate.

The second standard above is about the important issue of expiry of warnings. All readers should check that their disciplinary procedures have a time limit after which the warning will expire, and the process of a series of warnings would have to start again from scratch. The procedure must, the Commissioner maintains in the standard, state what actually happens on 'expiration'. Is the warning completely expunged from the record or is it still there but the warnings start from the beginning if there is a recurrence of the misconduct? The Commissioner does not say one or other procedure is correct, simply that it must be clear to all concerned and that the employer should have diary systems to ensure that the necessary changes are made and recorded.

None of these proposals are unduly onerous, unlike some other provisions of the Draft Code. No employer should change procedures yet, unless they are clearly failing to comply with *DPA 1998* in a major way in which case they should take action right away. In other cases it is necessary to wait until early 2002 when the Code is finalised.

Inaccurate CVs 16.23

Not all candidates go to the lengths of the lady who applying for a job as a reporter on The Sun newspaper wrote 'SEX' across the top of her application to draw attention to herself. (She got the job: see The Times 31 May 2000). However, many resort to leaving gaps on their CV, distorting facts or just telling lies. Many businesses now have procedures in place to try to identify inaccurate CVs and lying interviewees but this is not easy, particularly when the obligation also to comply with data protection legislation also arises.

In one case a well-known chef received a written apology from another chef after he was given a day to apologise or be sued for lying on his CV. A recruitment agency telephoned the chef to check that the candidate had worked for him as claimed on the CV. In fact they had apparently never met. The candidate wrote on his CV that he had worked for the chef as a senior souschef at a prestigious London restaurant. He had stated that the best food he had ever produced had been at that restaurant between 1994 and 1997, and that it has been hard, exacting work with very long hours. Moving from kitchen to office the situation is not much better. Many employees claim degree qualifications they do not have. They cover up gaps in their CV by saying they stayed longer at their previous employer than they did.

Libel and slander 16.24

There is no general law prohibiting telling lies. However some laws can be breached depending on what is said. If a libellous statement has been made about a third party they can bring an action for libel or, if it is not written down, for slander under the laws of defamation. This is unlikely to occur in an interview as most interviewees know it does not reflect very well on them if they start criticising their ex-employer.

Misrepresentation 16.25

Other relevant areas of law are the laws of negligent mis-statement and misrepresentation. A negligent mis-statement is a statement made to people who would be expected to rely on it and on which they do rely and suffer provable loss. Misrepresentation is also a tort or legal wrong which could be relevant where people lie on a CV or indeed any other document. The employer may be offering the job because the individual has a first from Oxford in law, when in fact they scraped a third in theatre studies at an ex-polytechnic and would not have even made the short list if this were the case. If when the lie comes to light the employer has to start the recruitment process over again, the employer has suffered loss, such as through having to spend money all over again on advertising and recruitment agencies' fees, then a recoverable loss against the employee can be shown and damages recovered. However in practice there is not sufficient money at stake to make an action worthwhile and the only issue is whether the lie is sufficiently bad to justify dismissing the employee. For example the woman with children who is known as Mrs Smith but has never married her partner may describe herself as married on the CV even though in law she is not. This may be completely irrelevant to her job on the till of the local supermarket but in a strict religious school it may be a justifiable policy not to recruit people 'living in sin' and the consequences might be different.

Some statements are of course open to opinion. A lot of prospective employees write about themselves in glowing terms such as 'team player', 'excellent all rounder' etc. Often this is very far from the truth. Such broad statements are unlikely to cause legal problems. In assessing whether a statement on a CV which is untrue is a misrepresentation or not, note that a statement of opinion is not a misrepresentation nor statement of intention. In one case a man said someone would make a very desirable tenant (knowing full well they were in arrears with their rent). A misrepresentation was found. A statement of intention may be actionable as a misrepresentation when at the time it was made the person making the statement had no intention to put it into effect.

Case law 16.26

In *Esso Petroleum Co v Mardon [1976] QB 801* back in 1976 the company had told a prospective tenant of a lease for a filling station a forecast of probable sales. Damages for negligent misrepresentation succeeded. When statements are made about the future, the courts look at whether it was reasonable for the person to have relied on that representation. Is the person just passing on information for what it is worth but clearly may not really know whether those facts are true or not? Damages can be recovered for fraudulent misrepresentation and often for negligent misrepresentation under *section 2(1)* of the *Misrepresentation Act 1967*. Where the misrepresentation was innocent, in most cases no damages can be recovered unless the representation is or becomes a contract term. Most lies on CVs risk being held to be fraudulent misrepresentations rather than innocent mistakes.

In *Box v Midland Bank [1981] 1 Lloyd's Rep 434*, in 1979 someone sought a large loan from Midland Bank. His manager gave the impression it would be a formality, but would need head office approval. The bank manager allowed him overdraft facilities in the meantime. The loan application was refused by the head office and the man claimed damages for misrepresentation as he had suffered loss through thinking the loan would be forthcoming. The court found that the bank manager owed a duty to the man not to mislead him with careless advice.

Section 8 of the *Unfair Contract Terms Act 1977* provides that where a term in a contract excludes or restricts liability for misrepresentations made before the contract was made or any remedy available to any part to the contract by reason of misrepresentation, then that term is not valid unless it satisfies the requirement of reasonableness in the Act.

Seeking legal advice 16.27

In any case, it is essential to speak to an employment lawyer before dismissing someone if a lie on their CV comes to light. Now that the maximum damages for unfair dismissal have been raised from £12,000 to up to £60,000 and there are unlimited rights to damages in certain areas, such as where there is sex discrimination, it is important to take advice before dismissing someone. It may be that a warning is more appropriate.

Practical tips **16.28**

In practice, it is best to try to put employees off lying on their application by using an application form rather than their own CV. This makes it much harder for them to lie as the information they have to supply is given on the form. Also, the employer has the opportunity to add to the form statements such as that all qualifications will be checked, and telling people to add all examinations which they passed, but not those they failed and asking for the full name of the institution they attended (e.g. 'Oxford' is not the same as 'Oxford University'). A statement such as:

> 'We require details on this form to be entirely accurate and up-to-date. If we subsequently find you have not completed this form accurately we reserve the right to treat this as serious misconduct and ultimately to dismiss you.'

Commissioner's advice **16.29**

In the Information Commissioner's Draft Code of Practice verification and data protection issues are addressed.

Applicants may not always give complete and accurate answers to the questions they are asked, the Commissioner writes. Employers are allowed to make reasonable checks on information 'but they should avoid asking questions and checking the responses for no other reason than to test an applicant's honesty. The verification process should be open. It necessarily involves the disclosure of information about the applicant, even if only identifying details, by the employer to a third party and the disclosure of personal information by the third party to the employer'.

The applicant should have understood and agreed to this. Where information obtained from a third party differs from that provided by the applicant, it should not be assumed that it is the information provided by the applicant that is necessarily incorrect or misleading. If necessary, further information should be sought and a decision reached on where the truth lies.

No enforced subject access **16.30**

The Commissioner has always been of the view that forcing potential employees to exercise their right of access in order to provide the employer with a copy of a record held by a third party is a breach of the law. Requiring the supply of certain records will become a criminal offence when *sections 112, 113* and *115* of the *Police Act 1997* come into force.

Standards: Verification **16.31**

The Information Commissioner proposes the following standards in the area of verification.

- Explain to applicants the nature and extent of the checks that will be undertaken to verify the information provided. Obtain their agreement both to the release of necessary details to third parties and the provision of personal information to the employer by these third parties (Principle 1).
- Do not obtain personal information from applicants and then seek to verify it solely to test their honesty unless:
  - the requirement for honesty is a particular feature of the job to be filled, because, for example, the postholder is likely to be called on to give evidence in court, or
  - there are clear grounds which call into question the honesty of the particular applicant from whom the information is obtained and, in both cases,
  - the information obtained is not particularly intrusive, and
  - the applicant has been informed that information supplied will be verified (Principle 1).
- Where information obtained from an applicant differs from that provided by a third party, give the applicant an opportunity to provide an explanation before reaching a conclusion (Principles 1 and 4).
- Do not require job applicants to exercise their right of access to information held about them by third parties as part of the recruitment process. (This will become a legal requirement in relation to police, prison and social security contribution records when *sections 112, 113* and *115* of the *Police Act 1997* come into force.) (*DPA 1998, s 56*)

Standards: Pre-employment vetting **16.32**

The Code deals separately with pre-employment vetting and proposes the following standards.

- Do not carry out pre-employment vetting unless
  - there are particular and significant risks to the security of the employer or others associated with the position being filled, and
  - the risks cannot be adequately addressed by asking the applicant to provide information that is then subject to verification (Principles 1 and 3).
- Only carry out vetting on an applicant once a decision has been taken that on all other grounds they should be appointed (Principles 1 and 3).
- Ensure vetting is 'tailor-made'. The extent and nature of information sought should be no more than is justified by the particular position being filled (Principles 1 and 3).
- Do not pursue untargeted 'fishing expeditions'. Only seek information from sources where it has been judged that there is a reasonable likelihood that information of relevance to the employment decision will be revealed (Principles 1 and 3).
- Explain to the subject of the vetting the nature, extent and range of sources of the information that will be sought. Obtain their agreement to the release of necessary details to third parties and the provision of personal information to the employer by these third parties (Principle 1).
- If, in exceptional cases, the collection of information about the applicant's family or close associates is justified, ensure that if sensitive data such as details of criminal convictions are involved, at least one of the sensitive data conditions is satisfied (Principle 1).
- If the collection of information about the applicant's family or close associates is justified, take particular care to ensure its reliability and accuracy, given the difficulty there might be in putting the information to the applicant or to a family member or associate (Principles 3 and 4).

The Code also contains useful standards on the areas of selection testing and interviews. The Commission suggests keeping records for those who were not successful when applying for jobs for no longer than 4 months. However, this is just a recommendation rather than a requirement of *DPA 1998*.

Advice to employers 16.33

1. Require that original examination certificates be brought to the interview or sent on beforehand. Make copies. It is worth checking at the institutions concerned. It is not particularly difficult to forge a certificate these days.
2. Ask the employees about their qualifications, particularly if they sound unusual or dubious and study their reaction.
3. Ask the obvious questions about gaps on the CV and take the employee through their career history. It is much better they are honest and say they spent 6 months between work unemployed than extend their departure date from the previous job.
4. Take up references and try to do this relatively early on. If only two out of three ex-employers are named, see if contact can be made with the missing one. It might have the most relevant information.
5. Look out for signs of lying in the interview such as individuals shifting in their seat, becoming less forthcoming, blushing or avoiding eye contact.
6. If it is found someone has lied do not recruit them. They may be dishonest in other ways and not prove a worthwhile employee.

Employment records 16.34

Section 3 of the Information Commissioner's Draft Code provides a huge amount of suggested advice and guidance for employers in the area of employment records which is too lengthy to consider here. The Commissioner considers the following areas set out at 16.35–16.37 below.

Standards: Collection of information ensuring employees are told how their data will be used 16.35

- Inform newly appointed staff what information will be kept about them, where it is obtained from, how it is used and who, if anyone, it will be disclosed to (Principle 1).
- Explain clearly how any sensitive data are to be used and obtain a clear indication of the employee's agreement (Principle 1).
- Do not seek personal information from new employees that is irrelevant or excessive to the employment relationship. If answers to some questions are optional make this clear (Principles 1 and 3).
- Inform new employees of their rights under *DPA 1998*, in particular their right of access to the information kept about them.

Standards: Maintaining records 16.36

Employers should not keep information longer than is necessary and should only keep sufficient data to be adequate.

- Put in place a system to ensure that the information in employee records is kept accurate and up-to-date (Principle 4).
- Provide every employee with a copy of his/her basic record annually and ask him/her to identify inaccuracies and amendments needed.
- Incorporate accuracy, consistency and validity checks into systems, such as automatic questioning of the input of a date of birth that suggests a new employee is over the normal retiring age.
- If an emergency contact is required, obtain and record this information not 'next of kin' (Principle 4).

Standards: Sickness records 16.37

Sickness records are likely to include sensitive data. The Information Commissioner sees a problem with requiring explicit consent requirements for sensitive data and the need for employers to keep sickness records. *DPA 1998* cannot have been intended to prohibit employers from keeping such data. The Information Commissioner proposes the following standards.

- Only hold sickness records of employees if you have the explicit consent of each employee or if one of the other conditions for processing sensitive data is satisfied (Principle 1).
- If you rely on explicit consent ensure each employee has been told the extent of information that will be held in sickness records and how this will be used and has given a positive indication of agreement (Principle 1).
- Do not make the sickness records of individual members of staff available to others, for example, by publishing a 'league table', other than to provide managers with information reasonably required in their management role (Principles 1 and 7).

Standards: Security 16.38

The Commissioner says 'Care should be taken with the use of e-mail. An employer that allows the transmission of confidential employee information by e-mail without taking appropriate security measures will be in breach of the Seventh Data Protection Principle'. Reference should be made here to CHAPTER 15 E-MAILS. Encryption may protect e-mail in transit but it is still vulnerable at either end. If a confidential e-mail is 'deleted' a copy may nevertheless be retained on the system. There are also risks with the use of fax. A confidential fax message may be received on a machine to which many people have access. It can also easily be misdirected, for example, by mis-keying the fax number of the intended recipient.

The Commissioner proposes the following standards.

- Apply proper security standards, such as those identified in *BS7799*, that take account of the risks of unauthorised access to or accidental loss or destruction of or damage to employment records (Principle 7).
- Institute a system of access controls and passwords that ensure staff access to employment records is strictly on a 'need to know' basis (Principle 7).

- Keep a log of non-routine access to employment records and, as far as possible, use systems that record an audit trail of all access to computerised records whether routine or not (Principle 7).
- Take steps to ensure the reliability of staff that have access to employee records (Principle 7).
- Treat accessing, disclosing or otherwise using employee records without authority as a serious disciplinary offence. Make staff aware of this and also that such conduct may constitute a criminal offence (Principle 7; *DPA 1998, s 55*).
- Pay particular attention to the risks of transmitting confidential employee information by e-mail or fax by:
  - only transmitting information between locations if a secure network or comparable arrangements are in place or if, in the case of e-mail, encryption is used;
  - ensuring that all copies of e-mails and fax messages received by managers are held securely;
  - providing a means by which managers can effectively expunge e-mails they receive or send from the system and make them responsible for doing so;
  - drawing attention of all employees to the risks of sending confidential, personal information by e-mail or fax.
  - ensuring that your information systems security policy properly addresses the risk of transmitting employee information by e-mail (Principle 7).

Standards: Data processors 16.39

The Information Commissioner's Code also looks at data processors such as a specialist business that runs the payroll and proposes the following.

- Satisfy yourself that any processor you choose adopts appropriate security measures both in terms of the technology it uses and how it is managed (Principle 7).
- Make sure the processor actually complies with these measures (Principle 7).

- Have in place a written contract with any processor that requires it to:
  - process personal information only on your instructions, and
  - maintain appropriate security (Principle 7).

Standards: Pension/insurance schemes **16.40**

It will not always be the case that information made available by an employee to the pension provider or medical insurer of the employer needs to be seen by the employer 'unless this is a necessary consequence of the funding or other arrangements of the scheme. For example, there is no obvious reason why an employer requires access to medical information in connection with private medical insurance', the Commissioner says. For permanent health insurance, however, the employer may need to know the information. The proposed standards are set out below.

- Remember that as the employer you do not have a right of access to personal information needed only by a third party for the administration of employment-related benefits. If you collect information on behalf of another data controller ensure there is a secure method of collection; for example, the employee places a completed questionnaire in a sealed envelope which is passed unopened by you to the scheme provider (Principles 1 and 7).
- Take particular care where the trustees of a company pension scheme are involved. Although the trustees may in some cases be your employees or directors, information that they receive in their capacity as trustees of the pension scheme, for example, a medical report on a new employee who has applied to join the scheme, may not be used for your purposes as employer (Principles 1, 2 and 7).
- Limit your exchange of information with a scheme provider to the minimum necessary for operation of the scheme bearing in mind the funding obligations (Principles 1 and 3).
- Ensure that when an employee joins a health or insurance scheme it is made clear what, if any, information is passed between the scheme controller and the employer and how it will be used. This may require an explanation of how the

funding obligations for the scheme fall on the parties involved. If sensitive data are involved, obtain the employees' explicit consent to the exchange of information (Principle 1).

- If you have a scheme that insures you against sickness by employees, seek to limit your disclosure of personal information about individual employees to the insurer to a minimum. To the extent that personal data are exchanged, obtain the explicit consent of employees to this (Principles 1 and 3).

Standards: Occupational health schemes **16.41**

As with other areas, the key to compliance here is to tell the employee how their data will be used. Explicit consent will usually be required for processing as this will be sensitive data. Standards proposed by the Information Commissioner in the Draft Code include the following.

- Set out clearly to employees the extent to which information they supply to a health professional directly or indirectly in the context of an occupational health scheme might be made available to and used by others. Obtain their explicit consent to this processing (Principles 1 and 2).
- Ensure security measures are appropriate to the nature of the sensitive data processed in connection with an occupational health scheme. In particular, ensure that no-one, whether a health professional or not, has access to personal health information that they do not 'need to know'. If non-health professionals have a 'need to know', require them to sign an undertaking that confirms they are under an equivalent duty of confidentiality (Principle 7).
- Meet the standards set out in the ethical guidelines of the Faculty of Occupational Medicine.

Standards: Equal opportunities **16.42**

Many employers monitor the racial make-up of their workforce, whether staff have a disability, or are male or female. This is permitted but the information should not be misused. The Commissioner proposes the following standards.

- Do not collect information about ethnic origin, sex, disability or other personal characteristics unless it is a legal obligation, a necessary element of an established programme for the promotion of equality of opportunity, or it is otherwise needed because of some special feature of a particular job (Principle 3).
- Design questions to ensure accurate data collection. For example, do not limit the range of choices of ethnic origin to the extent that individuals are forced to make a choice they consider does not properly describe them (Principle 4).
- Wherever possible keep information used for equal opportunities monitoring in an anonymised form so that it cannot be linked to particular employees (Principles 1 and 3).

Standards: Marketing **16.43**

It may seem unlikely that an employer would market to employees, but many will market their own products, particularly in bigger companies, perhaps offering a staff discount at the same time. There may also be marketing of aims or ideals, the Information Commissioner says. Employees have a right not to have their data used for this purpose.

- Inform employees if you intend to use their personal information in order to deliver marketing messages to them (Principle 1).
- If only basic information (e.g. name and work location) is used, and there is no disclosure to other organisations, give employees a clear opportunity to object and respect any objections whenever received (Principles 1 and 6).
- If more detailed information (e.g. trade union membership, sickness record) is used, or there is disclosure, do not proceed until individual employers have positively indicated their agreement (Principles 1 and 6).

Standards: Fraud prevention/detection **16.44**

Data matching is often undertaken, particularly by employers in the public sector to check things such as whether members of staff are claiming state benefits when they are not entitled to. Proposed standards are set out below.

- When considering carrying out data-matching consult employee representatives. The purpose of consultation should be to identify any legitimate concerns that employees may have about data matching itself and about the way in which any investigations into possible fraud are conducted. Exercises should be designed to address any legitimate concerns. The consultation process may also be a way of explaining and winning acceptance of the exercise.
- Inform employees upon appointment of the use of payroll or other data in fraud prevention exercises and again before any exercises are actually carried out (Principle 1).
- Do not disclose employee data to other organisations for the prevention or detection of fraud unless:
  - employees have given their consent,
  - you are required by law to make the disclosure, or
  - in the circumstances of a particular request, you are satisfied that if you fail to disclose, the prevention or detection of crime is likely to be prejudiced (Principle 1; *DPA 1998, s 29*).
- Ensure that guidance from the Data Protection Commissioner and any relevant Codes of Practice produced by other bodies are followed in any data-matching exercise.

Standards: Financial control **16.45**

Sometimes employees owe the employer money – they may be council tenants of the council for whom they work, for example. Such investigations are civil, not criminal in nature. The Information Commissioner says that 'If the standards set out below are not followed, an obligation of confidence to employees may prevent the use of their data for financial control'.

- As with data-matching exercises designed to prevent and detect fraud, first consult employee representatives with a view to identifying any legitimate concerns about either the data-matching itself or the way in which cases of staff debt are handled.
- Specify in contracts of employment (or your code of conduct) that employees are not permitted to have significant debts to

you, and that checks will be carried out to monitor compliance with this condition of employment. Draw the attention of new employees to this condition (Principle 1).

- As an alternative to amending conditions of employment, confine your exercises to those cases where a court has confirmed that you are owed a debt by your employee. Once a court has confirmed that a debt is legally enforceable you are entitled to take reasonable steps to recover the monies owed to you (Principle 1).
- In addition to informing employees of any amendment to conditions of employment, and informing new employees on appointment, advise employees before the start of any data-matching exercises (Principle 1).

Disclosure requests 16.46

Employers need to put in place policies so that staff handling employee subject access requests know where they stand.

Standards: Disclosure requests 16.47

- Establish a disclosure policy to guide staff likely to be on the receiving end of requests for information about employees on how to respond and where to refer requests that fall outside the policy rules (Principles 1 and 7).
- Ensure that disclosure decisions which are not covered by clear policy rules are taken by staff who are familiar with *DPA 1998* and this Code, and are able to give them proper consideration (Principles 1 and 7).
- Make staff aware that those seeking information may be using deception to gain access to information to which they are not entitled (Principle 7).
- Always establish the identity of the person making a request for disclosure before responding. Where practical, obtain the request in writing. Take particular care with telephone requests, for example by calling back to a known number (Principle 7).

- Inform the Commissioner where requests based on deception are detected and there is a reasonable prospect of obtaining evidence as to who is behind the deception.
- Where those requesting information maintain that the employer is under a legal duty to respond, ensure the request is received in writing and spells out the basis on which it is asserted there is a legal duty. Check the assertion is valid (Principles 1 and 2).
- Remember that although there is an exemption from the restrictions on disclosure where a failure to disclose would prejudice crime and taxation purposes, there is no legal requirement to disclose. The decision whether to disclose is still one for the employer.
- If the crime and taxation exemption is to be relied on, ensure that you are satisfied that a failure to disclose in the particular case in question would be likely to prejudice the prevention or detection of crime, the apprehension or prosecution of offenders or the assessment or collection of tax. Either include clear guidelines for staff, if and when information should be disclosed to the police and other law enforcement or similar agencies, or ensure that requests are always referred to an appropriate manager (Principles 1 and 2; *DPA 1998, s 29*).
- Where there is no legal duty to disclose, the disclosure is not covered by an exemption and you wish to respond positively, only do so if you are satisfied that in all circumstances it is fair to do so, bearing in mind that the duty of fairness is owed primarily to the employee, and that the purpose for which the information will be used after disclosure must not be incompatible with the purpose(s) for which you hold it.

  Circumstances to be taken into account include the employee's understanding of how his/her data might be used, the extent and nature of information requested, the person requesting it and the reason for the request, any view expressed by the employee or, if it is not practicable to ask for one, what the likely view would be if asked and whether the employee is likely to dispute the accuracy of the information (Principles 1 and 2).
- Always inform the employee at the time a non-routine disclosure is to be made unless prevented by law from doing so or the information would be a 'tip off' prejudicing the crime or taxation purposes (Principle 1).

- In the case of a non-routine disclosure, make available to the employee a copy of the information that has been disclosed. Where the accuracy of information may be challenged by the employee and it is practicable to do so, provide him/her with a copy before disclosure and address any concerns he/she might have at this stage (Principle 4).
- Keep a record of non-routine disclosures recording the person who made the disclosure, the person who authorised it, the person requesting the disclosure, the reasons, the information disclosed and the date and time (Principle 7).
- Check the record regularly to ensure the disclosure policy and the requirements of the *DPA 1998* are complied with. Address any deficiencies (Principle 7).
- Remind staff that it is a criminal offence to knowingly or recklessly disclose information about employees without the employer's consent. Incorporate this in disciplinary rules (Principle 7; *DPA 1998, s 55*).
- Inform the Commissioner when the security or confidentiality of employee records has been significantly prejudiced because they have been disclosed knowingly or recklessly without the employer's consent, and there is a reasonable prospect of obtaining evidence as to who was responsible.

Other disclosure requests 16.48

Some employers decide for policy reasons to disclose particular data. Examples might include information in a company's annual report or marketing material. Pictures of staff in a brochure or on a website are an example. Proposed standards of the Information Commissioner, not yet agreed are as set out at 16.49 below.

Standards 16.49

- Do not publish information about employees unless:
  - there is a legal obligation to do so,
  - the information is not intrusive and, taking into account the nature of the employer's business and the position held by the employee, publication would be expected, or
  - the employee has consented (Principle 1).

- If information is published with consent, ensure the employee is aware of the extent of information that will be published and how it will be published, including whether the information will be published on a website and the implications of this (Principle 1).
- Do not supply personal information about employees to trade unions for recruitment unless:
  - the trade union is recognised by the employer, the information is limited to name, job and work location/address and each employee has been told this will happen and has been given an opportunity to object, or
  - the employee has consented to the disclosure (Principles 1 and 2).
- Where staffing information is supplied to trade unions in the course of collective bargaining, ensure the information is such that individual employees cannot be identified (Principle 1).

Access to third party data 16.50

Sometimes employees will not want their names disclosed to those making subject access requests and third parties are entitled to protection in this way. The Commissioner has issued guidance on access to third party data in her Draft Employer/Employee Code.

Release of Third Party Information in Response to a Subject Access Request

1. Seek the consent of the third party to the release of the information unless it is impractical to do so (e.g. the third party's whereabouts are unknown) or consent cannot be given (e.g. the third party does not have sufficient mental capacity).
2. If consent has not been given, decide whether in all the circumstances it is nevertheless reasonable to give access. This involves balancing the employee's right of access with the third party's right to respect for his or her private life.
3. In doing so take into account:
   - whether you owe a duty of confidence to the third party,
   - any express refusal of consent,

- the impact the information has had or is likely to have on actions or decisions affecting the employee,
- the nature of the third party information, in particular whether its release will be damaging to the third party or whether it is sensitive,
- the extent to which the employee is already likely to be aware of the information,
- whether the information includes facts which might be disputed by the employee were he/she aware of them, and
- whether the third party information relates to the third party acting in a business or personal capacity.

4. Bear in mind that the release of confidential information, or information where there has been an express refusal of consent, is unlikely to be justified unless the information has had or is likely to have a significant adverse impact on the employee.

Mergers **16.51**

Whenever the assets of a business are sold a detailed schedule of employees will be drawn up and a due diligence exercise undertaken by the proposed buyer of *inter alia* the employment records. However data protection issues do arise. The proposed standards of the Information Commissioner below provide useful guidance on how to handle this issue.

Standards: Mergers **16.52**

- Where it is necessary to disclose information about employees in the run-up to a merger or acquisition, ensure that as far as possible the information is made anonymous so that individuals cannot be identified directly through the provision of names, job titles or similar details (Principle 1).
- Where the supply of personal data is unavoidable, for example, because it is obvious information relates to a particular senior manager even after identifiers have been removed, conditions should be applied to its release. These should include:

- ❍ the information must only be used for the preparation of a merger/acquisition bid,
- ❍ the information must not be further disclosed beyond the prospective purchaser and its corporate finance advisers,
- ❍ the information must be kept secure, and
- ❍ the information must be returned or destroyed once a bid has been submitted or there is a decision not to proceed (Principle 1).

- If, as a result of a merger or acquisition, employees are transferred to a new employer but with continuity of employment, then their employment records can be transferred. They should be advised that this is happening and be given an opportunity to check the accuracy of the key information that is passed on. The new employer should review the records to ensure the information it retains is relevant and not excessive to the new employment relationship (Principles 1, 3 and 4).
- If employees have their employment with the original employer terminated and they are re-employed by the new employer without continuity of employment, their records must not be transferred without their individual consent (Principle 1).

Other issues 16.53

The Information Commissioner's Draft Code also provides guidance on agency or contract staff and also a large section on employee monitoring (see CHAPTER 15 E-MAILS). Medical, discipline, dismissal and other employment topics are also addressed, but are not considered here.

Advice 16.54

Personnel managers and all those involved in the recruitment process, some of whom may know little about employment or data protection law if they are simply general managers interviewing a potential member of staff, do need guidance from their employer. They should therefore err on the side of caution. Such advice might include the following.

'• *DPA 1998* gives individuals such as prospective employees important rights in relation to their personal information. Employees should consult their legal department before doing anything with such personal data about which they are unsure or to which the potential employee may not have consented, even if the recruitment agency tells them this is acceptable. Areas to watch include sending a CV to offices outside the EU and passing on the details to anyone else, even if they believe the employee might be glad they have passed their CV to a manager in another company who is also looking for such members of staff.

- When interviewing be careful about the notes taken. *Section* 7 of *DPA 1998* gives individuals rights to see copies of the personal data held about them. This would include information written in e-mails and information you write down whether in handwriting, in a personal organiser or on the company's computer systems.
- If this information is inaccurate or biased it may be used against the company later if legal proceedings follow.
- There is nothing to stop notes being taken in interviews, and indeed it is a crucial part of the recruitment process that they are. For example, interviewers should note information that the employee mentions which had been left off the CV. However company policy on discrimination should always be followed.
- If in doubt take advice from the legal department.'

Further information 16.55

Draft Code Of Practice on The Use of Personal Data in Employer/Employee Relationships	www.dataprotection.gov.uk
European Commission Opinion 8/2001 (13 September 2001) 'on the processing of personal data in the employment context' (5062/01/EN/Final WP 48)	http://europa.eu.int/comm/internal_market/en/datprot/wpdocs/index.htm

In relation to inaccurate CVs see the following.

Lies We Live By: The Art of Self-Deception, Eduardo Gianetti and John Gledson, Bloomsbury, £12.79
Detecting Lies and Deceit, Aldert Vrij, Wiley, £24.99
Freedom, Fame, Lying and Betrayal, Lesek Kolakowski, Penguin, £6.99

17 – Enforcement, Remedies and Powers

At a glance 17.1

- Requests for assessment of compliance with the *Data Protection Act 1998* (*DPA 1998*) can be made to the Information Commissioner's office under *section 42* of *DPA 1998*.
- *Section 40* of *DPA 1998* entitles the Commissioner to issue an enforcement notice requiring compliance with the legislation.
- Information notices may be served by the Commissioner requiring information to be provided.
- Examples of undertakings given are provided in this chapter.
- Compensation can be awarded by the courts but not by the Commissioner.

Introduction 17.2

The Information Commissioner has substantial powers under *DPA 1998* to enforce the provisions of the Act. Her dual role also gives her powers under the *Freedom of Information Act 2000*. CHAPTER 4 COMMISSIONER looks at the assessment procedure, whereby a complainant or data controller can request the Commissioner to undertake an assessment. Section 7.2 of the Commissioner's Legal Guidance on the Act (October 2001) describes the assessment procedure in detail. CHAPTER 5 COMPENSATION/DAMAGES of this book examines the compensation which can be recovered under the legislation. This chapter looks at other enforcement issues under the legislation, including in particular remedies and powers under *DPA 1998* (see 17.9 below).

Assessment 17.3

Briefly, requests for assessment can be made by anyone who is directly affected by any processing of personal data under *section 42* of *DPA 1998*. The Commissioner has a wide discretion; see CHAPTER 2 COMMISSIONER in relation to how such assessments are handled.

Enforcement 17.4

Section 40 of *DPA 1998* empowers the Information Commissioner to serve enforcement notices on the data controller where there has been a contravention of one of the Data Protection Principles. The notice will specify what the controller must do, such as stop processing data in breach of *DPA 1998*. The Commissioner generally pursues a 'softly softly' approach to enforcement, and may well simply gently bring a breach to the attention of the controller rather than serving the notice in heavy-handed fashion (see CHAPTER 4 COMMISSIONER and the Commissioner's First Annual Report (June 2001), from which it can be seen that few enforcement notices are actually served). However, in assessing whether to serve such a notice, the Information Commissioner will consider if the contravention has caused or is likely to cause any person damage or distress.

> 'An enforcement notice must not require any of the provisions of the notice to be complied with before the end of the period within which an appeal can be brought against the notice unless the enforcement notice contains a statement of urgency. If an appeal is lodged the notice need not be complied with pending the determination or withdrawal of the appeal.'
>
> *Para 7.3, Data Protection Act 1998: Guidance of Information Commissioner (October 2001)*

There is power to enclose a requirement that the notice be dealt with urgently by way of a 'statement of urgency', but even then there is still a period ending seven days, beginning with the day on which the notice is served, before the requirement applies.

An enforcement notice may be cancelled or changed in particular circumstances, for example when the Commissioner considers that the notice (or part of it) need not be complied with in order to ensure compliance with the Data Protection Principle or Principles in question.

Information notices 17.5

DPA 1998 gives the Commissioner powers to serve an 'information notice' on a data controller once she has received a request for assessment or of her own volition. The notice will tell the data controller to provide information to the Information Commissioner and give a period in which to do so.

Special information notices **17.6**

Special information notices can also be served where the Information Commissioner suspects that personal data is not being processed only for 'special purposes' or with a view to publication for journalistic purposes.

'Special purposes' under *section 32* of *DPA 1998* mean purposes of journalism, artistic purposes or literary purposes. There is only an exemption for processing data for special purposes where the following conditions are met:

- the data is processed only for those purposes;
- it is undertaken to publish journalistic, literary or artistic material and the controller reasonably believes that it is in the public interest; and
- the data controller reasonably believes that compliance with the provision in respect of which the exemption is claimed is incompatible with the special purposes.

Fines **17.7**

CHAPTER 8 CRIME gives a chart of the fines which were imposed for breach of *DPA 1998* in the Commissioner's First Annual Report (June 2001). Fines may be imposed for breach of obligations under the legislation such as failure to notify the holding of data or breach of the Data Protection Principles under the legislation. Fines are a maximum of £5,000.

Example undertakings: Thames Water **17.8**

Undertakings under *DPA 1998* are relatively few and far between.

The Commissioner published undertakings given by Thames Water Utilities Limited following proceedings started in 1999.

In January 1999 the Commissioner served a notice to take enforcement action on Thames Water Utilities Limited over the contravention of the First Data Protection Principle. The enforcement notice said that Thames had unfairly processed personal data in breach of the First Principle. Thames had unfairly processed personal data held by individual customers for the supply of water for the purpose of marketing non-water-related goods and services both from Thames and others. However, Thames appealed on

11 February 1999 so the Commissioner reconsidered and decided that an undertaking about the future processing of personal data would suffice.

The undertaking was as follows:

1. Subject to paragraphs 2 to 5 below, in connection with marketing or trade promotion, the data controller shall only process personal data which is or has been obtained by the data controller or its predecessors (*a*) from its individual customers for the provision of water supply, sewerage, drainage and sewage disposal services (hereinafter called 'the Services') to premises for the purpose of the Services or (*b*) as a result of the Services to such customers, for the following purposes:

   (i) the provision of the Services to premises and informing customers of the existence and nature of loyalty schemes in connection with the Services; for the avoidance of doubt, the data controller shall be entitled to describe the nature and benefits available under any such loyalty scheme and any relevant conditions, but without identifying the third party provider of those benefits except as otherwise permitted under this undertaking;

   (ii) the marketing or promoting by the data controller, on its own behalf or on behalf of third parties, of the supply, installation, servicing or repair of appliances and goods relating to the Services, including water efficiency and conservation;

   (iii the marketing or promoting by the data controller, or by the data controller on behalf of an associated retail arm, of such goods or materials as are at the time of the marketing or promotion available for customers to purchase or hire at one or more retail premises of such retail company; and

   (iv informing customers as to where further information may be obtained from the data controller on the loyalty schemes,

   provided that the processing does not lead to the disclosure of personal data by the data controller to a third party.

2. Consent. No restriction as aforesaid shall apply to the processing of personal data of customers in the categories set out below:

(i) where individual customers have expressly consented to the type or types of marketing and promotions and disclosure (if any) for which their personal data is intended to be processed; or

(ii) where individual customers supplied by the data controller with the Services to their premises either:

(*a*) at or before the time when arrangements for the Services were made:

(i) have been informed of the type or types of marketing or promotions and disclosure (if any) for which their personal data is intended to be processed; and

(ii) have been given the choice to agree or not to such processing and either:

(*aa*) have responded then and there, and in their response have consented or not objected to such processing; or alternatively

(*bb*) thereafter and before such processing took place have returned a document to the data controller, or by other means of communication received by the data controller have indicated that they consent to, or by not filling in an 'opt-out' box, or by other means, have indicated that they did not object to such processing; or

(*b*) at any time when currently supplied by the data controller with Services to their premises:

(i) have been informed of the type or types of marketing or promotions and disclosure (if any) for which their personal data is intended to be processed; and

(ii) have been given the choice to agree or not to such processing, and either:

(*aa*) have responded then and there, and in their response have consented or not objected to such processing; or alternatively (*bb*) thereafter and before such processing took place have returned a document to the data controller, or by other means of communication received by the data controller have indicated that they consented to, or by not filling in an 'opt-out' box or by other means, have indicated that they did not object to such processing.

3. Where an individual customer supplied by the data controller with the Services at a premises is subsequently supplied by the data controller with the Services at other premises then, upon notice to the customer, any previous consent, non-objection or objection previously notified to the data controller in the manner set out in paragraph 2 above shall remain valid unless and until revoked by the customer.

4. Indirect disclosure. No processing under paragraphs 1 or 2 above shall be undertaken by reference to selected criteria whereby individual customers, to whom the data controller supplies the Services to premises, who respond to a third party marketing or promotion, would disclose to the third party personal information concerning themselves, other than name and address and the fact that they are a customer of the data controller, unless prior to, or at the time of receiving the marketing or promotional communication, the customers are informed of the type of personal information that might be disclosed by such response.

5. For the avoidance of doubt:

   (1) the prohibition above does not apply to personal data obtained and held for functions other than the regulated function/s of the supply of the Services;

   (2) marketing or promotions permitted under paragraph 1 may be independent of or accompanying a communication from the data controller (including the data controller's bills and circulars);

   (3) consent shall not be inferred from the failure of any person to return any leaflet or other document containing an opportunity to opt-out;

   (4) the prohibition above does not apply to the circulation of the annual charitable leaflet for Water Aid.

> ***Comment:*** The undertakings show how important it is to ensure compliance with the First Data Protection Principle. The points at paragraph 5 'for the avoidance of doubt' are illuminating. Consent is not implied where someone fails to return a document which contains a chance to opt out. Readers in similar utility companies should not necessarily assume that the same undertakings would precisely be permitted to avoid enforcement action in their own business, but they do provide useful guidance as to what the Commissioner finds acceptable.

Remedies and compensation 17.9

Compensation was addressed in CHAPTER 5 COMPENSATION/DAMAGES to which reference should be made, but the following is worthy of note in the context of remedies in this chapter. *DPA 1998* gives rights to those who suffer damage or damage and distress through a breach of the Act, allowing them to recover compensation where the data controller cannot prove it took reasonable care to comply. Normally compensation is only payable for damage, but will also be available for distress if the processing was for 'special purposes' (see 17.6 above). If the processing occurs there may also in certain cases be a breach of the law of confidence.

Applying for compensation 17.10

Compensation can be applied for either to the court or initially may simply be negotiated with the infringer of the data subject's rights. Unless a payment of compensation is agreed between the data controller and the data subject as a result of negotiations between them, the application may be made by the data subject to the court for compensation alone, or it may be combined with an application in respect of any breach of *DPA 1998*. The Commissioner has no power to award compensation.

In her Legal Guidance (October 2001) on *DPA 1998* the Commissioner poses the question 'How much will the court award if a claim for compensation is successful?' and replies as follows:

> 'There are no guidelines as to appropriate levels of compensation for a claim under the Act and the Commissioner is not routinely advised of the outcome of cases where individuals have made a successful claim for compensation under the Act. The judge hearing the case has discretion in these matters and would have to take into

consideration many factors including the seriousness of the breach and the effect upon the claimant, particularly when considering damages for distress.'

Case example 17.11

Extra-marital sexual relationships: *A v B plc and another (10th September 2001, Times Law Reports 2 November 2001)*

In *A v B plc and another* the High Court imposed an interlocutory injunction on a newspaper which was going to publish a story about sexual relationships which a married footballer had had with two women. The court said that the law of confidentiality could apply to facts concerning the existence of sexual relationships and details of sexual activities in those relationships both in and outside of marriage even if there was no express agreement between the parties to keep those details confidential. There was no public interest in the publication of the information and the information was not in the public domain, so in this case an injunction would be granted. The right to privacy given by the *Human Rights Act 1998* would prevail. This right should prevail over the human right of freedom of expression.

Further information 17.12

See also CHAPTER 5 COMPENSATION/DAMAGES and CHAPTER 4 COMMISSIONER where the assessment procedure is addressed.

18 – European Aspects

At a glance 18.1

- ✓ The *Data Protection Act 1998* (*DPA 1998*) implements the *EU Data Protection Directive* (*95/46/EC*) in the UK.
- ✓ All EU states should have implemented the Directive by now.
- ✓ Where a Government fails to implement a directive correctly, those suffering loss may be able to sue for damages under EU law.
- ✓ There are some areas where the UK may not have properly implemented the Directive.

Introduction 18.2

DPA 1998 implements the *Data Protection Directive* (*95/46/EC*) in the UK with effect from 1 March 2000. The Directive gives all Member States some choices and options in how they will implement the Directive so that laws will not be identical throughout the EU. However, they will be very similar indeed.

Effect of late implementation 18.3

All Member States should have implemented the Directive by 24 October 1998. The UK implemented it on 1 March 2000. The effect of this under European law is that from that date (24 October 1998) all state bodies or emanations of the state should already have been acting as if the Directive were in place.

Secondly, anyone who has suffered loss or damage through the failure to implement the Directive on time may be entitled to claim damages from the Government for the late implementation. However, this is unlikely as such cases are expensive and difficult to bring about.

Status of implementation of Directive 95/46/EC 18.4

The European Commission publishes a chart of implementation around the EU, and this is summarised below. However the position regularly changes so always check the latest position. It can be found at: www. europa.eu.int/comm/internal_market/en/dataprot/law/impl.htm

Member State	State of legislative procedure	Next steps
Austria	Directive implemented by the Data Protection Act 2000. Entry into force: 1.01.00.	
Belgium	Consolidated text of the Belgian law of December 8, 1992 on Privacy Protection in relation to the Processing of Personal Data as modified by the law of December 11, 1998. Secondary legislation adopted 13.2.01 (O.J. 13.3.01) Entry into force 1.9.01	
Denmark*	Parliament passed the Act on Processing of Personal Data (Act No 429) 31.05.00 Entry into force: 01.07.00.	
Finland	The Finnish Personal Data Act (523/1999) was given on 22.4.1999 Entry into force: 01.06.1999.	
France*	Bill discussed in the Parliament	
Germany*	Federal Data Protection Act adopted 18.5.01 Entry into force 23.5.01 Six Länder (Brandenburg, Baden-Württemberg, Bayern, Hessen. Nordrhein-Westfalen, Schleswig-Holstein) adopted new DPLs persuant to the Directive. These acts apply to the public sector of the respective 'Länder'.	The Bundesrat presented an opinion on 29.9.2000 (BR-Drs. 461/00 (Beschluss). First Reading by the Deutscher Bundestag on 27.10.2000.
Greece	Implementation Law 2472 adopted: 10.04.97. Protection of individuals with regard to the processing of personal data. Entry into force: 10.4.97.	

Italy	Protection of individuals and other subjects with regard to the Processing of Personal Data Act no. 675 of 31.12.96. Entry into force: 8.5.97	Parliamentary discussion about the renew of the delegation to the Government to complete Law 675.
Ireland*	Draft Bill to be approved by the Government and submitted to Parliament	
Luxembourg*	DPL approved by the Senate 6.7.00 Entry into force 1.9.01	
The Netherlands	DPL approved by the Senate on 06.07.00, (O.J. 302/2000). Personal Data Protection Act of 6.7.00 Estimated entry into force: Spring 2001	Secondary legislation to be adopted.
Portugal	Directive implemented by Law 67/98 of 26.10.1998. Entry into force: 27.10.1998	
Spain	Implementation law adopted 13.12.99. Ley Orgánica 15/1999, de 13 de diciembre de Protección de Datos de Carácter Personal. ('B.O.E.' núm. 298, de 14 de diciembre de 1999). Entry into force: 14.01.00.	
Sweden	Directive implemented by SFS 1998:204 of 29.4.98 and regulation SFS 1998:1191 of 03.09.98. Entry into force: 24.10.1998.	
United Kingdom	Date Protection Act 1998 passed 16.7.98 Entry into force: 01.03.00.	

* The Member State is subject to a Commission Decision to bring the Member State to the European Court of Justice for failure to notify the implementing measures within the deadline established by the Directive.

(Chart up to date 30 October 2001).

EU Data Protection Commissioners **18.5**

National Data Protection Commissioners **18.6**

Austria Bundeskanzleramt Büro der Datenschutzkommission und des Datenschutzrates Bundeskanzleramt Ballhausplatz 1 A–1014 Vienna Tel: 00 43 1 531 15 26 79 Website: www.bka.gv.at/datenschutz
Belgium Commission de la protection de la vie privée Avenue de la Porte de Hal 5–8 1060 Brussels Tel: 00 32 25 42 72 00 Website: www.privacy.fgov.be
Denmark Registertilsynet Christians Brygge, 28, 4 sal DK–1559 Copenhagen V Tel: 00 45 33 14 38 44 Website: www.datatilsynet.dk
Finland Office of the Data Protection Ombudsman Albertinkatu 25, 3.kerros PL 315 PO Box 315 Tel: 00 35 89 18 251 Website: www.tietosuoja.fi
France Commission Nationale de l'Informatique et des Libertés Rue Saint Guillaume, 21 75007 Paris Tel: 00 33 15 37 32 222 Website: www.cnil.fr
Germany Der Bundesbeauftragte für den Datenschutz Postfach 200112 53131 Bonn Tel 00 49 22 88 19 95 10 Website: www.bfd.bund.de

Greece Hellenic Data Protection Authority Ministry of Justice 96 Mesogion Avenue 115 27 Athens, Greece Tel: 00 30 17 79 58 05 Website: www.dpa.gr
Iceland Data Protection Commission Dómsmálaráouneytio Arnarhvoli 150 Reykjavik Tel: 00 35 45 60 90 10
Ireland Data Protection Commissioner Irish Life Centre, Block 4 Talbot Street Dublin 1 Tel: 00 35 31 87 48 544 Website: www.dataprivacy.ie
Italy Garante per la protezione dei dati personali Segretario generale Via della Chiesa Nuova 8 00186 Rome Tel: 00 39 06 68 89 21 34/5/6/7/8/9 Website: http://astra.garanteprivacy.it
Luxembourg Commission en matière d'utilisation des données nominatives dans les traitements informatiques Ministère de la Justice Boulevard Royal 16 L–2934 Luxembourg Tel: 00 35 24 78 45 46
Netherlands Registratiekamer Prins Clauslaan 20 Postbus 93374 NL – 2509 AJ's-Gravenhage Tel: 00 31 70 381 13 00 Website: www.registratiekamer.nl

Norway The Data Inspectorate Berhard-Getz-Gt. 2 PO Box 8177 Dep 003 4 Oslo 1 Tel: 00 47 22 42 19 10 Website: www.datatilsynet.no
Portugal Commissão Nacional de Protecção de Dados Pessoais Informatizados Rue de São Bento, 1483 1200 Lisbon Tel: 00 35 11 39 28 400 Website: www.cnpd.pt
Spain Agencia de Protección de Datos Paseo de la Castellana 41–5a planta E – 28046 MADRID Tel: 00 34 91 30 83 144 Website: www.agenciaprotecciondatos.org
Sweden The Data Inspection Board Box 8114 Fkennubggatan 14 8 Can 8 S–104 20 STOCKHOLM Tel: 00 46 86 57 61 00 Website: www.datainspektionen.se
United Kingdom The Office of the Data Protection Registrar Wycliffe House Water Lane Wilmslow Cheshire SK9 5AF Tel: 00 44 16 25 54 57 00 Website: www.dataprotection.gov.uk

Implementation issues 18.7

Areas where the UK may not have implemented the Directive properly include the fact that the Directive has a definition of 'consent'. The provisions in the Directive but not *DPA 1998* require data subjects to consent 'unambiguously'.

Other EU work 18.8

The Information Commissioner's Office participates in the Working Party of Data Protection Commissioners set up under *Article 29* of the *Data Protection Directive* (*95/46/EC*). In 2001 the Working Party principally worked on transborder data flow issues and the US Safe Harbor Agreement.

In 2001 the Working Party adopted a report from its Internet task force on data protection and the Internet (mentioned in the UK Information Commissioner's First Annual Report (June 2001)).

Retaining traffic data – proposals for e-security 18.9

The Working Party has also examined routine retention of traffic data for policing purposes. A proposal for a European Policy Approach for e-security was published by the European Commission on 6 June 2001. One of the main aims of this is to 'remedy the existing lack of security on a European level by finding effective solutions for securing networks and data transfers around the world'. The proposal aims to ensure:

- confidentiality (to avoid files interception and illegal computer access);
- network and information accessibility;
- actor's identification (to avoid misrepresentation of persons or entities);
- data integrity (to prevent modification or destruction of information).

The general legal issue of whether businesses should be obliged to keep logs of traffic data has been subject to some criticism.

The EU Draft Communications Data Protection Proposal contains similar provisions about retention of records. The Confederation of British Industry (CBI) has expressed concern that the EU plans would require Internet Service Providers (ISPs) to keep logs for lengthy periods about customers' activities. The CBI says it is a 'retrograde step' that could threaten privacy and e-commerce. Storage can lead to huge costs. The Government put forward proposals on 16 October 2001 which would require business to retain records of e-mails and Internet usage for 12 months under new anti-terrorist legislative proposals. The Home Office said that the measures would have a statutory base. Freeserve and AOL currently retain records for three months, so a twelve month period will involve some major changes for companies. Demon Internet was reported in October 2001 as saying that the extra costs could amount to hundreds of thousands of pounds. Few companies already retain data for as long as a year. The Government appears to have ruled out requiring ISPs to store the content of e-mails as that has proven too costly.

Recent developments 18.10

New legislation 18.11

In November 2001 the Government published its Anti-Terrorism, Crime and Security Bill. The Information Commissioner commented that 'The provisions could have a significant impact on the privacy of individuals whose data are retained. If there is a demonstrable and pressing need for these provisions, an appropriate balance must be struck between personal privacy and the legitimate needs of the law enforcement community. There are particular concerns that leaving matters to a voluntary code of practice, or to agreements, may pose difficulties for data protection and human rights compliance. Although recent events have prompted these measures to be brought forward, law enforcement agencies will make use of them on a day-to-day basis for a variety of matters. Careful consideration must be given to ensure that the provisions are appropriate to addressing these more routine needs.

Case law 18.12

In November 2001, in the case of *Brian Robertson v Wakefield City Council (High Court, 16 November 2001)*, the High Court held that the UK, in permitting the use of the electoral roll for commercial purposes had not, in *DPA 1998*, properly implemented the *EU Data Protection Directive* (*95/46/EC*). Voters should not have their data used for such purposes when it was gathered to enable them to vote.

Further information 18.13

Information on the implementation of the *Data Protection Directive* is on the European Commission's web site at www.europa.eu.int/comm/internal_market/en/dataprot/law/impl.htm

The EU European Policy Approach to E-security is on the Internet at http://europa.eu.int/information_society/eeurope/news_library/pdf_files/netsec_en.pdf.

19 – Exemptions

At a glance 19.1

- ✓ There are many exemptions from the *Data Protection Act 1998* (*DPA 1998*) including those for staff administration and some forms of marketing.
- ✓ Comprehensive coverage of the exemptions to *DPA 1998* appears in the Commissioner's Legal Guidance (Chapter 5, October 2001).
- ✓ The decision in *Baker v Home Department (October 2001)* held that the security services could not just apply a blanket ban on subject access in major areas.
- ✓ In a Swedish case the exemption under the *Data Protection Directive* (*95/46/EC*) for the processing of data for journalistic purposes in the public interest was held to apply.

Introduction 19.2

DPA 1998 contains many complex exemptions in a wide range of areas. Few are blanket exemptions. Most give exemption from one aspect only, such as the right of subject access under *section* 7 of *DPA 1998*. They therefore have to be considered very carefully indeed. This section simply provides a broad overview of the exemptions available. The staff administration exemption was also considered under CHAPTER 16 EMPLOYMENT.

Exemptions in notification regulations 19.3

The *Data Protection (Notification and Notification Fees) Regulations 2000* (the *Notification Regulations*) (*SI 2000/188*) appear wide-ranging, but in practice most companies will find the processing they do with their data takes them outside the exemptions. Few businesses will be able to avoid notification (registration) under *DPA 1998* simply because of these provisions. This was the same under the *Data Protection Act 1984* (*DPA 1984*) which contains some fairly similar exemptions.

Section 17 of *DPA 1998* provides that no one must process personal data without registration or notification. The exemption below provides an exemption from this provision. In effect the data controller does not have to register. However, all the other obligations under *DPA 1998* apply, such as the Eight Data Protection Principles and the requirement to give individuals access to their personal data under *section 7* of *DPA 1998*.

Staff administration exemption **19.4**

The staff administration exemption covers data processing for the purposes of appointments or removals, pay, discipline, superannuation, work management or other personnel matters in relation to the staff of the data controller where the personal data is in respect of a part, existing or prospective member of staff or any one the processing of whose personal data is necessary for the exempt purposes.

The exemption is limited to cases where the personal data is just the name, address and other identifiers of the data subject, information as to qualifications, work experience or pay, or other matters, the processing of which is necessary for the exempt purposes. In addition, the data must not be disclosed to a third party other than with the data subject's consent or where necessary for the exempt purposes. It must not involve keeping the personal data after the relationship has ceased.

Most employers will be outside this requirement.

Advertising, marketing and public relations exemption **19.5**

A very limited exemption applies where data processing is for the purposes of advertising or marketing the data controller's business or activity, and it:

- solely relates to data of past, existing or prospective customers or suppliers;
- is only the name, address or other identifier; and
- does not involve disclosure without data subject consent, as in relation to the staff administration exemption (see 19.4 above).

The information must not be kept after the relationship ends, except where necessary for the exempt purposes.

Accounts and records exemption **19.6**

Where data processing is:

- to keep accounts;
- to decide whom to accept as a customer or supplier;
- to keep records of purchases, sales or other transaction to ensure payments and deliveries are made; or
- for financial or management forecasts,

then it may be possible to be exempt from registration but not the other requirements of *DPA 1998*. This is limited as set out in *paragraph 4* of the *Schedule* to the *Notification Regulations* (*SI 2000/188*), by requirements such as the data must only consist of data about customers and suppliers, which consists just of their name, address and other identifiers, and which relates only to their financial standing. It must not involve disclosure to third parties nor any retention of the information after the relationship is over.

Non-profit making organisations **19.7**

There is an exemption from the *Notification Regulations* (*SI 2000/188*) where the processing is carried out by a body or association which is not established or conducted for profit. It applies where the data is just about past, existing or prospective members or any person in regular contact with the body or organisation, and must only be a name, address or other identifier and concern eligibility for membership. No disclosure may take place without the data subject's consent and after the relationship is over the data should be destroyed.

Other exemptions **19.8**

Other exemptions are contained in *DPA 1998*. However, it is essential to read *DPA 1998* in relation to these exemptions, as they provide exemptions from particular sections of *DPA 1998* rather than from the whole Act. A summary of the exemptions is contained in Chapter 5 of the Commissioner's Introduction which is on the website at www.dataprotection.gov.uk.

- National security (see the *Baker* decision at 19.13 below).
- Crime and taxation.
- Health and social work (in this respect note the *Data Protection (Subject Access Modification) (Social Work) Order 2000* (*SI 2000/415*), *Data Protection (Subject Access Modification) (Education) Order 2000* (*SI 2000/414*) the *Data Protection (Subject Access Modification) (Health) Order 2000* (*SI 2000/413*) (see 19.10 below).
- Regulatory activity.

- Journalism, literature and art – 'special purposes' (see the Swedish case at 19.15 below) under *DPA 1998* (this is an exemption from all the Data Protection Principles except the Seventh Principle (security) and also an exemption from *sections* 7, *10*, *12*, and *14(1)–(3)* of *DPA 1998* where:
  - the processing is with a view to the publication of journalistic, literary or artistic material;
  - the data controller reasonably believes it is in the public interest (not a very onerous requirement); and
  - the data controller believes that compliance with the provision in *DPA 1998* is incompatible with the special purpose.
- Research, history and statistics.
- Information available to the public under the law.
- Legal disclosures and legal proceedings (see *Totalise v Motley Fool* case at 19.14 below).
- Domestic purposes (family and householder affairs).
- *Schedule* 7 to *DPA 1998* exemptions:
  - confidential references;
  - armed forces;
  - judicial appointments and honours;
  - Crown employment;
  - management forecasts;
  - corporate finance (and note the provisions of the *Data Protection (Corporate Finance Exemption) Order 2000* (*SI 2000/184*));
  - negotiations;
  - examination marks;
  - examination scripts;
  - legal professional privilege; and
  - self incrimination.

Also relevant are exemptions under *DPA 1984* such as for manual data, processing otherwise than by reference to the data subject, back-up data etc., in cases where there are lengthy periods before *DPA 1998* will apply.

Information Commissioner's guidance on the exemptions 19.9

In October 2001 the Commissioner issued her Legal Guidance on *DPA 1998* which includes, in Chapter 5, comprehensive consideration of the exemptions under the Act briefly mentioned above. Her guidance, along with secondary legislation relevant to the exemptions, is considered in more detail at 19.10–19.11 below.

Orders made in relation to health, education and social work 19.10

The Orders made in relation to health, education and social work are made under *section 30* of *DPA 1998*. They include the *Data Protection (Subject Access Modification) (Health) Order 2000* (*SI 2000/413*) (the '*Health Order*'). This provides an exemption from subject access for data relating to the physical or mental health or condition of the data subject, to the extent to which the application of *section* 7 of *DPA 1998* would be likely to cause serious harm to the physical or mental health or condition of the data subject or any other person.

The Commissioner states in her Legal Guidance:

> 'Before deciding whether this exemption applies, a data controller who is not a health professional (as defined in *DPA 1998*) is obliged to consult the health professional responsible for the clinical care of the data subject, or if there is more than one, the most suitable one.'

The Commissioner recognises that in many cases there will be more than one health professional responsible for the patient's clinical care at the time a subject access request is made. Data controllers should ensure that they have systems in place to enable the most suitable health professional to be identified and consulted to enable the data controller to comply with a subject access request within the statutory time limit of 40 days.

Where a request for subject access is made by someone other than the data subject (i.e. by someone with parental responsibility for a child or, in relation to Scotland, by such a person on behalf of someone under the age of 16, or by a person appointed by a court to manage the affairs of the data subject), the data controller should consider the following:

- any expectation of confidentiality the data subject may have had at the time the information was provided or obtained; and
- any wishes expressed by the data subject with regard to the disclosure of personal data relating to his physical or mental health or condition.

In specific circumstances, which are set out in the *Health Order* (*SI 2000/413*) where certain personal data are processed by the Court, there is also an exemption from the subject information provisions.

The *Data Protection (Subject Access Modifications) (Education) Order 2000* (*SI 2000/414*) (the '*Education Order*') provides for modifications and exemptions:

- where the personal data consist of information constituting an education record;
- where disclosure of the information pursuant to a subject access request would be likely to cause serious harm to the physical or mental health or condition of the data subject, or to some other person; or
- in some circumstances, where disclosure would reveal that the data subject is, or may be at risk of child abuse

(as defined in the Order).

The *Data Protection (Subject Access Modifications) (Social Work) Order 2000* (*SI 2000/415*) (the '*Social Work Order*') provides for modifications and exemptions where the personal data relate to social work falling within any of the descriptions set out in the Order.

Processing for the special purposes **19.11**

Data processing for special purposes is governed by *section 32* of *DPA 1998.*

> 'Special purposes' means any one or more of the following:
>
> - the purposes of journalism;
> - artistic purposes;
> - literary purposes.'

Section 32 of *DPA 1998* provides four conditions which must all be present before the processing of personal data for the special purposes can qualify for any exemption from *DPA 1998* under this section. The conditions are that:

- the personal data are processed only for the special purposes;
- the processing is undertaken with a view to the publication by any person of any journalistic, literary or artistic material;
- the data controller reasonably believes that, taking account in particular of the special importance of the public interest in freedom of expression, publication would be in the public interest; and

- the data controller reasonably believes that, in all the circumstances, compliance with the provision in respect of which the exemption claimed is incompatible with the special purposes.

In her Legal Guidance under *DPA 1998* the Commissioner says:

> 'If all the conditions are satisfied, the exemption available is from the following provisions of the Act:
>
> - the *Data Protection Principles* except the *Seventh Data Protection Principle* (concerning security and other measures);
> - *section 7* of *DPA 1998* – subject access;
> - *section 10* of *DPA 1998* – right to prevent processing likely to cause damage or distress;
> - *section 12* of *DPA 1998* – rights in relation to automated decision-taking;
> - *section 12A* of *DPA 1998* – the rectification, blocking, erasure or destruction of certain inaccurate manual data during the transitional periods (see Chapters 4 and 6 [of the Commissioner's Legal Guidance]); and
> - *section 14(1)–(3)* of *DPA 1998* – provisions relating to rectification, blocking, erasure and destruction of inaccurate data.'

Confidential references **19.12**

Personal data which consist of a confidential reference given, or to be given, by the data controller for specified purposes (education, training or employment, appointment to office or provision of any service) are exempt from subject access. The Commissioner says:

> 'This exemption is not available to the data controller who receives such references. In other words, where Company A provides an employment reference concerning one of its employees to Company B, if the employee makes a subject access request to Company A, the reference will be exempt from the disclosure. If the employee makes the request to Company B, the reference is not automatically exempt from disclosure and the usual subject access rules apply.'

Section 28 exemption (national security): The Baker case 19.13

In the recent case of *Norman Baker MP v Secretary of State for the Home Department (1 October 2001)*, under *DPA 1998*, it was decided that the security service/Secretary of State was wrong to say that a blanket exemption (under national security exemption provisions) applied when a *section 7* of *DPA 1998* subject access request was refused. The security service had said subject access requests would only be permitted in the categories of staff administration, building security CCTV and commercial agreements, in which three categories in any event the security service held no data relating to the data subject, Mr Baker. This was held to be wrong in law by the Tribunal. It asked:

> '**When does national security take precedence over human rights?**
> Where the context is national security, judges and tribunals should supervise with the lightest touch appropriate; there is no area (foreign affairs apart) where judges have traditionally deferred more to the executive view than that of national security; and for good and sufficient reason'.

They found however, that there were no reasonable grounds for the Secretary of State to issue the certificate which led to the failure to disclose whether any information (except in the three categories mentioned at 19.11 above) was held.

Section 28 of *DPA 1998* provides an exemption from a number of provisions of the Act if exemption from any such provision is required for the purpose of safeguarding national security. In effect, such an exemption is, the Commissioner, says 'asserted by means of certificates, signed by a Minister of the Crown, certifying that exemption from all or any of the provisions is or was required for the requisite purpose. Such a certificate is conclusive evidence of that fact'. Any person directly affected by the issuing of such a certificate may appeal to the Data Protection Tribunal against the certificate.

The Tribunal is specially constituted to hear such appeals and is subject to different rules than in the case of appeals against enforcement and information notices under the *Data Protection Tribunal (National Security Appeals) Rules 2000* (*SI 2000/206*). The first appeal to be heard by this Tribunal was the one which considered the *Baker* case. As this was the first appeal, the parties consented to the proceedings taking place in public (subject to certain restrictions to protect the identity of some witnesses).

Section 35 exemption: Totalise v Motley Fool 19.14

Section 35 of *DPA 1998* provides that personal data are exempt from the non-disclosure provisions where the disclosure is required by or under any enactment, by any rule of law or by order of a court. Under *section 35(2)* of *DPA 1998* there is a similar exemption where the disclosure is necessary for the purpose of legal proceedings or for obtaining legal advice, or is otherwise necessary for the purposes of establishing, exercising or defending legal rights.

In the case *Totalise plc v Motley Fool Ltd and Another (2001)*, where the websites Motley Fool and Interactive Investor were reluctant to hand over confidential personal data of who was behind an alias, where the man operating the alias was posting defamatory material about Totalise on the bulletin boards concerned, the companies said *section 35* of *DPA 1998* would allow them to *resist* disclosure, not force them to disclose. They said it should be construed narrowly – that it should apply only for the data controller to obtain legal advice or to establish, exercise or defend legal rights. The court did not agree.

An interesting issue in relation to this area is raised. Totalise could not use *section 7* of *DPA 1998* to obtain the data they wanted because it is a company not an individual. Had a defamation of a director of Totalise occurred instead, the director exercising a right under *section* 7 against the websites might have obtained the identity of the anonymous poster, who went by the name of Z Dust, unless this allows another individual to be identified (the director would have made his request in order to have the third party individual, the person defaming him, identified. However, disclosure under *section* 7 is allowed which identifies third parties such as this where it is reasonable or where the individual consents. If the Internet Service Provider (ISP) website conditions did not offer people posting messages anonymity, then the ISP may be entitled to give the director in such a case the information required. In addition, a section 7 request is much cheaper than a high court application (£10 as opposed to presumably at least £10,000–£20,000).

Example of exemptions – Sweden 19.15

On 12 June 2001, the Swedish Supreme Court ruled in the first criminal case concerning the use and processing of personal data. The *Swedish Personal Data Act*, based on the *EC Data Protection Directive* (*95/46/EC*), came into force in 1998. Since then the Act has been heavily criticised, *inter alia*, for limiting the freedom of expression. The case involved a public Internet website on which a Swedish person (X) listed and named a number of individuals, several of them politicians and bank directors at Swedish banks. On the site X criticised several of the named individuals and accused them, among other things, of plundering. X also argued that some of them were responsible for the bankruptcy of X's company. The prosecutor claimed that the publishing of personal data constituted an unlawful distribution of personal data to a third country.

The website was held by the defence to be a 'forum' that threw light on the damage caused by Swedish banks, financial institutions and private capitalists during the Swedish bank crisis in the late 1980s and early 1990s. X further claimed that the personal data had been published solely with a journalistic purpose and was therefore exempt from the requirements of the legislation. An exemption exists for the processing and publication of personal data undertaken solely with a journalistic purpose (see 19.11 above). It is not clear if this provision relates to everyone or just mass media companies.

The lower court in Sweden found that part of the purpose behind the publishing of the personal data was to spread knowledge of the disparaging remarks on the site. Therefore the purpose behind X's listing of the personal data had not been solely journalistic. The court held the exemption applies however not just to professional journalists, but to others too.

The Supreme Court clarified the law concerning the exemption granted to journalistic publication stating that it applies not only to professional journalists and media enterprises, but to the ordinary people too. The court also identified a journalistic purpose underlying X's website and furthermore made it clear that the presence of disparaging or offensive remarks must be considered a normal part of the pubic debate. Therefore it was found that the publishing of the personal data did form part of a solely journalistic activity and thus was not a criminal offence under the Personal Data Act.

To read the case go to: http://www.notisum.se. For more information contact: Erik.Bergenstrahle@lindahl.se.

Further information 19.16

Information on the exemptions is contained in the Information Commissioner's Legal Guidance (October 2001).

20 – Export of Data

At a glance

20.1

- ✓ Data can be freely exported within the European Economic Area (EEA).
- ✓ Data can be exported freely to approved countries designated by the European Commission – currently only Switzerland and Hungary.
- ✓ Data can be exported under the US/EU Safe Harbor Agreement to those US companies who have registered under that agreement (few companies have registered to date). The Model Clauses are reproduced in APPENDIX 3.
- ✓ Data can be exported elsewhere as long as the Eighth Data Protection Principle is followed, e.g. by using the European Commission's model clauses for data export. The Information Commissioner has issued guidance on adequacy and transborder data flows.
- ✓ The European Commission has issued useful Frequently Asked Questions guidance about the model clauses for data export.

Introduction

20.2

On 18 June 2001 the European Commission approved important new standard clauses for those exporting data from the EEA. There are many misconceptions at large about export of personal data under the *Data Protection Act 1998* (*DPA 1998*). Many believe there is simply a ban on the export of data outside the EEA. In fact *DPA 1998* permits export in many situations. The Eighth Data Protection Principle in *Schedule 1* of DPA 1998 simply provides that export from the EEA is not permitted unless that country ensures an adequate level of protection in relation to the processing of personal data.

> 'Personal data shall not be transferred to a country or territory outside the European Economic Area, unless that country or territory ensures an adequate level of protection

of the rights and freedoms of data subjects in relation to the processing of personal data.'

(DPA 1998, Sch 1, Part I, Para 8.)

An adequate level of protection is one which is adequate in all the circumstances of the case, having regard in particular to:

- the nature of the personal data;
- the country or territory of origin of the information contained in the data;
- the country or territory of final destination of that information;
- the purposes for which and period during which the data are intended to be processed;
- the law in force in the country or territory in question;
- the international obligations of that country or territory;
- any relevant codes of conduct or other rules which are enforceable in that country or territory (whether generally or by arrangement in particular cases); and
- any security measures taken in respect of the data in that country or territory.

This is not an exhaustive list.

Schedule 4 of *DPA 1998* provides for circumstances in which the Eighth Data Protection Principle does not apply to a transfer of data. These are where:

(*a*) the data subject has given their consent to the transfer;

(*b*) the transfer is necessary:

  (i) for the performance of a contract between the data subject and the data controller; or

  (ii) for the taking of steps at the request of the data subject with a view to the data subject entering into a contract with the data controller;

(*c*) the transfer is necessary:

  (i) for the conclusion of a contract between the data controller and a person other than the data subject which:

    (A) is entered into at the request of the data subject, or

    (B) is in the interests of the data subject, or

  (ii) for the performance of such a contract;

(*d*) the transfer is necessary for reasons of substantial public interest.

The Secretary of State may specify by order the circumstances in which a transfer is to be taken to be necessary for reasons of substantial public interest. No order to this effect has been made to date;

(*e*) the transfer:

(i) is necessary for the purpose of, or in connection with, any legal proceedings (including prospective legal proceedings);

(ii) is necessary for the purpose of obtaining legal advice; or

(iii) is otherwise necessary for the purposes of establishing, exercising or defending legal rights;

(*f*) the transfer is necessary in order to protect the vital interests of the data subject;

(*g*) the transfer is part of the personal data on a public register and any conditions subject to which the register is open to inspection are complied with by any person to whom the data are or may be disclosed after the transfer;

(*h*) the transfer is made on terms which are of a kind approved by the Information Commissioner as ensuring adequate safeguards for the rights and freedoms of data subjects. It is not the practice of the Information Commissioner to consider or approve individual draft contracts submitted to her; and

(*j*) the transfer has been authorised by the Information Commissioner as being made in such a manner as to ensure adequate safeguards for the rights and freedoms of data subjects.

The Information Commissioner has issued guidance on transborder data flows which looks at how such requirements might be met.

Approved countries 20.3

Already the European Commission has approved data exports to Switzerland (Commission decision 2000/518/EC (OJ L 215 of 25.08.2000, p. 1–3) and Hungary (Commission decision 2000/519/EC (OJ L 215 of 25.08.2000, p. 4–6)).

Safe Harbor Agreement 20.4

The US/EU Safe Harbor Agreement (Commission decision 2000/520/EC (OJ L 215 of 25.08.2000, p. 7–47)) permits data exports to the US to those companies within the scheme.

In July 2000 after months of negotiation the United States and European Union reached an accord on data protection, which covers e-commerce but not financial services. It has been designed to aid businesses shipping personal data between the EEA and US. The *Data Protection Directive (95/46/EC)*, which was implemented in the UK by *DPA 1998* contains restrictions on export of data to countries such as the US which do not have the same type of data protection laws in place. Failure to comply with such laws will be considered a deceptive business practice and a prosecutable offence. The US Department of Commerce keeps a register of industry self-regulators and monitors those companies to ensure they comply with privacy rules. The Federal Trade Commission and the US judicial system can impose sanctions on companies that violate the rules.

The seven safe harbor principles' requirements 20.5

Organisations must comply with the seven safe harbor principles if exporting data to the US. The requirements of the principles are set out in 20.6–20.12 below.

Notice 20.6

Organisations must notify individuals about the purposes for which they collect and use information about them. They must provide information about how individuals can contact the organisation with any inquiries or complaints, the types of third parties to which it discloses the information and the choices and means the organisation offers for limiting its use and disclosure.

Choice 20.7

Organisations must give individuals the opportunity to choose (opt-out) whether their personal information will be disclosed to a third party, or used for a purpose incompatible with the purpose for which it was originally collected or subsequently authorised by the individual. For sensitive information, affirmative or explicit (opt-in) choice must be given if the information is to be disclosed to a third party or used for a purpose other than its original purpose or the purpose authorised subsequently by the individual.

Onward transfer (transfers to third parties) 20.8

To disclose information to a third party, organisations must apply the notice and choice principles. Where an organisation wishes to transfer information to a third party that is acting as an agent, it may do so if it makes sure that the third party subscribes to the safe harbor principles or is subject to the *EU Data Protection Directive (95/46/EC)*. As an alternative, the organisation can enter into a written agreement with such a third party requiring that the third party provide at least the same level of privacy protection as is required by the relevant principles.

Access **20.9**

Individuals must have access to personal information held about them by an organisation and be able to correct, amend, or delete that information where it is inaccurate, except where the burden or expense of providing access would be disproportionate to the risks to the individual's privacy in the case in question, or where the rights of persons other than the individual would be violated.

Security **20.10**

Organisations must take reasonable precautions to protect personal information from loss, misuse and unauthorised access, disclosure, alteration and destruction.

Data integrity **20.11**

Personal information must be relevant for the purposes for which it is to be used. An organisation should take reasonable steps to ensure that data is reliable for its intended use, accurate, complete, and current.

Enforcement **20.12**

In order to ensure compliance with the safe harbor principles, there must be:

(*a*) readily available and affordable independent recourse mechanisms so that each individual's complaints and disputes can be investigated and resolved and damages awarded where the applicable law or private sector initiatives so provide;

(*b*) procedures for verifying that the commitments companies make to adhere to the safe harbor principles have been implemented; and

(*c*) obligations to remedy problems arising out of a failure to comply with the principles. Sanctions must be sufficiently rigorous to ensure compliance by the organisation. Organisations that fail to provide annual self-certification letters will no longer appear in the list of participants and safe harbor benefits will no longer be assured.

To provide further guidance, the US Department of Commerce has issued a set of frequently asked questions and answers (FAQs) that clarify and supplement the safe harbor principles.

The Agreement began to operate in November 2000. After a slow start, with only Dun and Bradstreet registering (apart from some non-commercial bodies) Microsoft has announced it is joining the scheme, and in May 2001 the Direct Marketing Association also announced its support for the safe harbor agreement. It believes it will be the first trade association to offer its members free seals of approval through the arrangement.

The US authorities have a Safe Harbor website which is at www.export.gov/safeharbor/.

Commissioner's guidance 20.13

The Information Commissioner has issued detailed guidance on the export of personal data (see 20.17 below).

European Commission model clauses 20.14

The European Commission has recently issued model clauses which would ensure the adequacy required by the Eighth Data Protection Principle in any export of data and therefore it is likely that many companies will be agreeing with the imposition of such clauses on the recipients of their data outside the EU. At the same time, the Commission issued some very useful Frequently Asked Questions which complement those already issued in relation to the EU Safe Harbor agreement. The clauses are annexed to a Commission Decision (OJ L181/19, 4.7.2001). Article 1 of the Decision provides that the annexed standard clauses will ensure adequate protection on the export of data. Under Article 3 a member state is given power to withdraw the protection of the clauses, for example where a data importer has not complied with the clauses.

Export can be made even to countries without adequate levels of protection under *Schedule 4* of *DPA 1998* which concerns cases where the Eighth Principle does not apply. These are also contained in *Article 26* of the *Data Protection Directive (95/46/EC)* and include cases where:

- the data subject has given his or her consent unambiguously to the proposed transfer;
- the transfer is necessary for the performance of a contract between the data subject and the controller or the implementation of pre-contractual measures taken in response to the data subject's request;

- the transfer is necessary for the conclusion or performance of a contract concluded in the interest of the data subject between the controller and a third party;
- the transfer is necessary or legally required on important public interest grounds, or for the establishment, exercise or defence of legal claims;
- the transfer is necessary in order to protect the vital interests of the data subject; or
- the transfer is made from a register which according to laws or regulations is intended to provide information to the public and which is open to consultation either by the public in general or by any person who can demonstrate legitimate interest, to the extent that the conditions laid down in law for consultation are fulfilled in the particular case.

Finally, national authorities may authorise on a case-by-case basis specific transfers to a country not offering an adequate protection where the exporter in the EU adduces adequate safeguards with respect to the protection of privacy by fundamental rights and freedoms of individuals, and as regards the exercise of the corresponding rights. This could be undertaken for example by contractual arrangements between the exporter and the importer of data, subject to the prior approval of national authorities.

These clauses may be supplemented later. The European Commission, in its FAQ document on the clauses explains that it intends to start work on other standard contractual clauses 'in particular to deal with low risk transfers that may allow for a lighter approach to be followed. A first decision is likely to concern the transfer of data to a subcontractor for the mere processing, a category of transfers excluded from the scope of the Decision).' The Commission is hoping to receive drafts of clauses from Industry Associations for it to consider.

The way the new model clauses work is that each EU Member State will recognise the standard clauses as complying with the provisions of the legislation on data export. Member States will be free to impose a licensing system for such exports, although it is believed to be unlikely that the UK would do so. The European Commission also believes that some Member States may require the contract containing the model clauses to be 'deposited' at a central registry. Again it is unlikely to be required in the UK. The Commission has said that some Member States have already announced that they will request the deposit of the contract, which may cause confidentiality problems. Apparently it will be possible to ensure that only those clauses dealing with an individual's personal data will be in the public domain. There will also be cases where Member States will be able to block export of data. The European Commission says these include cases where:

(*a*) it is established that the law to which the data importer is subject imposes upon him the need to derogate from the relevant data protection rules beyond the restrictions necessary in a democratic society as provided for in *Article 13* of *Directive 95/46/EC* where those derogations are likely to have a substantial adverse effect on the guarantees provided by the standard contractual clauses;

(*b*) a competent authority has established that the data importer has not respected the contractual clauses; or

(*c*) there is a substantial likelihood that the standard contractual clauses in the annex are not being or will not be complied with and the continuing transfer would create an imminent risk of grave harm to the data subjects.

It is expected that this safeguard clause will be very rarely used.

The Commission says it is permissible to add additional clauses to the standard contractual clauses such as additional guarantees for the individuals (e.g. on-line procedures or relevant provisions contained in a privacy policy, etc.).

The clauses refer to joint and several liability. However if one party is not responsible for an event relating to data loss which causes damage then it would not then be liable. Data exporters may choose to sue the data importer, the data exporter or both. The European Commission states:

> 'Although an action against the data exporter before a European court seems the preferable way for an individual to obtain compensation, he or she may decide to take action against the data importer, if, for example the data exporter has disappeared or filed for bankruptcy. In these cases, the data importer may be sued before the data exporter's courts [clause 10] or before the courts of his own country if so permitted under private international law.'

Using the clauses 20.15

The clauses have now been adopted and some lawyers are having to struggle to provide practical advice on their use. Firstly, they are very long, although companies familiar with lengthy agreements should not encounter any difficulties. Others may find the provisions unacceptable. The Commission decision and clauses are 18 pages long and the clauses have three appendices of additional terms attached. There are also:

- a definitions section;
- a schedule which needs to be completed setting out the purposes for which the data will be exported;
- warranties from the data exporter and importer; and
- provisions about mediation and jurisdiction.

A data exporter might simply include a clause in a contract stating that the export would be governed by the Commission's Model Clauses (www.europa.eu.int/comm/internal_market/en/media/datprot/news/clausesdecision.pdf) rather than rewriting the clauses. Then, in the said contract, he should specify the variables required for the contract, such as the names of the data exporter and importer, purpose of export, the length of time the data will be held etc. This is probably not what is intended by the Commission. However, it seems legally permissible and may be more palatable to foreign data recipients who might otherwise be put off by the standard clauses' wording.

CBI clauses 20.16

Some bodies are still lobbying the EU about the model clauses. The CBI had earlier drawn up its own model clauses and these may still be submitted to the Information Commissioner and/or the EU for approval. As an alternative the CBI may redraft them in the light of the EU clauses. Other bodies have their own clauses as well which again may need to be redrafted.

CHAPTER 44 TRANSBORDER DATA FLOWS also makes mention of proposals in this area, including the International Chamber of Commerce's proposals.

Further information 20.17

The Information Commissioner's guidance, *The Eighth Data Protection Principle and Transborder Dataflows* is accessible under 'International Transfers' at http://wood.ccta.gov.uk/dpr/dpdoc.nsf.

The European Commission's model clauses can be found online at http://europa.eu.int/comm/internal_market/en/dataprot/news/1539en.pdf.

The European Commission's Frequently Asked Questions on its new model clauses for data export are at www.europa.eu.int/comm/internal_market/en/media/dataprot/news/clausesfaq.htm.

The US authorities have a Safe Harbor Agreement website which is at www.export.gov/safeharbor/.

See also CHAPTER 44 TRANSBORDER DATA FLOWS.

21 – Fair Processing

At a glance 21.1

- ✓ The First Data Protection Principle requires that personal data be processed fairly and lawfully.
- ✓ Data subjects should be told the purposes for which their data will be used.
- ✓ *Schedule 2* to the *Data Protection Act 1998* (*DPA 1998*) sets out the conditions required for processing and is known as the 'Fair Processing Code'.
- ✓ The Commissioner's Legal Guidance on *DPA 1998* (October 2001) contains further information on fair processing.

Introduction 21.2

Those who use personal data must comply with the Data Protection Principles set out in *DPA 1998*. In practice, the First Principle has the most impact. It requires that data must be processed fairly and lawfully. Specific information must be supplied to data subjects when the data is obtained, including details of the purposes for which the data will be processed. Sensitive personal data is subject to even more stringent requirements (see CHAPTER 43 SENSITIVE PERSONAL DATA).

First Principle 21.3

Paragraph 1 of *Schedule 1* to *DPA 1998* provides that personal data shall be processed fairly and lawfully and shall not be processed unless the conditions in *Schedule 2* to *DPA 1998* are met. For sensitive personal data, such as data about sex, race, religion, the conditions in *Schedule 3* to *DPA 1998* should be met, such as obtaining explicit consent.

The *Schedule 2* conditions are therefore crucial, and they comprise of what the Data Protection Commissioner calls the Fair Processing Code.

The 'information requirements' 21.4

Data subjects must be notified of:

(*a*) the identity of the data controller;

(*b*) the identity of any representative appointed for the purposes of *DPA 1998*, if any, by that data controller (this will usually not apply);

(*c*) the purpose or purposes for which the data are intended to be processed; and

(*d*) any further information which is necessary, having regard to the specific circumstances in which the data are to be processed to enable the processing in respect of the data subject to be fair.

Businesses need to ensure individuals are given the information listed above.

One of the new Orders under *DPA 1998*, the *Data Protection (Conditions under Paragraph 3 of Part II of Schedule 1) Order 2000* (*SI 2000/185*), addresses 'fair processing', and is examined in more detail at paragraph 21.5 below.

Disproportionate effort 21.5

The *Data Protection (Conditions under Paragraph 3 of Part II of Schedule 1) Order 2000* (*SI 2000/185*) deals with a number of areas under *DPA 1998* where data is not treated as fairly processed unless certain requirements have been met concerning the giving of information to data subjects. However, these information provisions vary, and sometimes the requirements can be ignored where disproportionate effort might be involved. Of course, it is not always easy to know exactly what 'disproportionate effort' is and the risk is that businesses will use this as an excuse to avoid the provisions of *DPA 1998*.

The Order therefore states that where a data controller seeks to rely on this provision, they must still provide the relevant information to any individual who requests it. If they cannot readily decide whether they are processing information about the individual because of a lack of identifying information, the data controller must write to the individual explaining the position. The controller must keep a record of the reasons why he believes the disapplication of the information provisions is necessary.

> 'Para. 3.1.7.6 of the Legal Guidance (October 2001) of the Commissioner provides that what does or does not amount

to disproportionate effort is a question of fact to be determined in each and every case.

In deciding this the Commissioner will take into account a number of factors, including the nature of the data, the length of time and the cost involved to the data controller in providing the information. The fact that the data controller has had to expend a substantial amount of effort and/or cost in providing the information does not necessarily mean that the Commissioner will reach the decision that the data controller can legitimately rely upon the disproportionate effort ground. In certain circumstances, the Commissioner would consider that a quite considerable effort could reasonably be expected. The above factors will always be balanced against the prejudicial or effectively prejudicial effect to the data subject and in this respect a relevant consideration would be the extent to which the data subject already knows about the processing of his personal data by the data controller.'

Conditions for processing under DPA 1998 21.6

Part II of *Schedule 1* to *DPA 1998* provides that in assessing whether the First Principle is complied with, regard must be had to the method by which the data is obtained, including whether anyone was deceived or misled about the purposes for which the data was processed. It goes on to provide that the information described above must be given at the 'relevant time' (when the data is first processed in most cases).

The Schedule 2 conditions 21.7

Schedule 2 sets out the Fair Processing Code. It comprises the conditions necessary for data to be fairly processed. The following six requirements can be met.

1. The data subject has consented to the processing.
2. The processing is necessary to perform a contract (necessary is a strong obligation and it means more than simply desirable).
3. The processing is necessary to comply with a legal obligation.
4. The processing is necessary to protect the data subject's 'vital interests' (this means a matter of life or death).
5. The processing is necessary for reasons such as the administration of justice.

6. The processing is necessary for the purposes of legitimate interests of the data controller or third parties.

The Commissioner takes the view that in assessing fairness, the first and paramount consideration must be given to the consequences of the processing to the interests of the data subject. Her Legal Guidance says:

> 'This view was supported by the Data Protection Tribunal in the context of the *Data Protection Act 1984* (*DPA 1984*) in the cases of *CCN Systems Limited and CCN Credit Systems Limited v The Data Protection Registrar [Case DA/90 25/49/9]* and *Infolink v The Data Protection Registrar [Case DA/90 25/49/9]*. The Commissioner will also look at the purposes and nature of the processing in assessing fairness. Even though a data controller may be able to show that information was obtained and personal data processed fairly and lawfully in general and on most occasions, if it has been obtained unfairly in relation to one individual there will have been a contravention of the First Principle.'

The *Schedule 3* conditions which apply to sensitive personal data are dealt with in CHAPTER 42 SENSITIVE PERSONAL DATA.

Consent 21.8

The Commissioner's Legal Guidance (which can be found at www.dataprotection.gov.uk) addresses the meaning of the provisions set out by *Article 2(h)* of *Directive 95/46/EC* in some detail, and in particular examines what is needed to establish consent. One of the conditions for processing is that the data subject must have consented to the processing.

The Commissioner's view is that consent is not particularly easy to achieve, and that data controllers should consider other conditions in *Schedule 2* to *DPA 1998* (and *Schedule 3* to *DPA 1998* if processing sensitive personal data) before looking at consent. No condition carries greater weight than any other. All the conditions provide an equally valid basis for processing. Consent is not defined in *DPA 1998*. The existence or validity of consent will need to be assessed in the light of the facts. To assist in understanding what may or may not amount to consent in any particular case, it is helpful to refer back to the *EU Data Protection Directive* (*95/46/EC*). This defines the data subject's consent as:

> '…any freely given specific and informed indication of his wishes by which the data subject signifies his agreement to personal data relating to him being processed'.

The Commissioner's view on giving consent 21.9

> 'The fact that the data subject must "signify" his agreement means that there must be some active communication between the parties. A data subject may "signify" agreement other than in writing. Data controllers cannot infer consent from non-response to a communication, for example from a customer's failure to return or respond to a leaflet.
>
> The adequacy of any consent or purported consent must be evaluated. For example, consent obtained under duress or on the basis of misleading information will not be a valid basis for processing.
>
> Where a data subject does not signify his agreement to personal data relating to him being processed, but is given an opportunity to object to such processing, although this does not amount to consent for the purposes of the Act, it *may* provide the data controller with the basis to rely upon another Schedule 2 condition, for example, the legitimate interests condition, provided that the data subject is given the right to object before the data are obtained.'

Appropriate consent 21.10

Consent must be appropriate to the particular circumstances. For example, if the processing is intended to continue after the end of a trading relationship, then the consent should cover those circumstances. The Commissioner adds:

> 'However, it must be recognised that even when consent has been given it will not necessarily endure forever. While in most cases consent will endure for as long as the processing to which it relates continues, data controllers should recognise that, depending upon the nature of the consent given and the circumstances of the processing, the individual may be able to withdraw consent.'

In her Frequently Asked Questions on data protection and the Internet the Commissioner states that in many cases a right to object is sufficient for non-sensitive personal data.

Explicit and non-explicit consent 21.11

There is a distinction in *DPA 1998* between the nature of the consent required to satisfy the condition for processing and that which is required in the case of the condition for processing sensitive data. The consent must be explicit in the case of sensitive data. The use of the word 'explicit', and the fact that the condition requires explicit consent to the processing of the personal data, suggests that the consent of the data subject should be absolutely clear. In appropriate cases it should cover the specific detail of the processing, the particular type of data to be processed (or even the specific information), the purposes of the processing and any special aspects of the processing which may affect the individual, for example, disclosures which may be made of the data.

Foreseeability of future data use 21.12

The Commissioner does say that the level of detail appropriate to a consent will vary and in some cases implied consent may be sufficient.

> 'A blanket consent to the processing of personal data is unlikely to be sufficient as a basis on which to process personal data, particularly sensitive personal data...As guidance...the Commissioner would advise that data controllers consider the extent to which the use of personal data by them is or is not reasonably foreseeable by data subjects. To the extent to which their use of personal data is not reasonably foreseeable, data controllers should ensure that they provide such further information as may be necessary.'

Timing 21.13

It does not say in *DPA 1998* when the data subject should be given the fair processing information where the data is obtained from data subjects. The Commissioner believes that this should be at the time when the data is obtained (Introduction, page 13, para 1.12.3).

Further information 21.14

See the Commissioner's Legal Guidance (October 2001), at www.dataprotection.gov.uk.

22 – Financial Services

At a glance 22.1

- ✓ The *Data Protection Act 1998* (*DPA 1998*) applies to financial services companies, many of whom hold considerable amounts of personal data about individuals.
- ✓ Importance guidance on the financial services sector can be purchased from the British Bankers' Association (BBA) and others.
- ✓ The consequences of personal data being incorrect in the hands of a financial services company are likely to be worse than with mere marketing data, thus particular caution should be exercised.
- ✓ Often financial services companies will process data by automated means (*DPA 1998, s 12*), such as when credit scoring.
- ✓ Monitoring of financial services companies' calls and e-mails may have data protection implications.
- ✓ An exemption from the subject access provisions exists in the category of corporate finance.

General 22.2

Financial services companies need to comply with *DPA 1998* in general. In particular, consideration should be given to fair processing of data (see CHAPTER 21 FAIR PROCESSING) and to automated decision-taking (see 22.3 below and CHAPTER 1 AUTOMATED DECISION-TAKING).

Automated decision-taking 22.3

Section 12 of *DPA 1998* provides that an individual is entitled, by written notice, to require a data controller to ensure that no decision which significantly affects that individual is based solely on the processing by automatic means of personal data of which that individual is the data subject. The Commissioner's Legal Guidance (October 2001) on *DPA 1998* says:

> 'The Act includes specific examples of the purposes for which such automated decision-taking might be employed, i.e. evaluating matters relating to the data subject such as his performance at work, his creditworthiness, his reliability or his conduct. This is not an exhaustive list.'

Many financial services companies make use of automated decision-taking and need to be conscious of their obligations in this respect. CHAPTER 1 AUTOMATED DECISION-TAKING also deals with this subject in general. If no notice has been given by an individual as mentioned above and a decision is based solely on automatic processing, the data controller must notify the individual that the decision was taken on that basis as soon as reasonably practicable. Within 21 days of receiving such notification, an individual is entitled by written notice (the 'data subject notice') to require the data controller to reconsider the decision, or to take a new decision on a different basis. Within 21 days of receiving the data subject notice, the data controller must give the data subject a written notice specifying the steps the data controller intends to take to comply with the data subject notice.

Exempt decisions 22.4

There is an exemption under *DPA 1998* for some decisions made this way, known as 'exempt decisions'. The Commissioner summarises this as follows.

> To qualify as an exempt decision certain conditions must be met as follows:
>
> Firstly:
>
> (*a*) the decision must be taken in the course of steps taken:
>
> (i) for the purpose of considering whether to enter into a contract with the data subject;
>
> (ii) with a view to entering into such a contract; or
>
> (iii) in the course of performing such a contract; or
>
> (*b*) the decision must be authorised or required by or under any enactment.
>
> Secondly:
>
> (*c*) the effect of the decision must be to grant a request of the data subject; or

(*d*) steps have been taken to safeguard the legitimate interests of the data subject (for example, by allowing, the data subject to make representations).

In addition, the Secretary of State may prescribe other circumstances in which an automated decision may qualify as an exempt decision. No order to this effect has been made to date.

Credit scoring is one obvious way in which a financial services company may become involved in automated decision-taking of this kind.

Monitoring 22.5

Financial services companies in particular engage in the monitoring of employees' telephone calls and e-mails. The *Telecommunications (Lawful Business Practice) (Interception of Communications) Regulations 2000* (*SI 2000/2699*) permit monitoring for most purposes under the *Regulations of Investigatory Powers Act 2000*. Those monitored should be informed that it is taking place. (See also CHAPTER 15 E-MAILS and CHAPTER 16 EMPLOYMENT. CHAPTER 29 INTERNET covers the *Telecommunications Regulations*.)

Corporate finance 22.6

DPA 1998 contains a corporate finance exclusion from the subject access provisions where the data are processed for 'a corporate finance service' (as defined in *DPA 1998, Sch 7, para 6*) provided by 'a relevant person' (*DPA 1998, Sch 7*). The exemption is only available to the extent to which the application of the subject information provisions could, or in the reasonable belief of the data controller could, affect the price or value of particular instruments of a price-sensitive nature. 'Instrument' is defined in *paragraph 6(3)* of *Schedule 7* to *DPA 1998* and includes, for example, company shares.

The Information Commissioner in her Legal Guidance (October 2001) says 'this exemption may be material in due diligence enquiries arising from company takeovers or mergers'.

Economic or financial interests 22.7

If required, the exemption is also available for the purpose of safeguarding an important economic or financial interest of the United Kingdom. *DPA 1998* provides that the Secretary of State may, by order, specify matters to be taken into account when determining whether exemption from the subject information provisions is required for the purpose of safeguarding an important economic or financial interest of the United Kingdom as specified in the *Data Protection (Corporate Finance Exemption) Order 2000* (*SI 2000/184*). The Order provides that one such matter is the inevitable prejudicial effect on the orderly functioning of financial markets or the efficient allocation of capital with the economy resulting from the occasional or regular application of the subject information provisions to data specified in the order.

The Information Commissioner says

> 'The court may make an order requiring a person taking a decision in respect of the data subject (referred to in the Act as "the responsible person") to reconsider the decision or to take a new decision which is not based solely on processing by automatic means. The court will only make such orders if it is satisfied that the responsible person has failed to comply with the data subject notice.'

Industry guidance 22.8

In September 2000 the main trade associations in the financial services sector published guidance on *DPA 1998* called 'The New Data Protection Act 2000: A Practitioner's Handbook'. Each chapter includes practical examples for banks and other financial institutions. Appended to the book are the following useful documents.

The Appendices

Appendix 1: Definitions within the Act.

Appendix 2: An explanation of transitional periods.

Appendix 3: Industry-wide examples of model notification. Wordings and ODPC's guidance leaflet on using her office's 'information padlock'.

Appendix 4: Putting it into practice: Who needs to do what to comply.

Appendix 5: Industry-wide examples of model subject access forms.

Appendix 6: BBA guidance: 'What banks need to tell customers about the personal information they collect: BBA Guidance on standard data protection notifications for customer application forms and data collection systems'.

Appendix 7: FLA model data protection notice (for implementation by FLA members 24 October 2000).

Appendix 8: FLA guidance for motor and caravan dealers (for implementation by FLA members 24 October 2000).

Appendix 9: CBI and ICC model contract clauses.

Further information 22.9

Copies of 'The New Data Protection Act 2000: A Practitioner's Handbook' can be ordered from the BBA web site at www.bba.org.uk under Publications.

For monitoring see CHAPTER 29 LAWFUL BUSINESS PRACTICE REGULATIONS.

23 – Forms

At a glance 23.1

- ✓ Companies seeking compliance with the *Data Protection Act 1998* (*DPA 1998*) will want to draw up various forms to be used by staff and those making subject access requests.
- ✓ In addition, there are forms which a data controller may use in notifying their holding of personal data under *DPA 1998* and an online questionnaire included in the Information Commissioner's Notification Handbook.
- ✓ In the employment and credit sector, companies often devise their own standards or use forms recommended by their relevant trade association.
- ✓ Two examples of the Information Commissioner's forms for aspects of notification are included for information.
- ✓ Solicitors can advise clients in drawing up forms in this field.

Introduction 23.2

DPA 1998 does not set down defined forms for use by data controllers so many companies have drawn up their own. Appendix 5 of 'The New Data Protection Act 2000: A Practitioner's Handbook' contains model forms for subject access in the financial services industry which may be used but are not mandatory (see CHAPTER 22 FINANCIAL SERVICES).

Notification form 23.3

A fee of £35 is payable for notification of the holding of data. This covers one year. Guidance on how to notify is found in the Notification Handbook (available from the Commissioner's Office or via the website at www.dataprotection.gov.uk).

Registrable particulars 23.4

Information to be provided on the notification form includes the following registrable particulars relating to the data controller.

(*a*) their name and address;

(*b*) if they have nominated a representative, the name and address of the representative;

(*c*) a description of the personal data being or to be processed and of the category(ies) of data subject to which they relate;

(*d*) a description of the purpose(s) for which the data are being or are to be processed;

(*e*) a description of any recipient(s) to whom the data controller intends or may wish to disclose the data;

(*f*) the name or a description of any countries or territories outside the European Economic Area to which the data controller transfers, intends to transfer or may wish to transfer the data; and

(*g*) where the personal data are of a type which is exempt from the prohibition against processing personal data without notification and where the notification does not extend to such data, a statement of that fact.

Security measures 23.5

When a notification is made by a data controller he must also provide, in addition to the registrable particulars, a general description of the security measures taken to protect the personal data. However, this information will not appear on the register.

Padlock symbol 23.6

Some companies have chosen to use the Commissioner's padlock sign to inform data subjects that their data is being gathered. Use of the symbol is not compulsory.

CHAPTER 34 PADLOCK (USE OF THE SIGN CALLED 'PADLOCK') examines the signpost. It is often used on forms.

Employment and credit 23.7

For details concerning forms in the credit field see CHAPTER 7 CREDIT REFERENCES. In relation to employment see CHAPTER 16 EMPLOYMENT.

Changing a register entry

Form DPR2

Application for Alteration or Removal of a Register Entry

Data Protection Act 1984

Form DPR2 3/93

87908 **H**

Name & address of applicant (Currently held on the Register)

Company Reg.No.

User Number (issued on the confirmation of your Register entry).

Post Code

Alteration of a Register entry (See Note 1)

Registration Numbers of Register entries to be altered

Removal of a Register entry (See Note 2)

Registration Numbers of Register entries to be removed

Describe Alterations overleaf

Declaration (See Note 3) **To be completed by all applicants**

To the best of my knowledge and belief, the particulars given in this form and on any continuation sheets are correct and complete. I confirm that I am the Data User or Computer Bureau named above or that I am authorised to act on behalf of that Data User or Computer Bureau.

Signature

Date

Name

Position

Tel.No.

Send your application to:
Changes Section, Office of the Data Protection Registrar,
Wycliffe House, Water Lane, Wilmslow, Cheshire SK9 5AF

See Notes 4-6 about confirmation of changes, and changes of name and address.

SPECIMEN

Notes

1. Write here the registration numbers of entries to be altered. Note that any alterations requested on this form will be applied to all of the Register entries listed here. Give details of alterations overleaf.
2. Write here the registration numbers of entries to be removed from the Register. Please note that once an entry has been removed it cannot be reinstated.
3. It is an offence knowingly or recklessly to furnish the Registrar with information which is false or misleading in any material respect.
4. Confirmation of the removal or alteration requested on this form will be sent by the Registrar to the contact name given in the Register entry.
5. Please remember there are 3 address sections which may be affected – data user, subject access and contact. Changes of contact name and address have no effect on the Register itself, but will be recorded for use by the Registrar and confirmed to the new address.
6. If a new name is that of a different legal person a new application should be made using forms DPR1 or DPR4.

NB There is no fee for an application for alteration or removal of a Register entry.

Details of Alterations to Register Entries

Please explain in your own words, and us clearly as possible, the nature of the alteration you wish to make. You should clearly indicate to which section of the Register entry the alteration applies.

If the alteration is particularly complex, or is to add a purpose to your Register entry, you may find it easier to complete a new Part B form. If you do this you must clearly mark the Part B form "For addition to Register entry" or "To replace previously submitted Part B on Register entry". The Register reserves the right to ask applicants who request an alteration to use this method if the proposed alteration described is unclear.

Now sign the Declaration overleaf

You are advised to keep a copy of your application

In making any requests for alterations to a Register entry, you should refer to the booklet *Notes—to help you apply for Registration, and where appropriate, to the Registrar's Guidelines. These, and copies fo Forms DPR1, DPR2 and DPR4 can be obtained from Information Services, Office of the Data Protection Registrar, Wycliffe House, Water Lane, Witmslow, Cheshire, SK9 5AF, Telephone Wilmslow (0625) 535777.*

A4 398/0962 Dd 03498 100M TP

Purpose form – to add a purpose to a register entry 23.9

PURPOSE FORM

DP Data Protection

(for adding a purpose to a notification)
A purpose form must be completed for **each** new purpose

You **must** quote your Security number or the form will be returned

Data controller name:		
Registration number:		
Security number/user number		
Purpose title:		See Notification Handbook Section 3.1.8 for full list
Write here a brief description only <u>none</u> of the standard purposes apply		
Data Subject Codes:		See Notification Handbook Section 3.1.9 for full list
Write here additional descriptions only if none of the standard descriptions apply.		
Data Class Codes:		See Notification Handbook Section 3.1.10 for full list
Write here additional descriptions only if none of the standard descriptions apply.		
Recipient Codes:		See Notification Handbook Section 3.1.11 for full list
Write here additional descriptions only if none of the standard descriptions apply.		
Transfers:	None outside EEA ☐ Worldwide ☐ Name individual countries below	See Notification Handbook page 18 for list of countries in the EEA
If there are more than ten countries indicate Worldwide		

SPECIMEN

The declaration overleaf **MUST** be completed

Declaration

To the best of my knowledge and belief, the particulars given in this form and on any continuation sheets are correct and complete. I confirm that I am the Data Controller named overleaf or that I am authorised to act on behalf of the Data Controller.

Signature ______________________________

Name ______________________________

Job Title ______________________________

Date ______________________________

Tel. No. ______________________________

Note:

Once you have notified you must keep your register entry up to date. When any part of your entry becomes inaccurate or incomplete you must inform us. This action must be taken as soon as practicable and in any event within a period of 28 days from the date on which your entry becomes inaccurate or incomplete. Failure to do so is a criminal offence.

Send this form with your Part I and Part 2 if making a new notification

or

If amending an existing notification send to:
Notification Changes Section, Information Commissioner's Office
Wycliffe House, Water Lane, Wilmslow, Cheshire SK9 5AF

Privacy policies 23.10

Many websites have forms or notices called privacy policies setting out how personal data will be used (see CHAPTER 36 PRINCIPLES). These are not in any statutory form but need to cover the issues of who is the data controller and how will that data be used.

Audit manual 23.11

The Information Commissioner publishes a detailed audit manual containing information and forms which can be used in checking whether internal procedures are compliant with the legislation. It includes *inter alia* audit and meeting pro formas. It is on the Information Commissioner's website at www.dataprotection.gov.uk under Guidance. It includes meeting record sheets and acts as a useful prompt as to the issues to be addressed in undertaking a data protection audit.

At the date of writing the manual for 2001 was still being finalised.

Further information 23.12

The Information Commissioner's Audit Manual 2001 can be found at www.dataprotection.gov.uk/dpr/dpdoc.nsf.

24 – Freedom of Information Act 2000

At a glance 24.1

- ✓ When it comes into force the *Freedom of Information Act 2000* (*FIA 2000*) will give individuals and businesses additional rights to information held about them by public bodies to complement the *Data Protection Act 1998* (*DPA 1998*).
- ✓ *FIA 2000* is due to be in force at the latest on 30 November 2005, but in November 2001 the Government announced that individuals' rights of access to data under the Act would come into force early in January 2005.
- ✓ Companies as well as individuals will be able to exercise rights under *FIA 2000*.
- ✓ The Information Commissioner is in charge of *FIA 2000* in a dual role which also encompasses *DPA 1998*.
- ✓ Public bodies may now want to align their subject access request procedures to accommodate the two regimes.
- ✓ Codes of practice and other documents on *FIA 2000* are accessible via the Commissioner's website.

Introduction 24.2

On 30 November 2000 *FIA 2000* received Royal Assent. The 'Information Commissioner', a new post which came into being on 30 January 2001, is in charge of enforcing the legislation – a combined role of freedom of information and data protection. Elizabeth France, the Data Protection Commissioner, is the first Information Commissioner. Both *FIA 2000* and *DPA 1998* relate to information handling, and the dual role will allow the Commissioner to provide an integrated and coherent approach.

Provisions of FIA 2000 — 24.3

Basic provisions — 24.4

FIA 2000 provides a statutory right of access to information held by public authorities. The Information Commissioner is an independent authority, with a statutory duty to promote good practice by public authorities and to disseminate information on good practice.

The implications of the Act will depend upon the organisation. Those in the public sector to whom *FIA 2000* will apply will need to consider carefully how their obligations to provide information to members of the public will now be expanded. Those in the private sector will find it has a much lesser impact, but it may be relevant when they wish to obtain information from public authorities.

Essential provisions — 24.5

FIA 2000:

- gives a general right of access to information of all kinds held by public authorities (and those providing services for them);
- sets out exemptions from that right of access; and
- places a number of obligations on public authorities.

The Act relates to individuals' rights and not to business relationships in the private sector.

Timing — 24.6

FIA 2000 must be brought fully into force within five years of Royal Assent, although it may be sooner. The long stop date is 30 November 2005.

On 13 November 2001 the Government announced the timetable for implementation. Implementation of the Act will be in stages with the duties on authorities to apply Publication Schemes (details of the information they will provide pro-actively) being introduced first. This will be staggered for different parts of the public sector. The individual right of access will come into force in January 2005, eleven months ahead of the original timetable.

The timetable for bringing Publication Schemes into effect is as follows.

November 2002: Central Government (except the Crown Prosecution Service and Serious Fraud Office), Parliament, National Assembly for Wales, Non-Departmental Public Bodies currently subject to the

Code of Practice on Access to Government Information (Part I, sections (1), (2), (3), (5) and some of Part IV of Schedule I of the Act).

February 2003: Local Government (except police authorities) (Part II).

June 2003: Police, police authorities, Crown Prosecution Service, Serious Fraud Office, Armed Forces (Part V not relating to Northern Ireland and Part I(6)).

October 2003: Health Service (Part III relating to England and Wales).

February 2004: Schools, Universities, remaining NDPBs (Part IV relating to England and Wales and some of Part IV).

June 2004: Remaining public authorities.

Public authorities in Northern Ireland will either be required to apply publication schemes at the same time as their counterparts in England and Wales, or alternative arrangements will be made. This is a matter for further discussion with the Northern Ireland Assembly. The Scottish Parliament is currently considering separate freedom of information legislation introduced by the Scottish Executive.

The Information Commissioner says 'The aim of a phased approach is both to allow for growth of the Information Commissioner's Office, to cope with the new regulatory regime, and to allow public authorities, in particular those which have not been subject to the Open Government Code, a reasonable period in which to develop their own internal procedures for compliance. It is in the clear interest of public authorities and the Information Commissioner alike to begin work now on the development of publication schemes and preparations for responding to individual requests for information. These responsibilities are considered further under separate headings.'

Work to date has included publication schemes. The Information Commissioner's Office has launched a consultation on three areas of work:

- a draft methodology for producing a publication scheme;
- a draft version of the Commissioner's own scheme; and
- draft criteria for scheme approval.

The complete document is available on the Commissioner's website under the heading of Drafts for Consultation: FOI Act 2000. The closing date for the receipt of responses to the consultation paper was 21 September 2001.

In June 2001 five Government departments and agencies undertook to pilot individual publication schemes and discussions within those bodies will be ongoing: more formal meetings between all the pilots and this office were scheduled for late 2001. The Information Commissioner's Office says 'It is the office's aim to be in a position to produce firm guidance on the production and approval of publication schemes, with particular reference to first wave bodies, at the turn of the year'.

In addition, by January 2005 Central Government will have been operating Electronic Records Management (ERM) for a year. This is separate from *FIA 2000* and is supervised by the Public Record Office. It introduces a requirement that all newly created public records are stored and retrieved electronically by 2004. The Government says that 'This initiative will enable the fast retrieval of information which will be necessary to meet the demands of the Freedom of Information Act 2000'.

Bodies covered 24.7

Only public authorities are covered by *FIA 2000.* These include:

- Government departments;
- local authorities;
- NHS bodies, such as hospitals, as well as doctors, dentists, pharmacists and opticians;
- schools, colleges and universities;
- the Police; and
- the House of Commons and the House of Lords, the Northern Ireland Assembly and the National Assembly for Wales.

It also includes a long list of other public bodies, ranging from various official advisory and expert committees, to regulators and organisations such as the Post Office, the National Gallery and the Parole Board. A list is provided in *Schedule 1* to *FIA 2000*. Readers whose company is public or quasi-public should check the list to see if their employer is on it.

Rights granted 24.8

Section 7 of *DPA 1998* provides a subject access right. As far as public bodies are concerned, *FIA 2000* will extend these rights to allow access to all the types of information held by public bodies, whether personal or non-personal. However, some of the information requested need not be provided if one of the exemptions in *FIA 2000* applies.

Who can make a request? 24.9

Anyone will be able make a request for information, although the request must be in permanent form (i.e. by e-mail or on paper, but not by telephone). *FIA 2000* gives applicants two related rights:

- the right to be told whether the information exists; and
- the right to receive the information and, where possible, in the manner requested, for example as a copy or summary; alternatively the applicant may ask to inspect a record.

The Introduction to FIA 2000 produced by the Information Commissioner states that:

> 'it is important to note that applicants will not be able to exercise their right of access until the body concerned has been phased in. However, applicants will then still be able to request information recorded before the Act was passed.'

New responsibilities 24.10

Publication schemes 24.11

FIA 2000 places a duty on public authorities to adopt and maintain publication schemes, which must be approved by the Information Commissioner. Such schemes must set out the types of information the authority publishes, the form in which the information is published and details of any charges. The Commissioner may also approve model schemes for groups of similar bodies, for example schools.

The Information Commissioner will be working with groups of public authorities to develop guidance on what should be included in publication schemes.

Responding to requests 24.12

In general, public authorities will have to respond to requests within 20 working days. They may charge a fee, which will have to be calculated according to regulations relating to fees, which are yet to be drafted. If a fee is required, the 20 working days will be extended by up to three months until the fee is paid.

In cases where information is covered by an exemption, but the authority is then required to consider the public interest in releasing it, the authority must provide the information within a reasonable time.

Exemptions 24.13

There are 23 exemptions in *FIA 2000*, some of which are familiar under data protection legislation, for example that information need not be released if it would prejudice national security or law enforcement.

Under *FIA 2000*, some exemptions apply to a whole category or class of information, for example:

- information relating to investigations and proceedings conducted by public authorities;
- court records; and
- trade secrets.

Any information covered by these class-based exemptions is always exempt.

Other exemptions are subject to a prejudice test, for example, where disclosure would or would be likely to prejudice:

- the interests of the United Kingdom abroad; or
- the prevention or detection of crime.

Information only becomes exempt if disclosing it would or would be likely to prejudice the activity or interest described in the exemption. In most cases, where information is exempt the public authority must then consider the public interest in providing the information. This public interest test involves considering the circumstances of each particular case and the exemption that covers the information. The information may only be withheld if the public interest in withholding it is greater than the public interest in releasing it.

Role of the Information Commissioner 24.14

The Information Commissioner is an independent public official reporting directly to Parliament. She is responsible for implementing *FIA 2000*. This involves:

- promoting good practice;
- approving and assisting in the preparation of publication schemes;
- providing information as to the public's rights under *FIA 2000*; and
- enforcing compliance with *FIA 2000*.

Guidance and codes of practice 24.15

In June 2001 the Commissioner issued an overview of *FIA 2000*, which is accessible via www.dataprotection.gov.uk/dpr/foi.nsf

Two codes of practice issued under *FIA 2000* will provide guidance to public authorities on:

- responding to requests for information and associated matters (a draft is available at www.lcd.gov.uk/foi/foidpunit.htm); and
- records management (draft available via: www.pro.gov.uk/records management/),

and are discussed in detail at 24.16–24.18 below.

Home Office Draft Code of Practice: discharge of functions of public authorities 24.16

The Home Office Draft Code of Practice under *Part I* of *FIA 2000* is issued under *section 45* of *FIA 2000*. It provides guidance to public authorities on desirable practices for them to follow under that part of the Act dealing with access to information held by them. The aims of the Code are to:

(*a*) facilitate the disclosure of information under *FIA 2000* by setting out good administrative practice which it is desirable for public authorities to follow when handling requests for information, including, where appropriate, the transfer of a request to a different authority;

(*b*) protect the interests of applicants by setting out standards for the provision of advice which it would be good practice to make available to them and to encourage the development of effective means of complaining about decisions taken under *FIA 2000*;

(*c*) ensure that the interests of third parties who may be affected by any decision to disclose information are considered by the authority by setting standards for consultation; and

(*d*) ensure that authorities consider the implications for the freedom of information before agreeing to confidentiality provisions in contracts and accepting information in confidence from a third party more generally.

The Code says that all public authorities should provide advice and assistance to those making requests for information and should publish their procedures for such requests. It is recommended that decisions be made within 20 working days where possible. Transfers to other bodies who in fact have the information requested should be made promptly.

Where the disclosure of information may affect the legal rights of a third party such as the right to have certain information treated in confidence, or rights under *Article 8* of the *European Convention on Human Rights*, then the authority should seek consent from that third party.

The Code and contracts 24.17

The Code's provisions on contracts are interesting. Many companies enter into contracts with public authorities. The Code says that when entering into contracts, public authorities should refuse to include:

> 'contractual terms which purport to restrict the disclosure of information held by the authority and relating to the contract beyond the restrictions permitted by the Act. Public authorities should not agree to hold information "in confidence" which is not in fact confidential in nature.'

When entering into contracts with non-public authority contractors, public authorities may be under pressure to accept confidentiality clauses so that information relating to the terms of the contract, its value and performance will be exempt from disclosure. Public authorities should not accept such clauses where this is commercially viable. This could have quite an impact in practice. Any acceptance of such confidentiality provisions must be for good reasons and capable of being justified to the Information Commissioner. In most cases it is for the public authority to disclose information under *FIA 2000*, and not the contractor. However, the public authority may need to protect from disclosure by the contractor information which would be exempt from disclosure under *FIA 2000*, by appropriate contractual terms. Apart from such cases, public authorities should not impose terms of secrecy on contractors.

The Code provides that a public authority should only accept information from third parties in confidence if it is necessary to obtain that information in connection with the exercise of any of the authority's functions. In addition, public authorities should not agree to hold information received from third parties 'in confidence' which is not confidential in nature. And again, acceptance of any confidentiality provisions must be for good reasons, capable of being justified to the Commissioner.

Public records 24.18

The Public Record Office (PRO) has produced guidance on data protection and there will be a Code of Practice on records management under *FIA 2000*. A working draft of the Lord Chancellor's Code of Practice on the Management of Records Under Freedom of Information is available at www.pro.gov.uk/recordsmanagement/CodeOfPractice.htm.

There are currently two model action plans to help public authorities reach compliance with the Code of Practice. One is for central government departments and agencies; the other is for local authorities.

The PRO has also produced a Manual of Guidance on Access to Public Records. This explains the current criteria for extended retention or closure of public records, and contains specialist guidance on specific topics or types of records. It has been approved by the Lord Chancellor's Advisory Council on Public Records.

The *Government of Wales Act 1998* made provision for a Public Record Office of Wales. However, until this has been established, the PRO will continue to look after Welsh public records and a Memorandum of Understanding has been drawn up to formalise this agreement.

Further information and the documents referred to in this paragraph are available at www.pro.gov.uk/recordsmanagement/access/default.htm.

Publication schemes 24.19

The Information Commissioner sought comments by 21 September 2001 on a consultation paper which outlined the obligation on public authorities to adopt and maintain publication schemes under *FIA 2000* and invited comment on three attached papers. The document was aimed at those who are required to adopt and maintain publication schemes, and also to those who are likely to want to consult them. The paper was prepared following the recommendations contained in the Code of Practice on Written Consultation, issued by the Cabinet Office, and can be found at www.dataprotection.gov.uk/dpr/foi.nsf.

Further information 24.20

Information published by the Information Commissioner can be obtained from the Freedom of Information part of the website www.dataprotection.gov.uk/dpr/foi.nsf

Information on the public records aspects is at www.pro.gov.uk/records management/access/default.htm.

The *Freedom of Information Act 2000* is available from the Stationery Office (ISBN 0105436003, price £9.55). The Explanatory Notes are available separately. The Act can also be accessed free via the Stationery Office website at www.tso-online.co.uk and the Parliament website at www.parliament.uk.

A useful website on freedom of information in the EU is 'Statewatch' and includes access to relevant EU documents in the privacy law area and case law in this field. See www.statewatch.org/foi.htm.

The report of the Advisory Group on Openness in the Public Sector can be read at ww.lcd.gov.uk/foi/foiadvgp.htm.

Details of the Public Record Office advice and guidance to records managers across Central Government on ERM can be read at ww.pro.gov.uk/recordsmanagement/default.htm.

25 – Health, Education and Social Work

At a glance 25.1

- ✓ Personal data relating to health, education and social work will often be classed as sensitive, personal data under the *Data Protection Act 1998* (*DPA 1998*).
- ✓ Limited exemption orders exist in these categories and are described in this chapter.
- ✓ Special rules on subject access and health records are examined in this chapter.
- ✓ Guidance has been issued on the issuing of school examination results to the media by the Information Commissioner.
- ✓ Other legislation with relevance to these areas is examined.

Introduction 25.2

A vast amount of personal data is held relating to individuals' health and in the education and social work context. Much of that data may be sensitive personal data (see CHAPTER 42 SENSITIVE PERSONAL DATA). Special regulations have been made under *DPA 1998* in relation to health, education and social work.

Health 25.3

The *Data Protection (Subject Access Modification) (Health) Order 2000* (*SI 2000/413*) (the 'Health Order') exempts from subject access requirements any data relating to the physical or mental health condition of the data subject, where the application of *section* 7 of *DPA 1998* would be likely to cause serious harm to the physical or mental health or condition of the data subject or any other person.

Data controllers have a legal obligation before they decide if this exemption applies to consult with a 'health professional' responsible for the clinical care of the data subject (if there is more than one, the most suitable health professional must be consulted). The Information Commissioner, in Guidance issued in October 2001, states:

> 'The Commissioner recognises that in many cases there will be more than one health professional responsible for the patient's clinical care at the time a subject access request is made. Data controllers should ensure that they have systems in place to enable the most suitable health professional to be identified and consulted to enable the data controller to comply with a subject access request within the statutory time limit of 40 days.
>
> Where a request for subject access is made by someone other than the data subject (i.e. by someone with parental responsibility for a child or, in relation to Scotland, by such a person on behalf of someone under the age of 16, or by a person appointed by a court to manage the affairs of the data subject) the data controller should consider any expectation of confidentiality the data subject may have had at the time the information was provided or obtained, and any wishes expressed by the data subject with regard to the disclosure of personal data relating to his physical or mental health condition.
>
> In specific circumstances set out in the Health Order where certain personal data are processed by the Court, there is also an exemption from the subject information provisions.'

If the data controller already has a written opinion from the appropriate health professional obtained in the previous six months that an exemption to the right of subject access exists because the disclosure is likely to cause serious harm to the physical or mental health of the data subject, or any other person, then there will not be a right of subject access in such a case. Where this is relied upon, the data controller should consider whether it is reasonable in all the circumstances to re-consult the health professional. This exemption does not apply if the request relates to information which the data controller is satisfied either:

(*a*) has previously been seen by the data subject; or

(*b*) is already within the knowledge of the data subject.

Access to a record containing information as to the data subject's physical or mental health or condition cannot be denied on the grounds that the identity of a third party would be disclosed if the third party is a health professional who has compiled, or contributed to, the health record, or has been involved in the care of the data subject in his capacity as a health professional, unless serious harm to that health professional's physical or mental health or condition is likely to be caused by giving access.

Subject access and medical data 25.4

In September 2000 the Information Commissioner issued guidance (see 25.17 below) on subject access requests and information in health records. A 'health record' is defined in *section 68(2)* of *DPA 1998* as any record which consists of information relating to the physical or mental health or condition of an individual, and has been made by or on behalf of a health professional in connection with the care of that individual. Appendix 1 to the Information Commissioner's guidance provides further details on the definition. The definition would apply to material held on an X-ray or an MRI scan, for example. This means that when a subject access request is made, the information contained in such material must be supplied to the applicant. The Information Commissioner states:

> 'It is clear, therefore, that many of the records being held by NHS Trusts, surgeries and other health care institutions will constitute "health records" and will therefore fall within the scope of the 1998 Act's subject access provisions.'

The old *Health Records Act 1990* has now been repealed.

The *Data Protection (Subject Access Modification) (Health) Order 2000* (*SI 2000/413*) provides that information need not be disclosed if it would be likely to cause serious harm to the physical or mental health of the data subject or any other person, and describes the mechanisms for ensuring that decisions as to whether to disclose or withhold information are taken by the appropriate health professional.

Fees for access 25.5

In March 2001 the Information Commissioner issued guidance on charging fees for subject access requests for medical data, which is on her website (see 25.17 below). The subject access rights are modified by two orders made under *DPA 1998*. Firstly, the *Data Protection (Subject Access Modification) (Health) Order 2000* (*SI 2000/413*) mentioned above, and secondly the *Data Protection (Subject Access) (Fees and Miscellaneous Provisions) Regulations 2000* (*SI 2000/191*). *Regulation 6* of *SI 2000/191* provides that whereas the normal maximum subject access fee that may be charged is £10, for health records there is a fee of up to £50 for access to non-automated records. This had been planned to cease to have effect on 24 October 2001. However, the *Data Protection*

(Subject Access) (Fees and Miscellaneous Provisions) (Amendment) Regulations 2001 (*SI 2001/3223*) extended the right to continue to charge the £50 fee.

The Commissioner's March 2001 guidance says that the subject access fee should be set no higher than that necessary to deter vexatious requests. 'The right to obtain a copy of personal data is a fundamental one. The provisions in *DPA 1998* reflect those of the *Data Protection Directive* (*95/46/EC*) and specify that data subjects should be able to gain access to their data "without excessive expense"'.

A fee of up to £10 appears to the Commissioner to achieve this. However *SI 2001/3223* mentioned above shows that lobbying by the health sector has succeeded and a fee of £50 can be charged. Even that fee often will not reflect the true cost of the exercise. The Commissioner thinks that if fees could be charged on a cost recovery basis for health data, this would inevitably lead to arguments by other types of data controller that they too should be able to set subject access fees according to the effort taken to respond. It could also mean those with poor record-management practices, for whom it is more expensive to extract the data, could charge more – a perverse result.

Fees, reportedly as high as £1000 for some requests under the former *Access to Health Records Act 1990*, are likely to deter most data subjects from exercising their rights and to lead to 'widespread mistrust of the standards to which health organisations process personal data', according to the Commissioner.

The Commissioner says if individuals ask for their whole record it is possible for the data controller to ask data subjects for information which they reasonably need in order to locate the data requested. In addition, under *section 8* of *DPA 1998* information need not be provided in permanent form where this would involve disproportionate effort.

Response periods 25.6

40 days is quite a short period for many in the health service, as the *Data Protection (Subject Access Modification) (Social Work) Order 2000* (*SI 2000/415*) requires consideration to be given by the appropriate health professional as to whether the disclosure of information might seriously harm the health of data subjects or other persons, particularly where, unusually, it may be necessary to consult more than one health professional. Perhaps those involved could make a case to the Secretary of State, the Commissioner says, although it is pointed out that others in industry also have to cope with the 40 day period.

On 30 July 2001 the Information Commissioner issued a paper entitled *Medical Records: Subject Access – Fees for Access* which confirms that the Commissioner believes higher fees are not justified. She also expresses the view that destroying X-rays after two years may breach other provisions of *DPA 1998* (the destruction might ease the burden of responding to subject access requests which have been growing in this sector with the rise in personal injury claims and conditional fee agreement).

Example – Disclosure of medical data **25.7**

In her first Annual Report (2001) the Information Commissioner gave one case example which related in part to confidential medical data.

A council employee sent into the office a large amount of employee personnel information found in a black bin liner in a skip at the council depot where he was employed. He alleged that the manager of the depot disposed of the personnel files of employees working there by placing them in black bin liners and then into skips to be transported to a public refuse tip. He said that two additional bags containing similar information had also been found.

The retrieved documents contained a large amount of personal data relating to the employees and their relatives, including pay and financial details, leave applications, medical information relating to sick leave and so on. Virtually all the documents retrieved were copies of manual documents, which did not come under the scope of *DPA 1998*.

However, there was one document (a sickness record relating to the complainant) which appeared to have been computer generated. On this basis the council concerned was notified that there had been a contravention of the Seventh Data Protection Principle in this case.

The council responded explaining that whilst systems and procedures were in place at the depot concerned these had not been strictly adhered to. As a result of the complaint all depots had been issued with shredders and management had been reminded of the procedures, which should be followed. In addition all employees were to receive data protection awareness training. Data protection liaison officers throughout the council were informed of the incident and asked to apply the lessons learned in their own areas.

Midwifery **25.8**

In a related sector in 2000, the Information Commissioner issued her views on a draft Nursing and Midwifery Order 2001 which would draw up a register of such staff. The comments were issued on 27 June 2001 and the Commissioner particularly objected to publication of home addresses of such staff. 'The Draft Nursing and Midwifery Order 2001: Comments by the Information Commissioner' are on the Commissioner's website under Guidance/Codes of Practice and other responses.

Health and Social Care Act 2001 25.9

In April 2000 the Information Commissioner issued her comments on the *Health and Social Care Act 2001* (*HSCA 2001*) (then in Bill form). *Part 5* of *HSCA 2001* deals with the control of patient information and the extension of prescribing rights as well as various other matters. *Section 60* of *HSCA 2001* contains provisions relating to patient information and *DPA 1998*.

Section 60 of *HSCA 2001* allows the Secretary of State to require or permit patient information to be shared for medical purposes where it is considered that this is in the interests of improving patient care or in the public interest. *Section 61* of *HSCA 2001* provides for the establishment of a statutory committee that is to be consulted about regulations to be made under *section 60*.

Section 60 of *HSCA 2001* should make it possible for patients to receive more information about their clinical care and for confidential patient information to be lawfully processed without informed consent to support prescribed activities such as cancer registries, the Government says in its explanatory note to *HSCA 2001*. *Section 60* of *HSCA 2001* does not amend *DPA 1998*, and any regulations must not derogate –and will not be able to derogate – from *DPA 1998*. *Section 60(2)(a)* of *HSCA 2001* enables regulations to be made that require specified communications about patients to be disclosed to them by NHS bodies, in certain circumstances. Such regulations may only provide for these communications to be disclosed to those persons to whom they relate or principally relate, or to a prescribed person on their behalf, for example a spouse. This is intended to support the NHS Plan commitment that clinicians will, in the future, be required to share information about patients with them.

What is 'patient information'? 25.10

Section 60(8) of *HSCA 2001* defines 'patient information' as any information that is, or is derived from, information concerning a patient's physical or mental health or condition, the diagnosis of their condition or their care or treatment.

In addition to information which directly identifies individuals, this would include information which is either anonymised (e.g. any information that cannot be tracked back to the individual) or coded (e.g. information that can be tracked back to an individual by persons in possession of a key to the code). It includes information recorded in any manner, whether electronically or manually. *Section 60(9) of HSCA 2001* provides that 'confidential patient information' for the purposes of the section is patient information that has been obtained by a person who owes an obligation of confidence to an individual where the identity of that individual is ascertainable from that information or from that information and other information which is in, or is likely to come into, the possession of the person processing the information.

Personal data in medical context 25.11

In her October 2001 Legal Guidance, when addressing the question of 'what is processing?', the Information Commissioner gives a medical example:

> 'It should be noted that the disclosure of personal data by a data controller amounts to processing under *DPA 1998*. For example:
>
> The obtaining of clinical information linked to a National Health Service number by a person having access to the National Health Service Central Register will amount to processing of personal data by that person because that person will have access to information enabling him to identify the individuals concerned.
>
> It will be incumbent upon anyone processing data to take such technical and organisational measures as are necessary to ensure that the data cannot be reconstituted to become personal data and to be prepared to justify any decision they make with regard to the processing of the data.'

Education 25.12

A similar order exists in relation to education as that relating to health (described at 25.3 above) in the *Data Protection (Subject Access Modification) (Education) Order 2000* (*SI 2000/414*).

SI 2000/414 applies to education records and allows for exemptions and modifications for such material, where disclosure of the information pursuant to a subject access request would be likely to cause serious harm to the physical or mental health or condition of the data subject, or to some other person or, in some circumstances, where disclosure would reveal that the data subject is, or may be at risk of, child abuse (as defined by *Reg 5(4)*). *SI 2000/414* does not apply to personal data to which the *Data Protection (Subject Access Modification) (Health) Order 2000* (*SI 2000/413*) applies.

Disclosure of examination results by schools to the media 25.13

The Information Commissioner has issued some guidance on disclosure of examination results by schools to the media. The Information Commissioner's Office regularly receives enquiries about the data protection implications of schools disclosing the examination results of their students to the local media for publication. Therefore in February 2001 an Advice Sheet was issued which explains the impact of *DPA 1998* on this use of personal data, and provides guidance on how such disclosures can be made within the remit of the Act. Schools should ensure that pupils and their parents are aware that examination results may be published. It may also be necessary to explain the form in which this will take place. Some pupils, for example, might object to their results being published if they know that they will be published in order of grades attained rather than alphabetically. The Commissioner does not think that pupils or their parents must give their consent to the publication of examination results, knowing from experience of complaints that in a small number of cases publication can cause distress. In informing pupils or their parents of the practice of publication of examination results, schools should therefore advise them of the right to object to publication.

The rights given to a data subject by *DPA 1998* are not affected by the data subject's age. The Commissioner generally advises that providing that people are able to understand their rights then it is them, and not their parents or guardians, who should be informed of uses and disclosures of data and who have the right to object to processing. In most cases, therefore, it is sufficient to provide the information described above to pupils. In a small number of cases, it may be that pupils are not capable of understanding their rights or of understanding the consequences of publication. In these cases, schools should provide the relevant information to parents or guardians.

Relevant person – education 25.14

For education records the *Data Protection (Subject Access Modification) (Education) Order 2000* (*SI 2000/414*) referred to above defines a 'relevant person' as:

(*a*) an employee of the local education authority which maintains the school, a teacher or other employee of an education and library board, or in the case of a voluntary aided, foundation or foundation special school or special school not maintained by a local education authority, a teacher or other employee of the school;

(*b*) a person employed by an education authority (within the meaning of *paragraph 6* of *Schedule 11* to *DPA 1998*) in pursuance of its function relating to education and the information relates to him, or he supplied the information in his capacity as such employee; or

(*c*) the person making the request.

Social work 25.15

The *Data Protection (Subject Access Modification) (Social Work) Order 2000* (*SI.2000/415*) provides for modifications and exemptions where the personal data relate to social work falling within any of the descriptions set out in the Regulations. *SI 2000/415* does not apply to personal data to which the *Data Protection (Subject Access Modification) (Health) Order 2000* (*SI 2000/413*) (see 25.3 above) and the *Data Protection (Subject Access Modification) (Education) Order 2000* (*SI 2000/414*) (see 25.12 above) apply.

It is not permissible to deny access to a social work record on the grounds that the identity of a third party would be disclosed where the third party is a 'relevant person' as defined by *DPA 1998*, unless serious harm to that person's physical or mental health or condition is likely to be caused by giving access.

Social work – conditions 25.16

If the information is 'social work' (defined by *SI 2000/415*)) and:

(*a*) (except in relation to Scotland) the data subject is a child and the request is made by someone with parental responsibility who is enabled to make the request by some enactment or rule of law; or

(*c*) in relation to Scotland, the data subject is a person under 16 and the request is made by someone with parental responsibility who is enabled to make the request by some enactment or rule of law; or

(*d*) the data subject is incapable of managing his own affairs and the person making the request has been appointed by a court to manage those affairs;

the information should *not* be supplied if:

(i) the information was supplied in expectation that it would not be disclosed to that person; or

(ii) the information results from an examination or investigation to which the data subject consented in the expectation that it would not be disclosed; or

(iii) the data subject has expressly indicated that the information should not be disclosed.

Further information 25.17

The Commissioner has issued the following separate guidance relevant in this field:

- Schools: exam results, publication.
- Subject access – education records in England.
- Subject access – health records.
- Subject access – health records: fees for access.
- Subject access – medical records: fees for access.
- Subject access – social services records.

The guidance is available on the website of the Information Commissioner (www.dataprotection.gov.uk under Compliance Advice).

26 – Human Rights Act 1998

At a glance 26.1

- ✓ The *Human Rights Act 1998* (*HRA 1998*) came into force on 2 October 2000 and makes the *European Convention on Human Rights* (*ECHR*) part of English law.
- ✓ *Article 8* of *ECHR* provides for a right to respect for private and family life, which has implications for privacy law.
- ✓ *Article 10* of *ECHR* provides a right of freedom of expression.
- ✓ The Information Commissioner takes account of *HRA 1998* in her interpretation of the *Data Protection Act 1998* (*DPA 1998*).
- ✓ The High Court has ruled that a breach of *DPA 1998* occurred when a voter was prosecuted for refusing to go on the electoral roll because his local council refused to allow him to opt-out of his details being commercially sold on by the council (*Brian Robertson v Wakefield City Council (High Court, 16 November 2001)*).

Introduction 26.2

Since 2 October 2000 *HRA 1998* has applied in the UK. The Act guarantees certain rights which may have implications in the data protection field, in particular a right to respect for private life. Therefore correspondence which breaches data protection legislation may also breach *HRA 1998*.

Commissioner's Legal Guidance 26.3

In her Legal Guidance to *DPA 1998* the Commissioner says:

> 'As I am required to do, I have sought to interpret the Act in the light of the provisions of the Human Rights Act 1998, which came into force on 2 October 2000. This will need to be kept under review. The full effect of the Human Rights Act on our legal system, and on society as a whole, has yet to be felt. It is, however, clear that the role of information in our society makes it increasingly important to develop respect

among data controllers for the private lives of individuals and to ensure good information handling practice. The Human Rights Act, and in particular Articles 8 and 10 of the European Convention on Human Rights provide the legal framework within which interpretation of the Act, and the Data Protection Principles which underpin it, can be developed.'

Lawful obtaining 26.4

Under the Eight Data Protection Principles data must be lawfully obtained. Data which is obtained in breach of confidence or in breach of an enforceable contractual agreement comes within this category, as does breach of *HRA 1998* by a data controller bound by that Act (this is an example given by the Information Commissioner in her Legal Guidance).

Convention rights 26.5

In her Draft Code of Practice on the Use of Personal Data in Employer/Employee Relationships, the Commissioner writes the following about *HRA 1998*:

> '…the Act gives effect to rights and freedoms guaranteed under the European Convention on Human Rights. Public authorities including the courts and tribunals such as the Data Protection Tribunal must not act in a way that is incompatible with a Convention right unless the need to apply primary legislation leaves them with no choice'.

The Convention rights most relevant to the area of data protection, those given by *Article 8* and *Article 10* of the *ECHR*, are set out at 26.6–26.7 below.

Article 8 26.6

Right to respect for private and family life

1. Everyone has the right to respect for his private and family life, his home and his correspondence.
2. There shall be no interference by a public authority with the exercise of this right except such as is in accordance with the law and is necessary in a democratic society in the interests of national security, public safety or the economic well-being of the country, for the prevention of disorder or crime, for the protection of health or morals, or for the protection of the rights and freedoms of others.

Article 10 26.7

Freedom of expression

1. Everyone has the right to freedom of expression. This right shall include freedom to hold opinions and to receive and impart information and ideas without interference by public authority and regardless of frontiers. This Article shall not prevent States from requiring the licensing of broadcasting, television or cinema enterprises.

2. The exercise of these freedoms, since it carries with it duties and responsibilities, may be subject to such formalities, conditions, restrictions or penalties as are prescribed by law and are necessary in a democratic society, in the interests of national security, territorial integrity or public safety, for the prevention of disorder or crime, for the protection of health or morals, for the protection of the reputation or rights of others, for preventing the disclosure of information received in confidence, or for maintaining the authority and impartiality of the judiciary.

Interception 26.8

The interception of communications can breach *HRA 1998* as well as *DPA 1998*. The *Telecommunications (Lawful Business Practice) (Interception of Communications) Regulations 2000* (*SI 2000/2699*) set out the relevant law in this area and permit the carrying out of covert, directed surveillance of individuals by public authorities. It sets out arrangements for the authorisation of such surveillance and the grounds on which an authorisation can be given. An example given by the Commissioner is as follows.

A local authority sets up a secret camera in the office of the Deputy Director of Social Services, who it suspects of sexually harassing another member of staff. The surveillance has not been authorised in accordance with the provisions of *section 28* of the *Regulation of Investigatory Powers Act 2000*. The processing of personal data involved in the surveillance will be unlawful, putting the local authority in breach of the First Data Protection Principle. This is because the surveillance is not carried out in accordance with the law, in this case the *Regulation of Investigatory Powers Act 2000*. Furthermore, it contravenes *Article 8* of the *European Convention on Human Rights* as given effect by the *Human Rights Act 1998* in that there is an interference with the Deputy Director's exercise of his right to respect for his private life that is not in accordance with the law.

Case law 26.9

A v B plc and another (10 September 2001, Times Law Reports 2 November 2001)

As described at paragraph 17.11 in CHAPTER 17 ENFORCEMENT, REMEDIES AND POWERS, on 10 September 2001 the High Court granted an interlocutory injunction to prevent an unnamed first defendant from disclosing or publishing any information about the extra-marital sexual relationships a married professional footballer had allegedly had with two women. The court said that facts concerning the existence of a sexual relationship and details of the sexual activity in the relationship, whether within a marriage or outside of it, were confidential. Here there was no public interest in the publication of the details and the information was not already in the public domain. The information was confidential and publication would be a breach of the claimant's right of privacy enshrined in *HRA 1998*. The right to privacy prevailed over the newspaper's right to freedom of expression.

A v B plc is consistent with earlier cases which have held that famous people who choose to sunbathe on a public beach did not have any right to privacy sufficient to prevent publication of photographs taken of them, whereas those inviting guests to a very private wedding at which photography is banned and tight security imposed with the aim of ensuring confidentiality would be protected. In the latter case, the courts have held that the individuals may then restrain publication of illicit photographs taken there in breach of confidentiality and privacy rights. Similarly, the careless, or public, adulterer may find their lack of discretion held against them where similar injunctions are sought, whereas the discreet will find that their privacy rights prevail.

Commissioner's views 26.10

DPA 1998 derives from the *ECHR* as it is based upon the Council of Europe *Convention on Data Protection*, which seeks to give particularity to the provisions of *Article 8* of *ECHR*. This makes it unlike many other statutes. When commenting on the proposed Social Security Fraud Bill in January 2001, the Commissioner noted that the exemptions contained in *DPA 1998* are based upon those provided for in *ECHR*.

Social Security Fraud Act 2000 26.11

In the context of the *Social Security Fraud Act 2000*, the Commissioner took advice from counsel about the compatibility of the proposals in the Bill with the European Court of Human Rights (ECtHR).

Article 8(1) of *ECHR* provides that:

> 'Everyone has the right to respect for his private and family life, his home and his correspondence.'

This right is qualified by *Article 8(2)* of *ECHR* which states:

> 'There shall be no interference by a public authority with the exercise of this right except such as in accordance with the law and is necessary in a democratic society in the interests of national security, public safety or the economic well-being of the country, for the prevention of disorder or crime, for the protection of health or morals or for the protection of the rights or freedoms of others.'

It is useful to examine the Commissioner's comments which show her own and counsel's views of the impact of *HRA 1998* in this field. She said she:

> 'considers that the test of necessity may be failed for other reasons. c.1 of the Bill lists organisations which may be required to provide information to "authorised officers". However, it seems…that in a significant number of cases the organisations described either do not have the information required or will have considerable difficulty in ensuring that the information they do possess relates to the subject of an officer's enquiries…'

In considering 'necessity' the ECtHR has considered the matter of proportionality. The Commissioner writes the following:

> 'It is hard to see how the proposed powers may be justified when they are compared, say with those of the police, who even where the matters under investigation are extremely serious, must either seek evidence from the suspect, must persuade others of their need for information or, as a last resort seek judicial authority for the collection of information without consent.

Wide information gathering can breach *HRA 1998*. The ECtHR has also found that for an interference with the right to privacy to be justified, there must be adequate, enforceable safeguards. The provisions from the Bill are now contained in the *Social Security Fraud Act 2000*, and include the powers criticised above for state bodies to cross-check data of claimants for DSS benefits. Whilst the above quotes are comments on only one piece of legislation, they do illustrate the Commissioner's views on the application of *HRA 1998* in this area.

E-mails **26.12**

In the area of subject access rights and e-mails, in her guidance the Information Commissioner is of the view that if an e-mail were written in a private rather than an official capacity, then only exceptional circumstances will justify the disclosure of third party information without the consent of the individual concerned. 'Cases which involve possible breaches of *Article 8* provisions will be considered on their individual merits', the Commissioner says.

Traffic and billing data **26.13**

The *EU Directive on the Processing of Personal Data and the Protection of Privacy in the Telecommunications Sector (97/66/EC)* recognises the importance of safeguarding traffic and billing data, and lays down strict rules about the retention and use of this information by telecoms providers. It is the Commissioner's view that access to traffic and billing data should also be made subject to prior judicial scrutiny, so that consideration could be given to *Article 8* of *ECHR*. The Anti-Terrorism, Crime and Security Bill proposed in the UK in 2001 may, under its Code of Practice, lead to a requirement for the retention of traffic data for up to 12 months, however this is the traffic data rather than the contents of the traffic itself.

Human rights and monitoring **26.14**

In 2001 the Institute of Management suggested that some monitoring by managers of staff e-mail and telephone calls could breach *HRA 1998*. Ringing staff at home to discuss work matters could, under UK human rights legislation, be construed as an invasion of privacy.

> 'An employer does not have the right to demand an employee's telephone number, unless it is specified in the contract that the employee has a duty to be available outside normal working hours.'

The Institute also warned that the unauthorised vetting of e-mails and phone calls could be considered an invasion of privacy, even if employees are thought to be sending personal messages through company lines.

Recent case law **26.15**

In the case of *Brian Robertson v Wakefield City Council (High Court, 16 November 2001)*, the High Court held a breach of *Article 8* of *ECHR*, as given effect by *HRA 1998*, when a voter was prosecuted for refusing to register to vote on the grounds that his local council allowed the electoral roll to be used for commercial purposes by third parties. They would not let him opt-out of such use. Mr Justice Maurice Kay said that there was a breach of *Article 8*, and also this resulted in a disproportionate and unjustified restriction on Mr Robertson's right to vote.

The judge also said on this issue that the British Government had not properly implemented the *EU Data Protection Directive* (*95/46/EC*) in *DPA 1998*. Mr Robertson argued through his solicitors that his details should only be used for electoral purposes for which he had consented, or other purposes justified in the public interest, and yet for years (at least since 1918) all local authorities have sold their electoral registers for commercial use.

At the time of writing the full judgment is not available, nor a follow-up decision on whether Mr Robertson is entitled to the £1000 damages which he claimed for the 'loss' of his right to vote.

Further information 26.16

See *A v B plc and another (10 September 2001, Times Law Reports 2 November 2001).*

27 – International Aspects

At a glance 27.1

- ✓ The *Data Protection Act 1998* (*DPA 1998*) implements the *EU Data Protection Directive (95/46/EC)* in the UK.
- ✓ Internationally, in 1980 the Organisation for Economic Co-operation and Development (OECD) agreed guidelines on data protection.
- ✓ Further international development of such guidelines may occur in due course.
- ✓ In September 2001 the Council of Europe agreed the Cyber-crime Convention which has data protection implications.

Introduction 27.2

DPA 1998 implements the *EU Data Protection Directive (95/46/EC)*. However, the UK Information Commissioner liaises with international data protection bodies in the course of her work. In 1980 the OECD agreed guidelines in the data protection field, and the Information Commissioner has also been involved in a long running series of international conferences of data protection commissioners.

OECD data protection guidelines 27.3

Guidelines on the Protection of Privacy and Transborder Flows of Personal Data (the 'Privacy Guidelines') were adopted on 23 September 1980 as a Recommendation of the Council of the OECD. In adopting these Guidelines, the OECD member countries clearly intended to 'help to harmonise national privacy legislation and, while upholding such human rights, to prevent at the same time interruptions in international flows of data'. According to the OECD, since then the Recommendation has 'proved to represent international consensus on general guidance concerning the collection and management of personal information'.

The principles contained in the OECD Privacy Guidelines are reflected in legislation and practices for the protection of privacy worldwide. The principles were designed in a technology-neutral way to accommodate future developments; they are still applicable with regard to any technology used for collecting and processing data, including network technologies.

The last international conference of data protection commissioners examined whether the time was right for a review of the international instruments which address data protection and the preparation of a more global multi-lateral convention.

The Information Commissioner, in her First Annual Report (June 2001), states that 'the predominant view was that it would be more constructive for the moment to concentrate on pragmatic means of securing the implementation of and compliance with the acknowledged international principles declared in instruments such as the OECD Guidelines.' In September 2001 the OECD conference met again to discuss these issues in Paris.

The aim of the Privacy Guidelines which arose from the Council of Europe Convention is to provide protection for individuals whilst also allowing a free flow of information for trade purposes. The Commonwealth Centre for Electronic Governance, which has been recently set up, also works in these areas.

OECD Privacy Statement Generator 27.4

In 2000 the OECD adopted the *OECD Privacy Statement Generator* for websites at http://cs3-hq.oecd.org/scripts/pwv3/pwhome.htm. Privacy policies are also addressed in CHAPTER 37 PRIVACY POLICIES AND AUDITS.

The Generator has been endorsed by the OECD's 29 member countries, and aims to:

- offer guidance on compliance with the Privacy Guidelines and to help organisations develop privacy policies and statements for display on their websites;
- provide guidance on conducting an internal review of existing personal data practices and on developing a privacy policy statement;
- give links to private sector organisations with expertise in developing a privacy policy; and
- offer links to governmental agencies, non-governmental organisations and private bodies that give information on applicable regulations.

The OECD say: 'The Generator makes use of a questionnaire to learn about your personal data practices. A Help Section provides explanatory notes and practical guidance. Warning flags appear where appropriate. Your answers are then fed into a pre-formatted draft policy statement. You must assess this statement: is it an accurate reflection of your personal data practices and policy? Note that the OECD does not guarantee that such a draft privacy policy statement meets applicable legal or self-regulatory requirements. The statement merely reflects the answers given to the Generator's questions. However, the draft statement will furnish an indication of the extent to which your privacy practices are consistent with the OECD Privacy Guidelines.'

The OECD feels that by making the Generator freely available online, it will help:

- foster awareness of privacy issues amongst web site owners.;
- increase awareness among visitors about privacy practices on the websites which they browse; and
- encourage user and consumer trust in global networks and electronic commerce.

Use of the OECD Generator does not, however, necessarily imply that a website complies with the OECD Privacy Guidelines. Those are accessible on the OECD website (see 27.7 below).

E-commerce privacy disputes and other work of OECD 27.5

The OECD began work in 2000 on creating methods of online alternative dispute resolution for addressing privacy and consumer disputes in the e-commerce area.

The OECD is also examining the special privacy problems arising from genetic research data.

Council of Europe Convention on Cybercrime 27.6

On 19 September 2001 the Council of Europe Ministers' Deputies approved the Convention on Cybercrime. The Convention was presented for formal adoption to Foreign Affairs Ministers meeting in Strasbourg on 8 November 2001, with the opening for signature by member states taking place at an international conference in Budapest at the end of November 2001. It will enter into force when five states, at least three of which are members of the Council of Europe, have ratified it.

The Convention on Cybercrime will be the first international treaty on crimes committed via the Internet and other computer networks, dealing particularly with infringements of copyright, computer-related fraud, child pornography and violations of network security. It also contains a series of powers and procedures relating to the search of computer networks and the interception of data. Its main objective, set out in the preamble, is to pursue a common criminal policy aimed at the protection of society against cybercrime, especially by adopting appropriate legislation and fostering international co-operation. The Convention is the product of four years of work by Council of Europe experts, but also by the United States, Canada, Japan and other countries which are not members of the organisation. It will be supplemented by an additional protocol making any publication of racist and xenophobic propaganda via computer networks a criminal offence.

Further information 27.7

The OECD's website is at www.oecd.org.

The OECD Privacy Statement Generator for websites is at http://cs3-hq.oecd.org/scripts/pwv3/pwhome.htm

28 – Internet

At a glance 28.1

- ✓ Personal data is often gathered on Internet websites and must be handled in accordance with the applicable sections of the *Data Protection Act 1998* (*DPA 1998*).
- ✓ The Information Commissioner has issued guidance for data controllers and for data subjects relating to the Internet, and in June 2001 also issued a list of Frequently Asked Questions in relation to the Internet and personal data.
- ✓ The Information Commissioner's Draft Code of Practice on the Use of Personal Data in Employer/Employee Relationships also looks at Internet use by employees and the data protection implications thereof, including those relating to surveillance (see CHAPTER 15 E-MAILS, CHAPTER 29 LAWFUL BUSINESS PRACTICE REGULATIONS and CHAPTER 40 REGULATION OF INVESTIGATORY POWERS ACT 2000).
- ✓ Many companies have a privacy policy on their website.

Introduction 28.2

Many companies gather personal data through use of a website. They must comply with *DPA 1998*. Many display a privacy policy on the website (see CHAPTER 37 PRIVACY POLICIES AND AUDITS). The Organisation for Economic Co-operation and Development (OECD) has also issued some guidance on privacy policies also addressed in CHAPTER 37.

Information to be given to users of a website 28.3

Some websites collect no personal data at all; they are simply online catalogues displaying the goods or services offered by a business. There may be no data protection implications and no need for a privacy policy or other notice on the website. However, in other cases, for the processing of personal data to be fair and compliant with the law, website operators who collect personal data directly from individuals must always ensure that individuals are aware of:

(*a*) the identity of the person or organisation responsible for operating the website and of anyone else who collects personal data through the site;

(*b*) the purposes for which they intend to process the personal data; and

(*c*) any other information needed to ensure fairness to individuals, taking into account the specific circumstances of the processing. This will include informing individuals of any disclosure of information about them to third parties, including disclosure to companies within the same group.

The Information Commissioner states that:

> 'Unless it is obvious, website operators must give this information to individuals before they collect any personal data from them. It should be remembered that visitors to a website will not necessarily enter it through its homepage. They may, for example, come directly to a particular page via a hypertext link. The above information should therefore be provided at any point at which personal data are collected.'

In some cases there will be more than one data controller collecting data, for example where there is banner advertising placed by a third party, or where a third party provides a secure payment mechanism. In such cases all data controllers should be identified, the Information Commissioner advises.

Where information collected is to be used or disclosed for direct marketing purposes, individuals should be provided with the opportunity to prevent this. Website operators may wish to adopt the Information Commissioner's padlock symbol (available at www.dataprotection.gov.uk/#info_padlock_signpost) (see CHAPTER 34 PADLOCK (USE OF SIGN CALLED PADLOCK)). This alerts individuals to the fact that their information is being collected, and draws their attention to the explanation of how it is to be used. Further information about the symbol is available under News and Events on the Commissioner's website (www.dataprotection.gov.uk).

Using privacy statements is a good way to ensure individuals are given the information they need. It does not, however, remove the requirement for notification. The Commissioner says that although a privacy statement is important, it is not sufficient to provide the above information simply in the form 'click here to view our privacy statement'. At least the basic messages and choices should be displayed in an intelligible and prominent form wherever personal data are collected, even where a more detailed explanation is provided elsewhere by means of a privacy statement. Clearly, any basic messages or information given about choices should correspond with the contents of any privacy statement.

Help in designing a privacy statement is available. The OECD has developed a Privacy Policy Generator (see CHAPTER 27 INTERNATIONAL ASPECTS and CHAPTER 37 PRIVACY POLICIES AND AUDITS). This is available at www.oecd.org under 'OECD Tools'. The Information Commissioner advises that:

> 'As a matter of good practice and as an aid to encouraging confidence, a privacy statement should describe not only what a website operator does with personal data but also what it does not do. It should also tell individuals something about their rights and how to exercise them. For example, individuals have a right to be told whether data about them are being processed and to have a copy of the data. They should be told how to go about this. The privacy statement must include the physical address of the website operator unless this is clearly available on the site.'

Is opting-in or opting-out required? 28.4

A major issue for businesses gathering personal data is whether they can use information unless someone objects (opting-out), or whether they can only use it if the individual expressly agrees (opting-in). For many businesses, particularly where the data is not sensitive, the practice has been to give individuals a right to tick a box to indicate they object, and if they do not indicate this then to make use of the data as set out on the notice accompanying the box (opting-out). Commercially this is the easiest method for businesses keen to use personal data for particular marketing purposes.

One question posed by the Information Commissioner in her guidance is whether those supplying data to a website should be required to opt-in or opt-out to the further use of their data (see CHAPTER 33 OPT-IN AND OPT-OUT). The Commissioner states:

> 'The general standard to ensure compliance with the *Data Protection Act 1998* is for a website to provide an individual with an opportunity to opt-out of the use or disclosure of their personal data for direct marketing, whether by e-mail or other means. This requires a statement along the following lines:
>
> "We would like to e-mail you with offers relating to products of ours that we think you might be interested in. Click here if you object to receiving such offers."; and/or

> "We would like to pass your details on to other businesses so they can e-mail you with offers of goods/services that you might be interested in. Click here if you don't want your details to be passed on."
>
> It should be easy for the individual to register his or her wishes. It would not be acceptable, for example, to expect an individual to visit another site to register his or her wishes, or to register his or her wishes by post.
>
> In some cases an opt-out facility will not be sufficient. This is likely to be the case where the processing of sensitive personal data is involved. Where sensitive data about an individual are collected it will usually be necessary to obtain the data subject's explicit consent to the processing before collecting the information. Sensitive data, as defined in *DPA 1998*, are information as to a person's:
>
> - racial or ethnic origin;
> - political opinions;
> - religious or similar beliefs;
> - trade union membership;
> - physical or mental health;
> - sexual life;
> - commission of criminal offences; and
> - involvement in criminal proceedings.
>
> Where explicit consent is required a statement along the following lines will be needed:
>
> "We keep information you have provided us with about your health in order to send you offers of vitamin supplements we think you are likely to be interested in. Click here to show that you agree to this."
>
> It should be noted that explicit consent cannot be obtained by the presence of a pre-crossed box. The individual must take some positive action to signify consent and must be free not to consent.'

In some other countries an opt-in clause is required which raises an interesting jurisdictional issue. It is understood that the general standard is 'opt-in' in Germany, Denmark, Finland, Sweden and Italy. There are also developments which may lead to an 'opt-in' standard being adopted throughout the EU in the draft *Communications Data Protection Directive*.

There is nothing to stop a website operator using an opt-in clause if they prefer to.

Marketing 28.5

Many companies ask for personal data from those visiting the site for marketing purposes. This is lawful as long as the individuals are told that their data will be used for such a function. If personal information is only required for marketing and is not strictly necessary for the supply of a product or service it should be made clear to visitors why the information is being requested, and its supply should be optional.

Wording along the following lines is suggested by the Information Commissioner:

> 'You do not have to answer the following questions but if you do so your answers will help us understand you better as a customer. We will then be able to bring to your attention offers that we believe you are likely to be interested in.'

Cookies 28.6

Many websites gather data through the use of 'cookies'. A cookie is a message given to a web browser by a web server. The message is then stored by the browser in a text file called cookie.txt. Each time the browser requests a page from the server, the message is sent back. A cookie's main objective is to identify users and personalise their visit by customising web pages for them, for example by welcoming them by name next time they visit the same site. A site using cookies will usually invite the user to provide personal information such as their name, e-mail address and interests.

Internet users who have not disabled the cookie function will find that their internet use can be tracked and a profile developed of them (without the collection of traditional identifiers) which is used in advertising to them later. The Information Commissioner advises that if the operator intends to link this profile to a name and postal address or even an e-mail address, there is no doubt that the profile information is personal data subject to the requirements of *DPA 1998*. The Commissioner is of the opinion that in the context of the online world 'the information that identifies an individual is that which uniquely locates him or her in that world, by distinguishing him or her from others. Thus profiles that are based on cookies and that are used to deliver targeted marketing messages to particular individuals are personal data.'

There are many different methods in which cookies are used in websites. The important legal issue is to ensure visitors know what is going on, for example by way of an online notification or in the privacy statement. Advice from the Office of the Information Commissioner is that 'if a notification provided via an online privacy statement is to be relied upon it is important that at least some reference to the use of tracking technology is clearly displayed to all site visitors.'

Profiling visitors 28.7

The position is the same if a profile of visitors is built up although it can be hard to use internet protocol (IP) addresses to build up personalised profiles. These are often dynamic so that each time a user connects to his or her Internet Service Provider (ISP) he or she is allocated an IP address. The Information Commissioner states that:

> 'This IP address will be different each time. Thus it is only the ISP that can link the IP address to an individual. It is hard to see how the collection of dynamic IP addresses without other identifying information would bring a website operator within the scope of the *Data Protection Act 1998*. Static IP addresses are different. As with cookies they can be linked to a particular computer which may actually or by assumption be linked to an individual user. If static IP addresses were to form the basis for profiles that are used to deliver targeted marketing messages to particular individuals they, and the profiles, would be personal data subject to the *Data Protection Act 1998*. However, it is not easy for a website operator to distinguish between dynamic and static IP addresses. Thus the scope for using IP addresses for personalised profiling is limited.'

If dynamic or static IP addresses are collected simply to analyse aggregate patterns of website use they are not necessarily personal data. They will only become personal data if the website operator has some means of linking IP addresses to a particular individual, perhaps through other information held or from information that is publicly available on the internet. ISPs will of course be able to make this link but the information they keep will not normally be available to a website operator.

Using Internet information: spiders etc. 28.8

One of the Information Commissioner's FAQs is whether information on the Internet can be used by people for their own purposes. The Commissioner advises that 'Website operators should exercise caution when obtaining personal data from a source other than the individual him or herself. It is by no means the case that the processing of personal data obtained via the Internet is free from restriction. Simply because individuals have put their e-mail addresses in the public domain, perhaps by participating in a chat-room, does not mean they can be used for marketing or other purposes. Those who use "spiders" or other scavenging type programmes to harvest e-mail addresses, or other personal data from the Internet, are likely to breach the Act unless the use they are making of the information is consistent with the purpose for which it was first made available. If e-mail marketing lists are used there is a responsibility to ensure that the personal data on the list were obtained fairly in the first place, bearing in mind the intended use of the list. The user of the list must also respect any relevant conditions put on its use by the source.'

Lots of data subjects, of course, put up often highly personal information on the Internet at their own option. They display pictures of their children (whether with or without the child's consent is not always clear) and give other details. The Information Commissioner advises that individuals should be wary of doing this. However this does not absolve others from ensuring the information is used fairly with regard to the purpose for which it was posted on the Internet.

Web bugs 28.9

Web bugs (see definition below) may be used as can similar software. However if they are invisible to the user it is hard to see how they can be used in compliance with *DPA 1998*.

The Commissioner says that 'individuals being monitored through the use of a web-bug or similar device should be informed that monitoring is taking place, who the monitoring is being performed by and for what purposes the monitoring is taking place. The Information Commissioner suggests that data controllers who intend to place a web-bug or similar device give the individual a simple means of refusing or disabling the device prior to any personal information being collected through it.'

> A web-bug is a graphics file, generally only 1 x 1 pixel in size, that is designed to monitor who is reading a web page or e-mail message. As with the use of a cookie the use of such a device may well result in personal data being processed.
>
> *IC FAQs – Internet June 2001*

FAQs 28.10

The Commissioner has issued the following additional Frequently Asked Questions relating to the Internet.

A: If we have collected information about someone other than directly from them, do we have to tell them that we have got it?

Where information is obtained from a third party, for example where one website operator obtains information about an individual from another website operator, there is still a duty to ensure that the subsequent processing of information about the individual is fair, i.e. that the individual is aware of such matters as the identity of the person or organisation that now holds the information and the purposes for which it is to be used. In some cases it may be possible for operators to inform individuals of the fact that information about them is to be obtained indirectly, and the purposes for which the data are to be used, before the data are obtained. This might be the case where the operator has already had contact with the individual, perhaps when he or she has registered with a website, and has informed him or her that there is an intention to obtain information from other sources. In other cases the source may already have provided a full explanation to the individual on behalf of the third party website operator. This might be the case where two operators routinely exchange information about individuals, and their respective fair processing notices explain this.

Where individuals do not have the information necessary to make the processing of personal data about them fair, operators should provide the necessary information as soon as is practicable. If there is an intention to disclose personal data, the explanation should certainly be provided no later than the time when the information is first disclosed.

The website operator does not have to contact the individual where it would involve "disproportionate effort" to do so. If an operator believes this to be the case it will have to ensure that it can provide the necessary explanation to any individual who asks for it. It must also keep a record of the reasons why it concluded that providing the information would involve disproportionate effort. Website operators should be aware that the ease by which explanations can be provided on-line, for example by the automated sending of an e-mail, means that the circumstances in which they can rely on this exemption are limited. However, the Commissioner would not normally seek to challenge a website operator's compliance with the Act if after obtaining a legitimate e-mail marketing list, the operator provided the necessary explanation with its first marketing approach rather than separately, as long as the first marketing approach came soon after the list was obtained.

B: Our website is directed at children. Are there any special rules that we have to follow?

Websites that collect information from children may have to put more rigorous safeguards in place to ensure the processing of those children's information is fair. Website operators should recognise that children generally have a lower level of understanding than adults and notices explaining the way their data will be used should be appropriate to this level of understanding and should not attempt to exploit any lack of understanding. The consent of a parent or guardian is necessary where a child is asked to provide personal data unless it is reasonable to believe the child clearly understands what is involved and is capable of making an informed decision.

The Act does not lay down a precise age at which a child can act in his/her own right and the Commissioner does not consider it is valid to try and do so. Much depends on the capacity of the child and the complexity of the proposition that is being put to him/her. As a general rule the Commissioner considers the standard adopted by Trust UK (www.trustuk.org.uk) in its accreditation criteria to be a reasonable one. This is that: "Personal data must only be collected from children with the explicit and verifiable consent of the child's parent/guardian unless that child is aged 12 years or over, the information collected is restricted to that necessary to enable the child to be sent further but limited on-line communications and it is clear that the child understands what is involved".

The above standard is based on the definition of a child as a person aged 16 years or under. There are certain practices that, if adopted, are likely to breach the requirements of the Act. These include collecting personal data relating to other people (for example parents) from children and enticing children to divulge personal data with the prospect of a game prize or similar inducement. If personal data collected from children are to be disclosed or transferred to third parties this should not take place without the explicit and verifiable consent of the child's parent/guardian unless it can be demonstrated that the child really appreciates what is going on and the consequences of his or her actions. Similarly, where a website operator wishes to publish personal data relating to a child on the Internet the verifiable consent of the child's parent/guardian should usually be obtained. Whether it is necessary to seek the parent or guardian's consent to publication, rather than that of the child, will again depend on the circumstances, in particular the age of the child, and whether or not the data controller can be certain that the child fully understands the implications of making their information available on the Internet. Where parental consent is required the website operator must have some way of verifying that this has been given. It will not usually be sufficient to simply ask children to confirm that their parents have agreed by means of a mouse click. It will in all likelihood be necessary to revert to postal communication. If parental consent is the required standard but the website operator concludes that the effort in verifying the consent is disproportionate, the proposed marketing activity or other course of action should not be pursued.

C: We collect personal information through our website. Do we have to use an encryption based transmission system?

A website operator is responsible for the security of its processing of personal data. It must adopt appropriate technical and organisational measures to protect the personal data. The processing of personal data includes its obtaining. A website operator is therefore required to obtain personal data in a way that is sufficiently secure. It is hard to see how this can be done without the use of a secure, encryption-based transmission system if the personal data are in any way sensitive or otherwise pose a risk to individuals, for example because they include credit card numbers.

Website operators should be aware that whilst the use of a secure, encryption-based transmission system will protect personal data whilst in transit, there is a potentially greater threat to the security of personal data once the data have been decrypted and they are held in unencrypted form on a website operator's server. Personal data that are in any way sensitive or otherwise pose a risk to individuals should not be held on a website server or, if they are, should be properly secured by encryption or similar techniques.

D: If we use another company to host our website who is responsible for data protection?

Responsibility for compliance with the Data Protection Act 1998 rests with the data controller, that is the person who determines the purposes for which and the manner in which the personal data are or are to be processed. This is likely to be the website operator rather than the host. A data controller does not have to own the equipment on which the processing actually takes place. A website operator that uses a separate processor, i.e. a person who processes personal data on the operator's behalf, must have a written contract with the processor under which the processor is required to act only on instructions from the website operator and to have in place appropriate technical and organisational security measures.

E: Can we publish personal data on our website?

The eighth principle of the Act states that personal data shall not be transferred outside the European Economic Area if the country to which the data are transferred does not ensure an adequate level of protection for the individual in each case. Placing personal data on the Internet potentially involves a transfer to any country worldwide. In many countries the processing of personal data is not protected by legislation so it will not always be possible for website providers to guarantee the protection of personal data placed on their website. However, all the circumstances of such a transfer can be taken into account when assessing the adequacy of protection provided for the data. In some cases the risks arising as a result of a transfer, even in the absence of protective legislation, may be negligible. This may be the case with information that is already in the public domain, for example publication of details of the sporting achievements of well known athletes. It may also be a relevant factor if the information published does not enable the individual to be contacted, although the sensitivity of the information will have to be taken into account. In other cases it will be necessary to obtain the individual's consent for their data to be published on the Internet. This consent must be 'informed', in that the website operator must explain the possible consequences of publishing the data. Consent must also be 'freely given' in that the individual must be able to decline without penalty.

Although likely to lead to similar conclusions, in most cases the general requirement of fairness in the processing of personal data must also be addressed when considering publication on a website. For example, a yacht club may have traditionally published the names and contact details of its members in a handbook distributed to all members and placed in local libraries. The club now intends to publish these details on its website.

Although the information has always been publicly available, the implications for members of publication on the web are significantly different. Fairness requires that the individuals concerned are told that there is an intention to publish information about them on the website and that the wishes of individuals who object are respected. If the intention is that information about the club's membership is only made available to other club members, the club should employ technical means to prevent access by unauthorised individuals, for example, by preventing general access to the site or to the part of the site where information about the club's members is published through the use of password protection.

F: If we want to use the personal data we have obtained through our website differently can we simply change our privacy statement?

The simple answer is no. Changing the privacy statement and other information on the site can only affect how you can use personal data that are obtained after the date of the change. Visitors who provided you with personal data prior to the change will have done so on the basis of the privacy statement and other information you provided at that time. You must honour the assurances you gave them.

If you want to use the personal data differently the safest course of action is to obtain your customers' consent to the new use. In other words you must explain the proposed new use to them and only proceed when they have given you a positive indication of their agreement. Failure to respond to an e-mail message would not be sufficient. This is sometimes referred to as 'opt-in'. The opt-in approach will be necessary if the data you have obtained are to be used by you or others for a new purpose or are to be disclosed either for the first time or to different organisations from those referred to in your privacy statement. It will also be necessary if the personal data are sensitive or if they are subject to a duty of confidentiality which would be breached by the new use.

In some cases it will be sufficient to advise your customers of the new use and to give them an opportunity to object. This will be the case if the new use does not amount to use for a new purpose or where the nature and purpose of a new disclosure remains close to the terms described in the privacy statement. For example, your site was originally set up to sell books, your customers were advised only that you would use their information for marketing and they were given an opportunity to opt-out. In the absence of any indication to the contrary they would have assumed your marketing was confined to books. You are now expanding into the sale of CDs and want to market these. As this activity is close to but nevertheless outside the terms of your original privacy statement, you should at least advise those customers that did not opt-out originally of the new use and give them another opportunity to opt-out, either from all marketing or from the marketing of CDs. Those customers that opted out originally should not be contacted. If in the above example the new marketing is of financial services or holidays, for example, or if customer details are to be provided to a third party for their marketing, the standard has to be opt-in. This will certainly be the case if, for the first time and with no previous explanation the marketing is to be based on a profile of the individual's book buying habits.

In other cases the new use might fall within the original privacy statement. For example, the privacy statement might have referred to the intention to market a range of products even though at the time this was confined to books. Now it will include CDs. There is no need to advise customers specifically of this as the products are sufficiently closely related. Clearly the wishes of any customers that subsequently object to the receipt of the new marketing message should be respected.

If the new products are substantially different, for example if they now include financial services, the marketing of these would not have been within customers' expectations even though arguably the privacy statement might have covered it. It is the interpretation customers are likely to have placed on the privacy statement rather than its precise wording that is important. Depending on how far removed from this likely interpretation the new use is, the standard may be opt-in rather than opt-out.

G: Can we disclose personal data if our web-based company is subject to a take-over or merger?

The Act would not necessarily prevent this. Essentially the position on disclosure is no different simply because a web-based company goes out of business or is otherwise subject to a take-over or merger. A disclosure could breach the Act where individuals have previously been assured that personal data about them will not be disclosed, where the personal data are subject to a duty of confidentiality or where once disclosed the personal data are processed in a manner that has a markedly different effect on individuals. In such cases the consent of individuals will be required before the disclosure takes place. Before making a disclosure of personal data careful consideration should be given as to how the data were originally obtained. If a disclosure is to take place, in order to prevent unfairness to individuals it may be necessary to place restrictions on the purposes for which and the manner in which the data may be processed. So long as individuals were not led to believe their data would never be disclosed, the new owner in effect takes over the existing business and the personal data will be used in substantially the same way as previously. The Act is likely to be satisfied if individuals are told of the change of ownership and have an opportunity to object to the new owner holding their details.

H: Do we have to notify the commissioner if we put personal data on our website or obtain personal data through it?

Website operators who are established in the UK and who process personal data will need to notify the Commissioner unless exempt. Failure to notify is a criminal offence for those required to do so. There are conditional exemptions from notification where personal data are only processed for certain core business purposes. These include advertising and marketing your own business and keeping accounts and records. The exemptions will not necessarily be lost because personal data are obtained through a website or used for marketing by electronic means. They are more likely to be lost through publishing personal data on a website.

Many website operators will need to notify under the Act. You should visit www.dpr.gov.uk for more information about this and to notify. The current fee for notification is £35 for one year.

I: Does the Data Protection Act 1998 apply if our website is operated outside the UK?

Website operators not established in the UK but established elsewhere within the European Economic Area (EEA) will be subject to the data protection laws of the countries where they are established. In some circumstances website operators established outside the EEA might be subject to UK data protection law. If a website operator established outside the EEA uses equipment in the United Kingdom to process personal data, the processing will be subject to the Act even though the operator is not established in the UK. This might be the case where the operator's site is hosted in the UK or where the operator places a 'cookie' on the computer of a UK internet user in order to create a profile of that individual's on-line behaviour.

J: What is the position if i only use my website for domestic purposes?
Where personal data are processed only for an individual's personal, family or household affairs, including recreational purposes, the data are exempt from the Act's notification requirements and from the requirements of the data protection principles. However, the Information Commissioner retains her powers of investigation and enforcement to determine whether the scope of the exemption has been exceeded, for example because the site is also used for business purposes.

Commissioner's Guidance 28.11

The IC has issued some general guidance for data controllers and separately for data subjects which is reproduced with permission below.

Internet: Protection of Privacy-Data Controllers
In using the Internet for their business dealings, data controllers must take into account the privacy rights of individuals and their own responsibilities under privacy and data protection legislation. The following points should be considered by data controllers in planning their Internet strategies.

Personal data placed on the Internet is available world-wide. In many countries the use of personal data is not protected by legislation. Because of this it is always advisable and will often be essential to obtain consent from individuals before publishing their personal data on your website.

When collecting information via the Internet always inform the user of who you are, what personal data you are collecting, processing and storing and for what purpose. Do this before a user gives you *any* information, when they visit your site and wherever they are asked to provide information, for example via an on-line application form. It is good practice to ask for consent for the collection of all data and it is usually essential to get consent if you want to process sensitive personal data.

It is good practice for a data controller who sets up a website to provide a statement of its privacy policy. A 'privacy statement' helps individuals to decide whether or not to visit a site and, when they do visit, whether or not to provide any personal information to the data controller.

Always let individuals know when you intend to use 'Cookies' or other covert software to collect information about them.

Never collect or retain personal data unless it is strictly necessary for your purposes. For example you should not require a person's name and full address to provide an on-line quotation. If extra information is required for marketing purposes this should be made clear and the provision of the information should be optional.

Design your systems in such a way as to avoid or minimise the use of personal data.

Upon a user's request you should correct, change or delete inaccurate details. If information is altered notify the third parties to whom the original information was communicated. Regularly delete data which is out of date or no longer required.

Stop processing data if the user objects to it because the processing is causing them damage or distress.

Only use personal data collected on-line for marketing purposes where the user has already been told that his or her information was to be used in this way. If a user asks you to stop using his or her data for marketing purposes you must do so and the individual should always be given the opportunity to opt of the use of his or her data for marketing. It is also good practice to get the individual's consent before using their information for marketing. It will always be necessary to get their consent where if the data is sensitive.

Use the most up-to-date technologies to protect the personal data collected or stored on your site. Especially sensitive or valuable information, such as financial details should be protected by reliable encryption technologies.

Internet: Protection of Privacy – Data Subjects

It is easy to see and understand the benefits the Internet offers individuals, allowing immediate access to global information and markets and facilitating direct global communications. It is however worth remembering a few points:

The Internet is not secure. There is a risk that information provided over the Internet might be intercepted by people you wouldn't want to read it.

Information you provide to a website or send via e-mail may be made available anywhere in the world and may not be protected by data protection legislation.

Never provide information on-line unless you are confident you know what the website intends to use the information for.

Is more information being collected than is absolutely necessary? Be aware of this when accessing a site or making a transaction, especially if it not clear why this additional information is being requested. Don't be afraid to ask. Just because you are asked a question doesn't mean you have to answer it.

Show caution with your credit card and account numbers, for example, are your details security protected? Remember your information can be used and abused.

The best way to protect your privacy when using services over the Internet is to avoid giving your name or other personal details out over the Internet. If anonymity is impractical you may use a pseudonym (if permitted by law) so that only yourself and your ISP (Internet Service Provider) know your personal identity, for example when signing on to use a chatroom

Information may be collected from you on the Internet without your knowledge. Your ISP will have access to a lot of detailed information relating to you. Always choose a reliable ISP. Enquire what data they collect, process and store, in what way and for what purpose. Do this periodically. If you want to know what information your ISP or any other service or website provider (based in the European Economic Area) holds about you can make a subject access request.

Websites you visit may also implant software known as 'cookies' on your machine. Some of these cookies serve a useful purpose, for example they can be used to facilitate on line 'shopping baskets but some are used to track your movements on the Internet. Check your 'Cookie' files and consider deleting those you do not want.

E-mail addresses are personal data. If you find yourself on a directory or user list you can request to be omitted from it.

You can also ask not to be sent 'junk e-mail or SPAM' and where the sender is based in the EEA they should comply with your request.

Consider using reliable encryption techniques for confidential e-mail

Try and keep up to date with the latest privacy and security risks on the Internet. Try the Internet search engine facilities using the words 'privacy' and 'security'.

All guidance is current at the date of this book but is updated from time to time, and reference should always ideally be made to the website of the Information Commissioner at www.dataprotection.gov.uk

Further information 28.12

See also CHAPTER 15 E-MAILS, CHAPTER 20 LAWFUL BUSINESS PRACTICE REGULATIONS and CHAPTER 40 REGULATION OF INVESTIGATORY POWERS ACT 2000.

For privacy policies see CHAPTER 37 PRIVACY POLICIES.

More information on the padlock symbol is available on the Information Commissioner's website under News and Events at www.dataprotection.gov.uk.

For information on employment and data protection issues, see the Information Commissioner's Draft Code of Practice on the Use of Personal Data in Employer/Employee Relationships, which when reissued may be known as the HR Code of Practice. The provisional timetable for this Code at the time of writing is that it will be amended and released in four stages:

- recruitment and selection (published by 30 November 2001);
- general records maintenance (end of December 2001);
- monitoring (January 2002); and
- testing (March/April 2002).

29 – Lawful Business Practice Regulations

At a glance **29.1**

- ✓ The *Telecommunications (Lawful Business Practice) (Interception of Communications) Regulations 2000* (*SI 2000/2699*) are made under the *Regulation of Investigatory Powers Act 2000* (*RIPA 2000*).
- ✓ The Regulations permit interception of e-mails and telephone calls by employers and others without consent for a vast range of purposes.
- ✓ In addition, compliance with the *Data Protection Act 1998* (*DPA 1998*) must be achieved.
- ✓ The Information Commissioner's Draft Code of Practice on the Use of Personal Data in Employer/Employee Relationships addresses these issues in relation to the employment aspects (see CHAPTER 16 EMPLOYMENT).

Introduction **29.2**

The *Telecommunications (Lawful Business Practice) (Interception of Communications) Regulations 2000* (*SI 2000/2699*) came into force on 24 October 2000 under *RIPA 2000*. *RIPA 2000* is considered in CHAPTER 40 REGULATION OF INVESTIGATORY POWERS ACT 2000. Recording of telephone calls and e-mails is also considered in CHAPTER 38 RECORDING TELEPHONE CALLS AND E-MAILS, CHAPTER 15 E-MAILS, CHAPTER 16 EMPLOYMENT are also relevant in this field.

What the Regulations do **29.3**

The *Lawful Business Practice Regulations* (*SI 2000/2699*) authorise businesses to monitor or record communications on their telecommunications systems *without consent* for the purposes set out below. These cover most of the reasons why employers might want to intercept communications, except perhaps snooping on employees' personal relationships.

However, people must be notified of the surveillance and this includes both employees and third parties sending e-mails to a business. This can easily be achieved in an employment contract, staff handbook or e-mail to members of staff. Interception without consent is permitted for the following reasons under the Regulations:

- to establish the existence of facts relevant to the business (e.g. keeping records of transactions and other communications in cases where it is necessary or desirable to know the specific facts of the conversation);
- to ascertain compliance with regulatory or self-regulatory practices or procedures relevant to the business (e.g. monitoring as a means to check that the business is complying with regulatory or self-regulatory rules or guidelines);
- to ascertain or demonstrate standards which are or ought to be achieved by persons using the telecoms system (e.g. monitoring for purposes of quality control or staff training);
- to prevent or detect crime (e.g. monitoring or recording to detect fraud or corruption);
- to investigate or detect the unauthorised use of the telecoms systems (e.g. monitoring to ensure that employees do not breach company rules regarding use of the telecoms system); and
- to ensure the effective operation of the system (e.g. monitoring for viruses or other threats to the system; automated processes such as caching or load distribution).

The Regulations also authorise businesses to monitor (but not record) without consent in the following cases:

- for the purpose of determining whether or not they are communications relevant to the business (e.g. checking e-mail accounts to access business communications in staff absence); and
- in the case of communications to a confidential anonymous counselling or support helpline (e.g. monitoring calls to confidential welfare helplines in order to protect or support helpline staff).

Staff whose communications may be intercepted without their consent should be told, according to the Department of Trade and Industry, who state:

> 'Businesses could place a note in staff contracts or in other readily available literature informing staff that interceptions may take place. The persons who use a system are the people

who make direct use of it. Someone who calls from outside, or who receives a call outside, using another system is not a user of the system on which the interception is made.'

Interceptions outside the Regulations 29.4

Some interceptions will be outside the scope of the *Lawful Business Practice Regulations* (*SI 2000/2699*). In those cases business must obtain consent of the sender and recipient.

Examples given by the Department of Trade and Industry (DTI) are:

- interceptions for purposes such as marketing or market research; and
- interceptions for any other purposes that fall outside the list described above.

The types of steps businesses can take to gain consent of staff and others are:

- the business could insert a clause in staff contracts by which employees consent to calls being monitored or recorded;
- the call operator could ask outsiders at the start of a call whether they consented to their call being monitored or recorded; and/or
- the business could begin calls with a recorded message stating that calls might be monitored or recorded unless outsiders requested otherwise.

The DTI believes that, as a minimum, a business would need to give outsiders a clear opportunity to refuse consent to interception and to be able to continue with the call.

Overlap with DPA 1998 29.5

Consideration should be given to *DPA 1998*. If the interceptions involve obtaining, recording or otherwise processing personal data by means of automated equipment (for example recording calls or filtering e-mails) it also falls within the scope of *DPA 1998*. So too does the holding or processing of personal data after the interception has taken place.

The *Lawful Business Practice Regulations* (*SI 2000/2699*) also specifically state that compliance must be achieved with *DPA 1998*. The Information Commissioner's Draft Code of Practice on the Use of Personal Data in Employer/Employee Relationships examines such interception in the context of employment relationships and advocates data controllers taking the least intrusive surveillance method possible to achieve their objective, in order to ensure compliance with *DPA 1998*. This is considered in CHAPTER 15 E-MAILS and CHAPTER 16 EMPLOYEES.

Further information 29.6

A copy of the *Telecommunications (Lawful Business Practice) (Interception of Communications) Regulations 2000* (*SI 2000/2699*) is on the HMSO website, www.hmso.gov.uk, under Statutory Instruments 2000.

30 – Manual Records

At a glance 30.1

- ✓ The *Data Protection Act 1998* (*DPA 1998*) applies to manual records which form part of a structured set.
- ✓ A first transitional period for certain such manual records expired on 23 October 2001 after which time subject access requests for all such records became available.
- ✓ The precise meaning of 'manual records' is not always clear.

Introduction 30.2

The *Data Protection Act 1984* (*DPA 1984*) applied only to data on computer systems. *DPA 1998* also applies to certain, but not all, manual data. This chapter examines what is caught. *DPA 1998* has applied to such data since it came into force on 1 March 2000. However, some businesses had manual data in relation to which processing was already underway on 24 October 1998 (the date when the EU *Data Protection Directive* (*95/46/EC*) should have been implemented). For those businesses the right of subject access to that manual data did not apply until three years later when the first transitional period under *DPA 1998* expired on 24 October 2001.

Types of manual data caught 30.3

The legislation applies to information 'recorded as part of a relevant filing system or with the intention that it should form part of a relevant filing system' (*DPA 1998, s 1(1)(c)*).

Relevant filing system means any 'set of information relating to individuals to the extent that…the set is structured, either by reference to individuals or by reference to criteria relating to individuals, in such a way that specific information relating to a particular individual is readily accessible' (*s 1(1), DPA 1998*). In the *Data Protection Directive (95/46/EC)* a 'personal data filing system' is defined as 'any structured set of personal data which are accessible according to specific criteria, whether centralised, decentralised or dispersed on a functional or geographical basis'. It also provides that the scope of protection of individuals does not cover 'unstructured files'.

Examples 30.4

Examples of manual data given by the Information Commissioner are:

- employees' filing cabinets in their rooms;
- employees' work address books and diaries;
- wall charts;
- rotas and rosters;
- black and white boards;
- rolodex systems;
- card indexes or records; and
- non-automated microfiches (and other microfiches too which were always covered).

Businesses should ideally have completed an audit of their manual records to ascertain what is held within their organisation and where. If they have not done so to date they should undertake this as a matter or urgency.

Sets 30.5

Data controllers need to assess whether the manual documents they hold are part of sets or not. Sets might be sets of information about customers or employees, but need not be in files. Information dispersed around branches or between home workers could still fall within the margins of *DPA 1998*. Therefore, businesses which have staff working from home will need to ensure any auditing also includes information at those locations. For the Information Commissioner's guidance as to the definition of sets of manual data, see 30.8 below.

However, in many cases some manual information will not be part of a structured set and thus is outside *DPA 1998*. The provisions in *DPA 1998*, as an examination of relevant passages in Hansard reporting on the Parliamentary debates as the Bill went through show, were created to achieve a compromise and exclude on practical grounds manual records in which personal data was not readily accessible, so that businesses would not have to hunt through unstructured files looking for data.

Criteria 30.6

The Commissioner says that the criteria may be a reference to the individuals themselves, such as their name or a reference number, or it could be in relation to criteria about the individuals. Examples include:

- age;
- sickness record;
- type of job;
- credit history;
- shopping habits;
- entitlement to particular benefits; and
- membership of particular organisations.

The information must be specific about that individual, rather than being all of the information about that person. Separately it must be readily accessible.

Paper files 30.7

Transitional arrangements will exempt manual records held in a 'relevant filing system' before 24 October 1998 from full compliance until 2007. However, the right of subject access to information held in paper files covered by *DPA 1998* is available from 24 October 2001 regardless of the date from which the information was held.

Commissioner's guidance 30.8

In October 2001 the Information Commissioner issued her *Legal Guidance* on *DPA 1998* which addresses manual data.

The advice in that guidance is that data controllers should examine all their non-automated information systems in order to determine how far *DPA 1998* applies to personal data processed in those systems. The Information Commissioner states:

> 'It is not wholly clear how this definition translates in practical terms in all conceivable situations. The Commissioner can only give general guidance; the final decision in cases of dispute is a question for the Courts. Whether or not manual information falls within this definition will be a matter of fact in each case. It is not possible for the Commissioner to state categorically whether or not certain types of information or files are caught by *DPA 1998* although it is recognised that there are certain areas of business where

the question of whether manual information falls within the definition will be of particular significance, e.g. personnel files. In deciding whether manual information falls within the definition, data controllers should consider the following:

- There must be a set of information about individuals. The word "set" suggests a grouping together of things by reference to a distinct identifier i.e. a set of information with a common theme or element. Examples might include a set of information on customers or employees. Sets of information about individuals need not necessarily be grouped together in a file or files. They may be grouped together in some other way, for example, by prefix codes, or by attaching an identifying sticker within a file or files. Similarly, the information does not necessarily have to be grouped together in the same drawer of the filing cabinet or the same filing cabinet; nor does it necessarily have to be maintained centrally by an organisation. The set of information might be dispersed over different locations within the organisation, for example, different departments, branch offices, or via home workers.

- The set of information must be structured in such a way that specific information about a particular individual is readily accessible. What does or does not amount to such specific information will be a matter of fact in each individual case. *DPA 1998* does not define what is meant by "readily accessible". In deciding whether or not it is readily accessible, a suggested approach is to assume that a set or sets of manual information which are referenced to individuals (or criteria relating to individuals), are caught by *DPA 1998* if they are, as matter of fact, generally accessible at any time to one or more people within the data controller's organisation in connection with the day to day operation of that organisation.

In practice, data controllers may find that their manual files consist partly of information which forms, or is intended to form, part of a "relevant filing system", and partly of information which does not. It is essential for data controllers to keep in mind that it is the information and the ease with which it may be located which they should assess rather than whether it is in itself a file or filing system. In other words a file is not synonymous with "relevant filing system". Manual information which forms part of clearly highly structured files, for example, card indexes or records, is likely to fall within the definition.

The Commissioner recognises that data controllers may find that there are grey areas in determining whether or not certain manual information is subject to the requirements of *DPA 1998*. It is suggested that in those cases where data controllers are unsure whether or not manual information comes within the definition of data/"relevant filing system" they should evaluate how accessible the data are by making reasoned judgements. Data controllers should consider whether or not and, if so, the extent to which, a decision not to treat the information as being covered by *DPA 1998* will prejudice the individual concerned. Where the risk of prejudice is reasonably likely then data controllers would be expected to err on the side of caution and take steps to ensure compliance. Whether the Commissioner decides to enforce any particular case does not affect the rights of individuals to seek redress from the Courts under *DPA 1998* on the basis of a different or wider interpretation of "relevant filing system".

Where manual information falls within the definition, data controllers may not have to comply with the requirements of *DPA 1998* in full immediately as transitional relief may apply Where the data controller does not qualify for transitional relief manual data should have been processed in compliance with *DPA 1998* from 1 March 2000.'

The second transitional period 30.9

From 24 October 2001 to 23 October 2007 a very limited exception applies to manual data that was being processed at 24 October 1998. This also covers credit reference agency records and accessible records. This does not apply where manual data are added on or after 24 October 1998. The Commissioner says 'Note that the important consideration here is the date of creation of the record itself rather than the date when the overall processing operation began. Data subjects will have rights of access to their files; data must be fairly processed, kept securely and not transferred outside the European Economic Area unless there are adequate safeguards. However other provisions, particularly those relating to data quality (Principles 2–5) do not come fully into force until the end of this period.'

Action 30.10

The following action is recommended.

- Audit manual records and list what is found.
- Ensure the audit covers data held off site (such as at home workers' homes) as well as on site.
- Ensure all employees know the right of subject access will now apply to all manual data which falls within *DPA 1998*.
- Prepare for subject access requests relating to information held in manual data.

Further information 30.11

The Information Commissioner's Guidance is on the Data Protection website at www.dataprotection.gov.uk.

31 – Marketing

At a glance 31.1

- ✓ Many forms of marketing have data protection implications.
- ✓ Individuals have a right under *section 11* of the *Data Protection Act 1998* (*DPA 1998*) to prevent the processing of their personal data for direct marketing purposes.
- ✓ Data must be fairly processed in accordance with *Schedule 2* to *DPA 1998*.
- ✓ Marketing to employees must be handled with particular care.

Introduction 31.2

The process of marketing involves substantial amounts of personal data in most cases. Thus marketing must be approached with great care to ensure that the requirements of *DPA 1998* are met. (See also CHAPTER 12 DIRECT MAIL, CHAPTER 13 DIRECT MARKETING and CHAPTER 33 OPT-IN AND OPT-OUT.) However, many other forms of marketing exist which may have data protection implications. Where marketing is done via the Internet, reference should be made to CHAPTER 28 INTERNET, and in particular to the Information Commissioner's guidance in this field.

Right to prevent processing for purposes of direct marketing 31.3

Under *section 11* of *DPA 1998* an individual can, by written notice, require a data controller to cease, or not to begin, processing his personal data for the purpose of direct marketing. When a data controller receives such a notice, he must comply as soon as he can. There are no exceptions to this under *DPA 1998*. The data subject may apply to court for an order if the data controller fails to comply with the notice.

'Direct marketing' is defined in *DPA 1998* for the purposes of this provision as meaning the communication, by whatever means, of any advertising or marketing material which is directed to particular individuals. In her Legal Guidance (October 2001) the Commissioner says that she regards the term 'direct marketing' as covering a wide range of activities, applying not just to the offer for sale of goods or services, but also to the promotion of an organisation's aims and ideals.

Preference services 31.4

An individual who wishes to prevent personally addressed marketing material being sent to him may register with the Mailing Preference Service. Contact details for the Mailing Preference Service can be found at 31.10 below.

Uninvited telesales calls and uninvited telemarketing faxes can be prevented by registering with the Telephone Preference Service on 0845 070 0707 and the Fax Preference Service on 0845 070 0702. CHAPTER 12 DIRECT MAIL and CHAPTER 13 DIRECT MARKETING contain further information on this area.

Fair processing 31.5

Under the First Data Protection Principle (see CHAPTER 21 FAIR PROCESSING) data must be processed fairly and lawfully. Under *Schedule 2* to *DPA 1998* this is shown for data which is not sensitive personal data where:

(*a*) the data subject has given his consent to the processing;

(*b*) the processing is necessary:

- (i) for the performance of a contract to which the data subject is a party; or
- (ii) for the taking of steps at the request of the data subject with a view to entering into a contract,

(*c*) the processing is necessary to comply with any legal obligation to which the data controller is subject, other than an obligation imposed by contract; or

(*d*) the processing is necessary in order to protect the vital interests of the data subject.

In most cases consent is the key issue. Consent is addressed in CHAPTER 33 OPT-IN AND OPT-OUT. Sensitive personal data is deal with in CHAPTER 42 SENSITIVE PERSONAL DATA.

Marketing to employees 31.6

Some employers distribute marketing material to their employees to sell them goods or services, or give them details of third parties' goods or services such as insurance and charities. The Information Commissioner in her Draft Code of Practice on the Use of Personal Data in Employer/Employee Relationships says that marketing includes the promotion of aims and ideals as well as goods and services, and that employees have a right not to have their data used for this purpose. She proposes the following standards.

Standards 31.7

- Inform employees if you intend to use their personal information in order to deliver marketing messages to them (Principle 1).
- If only basic information, e.g. name and work location, is used and there is no disclosure to other organisations, give employees a clear opportunity to object and respect any objections whenever received (Principles 1 and 6).
- If more detailed information, e.g. trades union membership or sickness record, is used or there is disclosure, do not proceed until individual employers have positively indicated their agreement (Principles 1 and 6).

Marketing using employees' personal data 31.8

Sometimes employees' personal data will appear in the marketing literature of the employer such as pictures of members of staff on a web site or in a brochure. The IC proposes the following standards in this field.

Standards 31.9

- Do not publish information about employees unless:
  - there is a legal obligation to do so;
  - the information is not intrusive and, taking into account the nature of the employer's business and the position held by the employee, publication would be expected; or
  - the employee has consented (Principle 1).

- If information is published with consent, ensure the employee is aware of the extent of information that will be published and how it will be published, including whether the information will be published on a website and the implications of this (Principle 1).

Further information 31.10

See also CHAPTER 12 DIRECT MAIL and CHAPTER 13 DIRECT MARKETING.

See CHAPTER 28 INTERNET for Internet marketing.

Opting-in and opting-out are addressed in CHAPTER 33 OPT-IN AND OPT-OUT.

Sensitive personal data are addressed in CHAPTER 42 SENSITIVE PERSONAL DATA and fair processing in CHAPTER 21 FAIR PROCESSING.

Mailing Preference Service
FREEPOST 22
London
W1E 7EZ
Tel: 020 7766 4410.

The Direct Marketing Association (UK) Ltd's Guide to the DPA for Direct Marketers is available from www.dma.org.uk and costs £75 (members) and £150 (non-members).

32 – Offences

At a glance

32.1

- ✓ Many offences are created by the *Data Protection Act 1998* (*DPA 1998*).
- ✓ In some circumstances individuals such as directors and company secretaries can be prosecuted for breach of the legislation.
- ✓ A specific offence of unlawfully selling personal data is also created.
- ✓ Enforced subject access is also an offence.

Introduction

32.2

The enforcement of the *Data Protection Act 1984* (*DPA 1984*) was characterised by the 'softly softly' approach of the Data Protection Registrar. Prosecutions were few and fines low. Although introducing more offences, *DPA 1998* is unlikely to result in a huge change to that approach. The Information Commissioner still principally intends to educate companies, and enforcement proceedings have so far been few.

Fines of up to £5000 can be imposed, and this is likely to be per offence, so if high deterrent damages were to be awarded then the £5,000 fines could be cumulated. However, in the Commissioner's First Annual Report (June 2001), the Commissioner's fines displayed in that report tended to be around £1,000–£3000.

It must be remembered that offences bring bad publicity for commercial companies. An even greater cost can the obligation to change their practices to comply with the legislation. Therefore companies must take the obligations imposed under *DPA 1998* seriously.

Criminal offences

32.3

DPA 1998 includes various criminal offences which can be prosecuted by the Information Commissioner or by the Director of Public Prosecutions. Special rules apply in Scotland and Northern Ireland.

Someone accused of the offences of:

- intentionally obstructing a person in the execution of a search warrant issued in accordance with *DPA 1998*; or
- failing without reasonable excuse to give any person executing such a warrant such assistance as he may reasonably require for the execution of the warrant,

cannot elect a Crown Court trial and will be tried in the Magistrates' Court, or the Sheriff Court of Scotland.

In her Legal Guidance (October 2001), the Information Commissioner says that if someone is found guilty of one of the above offences, then the court can impose a fine not exceeding Level 5 on the standard scale of fines contained in the *Criminal Justice Act 1982* (as amended) and the *Criminal Procedure (Scotland) Act 1995*, which is at present £5,000.

All other offences under *DPA 1998* can be tried either way:

- in England and Wales either in the Magistrates' Court (summary trial) or the Crown Court (on indictment); or
- in Scotland on indictment in the Sheriff Court or High Court of Justiciary.

A person found guilty of any of these offences can be sentenced on summary conviction to a fine not exceeding the statutory maximum, which is currently £5,000, or upon conviction on indictment to an unlimited fine.

Strict liability 32.4

Liability without fault, that is without the usual *mens rea* or knowledge needed for criminal offences, exists for the offences of:

- processing without notification;
- processing before the expiry of the assessable processing time limits; and
- enforced subject access.

On conviction the court may order any data apparently connected with the crime to be forfeited, destroyed or erased. Anyone other than the offender who claims to own the material may apply to the court that such an order should not be made.

Personal liability 32.5

An important issue for companies is the extent to which individuals can be personally liable for an offence under *DPA 1998*. Many personnel and human resources managers who are charged with achieving data protection compliance, and who are wrestling to ensure their departments are given sufficient resources in this field, will find it helpful to show their finance and other directors that personal liability can attach to individuals. Such liability may arise unless sufficient resources are devoted to data protection to ensure that *DPA 1998* is less likely to be breached.

Under *section 61* of *DPA 1998*, if a company commits a criminal offence under the Act, any director, manager, secretary or similar officer, or someone purporting to act in any such capacity, is personally guilty of the offence in addition to the corporate body if:

- the offence was committed with their consent or connivance; or
- the offence is attributable to any neglect on their part.

Where the affairs of a corporate body are managed by its members, any member who exercises the functions of management as if he were a director can also be guilty of the offence that results from any of their acts or omissions.

Government liability 32.6

Much personal data is handled by state bodies. Their liability must also be considered. In her Legal Guidance the Information Commissioner states that Government departments are not liable to prosecution under *DPA 1998*. However, individual civil servants may be prosecuted if they are believed to be personally guilty of an offence under *section 55* of *DPA 1998,* which covers the unlawful obtaining or disclosure of personal data, or believed to be obstructing or failing to assist in the execution of a warrant issued in accordance with the Act (*DPA 1998, Sch 9, para 12*).

Offences 32.7

The offences included in *DPA 1998* are:

(*a*) processing without notification (*DPA 1998, s 21(1)*);

(*b*) failure to notify the Commissioner of changes to the notification register entry (*DPA 1998, s 21(2)*);

(*c*) processing before expiry of assessable processing time limits or receipt of assessable processing notice within such time (*DPA 1998, s 22(6)*);

(*d*) failure to comply with written request for particulars (*DPA 1998, s 24*);

(*e*) failure to comply with an enforcement notice, information notice or special information notice (*DPA 1998, s 47(1)*);

(*f*) knowingly or recklessly making a false statement in compliance with an information notice or special information notice (*DPA 1998, s 47(2)*);

(*g*) intentional obstruction of, or failure to give reasonable assistance in, execution of a warrant (*DPA 1998, Sch 9*).

(*h*) unlawful obtaining etc., of personal data (*DPA 1998, s 55(1)*); there is a defence to this offence if the person can show:

(i) that the obtaining, disclosing or procuring of the data:

- was necessary to prevent or detect crime; or
- was required or authorised by law;

(ii) that he acted in the reasonable belief that he had the legal right to obtain, disclose or procure the disclosure;

(iii) that he acted in the reasonable belief that the data controller would have consented to the obtaining, disclosing or procuring if the data controller had known; or

(iv) that in the particular circumstances the obtaining, disclosing or procuring was justified as being in the public interest.

Where employees use data belonging to their employer for personal or unrelated purposes outside their job, then they commit offences if they use their position to obtain, disclose, or procure the disclosure of personal data for their own purposes. Examples of individuals who have misused data in this way in the Commissioner's First Annual Report (June 2001).

Unlawful selling 32.8

It is an offence for someone who obtains data in breach of *section 55(1)* of *DPA 1998* to then sell that data. Advertising data for sale is counted as offering it for sale.

Enforced subject access 32.9

Under *section 56* of *DPA 1998* it is an offence to require someone to exercise their right of subject access unless an exception applies (see 32.10 below).

Section 56 of *DPA 1998* states that:

> 'A person must not, in connection with:

(a) the recruitment of another person as an employee;

(b) the continued employment of another person; or

(c) any contract for the provision of services to him by another person,

require that other person or a third party to supply him with a relevant record or to produce a relevant record to him.'

Statutory exceptions 32.10

The statutory exceptions to liability for the offences set out at 32.7 above are:

(a) that the imposition of the requirement was required or authorised by law; or

(b) that in the particular circumstances the imposition of the requirements was justified as being in the public interest.

DPA 1998 provides that the imposition of the requirement is not to be regarded as being justified in the public interest on the ground that it would assist in the prevention or detection of crime.

The Information Commissioner says that 'The term "relevant record" is defined in *section 56* of *DPA 1998* by reference to a table which lists data controllers and the subject matter of subject access requests that may be made to them by data subjects. Generally, the term relates to records of cautions, criminal convictions and to certain social security records relating to the data subject.'

Section 56 of *DPA 1998* does not come into force until the Criminal Records Bureau is up and running, which is likely to be in 2002. The Commissioner says that the 'practice of requiring subject access may still breach other provisions of the Act, or the *Human Rights Act 1998* or the *Rehabilitation of Offenders Act 1974*.'

Disclosure by the Commissioner 32.11

CHAPTER 4 COMMISSIONER examined *section 59* of *DPA 1998*, which makes it an offence for the Commissioner or her staff to disclose information. Some of the provisions of *section 59* appear to curb the Commissioner's power too much and she has suggested the provisions be modified.

Further information 32.12

CHAPTER 4 COMMISSIONER deals with compensation, damages and prevention of processing,

Criminal issues are covered in CHAPTER 8 CRIME which includes a summary of the prosecutions in the First Annual Report of the Information Commissioner (June 2001).

The powers of the Commissioner are covered in CHAPTER 3 CODES OF PRACTICE.

Enforcement remedies and powers are addressed in CHAPTER 17 ENFORCEMENT, REMEDIES AND POWERS.

33 – Opt-in and Opt-out

At a glance 33.1

- ✓ Data subjects must in many cases consent to the processing of their personal data.
- ✓ Consent can be obtained on forms and one difficult question is whether opting-in or opting-out is required.
- ✓ The safest course is opting-out and this will normally be required at least where sensitive personal data is concerned.
- ✓ The decision in *Brian Robertson v Wakefield City Council (High Court, 16 November 2001)* held that current use of electoral registers for commercial purposes breached the *Human Rights Act 1998* (*HRA 1998*), and that the UK had not properly implemented the *EU Data Protection Directive* (*95/46/EC*) in this regard.

Introduction 33.2

The *Data Protection Act 1998* (*DPA 1998*) requires that data subjects must in many cases consent to the processing of their data (see CHAPTER 21 FAIR PROCESSING). For sensitive personal data explicit consent is required (see CHAPTER 42 SENSITIVE PERSONAL DATA). Here consideration is given to ordinary personal data which does not fall into that category. For such data the issue is whether 'consent' has been given or not.

Many people will be familiar with the box one ticks when filling in forms to 'opt-out' of personal data being used for other purposes. Some companies now use an 'opt-in' box, to be ticked if the user consents to their personal data being so used. *DPA 1998* is not entirely clear as to which is legally required. If there is a lot of money at stake, which will be lost by not having personal data freely useable, then it is advisable for companies to remain using an opting-out method. In practice, data subjects will often do nothing – thus when opting out is used the data controller can use the data for other purposes. If opting-in is chosen, and again the data subject does nothing, then the data cannot be used.

However, for those clients who want to be entirely sure they comply with *DPA 1998* and there is little financial loss likely to ensure from a failure of individuals to opt in, then the safest course to achieve compliance with the legislation will be to change to opting-in. Those companies wanting to appear a standard bearer for good practice and privacy will also want for obvious reasons to move to opting-in as well.

In *Brian Robertson v Wakefield City Council (High Court, 16 November 2001)*, Mr Justice Maurice Kay held that Wakefield Council's refusal to comply with a request from Mr Robertson to register to vote without his personal data being used for commercial purposes breached *Article 8* of *ECHR*, as given effect by *HRA 1998* (see CHAPTER 26 HUMAN RIGHTS ACT 1998). In addition, the court held that the UK had not properly implemented the *EU Data Protection Directive* (*95/46/EC*) in *DPA 1998* in this regard. It is likely that this judgment, which has not yet been published at the time of writing, may have a substantial impact on the opt-in and opt-out issues considered in this chapter, so the latest position will need to be checked.

Mr Robertson's lawyers argued that his data should only be used for the purposes for which it was provided, that is electoral purposes or where it is justified in the public interest, such as the use of data for political parties, by police, security forces or public authorities.

Commissioner's guidance 33.3

In the Frequently Asked Questions (June 2001) relating to the Internet issued by the Information Commissioner, that the following position is taken:

> 'The general standard to ensure compliance with the *DPA 1998* is for a website to provide an individual with an opportunity to opt-out of the use or disclosure of their personal data for direct marketing, whether by e-mail or other means. This requires a statement along the following lines:
>
> - "We would like to e-mail you with offers relating to products of ours that we think you might be interested in. Click here if you object to receiving such offers."; and/or
> - "We would like to pass your details on to other businesses so they can e-mail you with offers of goods/services that you might be interested in. Click here if you do not want your details to be passed on."

It should be easy for the individual to register his or her wishes. It would not be acceptable, for example, to expect an individual to visit another site to register his or her wishes, or to register his or her wishes by post.

In some cases an opt-out facility will not be sufficient. This is likely to be the case where the processing of sensitive personal data is involved.

Some countries provide expressly for 'opt-in': Germany, Denmark, Finland, Sweden and Italy.'

Signifying consent 33.4

In her Legal Guidance (October 2001) the Information Commissioner says that 'consent is not particularly easy to achieve and that data controllers should consider other conditions in *Schedule 2* (and *Schedule 3* if processing sensitive personal data) before looking at consent. No condition carries greater weight than any other. All the conditions provide an equally valid basis for processing. Merely because consent is the first condition to appear in both *Schedules 2* and *3*, does not mean that data controllers should consider consent first.' (The Schedules referred to above are in *DPA 1998*.)

The problem is in part caused by there being no definition of 'consent' in *DPA 1998*. However, *Article 2(h)* of the *EU Data Protection Directive (95/46/EC)* defines 'the data subject's consent' as:

> '…any freely given specific and informed indication of his wishes by which the data subject signifies his agreement to personal data relating to him being processed'.

As can be seen above the word 'signify' is used. The Commissioner says that this means there must be some active communication between the parties. A data subject may 'signify' agreement other than in writing. 'Data controllers cannot infer consent from non-response to a communication, for example from a customer's failure to return or respond to a leaflet.' This statement from the Commissioner appears to be at odds with the e-mail guidance referred to at 33.2 above.

Importantly the Commissioner goes on to say that 'where a data subject does not signify his agreement to personal data relating to him being processed, but is given an opportunity to object to such processing, although this does not amount to consent for the purposes of *DPA 1998*, it may provide the data controller with the basis to rely upon another *Schedule 2* to *DPA 1998* condition, for example, the legitimate interests condition, provided that the data subject is given the right to object before the data are obtained.'

Arguably there is no reason why the act of signifying cannot be undertaken passively although the verb 'sign' is an active verb, therefore the Commissioner's view is unsurprising. It may be possible to argue that the requirement for 'explicit consent' for processing sensitive personal data must be different from any other consent and that such a difference might exist between opting-in and opting-out. Many commercial contract terms are legally accepted under English law by failure to object – standard terms and conditions of supply for example, which are not required to be signed.

Appropriate consent 33.5

Consent must be appropriate to the particular circumstances. The Commissioner gives the example of processing intended to continue after the end of a trading relationship. Where such processing is intended, then the data controller must ensure that it obtains a consent which expressly covers such an eventuality.

Enduring consent 33.6

Consents do not last forever. In most cases the Information Commissioner says '…consent will endure for as long as the processing to which it relates continues. Data controllers should recognise that, depending upon the nature of the consent given and the circumstances of the processing, the individual may be able to withdraw consent.'

Sensitive data 33.7

As mentioned above there is a distinction in *DPA 1998* between the nature of the consent required to satisfy the condition for processing and that which is required in the case of the condition for processing sensitive data. The consent must be 'explicit' in the case of sensitive data.

The Information Commissioner writes that:

> 'The use of the word "explicit" and the fact that the condition requires explicit consent "to the processing of the personal data" suggests that the consent of the data subject should be absolutely clear. In appropriate cases it should cover the specific detail of the processing, the particular type of data to be processed (or even the specific information), the purposes of the processing and any special aspects of the processing which may affect the individual, for example, disclosures which may be made of the data."

Direct Marketing Association 33.8

The Direct Marketing Association (DMA) issued a booklet *A Guide to the Data Protection Act 1998 for Direct Marketers*. Here, the author Colin

Fricker states '…not ticking an opt-out box on a completed and returned order form might, depending on the clarity and wording of any "notification", constitute consent (except in regard to sensitive data)'.

Conclusion 33.9

The safest course is to have an opting-in option. However where this is not commercially viable and the information is not sensitive data, opting-out will be sufficient as long as it is clearly stated. This may be an area for businesses to take legal advice appropriate to their individual circumstances.

Further information 33.10

A Guide to the Data Protection Act 1998 for Direct Marketers (2000) by Colin Fricker is available from the DMA (website:www.dma.co.uk).

34 – Padlock (Use of Sign Called 'Padlock')

At a glance 34.1

- ✓ The Information Commissioner has issued a system known as the 'information padlock' which businesses can use when personal data is gathered.
- ✓ Use of the symbol is not compulsory and has not been widely used to date.
- ✓ Some companies, however, display it on their marketing materials when they gather personal data.

Introduction 34.2

The *Data Protection Act 1998* (*DPA 1998*) requires that in many cases individuals be told how their personal data will be used. Such information therefore often appears on application forms and similar materials.

No precise form of words is prescribed but the Information Commissioner suggests businesses may like to use a symbol or padlock device on places where such data is gathered so that individuals can see that personal data about them is being gathered on that website or in that place.

When to use the symbol 34.3

The Information Commissioner issued a leaflet concerning the symbol in which it is stated that the principles of 'good information handling' lay clear obligations on data controllers. However, individuals can take steps to prevent any mishandling of their information by ensuring that they are aware of the purpose(s) for which information is being collected from them, at the time it is collected.

The Commissioner writes: 'To assist in this, the Information Commissioner and the National Consumer Council have devised an 'information padlock' symbol to act as a signpost which will, at a glance, tell data subjects that personal information about them is being collected to be processed. The symbol is available to data controllers to use on their media to signpost individuals towards information regarding the use of their personal data.'

Where to site the signpost 34.4

The following information is contained in the leaflet mentioned above:

> 'The "information padlock" signpost is intended for use by all data controllers. It should be clearly positioned at any point where information is requested – this could be within any medium, such as an advertisement coupon, application form or Internet site. If an option box is used, the signpost should be placed next to it.
>
> Wherever the signpost appears, an explanation of why the information is requested should be detailed, or directions given to where such an explanation is provided. The signpost can be reproduced in any colour and may be reversed-out if necessary. No minimum or maximum size is recommended, but the symbol should always be clear to any reader.
>
> Electronic copies of the signpost and this leaflet can be downloaded from the Data Protection Commissioner's website at www.dataprotection.gov.uk.'

Printed copies of the symbol for use as bromides are also available, details of which are given in the leaflet (for availability, see 34.6 below).

The padlock 34.5

This symbol alerts people to the fact that their information is being collected, and directs them to sources which will clearly explain how their information is to be used.

Further information 34.6

The Information Commissioner's leaflet on the padlock and the padlock symbol itself are on the data protection website (www.data protection.gov.uk).

35 – Personal Data

At a glance 35.1

- ✓ The *Data Protection Act 1998* (*DPA 1998*) applies to those processing 'personal data'.
- ✓ For the data to be personal it must relate to an individual and must apply to living individuals only, not companies or the deceased.
- ✓ The issue of whether data can be made anonymous also needs to be addressed.

Introduction 35.2

DPA 1998 regulates personal data which is processed. *Section 1* of *DPA 1998* defines personal data as data 'which relate to a living individual who can be identified:

(*a*) from those data; or

(*b*) from those data and other information which is in the possession of, or is likely to come into the possession of the data controller,

and includes any expression of opinion about the individual and any indication of the intentions of the data controller or any other person in respect of the individual'.

Which personal data is caught? 35.3

Data will be personal data where the individual can be identified either from the data itself, from that data and other information held by the data controller, or information which is likely to come into the possession of the data controller. Under the *Data Protection Act 1984* (*DPA 1984*) personal data was information relating to a living individual who could be identified from the information, or from that and other information in the possession of the data user.

A list of names and addresses of individual customers would be personal data, as the individuals can be identified from the data. In such cases there is no doubt the information is personal data. An exemption may apply but subject to that, *DPA 1998* will apply. However, it can often be unclear whether some types of data are personal data.

Article 2 of the *EU Data Protection Directive (95/46/EC)*, which *DPA 1998* implements in the UK, defines an identifiable person as 'one who can be identified, indirectly, in particular by reference to an identification number or to one or more factors specific to his physical, physiological, mental, economic, cultural or social identity'. If images of distinguishable individuals' features are processed and an individual can be identified from it, this will amount to personal data (see the Information Commissioner's CCTV draft guidance at www.data protection.gov.uk/cctvcop.htm).

The individual must be a living individual. A database of people who have just died with perhaps the size of their estates, details from their wills etc. will not be personal data of the individuals (although disclosure of legacies to individual beneficiaries may itself be personal data about those individuals).

Animals are not living individuals under English law.

It is not clear at what point an unborn child becomes a living individual; whether at conception, after most abortions are prohibited in law, or after birth. A hospital, for example, taking DNA samples from unborn children in a mass screening of those whose mothers have had a test for other purposes would need to consider if the data held about the foetuses is personal data.

Data will still be personal data even if the individual cannot be identified from the data if an identification can be made by other information the data controller has or could obtain. Having a list of people identified by a code number is still personal data if the data controller also has a separate system to identify, for example, who numbers 12345 or 34567 are.

Similarly, photographs of people's homes with an accompanying post code may be sufficient to make the photographs personal data because it is possible to purchase a CD-ROM of post codes from which the data controller, or indeed any third party, could then make the necessary connection. If the data controller swore an affidavit that it would never put such a CD-ROM into its possession could it avoid the data becoming personal data? The 'other information' would never come into the possession of the controller so it is possible that the *DPA 1998* could then be circumnavigated, in relation to that data controller.

The Information Commissioner, in her Legal Guidance published in October 2001 (see 35.14 below) states:

> 'The definition in *DPA 1998* is not without difficulty and the Commissioner recognises that, potentially, the definition has a very broad scope. This, in turn, will have a considerable impact on data controllers in terms of compliance with the Data Protection Principles, in particular, the First Data Protection Principle.
>
> It is important not to look at the definition of personal data in isolation as it is the Commissioner's view that for the scope of the definition to be understood properly, it should be considered in the context of the definitions of "data", "data controller" and "data subject" in *DPA 1998*.'

CCTV 35.4

CCTV pictures of individuals are 'personal data' under *DPA 1998*. *Article 14* of the *Data Protection Directive (95/46/EC)* provides that the Directive applies to 'the techniques used to capture, transmit, record, store or communicate sound and image data relating to natural persons'. The Information Commissioner has issued a Code of Practice For Users of CCTV under *DPA 1998* (www.dataprotection.gov.uk/cctvcop.htm) (for further information see CHAPTER 2 CCTV). Similarly the Draft Code of Practice on the Use of Personal Data in Employer/Employee Relationships provides similar guidance in the employment field.

The following is a non-exhaustive list of personal data.

- Names and addresses of individuals.
- Still photographs of individuals.
- Moving pictures of individuals.
- E-mail addresses of individuals, particularly if they give a person's name – for example john.smith@butterworths.com or susan@singlelaw.com.
- Information about individuals identified by reference number where the number in another listing reveals the identity of the individual.

The Information Commissioner has issued specific guidance on provisions under *DPA 1998*, including guidance as to the definition of personal data. The section below is based largely on that guidance.

What determines whether data relate to an individual? 35.5

This will be a question of fact. One question is 'whether a data controller can form a connection between the data and the individual'. Data does not have to relate solely to one individual and the same data may relate to two or more people and still be personal data about each of them. For example, joint tenants of a property, or holders of a joint bank account, or even individuals who use the same telephone or e-mail address. Information may relate to an individual in a business capacity and not just to their private life. Information about the business of a sole trader will amount to personal data as information about the business will be about the sole trader. Information about an individual in a partnership will be personal data if it relates to a specific partner. This will be more likely in a small partnership.

Although *DPA 1998* refers to individuals and not other legal entities such as limited companies, there will be situations where information about a limited company or other legal entity amounts to personal data because it relates to a specific individual, for example, the performance of a department. Information relating solely to the legal entity will not be personal data.

Does DPA 1998 only relate to living individuals? 35.6

DPA 1998 is only concerned with living individuals and so if the subject of the information is deceased, then the information cannot be personal data.

Identifying the individual 35.7

The Information Commissioner recognises that an individual may be 'identified' without necessarily knowing the name and address of that particular individual. The Commissioner's view is that it is sufficient if the data are capable of being processed by the data controller to enable the data controller to distinguish the data subject from any other individual. This would be the case if a data subject could be treated differently from other individuals.

Future possession of data 35.8

In the majority of cases the ability to 'identify' an individual will be achieved by knowing the name and address of an individual or by the data controller being in possession of some other information. The definition also allows for an individual to be identified from data together with information 'likely to come into the possession of' the data controller. It will be for a data controller to satisfy himself whether it is likely that such information will come into his or her possession to render data personal data. This will depend largely on the nature of the processing undertaken by a data controller, the Commissioner says.

This issue is clearly relevant in the context of personal data which a data controller wishes to make anonymous (see 35.11 below).

Example – identifying an individual 35.9

The following example is given by the Information Commissioner.

If information about a particular web user is built up over a period of time, perhaps through the use of tracking technology, with the intention that it may later be linked to a name and address, that information is personal data. Information may be compiled about a particular web user, but there might not be any intention of linking it to a name and address or e-mail address. There might merely be an intention to target that particular user with advertising, or to offer discounts when they re-visit a particular website, on the basis of the profile built up, without any ability to locate that user in the physical world. The Commissioner takes the view that such information is, nevertheless, personal data. In the context of the online world the information that identifies an individual is that which uniquely locates him in that world, by distinguishing him from others.

What is meant by the expression "possession" in this context? 35.10

The concept of possession is very wide. In the Information Commissioner's view possession does not necessarily mean that the identifying data are in the physical control of the data controller, or likely to come under the data controller's physical control. A data controller enters into a contract with a data processor for the processing of personal data. The arrangement is that the data processor may receive some of the identifying data from a third party and some from the data controller. The data are processed in accordance with the terms of the contract. The data controller determines the purposes for which, and the manner in which the personal data are to be processed by the data processor but may not have sight of all or any of the information which identifies a living individual. The data controller would, however, be deemed to be in possession of those data. The data controller could not argue in such a situation that the identifying data are not in his or her 'possession' and therefore is unable to absolve themselves of responsibilities as a data controller.

Can personal data be made anonymous? 35.11

The issue of information in the possession of, or likely to come into the possession of, a data controller has an impact on a data controller who seeks to make anonymous the personal data they are processing by stripping those data of all personal identifiers.

On this matter the Information Commissioner says:

> 'The fact that personal data may be anonymised is referred to in *Directive 95/46/EC* (the "Directive"), at *Recital 26*, and in the matter of *R v The Department of Health ex parte Source Informatics Limited [2000]1 All ER 786*. In that case it was acknowledged by the Court of Appeal that the Directive does not apply to anonymised data. In anonymising personal data the data controller will be processing such data and, in respect of such processing, will still need to comply with the provisions of the Act.'

The Commissioner recognises that the aim of anonymisation is to provide better data protection, although some people use it to avoid the onerous obligations of *DPA 1998*. The Commissioner believes it is essentially a good thing but very hard to achieve. The fact that the data controller is in the possession of this data set which, if linked to the data which have been stripped of all personal identifiers, will enable a living individual to be identified, means that all the data, including the data stripped of personal identifiers, remain personal data in the hands of that data controller and cannot be said to have been anonymised. The fact that the data controller may have no intention of linking these two data sets is immaterial.

A data controller who destroys the original data set retaining only the information which has been stripped of all personal identifiers and who assesses that it is not likely that information will come into his possession to enable him to reconstitute the data, ceases to be a data controller in respect of the retained data. This is because it will then not come within the definition of personal data under *section 1(1)* of *DPA 1998*, in the view of the Information Commissioner.

Whether or not data which have been stripped of all personal identifiers are personal data in the hands of a person to whom they are disclosed will depend upon that person being in possession of, or likely to come into the possession of, other information which would enable that person to identify a living individual (data is only 'personal data' when it can be identified as such – *DPA 1998, s 1(1)*).

It should be noted that the disclosure of personal data by a data controller amounts to processing under *section 1(1)* of *DPA 1998*.

Examples 35.12

The obtaining of clinical information linked to a National Health Service number by a person having access to the National Health Service Central Register will amount to processing of personal data by that person because that person will have access to information enabling him to identify the individuals concerned.

It will be a duty upon someone processing data to take steps to ensure that the data cannot be reconstituted to become personal data and to be prepared to justify any decision made on processing of the data.

In the case of data collected by the Office of National Statistics, where there is a disclosure of samples of anonymised data, it is conceivable that a combination of information in a particular geographic area may be unique to an individual or family who could therefore be identifiable from that information. In recognition of this fact, disclosures of information are done in such a way that any obvious identifiers are removed and the data presented so as to avoid particular individuals being distinguished.

If data have been stripped of all personal identifiers such that the data controller is no longer able to single out an individual and treat that individual differently, the data cease to be personal data. Whether this has been achieved may be open to challenge. Data controllers may therefore be required to justify the grounds for their view that the data are no longer personal data. When a subject access request is received, a data controller must be able to identify the data relating to the data subject making the request, to enable him to provide information specific to that data subject. In making a subject access request, a data subject might provide the data controller with sufficient information to enable their data to be distinguished from data relating to other individuals, in a situation where the data controller would not otherwise be able to do so from the information in his possession, which he may have stripped of all personal identifiers. In this case the data relating to the individual making the request become personal data, but the information provided by the data subject does not render the other data being held personal data, unless the data controller believes that it is likely that information will come into his possession to render the other data personal data.

If there are any doubts as to whether data are personal data the Commissioner's advice would be to treat the data as personal data, having particular regard to whether those data are *sensitive* personal data.

In respect of such data, if a subject access request is received and the data controller cannot satisfy himself as to the identity of the person making the subject access request, or as to his ability to locate the information to which the subject access request relates because the data have been stripped of identifiers, then the data controller would not be obliged to comply with that subject access request, advising the data subject accordingly.

Expressions of opinion or intention 35.13

The definition of personal data contained in *DPA 1998* now expressly includes any indication of the intentions of the data controller or any other person in respect of an individual. This aspect of the definition was not included in the definition of 'personal data' in *DPA 1984*. The consequence of this may mean, for example, that an employer who processes appraisals of employees would have to disclose not only his opinions of the employees but also any intention to offer or decline promotion on the basis of those opinions subject to any exemption available at any particular time.

This is a major change which not all personnel or human resources departments have as yet noted.

Further information 35.14

The Information Commissioner's Legal Guidance is on the website (www.dataprotection.gov.uk).

36 – Principles

At a glance 36.1

- ✓ The Eight Data Protection Principles set out a code by which data controllers must gather and handle personal data.
- ✓ The Principles must be complied with even if the data controller has failed to register its holding of personal data.
- ✓ The Principles address issues such as fair processing of the data, use of the data for the purposes for which it was gathered and export of the data.
- ✓ Guidance is available from the Information Commissioner on the Principles and their application.

The Principles 36.2

The Eight Data Protection Principles must be followed by data controllers in their handling of personal data and the obtaining of such data. The Principles are slightly different from the eight previous Principles in the *Data Protection Act 1984* (*DPA 1984*), which they replaced.

First Principle: Fair and lawful processing 36.3

The First Principle provides that 'Personal data shall be processed fairly and lawfully and, in particular, shall not be processed unless:

- at least one of the conditions in *Schedule 2* of the *Data Protection Act 1998* (*DPA 1998*) is met; and
- in the case of sensitive personal data, at least one of the conditions in *Schedule 3* to *DPA 1998* is also met.'

Fair and lawful processing is covered in CHAPTER 21 FAIR PROCESSING. 'Fair' essentially means with the data subject's consent. 'Lawful' is not defined. The Information Commissioner suggests that it may broadly be described by the courts as 'something which is contrary to some law or enactment or is done without lawful justification or excuse' (see *R v R [1991] 4 All ER 481*). The term applies equally to the public and private sector and to breaches of both statute and common law, whether criminal or civil. According to the Commissioner, an example of information unlawfully obtained might be information which is obtained as a result of a breach of confidence or in breach of an enforceable contractual agreement. Since 2 October 2000 it applies to a breach of the *Human Rights Act 1998* (*HRA 1998*) by a data controller bound by that Act (see CHAPTER 26 HUMAN RIGHTS ACT 1998).

Areas of law relevant to lawfulness listed by the Commissioner in her Legal Guidance (October 2001) are:

- confidentiality arising from the relationship of the data controller with the data subject;
- the *ultra vires* rule and the rule relating to the excess of delegated powers, under which the data controller may only act within the limits of its legal powers;
- legitimate expectation, that is, the expectation of the individual as to how the data controller will use the information relating to him or her; and
- *Article 8* of the *European Convention on Human Rights* (the right to respect for private and family life, home and correspondence).

Confidentiality **36.4**

Some relationships imply confidentiality, such as those existing between banker and client. In *A v B plc (Times Law Reports, 2 November 2001)* the court held that a lover in a secret affair was legally restrained from revealing all to the newspapers because of obligations of confidentiality which would be implied by the relationship and because of *HRA 1998*. The Information Commissioner says that 'the effect of an obligation of confidence is that a data controller is restricted from using the information for a purpose other than that for which it was provided or disclosing it without the individual's permission. It would be unlawful for a data controller to do this unless there was some overriding reason in the public interest for this to happen. Where such personal data are processed for a purpose other than that for which the information was provided, the processing is likely to be unlawful processing.'

Public bodies and other organisations have data for certain statutory functions. They must act solely in accordance with their powers.

The Commissioner advises:

> 'Where a public body obtains information of a confidential nature in order to carry out its statutory functions then processes that information for other purposes, there is likely

to be a breach of the obligation of confidence to that individual, unless there is a good reason or some legal justification for using the information in that way.'

In *Brian Robertson v Wakefield City Council (High Court, 16 November 2001)*, the court held that refusing to allow a Mr Robertson to register to vote without his data being used by way of the electoral roll being sold on for commercial purposes was a breach of *HRA 1998*. Allowing such sales showed that the UK had not properly implemented the *EU Data Protection Directive* (*95/46/EC*) properly through *DPA 1998*.

Second Principle: Purposes 36.5

The Second Principle of *DPA 1998* requires that personal data should be obtained only for one or more specified and lawful purposes, and shall not be further processed in any manner incompatible with that purpose or those purposes. The purpose may, by *Schedule 1, Part II, paras 5–6* of *DPA 1998*, be specified in a notice given for that purpose or in a notification (registration) given to the Commissioner under *DPA 1998*. The Second Principle states that 'personal data shall be obtained only for one or more specified and lawful purposes, and shall not be further processed in any manner incompatible with that purpose or those purposes'.

In deciding whether any disclosure of personal data is compatible with the purpose or purposes for which the data were obtained, consideration will be given to the purpose or purposes for which the personal data are intended to be processed by any person to whom they are disclosed, the Commissioner says. Such decisions cannot be made retrospectively by data controllers once the data are obtained.

For the purposes of the Second Principle, the further processing of personal data in compliance with the conditions set out in *section 33* of *DPA 1998* is not to be regarded as incompatible with the purposes for which they were obtained. If the data controller has complied with *Schedule I, Part II, Para I* of *DPA 1998* then this is likely to indicate that a data subject has not been deceived or misled as to the purposes for which their personal data are to be processed.

In practice, letting users know in a lot of detail what will be done with their data is much better than simply saying their data may be used generally for all manner of things. A general notification may not satisfy the Commissioner.

Third Principle: Adequate, relevant and not excessive 36.6

The Third Principle requires that personal data must be adequate, relevant and not excessive in relation to the purposes for which it is processed. Concerning this, the Information Commissioner states in her October 2001 Legal Guidance:

> 'In complying with this Principle, data controllers should seek to identify the minimum amount of information that is required in order properly to fulfil their purpose and this will be a question of fact in each case. If it is necessary to hold additional information about certain individuals, such information should only be collected and recorded in those cases.
>
> This guidance has been endorsed by the Data Protection Tribunal in the context of *DPA 1984* in the case of *Runnymede Borough Council CCRO and Others v The Data Protection Registrar (November 1990).* Where a data controller holds an item of information on all individuals which will be used or useful only in relation to some of them, the information is likely to be excessive and irrelevant in relation to those individuals in respect of whom it will not be used or useful and should not be held in those cases.
>
> It is not acceptable to hold information on the basis that it might possibly be useful in the future without a view of how it will be used. This is to be distinguished from holding information in the case of a particular foreseeable contingency which may never occur, for example, where an employer holds details of blood groups of employees engaged in hazardous occupations.'

Practical guidance 36.7

The Information Commissioner suggests data controllers should consider for all data in this context:

- the number of individuals on whom information is held;
- the number of individuals for whom it is used;
- the nature of the personal data;
- the length of time it is held;
- the way it was obtained;

- the possible consequences for individuals of the holding or erasure of the data;
- the way in which it is used; and
- the purpose for which it is held.

Fourth Principle: Accurate and up-to-date **36.8**

Personal data should be accurate and, where necessary, kept up-to-date. It is a matter of fact whether data is incorrect or misleading in each case. *Schedule 1, Part II, para* 7 of the *DPA 1998* states that this Principle is not to be taken as contravened where the data controller has taken reasonable steps to ensure the accuracy of the data.

'Necessary' **36.9**

An interesting issue is when is it 'necessary' to keep the data up to date. The Information Commissioner's Legal Guidance indicates that if the data are intended to be used merely as an historical record of a transaction between the data controller and the data subject, updating would be inappropriate. To change the data so as to bring it up to date would defeat the purpose of maintaining the historical record. However, according to the Commissioner 'sometimes it is important for the purpose that the data reflect the data subject's current circumstances, for example, if the data are used to decide whether to grant credit or confer or withhold some other benefit. In those cases either steps should be taken to ensure that the data are kept up to date, or when the data are used, account should be taken of the fact that circumstances may have changed.'

A data controller will need to consider the following questions.

- Is there a record of when the data were recorded or last updated?
- Are all those involved with the data – including people to whom they are disclosed as well as employees of the data controller – aware that the data do not necessarily reflect the current position?
- Are steps taken to update the personal data – for example, by checking back at intervals with the original source or with the data subject? If so, how effective are these steps?
- Is the fact that the personal data are out of date likely to cause damage or distress to the data subject?

Fifth Principle: Data not to be kept longer than purposes require 36.10

Personal data processed for any purpose or purposes shall not be kept for longer than is necessary for that purpose or those purposes.

Some Acts of Parliament deal with this issue in particular for certain types of data, such as the *Police and Criminal Evidence Act 1984*. Reference should be made here to the CCTV Code of Practice (see CHAPTER 2 CCTV) which makes recommendations for retention periods.

If personal data have been recorded because of a relationship between the data controller and the data subject, the need to keep the information should be considered when the relationship ceases to exist. For example, the data subject may be an employee who has left the employment of the data controller. The end of the relationship will not necessarily cause the data controller to delete all the personal data. It may well be necessary to keep some of the information so that the data controller will be able to confirm details of the data subject's employment for, say, the provision of references in the future or to enable the employer to provide the relevant information in respect of the data subject's pension arrangements. The Information Commissioner makes the point that 'it may well be necessary in some cases to retain certain information to enable the data controller to defend legal claims, which may be made in the future. Unless there is some other reason for keeping them, the personal data should be deleted when the possibility of a claim arising no longer exists i.e when the relevant statutory time limit has expired.'

Sixth Principle: Data processed in accordance with data subjects' rights 36.11

Personal data shall be processed in accordance with the rights of data subjects under *DPA 1998*. This provision is contravened if, but only if, a person contravenes:

- *section 7* of *DPA 1998* by failing to supply information which has been duly requested in accordance with that section;
- *sections 10–11* of *DPA 1998* by failing to comply with a notice duly given under that section; or
- *section 12* of *DPA 1998* by failing to give a notice under that section.

Seventh Principle: Security **36.12**

Appropriate technical and organisational measures shall be taken against unauthorised or unlawful processing of personal data and against accidental loss or destruction of, or damage to, personal data.

Security measures should be taken at all stages (see CHAPTER 5 CONFIDENTIALITY). The *Data Protection Directive (95/46/EC)* provides that such measures should be taken both at the time of the design of the processing system and at the time of the processing itself, particularly in order to maintain security and thereby to prevent any unauthorised processing. Data controllers are, therefore, encouraged to consider the use of privacy-enhancing techniques as part of their obligations under the Seventh Principle.

In her *Legal Guidance* the Information Commissioner suggests as follows.

Some of the security controls that the data controller is likely to need to consider are set out below. (This is not a comprehensive list but is illustrative only.)

Security management:

- Does the data controller have a security policy setting out management commitment to information security within the organisation?
- Is responsibility for the organisation's security policy clearly placed on a particular person or department?
- Are sufficient resources and facilities made available to enable that responsibility to be fulfilled?

Controlling access to information:

- Is access to the building or room controlled or can anybody walk in?
- Can casual passers-by read information off screens or documents?
- Are passwords known only to authorised people and are the passwords changed regularly?
- Do passwords give access to all levels of the system or only to those personal data with which that employee should be concerned?
- Is there a procedure for cleaning media (such as tapes and disks) before they are reused or are new data merely written over old? In the latter case is there a possibility of the old data reaching somebody who is not authorised to receive it? (e.g. as a result of the disposal of redundant equipment).
- Is printed material disposed of securely, for example, by shredding?

- Is there a procedure for authenticating the identity of a person to whom personal data may be disclosed over the telephone prior to the disclosure of the personal data?
- Is there a procedure covering the temporary removal of personal data from the data controller's premises, for example, for staff to work on at home? What security measures are individual members of staff required to take in such circumstances?
- Are responsibilities for security clearly defined between a data processor and its customers?

Ensuring business continuity:

- Are the precautions against burglary, fire or natural disaster adequate?
- Is the system capable of checking that the data are valid and initiating the production of back-up copies? If so, is full use made of these facilities?
- Are back-up copies of all the data stored separately from the live files?
- Is there protection against corruption by viruses or other forms of intrusion?

Staff selection and training:

- Is proper weight given to the discretion and integrity of staff when they are being considered for employment or promotion or for a move to an area where they will have access to personal data?
- Are the staff aware of their responsibilities? Have they been given adequate training and is their knowledge kept up to date?
- Do disciplinary rules and procedures take account of the requirements of *DPA 1998*? Are these rules enforced?
- Does an employee found to be unreliable have his or her access to personal data withdrawn immediately?
- Are staff made aware that data should only be accessed for business purposes and not for their own private purposes?

Detecting and dealing with breaches of security:

- Do systems keep audit trails so that access to personal data is logged and can be attributed to a particular person?
- Are breaches of security properly investigated and remedied; particularly when damage or distress could be caused to an individual?

DPA 1998 introduces express obligations upon data controllers when the processing of personal data is carried out by a data processor on behalf of the data controller. In order to comply with the Seventh Principle the data controller must:

- choose a data processor providing sufficient guarantees in respect of the technical and organisational security measures they take;
- take reasonable steps to ensure compliance with those measures; and
- ensure that the processing by the data processor is carried out under a contract, which is made or evidenced in writing, under which the data processor is to act only on instructions from the data controller. The contract must require the data processor to comply with obligations equivalent to those imposed on the data controller by the Seventh Principle.

Further advice may be found in *BS 7799* and *1S0/IEC Standard 17799*.'

Eighth Principle: Data export **36.13**

Personal data shall not be transferred to a country or territory outside the European Economic Area, unless that country or territory ensures an adequate level of protection of the rights and freedoms of data subjects in relation to the processing of personal data.

This would appear to prevent a data export, however *Schedule 4* to *DPA 1998* sets out exceptions. CHAPTER 20 EXPORT OF DATA, CHAPTER 41 'SAFE HARBOR' AGREEMENT and CHAPTER 44 TRANSBORDER DATA FLOWS examine this Principle in more detail.

Schedule 4 of *DPA 1998* sets out when the Eighth Principle will not apply, and often seems to be overlooked by companies. It provides that this is the case where:

(*a*) the data subject has given their consent to the transfer;

(*b*) the transfer is necessary:

(i) for the performance of a contract between the data subject and the data controller, or

(ii) for the taking of steps at the request of the data subject with a view to the data subject entering into a contract with the data controller;

(*c*) the transfer is necessary:

(i) for the conclusion of a contract between the data controller and a person other than the data subject which:

(A) is entered into at the request of the data subject, or

(B) is in the interests of the data subject, or

(ii) for the performance of such a contract;

(*d*) the transfer is necessary for reasons of substantial public interest.

The Secretary of State may specify by order the circumstances in which a transfer is to be taken to be necessary for reasons of substantial public interest. No order to this effect has been made to date;

(*e*) the transfer:

(i) is necessary for the purpose of, or in connection with, any legal proceedings (including prospective legal proceedings);

(ii) is necessary for the purpose of obtaining legal advice; or

(iii) is otherwise necessary for the purposes of establishing, exercising or defending legal rights;

(*f*) the transfer is necessary in order to protect the vital interests of the data subject;

(*g*) the transfer is part of the personal data on a public register and any conditions subject to which the register is open to inspection are complied with by any person to whom the data are or may be disclosed after the transfer;

(*h*) the transfer is made on terms which are of a kind approved by the Information Commissioner as ensuring adequate safeguards for the rights and freedoms of data subjects. It is not the practice of the Commissioner to consider or approve individual draft contracts submitted to her; or

(*j*) the transfer has been authorised by the Commissioner as being made in such a manner as to ensure adequate safeguards for the rights and freedoms of data subjects.

Audits and networks of privacy offices – EPON 36.14

All businesses which process personal data need to ensure on a regular basis that they are compliant with the Principles. The Information Commissioner's website gives access to a data protection audit process with forms which businesses can use in assessing their compliance with the legislation.

Privacy Laws and Business organises a network of data protection or privacy officers known as EPON (European Privacy Offices Network), who meet three times a year to discuss privacy and data protection issues, form working groups and exchange information. For further information see www.privacylaws.com, email sandra@privacylaws.com. Tel: 020 8423 1300.

CHAPTER 37 PRIVACY POLICIES AND AUDITS looks at audits in more detail and in particular the Commissioner's Audit Manual.

Further information 36.15

With regard to CCTV and employers and employees, reference should be made to the Information Commissioner's Code and draft Code of Practice respectively – available online at www.dataprotection.gov.uk.

Details of the Privacy Laws and Business network of privacy officers are at www.privacylaws.com. E-mail: sandra@privacylaws.com.
Tel: 020 8423 1300. Fax: 020 8423 4536.

37 – Privacy Policies and Audits

At a glance 37.1

- ✓ Many companies which handle personal data choose to set up a privacy policy which gives data subjects access to information about how their data will be used.
- ✓ Auditing systems to ensure compliance should be the first stage before setting up such a policy. The Information Commissioner has produced an Audit Manual to provide guidance on this.
- ✓ There is no legal obligation to set up such a policy, although there are obligations to notify data subjects of certain matters in one form or another such as who is the data controller.
- ✓ Many websites which gather personal data have privacy policies.
- ✓ The Organisation for Economic Co-operation and Development (OECD) has an online tool for the setting up of a privacy policy.
- ✓ An example of a simple Internet privacy policy is given in this chapter.

Introduction 37.2

The *Data Protection Act 1998* (*DPA 1998*) obliges data controllers to notify data subjects of important information about who the data controller is, how the data will be used etc. That information must be provided to individuals in whatever is the best form as regards the data concerned. There will be less space on a short paper form on which individuals provide personal data then there will be on a website where a lengthy document can be accommodated.

In practice, putting such information into one document known as a 'privacy policy' is a good idea. However, it is not a substitute for general compliance. The data controller must, for example, ensure that the information can be accessed. A privacy policy hidden in an obscure part of a website is worse than useless. The information should at least be visible when individuals supply the information concerned. In addition, before a privacy policy or general data protection policy can be set up, an audit should be done of the business' systems.

Websites 37.3

The information to be given on a website where data is gathered is:

(*a*) the identity of the person or organisation responsible for operating the website and of anyone else who collects personal data through the site;

(*b*) the purposes for which they intend to process the personal data; and

(*c*) any other information needed to ensure fairness to individuals, taking into account the specific circumstances of the processing. This will include informing individuals of any disclosure of information about them to third parties, including disclosure to companies within the same group.

The Information Commissioner says that

> 'Unless it is obvious, website operators must give this information to individuals before they collect any personal data from them. It should be remembered that visitors to a website will not necessarily enter it through its homepage. They may, for example, come directly to a particular page via a hypertext link. The above information should therefore be provided at any point at which personal data are collected.'

Information Commissioner FAQs – Internet

CHAPTER 28 INTERNET considers the data protection issues relating to the Internet in particular.

Developing a privacy policy 37.4

Before a privacy policy can be set up it is useful to carry out some kind of an audit. Lots of information is available on the Information Commissioner's website. Under the Compliance Advice section of the Commissioner's website, guidance is given to businesses in achieving compliance with *DPA 1998*.

The Commissioner's Audit Manual 37.5

The Information Commissioner intended to issue a comprehensive Audit Manual to be used by businesses to achieve compliance under *DPA 1998* in late 2001. The proposed contents are as follows.

Part 1: Introduction

1. Aims of Data Protection Compliance Audits.
2. Why Should We Audit?
3. Audit Objectives.
4. What is an Audit?
5. Audit Categories.
6. Audit Benefits.

Part 2: The Audit Method

1. Audit Categories.
2. Adequacy Audit Outcomes.
3. Compliance Audit.

Part 3: The Audit Process

1. Audit Planning
2. Audit Preparation
3. Conduct of the Compliance Audit
4. Compliance Audit Reporting
5. Audit Follow-up

Part 4: Guide to Auditing

1. The Role of an Auditor
2. Auditing Tasks
3. Human Aspects
4. Audit Techniques
5. Practical Considerations

Annex A: Risk Assessment.

Annex B: Sampling Criteria.

Annex C: Audit Pro formas.

Annex D: Meeting Pro formas.

Annex E: Adequacy Audit Checklist.

Annex F: Compliance Audit Checklists: Organisational & Management Issues.

Annex G: Compliance Audit Checklists: The Eight Data Protection Principles.

Annex H: Compliance Audit Checklists: Other Data Protection Issues.

Annex J: Process Audit Checklist.

The contents above show how useful this document is likely to be for data protection manuals when the manual is available in late 2001. The manual was piloted by Privacy Laws and Business in public and private sector organisations. It follows common auditing principles and is based on a two stage risk assessment:

(*a*) an adequacy audit to assess whether a business' policy, code of practice, guidelines and procedures meet the requirements of *DPA 1998*; and

(*b*) a compliance audit to check that the business is in compliance, giving guidance to data controllers in assessing the risks, and using pro formas and audit checklists.

Guidance and training 37.6

Training 37.7

Privacy Laws and Business, who wrote the Audit Manual for the Information Commissioner (see 37.5 above) also provide audit workshops (see www.privacylaws.com) and they publish a regular UK and EU newsletter of data protection developments. In addition, many companies offer courses and conferences on data protection legal issues, including Butterworths Tolley.

Online seminars 37.8

On 30 October 2001 the Information Commissioner announced a series of online seminars to help individuals and organisations who hold personal information (data controllers) to understand *DPA 1998*. These consisted of a voiceover recording accompanied by a Powerpoint presentation. The seminars can be downloaded from the Information Commissioner's website at www.dataprotection.gov.uk/seminars.htm. The Information Commissioner Elizabeth France said that the seminars will be of particular use to data protection officers, and that further specialist seminars will be added to the programme over the coming months to build up a comprehensive training package.

OECD guidance 37.9

OECD have issued guidance on how to set up a privacy policy at http://cs3-hq.oecd.org/scripts/pwv3/PWPart1.htm.

Step 1 **37.10**

The OECD suggest first reviewing internal systems by asking the following questions.

- Do you collect personal data?
- What kinds of personal data do you collect?
- How are they collected? From individuals, from third parties, from public bodies or authorities? Are individuals aware that their personal data are being collected?
- Who in your organisation is responsible for deciding what personal data are collected and how?
- Why do you collect personal data?
- How are they used?
- Who controls personal data once they are collected?
- Are personal data disclosed to third parties, and if so, why?
- How and where are they stored?
- Do you have standards, guidelines and regulations which apply to your collection and use of personal data?
- Do you allow visitors access to the personal data you have about them?
- What happens if a visitor has a query about their personal data? What if they are not satisfied with how you deal with their query?

Step 2 **37.11**

OECD suggest that the second step would then be a review of laws which apply to the company concerned which of course differ around the world.

Step 3 **37.12**

Once this is done, the next step is to use the OECD's generator answering the questions there. After a data controller has completed the questionnaire as accurately as possible, a draft privacy policy statement is automatically generated. It proposes pre-formatted sentences based on the answers given and choices made.

Step 4 **37.13**

The fourth step is to ensure:

- that the draft privacy statement accurately reflects your organisation's personal data practices;
- that the draft privacy statement complies with applicable national, regional and international laws or (self) regulatory schemes; and
- that errors are corrected and that the privacy statement reads smoothly.

Step 5 37.14

The final step is to place the privacy policy on the website. The OECD states:

> 'Regulations to which you may be subject may require a specific location for such a statement, such as on your homepage, or at the point(s) where personal data are collected. In the absence of specific regulatory requirements, you may wish to consider creating a link between your homepage and your privacy statement, or between pages where you collect personal data and your privacy statement. The OECD Privacy Guidelines recommend that individuals should be able to gain access to information about personal data practices without unreasonable effort as to time, knowledge and expense. You may also wish to create links to relevant web sites to make visitors aware of any relevant regulation.'

They end with the following warning:

> '**REMEMBER:** Once your privacy statement is publicly posted, you may be legally liable if you fail to abide by your privacy policy statement or if that statement does not comply with local laws.'

Example of a simple internet privacy policy 37.15

The OECD online privacy policy statement was revised using the OECD Generator. This example is not intended to be a 'model' statement. It is intended only to provide an indication of what you can expect your final privacy statement to look like.

Below is an example of a simple privacy policy for a fictional company, EFG Limited.

Privacy policy

EFG's commitment to privacy
EFG Limited is committed to protecting the privacy of those using our site and the confidentiality of the personal information with which our subscribers provide us.

Data Protection Act 1998
We are registered under the *Data Protection Act 1998* and comply with the Act in all our dealings with your personal data.

Your personal information is safe with us.

EFG will never sell personal information or share personal information with third parties unrelated to it. At EFG we use the information we collect to serve our customers in the following ways.

- If you become a subscriber to EFG or a user of other EFG services your name, e-mail address, address and other information on the subscription form are kept by us and used to remind you when your next subscription is due and to send you the EFG Report.
- We may also use your contact information to let you know about enhancements to the site and your subscription entitlements. If you would rather not receive this information please inform us by e-mail at privacy@efg.co.uk.
- We do not use cookies (defined below) for collecting user information from the site and we will not collect any information about you except that required for system administration of the Web server.

Cookies

Message given to a web browser by a web server. The message is then stored by the browser in a text file called *cookie.txt*. Each time the browser requests a page from the server, this message is sent back. A cookie's main objective is to identify users and personalise their visit by customising web pages for them, for example by welcoming them by name next time they visit the same site. A site using cookies will usually invite you to provide personal information such as your name, e-mail address and interests.

Further information

For further information on data protection and privacy contact:-

The Data Protection Manager, EFG Limited, ________________.

Telephone (+44) (0) 20 7__________. Facsimile (+44) (0) 20 7.

Email privacy@efg.co.uk.

Information on the Data Protection Act 1998 is also on the Data Protection Commissioner's web site at www.dataprotection.gov.uk

Use of this Site is subject to our Terms and Conditions

Further information 37.16

OECD's guidance on forming a privacy policy is at http://cs3-hq.oecd.org/scripts/pwv3/PWPart1.htm

OECD says that further guidance on carrying out an internal review can be found on the web sites of SIIA, USCIB,or CSA Model Code CAN/CSA-Q830.

They say businesses may also wish to consult the following websites.

www.jipdec.or.jp/security/privacy/index-e.html

www.research.att.com/projects/p3p/propgen

www.the-dma.org

www.truste.org/wizard

Details of Privacy Laws and Business who wrote the Information Commissioner's Audit Manual and their network of privacy officers is at www.privacylaws.com. Tel: 020 8423 1300. Fax 020 8423 4536.

38 – Recording Telephone Calls and E-mails

At a glance 38.1

- ✓ The *Regulation of Investigatory Powers Act 2000* (*RIPA 2000*) regulates the interception of communications.
- ✓ The *Telecommunications (Lawful Business Practice) (Interception of Communications) Regulations 2000* (*SI 2000/2699*) regulate this area. These are known as the 'Lawful Business Practice Regulations'.
- ✓ In most cases recording is permitted if the other person is aware that it is occurring or may occur.
- ✓ The Government's Office of Telecommunications (Oftel) has provided guidance for consumers in this field.
- ✓ Employers can include statements to this effect in employment contracts.

Introduction 38.2

The legislation relating to the recording of telephone calls and e-mails is contained in *RIPA 2000* (see CHAPTER 40 REGULATION OF INVESTIGATORY POWERS ACT 2000). In addition, businesses must comply with the requirements set out in the *Data Protection Act 1998* (*DPA 1998*). In this respect, the Information Commissioner's Draft Code of Practice on the Use of Personal Data in Employer/Employee Relationships should be considered (see CHAPTER 16 EMPLOYMENT and CHAPTER 28 INTERNET). The *Lawful Business Practice Regulations* (*SI 2000/2699*) were made under *RIPA 2000*, and set out the law in this field. They are considered in 38.3 below, and in more detail in CHAPTER 29 LAWFUL BUSINESS PRACTICE REGULATIONS.

Lawful Business Practice Regulations 38.3

The *Lawful Business Practice Regulations* (*SI 2000/2699*) provide that the interception has to be by or with the consent of a person carrying on a business for purposes relevant to that person's business, and using that business's own telecommunication system. The term 'carrying on a business' includes the activities of government departments, public authorities and others exercising statutory functions.

Interceptions are authorised for:

(*a*) the monitoring or recording of communications:

- (i) to establish the existence of facts, to ascertain compliance with regulatory or self-regulatory practices or procedures or to ascertain or demonstrate standards which are or ought to be achieved (quality control and training);
- (ii) in the interests of national security (in which case only certain specified public officials may make the interception);
- (iii) to prevent or detect crime;
- (iv) to investigate or detect unauthorised use of telecommunication systems; or
- (v) to secure, or as an inherent part of, effective system operation;

(*b*) the monitoring of received communications to determine whether they are business or personal communications; and

(*c*) the monitoring of communications made to anonymous telephone helplines.

Interceptions are authorised only if the controller of the telecommunications system on which they are effected has made all reasonable efforts to inform potential users that interceptions may be made.

The *Lawful Business Practice Regulations* (*SI 2000/2699*) do not authorise interceptions to which the persons making and receiving the communications have consented; they are not prohibited by *DPA 1998*.

Oftel guidance 38.4

Oftel, the Telecoms Regulator, provide a helpful summary of the laws in this field for consumers at www.oftel.gov.uk/consumer/advice/FAQs/prvfaq3.htm. This guidance is below.

Recording and monitoring telephone calls or e-mails

A general overview of interception, recording and monitoring of communications

The interception, recording and monitoring of telephone calls is governed by a number of different pieces of UK legislation. The requirements of all relevant legislation must be complied with. The main ones are:

- *RIPA 2000*;
- *Telecommunications (Lawful Business Practice) (Interception of Communications) Regulations 2000* (*SI 2000/2699*);
- *DPA 1998*;
- *Telecommunications (Data Protection and Privacy) Regulations 1999* (*SI 1999/2093*); and
- *Human Rights Act 1998*.

It is not possible to provide comprehensive detail of that legislation here. Any person considering interception, recording or monitoring of telephone calls or e-mails is strongly advised to seek his/her own independent legal advice and should not seek to rely on the general information provided below. It should be borne in mind that criminal offences and civil actions may occur when the relevant legislation is not complied with. Accordingly, Oftel accepts no liability for reliance by any person on the following information.

Can I record telephone conversations on my home phone?

Yes. The relevant law, *RIPA 2000*, does not prohibit individuals from recording their own communications provided that the recording is for their own use. Recording or monitoring are only prohibited where some of the contents of the communication – which can be a phone conversation or an e-mail – are made available to a third party, i.e. someone who was neither the caller or sender nor the intended recipient of the original communication. For further information see the Home Office website where *RIPA 2000* is posted.

Do I have to let people know that I intend to record their telephone conversations with me?

No, provided you are not intending to make the contents of the communication available to a third party. If you are you will need the consent of the person you are recording.

Can a business or other organisation record or monitor my phone calls or e-mail correspondence with them?
Yes they can, but only in a limited set of circumstances relevant for that business which have been defined by the *Lawful Business Practice Regulations* (*SI 2000/2699*). The main ones are:

- to provide evidence of a business transaction;
- to ensure that a business complies with regulatory procedures;
- to see that quality standards or targets are being met in the interests of national security;
- to prevent or detect crime to investigate the unauthorised use of a telecom system; and
- to secure the effective operation of the telecom system.

In addition, businesses can monitor, but not record, phone calls or e-mails which have been received to see whether they are relevant to the business, for example open an employee's voicemail or mailbox systems while they are away to see if there are any business communications stored there. Further information can be found on the Department of Trade and Industry (DTI) website.

However, any interception of employees' communications must be proportionate and in accordance with the Data Protection Principles. The Data Protection Commissioner is consulting on a Draft Code of Practice on the Use of Personal Data in Employer/ Employee Relationships. It is proposed that where the standards in the Code of Practice are, in the Commissioner's opinion, necessary for compliance with *DPA 1998*, they may be directly enforceable as a breach of the Data Protection Principles. Accordingly, this Code of Practice and *DPA 1998* must also be considered by any business before it intercepts employees' communications. For further information see the Information Commissioner's website.

Do businesses have to tell me if they are going to record or monitor my phone calls or e-mails?
No. As long as the recording or monitoring is done for one of the above purposes, then the only obligation on businesses is to inform their own employees. If businesses want to record for any other purpose, such as market research, they will have to obtain your consent.

Can a helpline record my calls?
No. If you phone an anonymous helpline that offers its services for free your conversation may be monitored but not recorded.

What do I do if my calls have been recorded unlawfully?
Under *RIPA 2000* it is a tort to record or monitor a communication unlawfully. This means that if you think you have suffered from unlawful interception of your phone calls or e-mails you have the right to seek redress by taking civil action against the offender in the courts.

Further information 38.5

For the employment issues see CHAPTER 16 EMPLOYMENT, CHAPTER 28 INTERNET and CHAPTER 29 LAWFUL BUSINESS PRACTICE REGULATIONS. For information on *RIPA 2000* see CHAPTER 40 REGULATION OF INVESTIGATORY POWERS ACT 2000.

The Home Office has a special section of its website devoted to *RIPA 2000*. This can be found via www.homeoffice.gov.uk, and includes drafts of codes of practice made under *RIPA 2000* and consultations.

The DTI consultation on the *Lawful Business Practice Regulations* (*SI 2000/2699*) is on the Internet at www.dti.gov.uk/cii/regulatory/telecomms/telecommsregulations/lawful_business_practice_regulations.shtml.

Oftel's guidance on recording of calls is at www.oftel.gov.uk/consumer/advice/FAQs/prvfaq3.htm.

39 – Registration/ Notification

At a glance 39.1

- ✓ Data controllers have to notify the Information Commissioner of their holding of personal data and pay an annual fee, which is currently £35. This process is called notification, or sometimes registration.
- ✓ Some EU states provide for a notification or deposit of contract terms under which data is exported from the European Economic Area (EEA).
- ✓ The Information Commissioner's website has an online notification form, as well as a question and answer section to check whether notification is necessary.
- ✓ Chapter 8 of the Information Commissioner's Legal Guidance (October 2001) provides information on Notification.
- ✓ Some companies who deal little with personal data do not have an obligation to notify as they benefit from various exemptions under the *Data Protection Act 1998* (*DPA 1998*).

Introduction 39.2

The first obligation of those handling personal data is to notify (register) with the Data Protection Office. *Part III* of *DPA 1998* contains the relevant law. Regular fees must be paid to keep a notification in effect. All those who are registered appear on the website at www.dpr.gov.uk. Further information on notification appears in Chapter 8 of the Commissioner's Legal Guidance (October 2001).

The European Commission, in providing general information on the *EU Data Protection Directive* (*95/46/EC*), describes the notification obligation as follows.

> 'In order to ensure that the public are properly informed about data processing operations, and also so as to allow the supervisory authorities to perform their tasks, the Directive

devises a system of notification for processing operations. National data protection authorities are required to keep a public register indicating details of the data controllers and of the processing undertaken.'

Some countries in the EU have opted to provide a deposit system for those entering into agreements for the export of personal data from the EEA within the Eighth Data Protection Principle under the Commission's model clauses for data export (see APPENDIX 3). The model clauses are considered in CHAPTER 20 EXPORT OF DATA and CHAPTER 44 TRANSBORDER DATA FLOWS. The UK has not adopted this optional requirement.

Duty to notify 39.3

Section 16 of *DPA 1998* sets out the registrable particulars which those notifying must give. They include information such as the name and address of the person and a description of the data (see 39.4 below). Under the *Data Protection Act 1984* (*DPA 1984*) someone who was exempt from registration was exempt from compliance with the Act. Under *DPA 1998* the link has gone. Every data controller has to comply with *DPA 1998*, even if they are exempt from notification.

When is it necessary to notify and what information is provided? 39.4

Those who process personal data have to notify under *DPA 1998*. An online questionnaire on the Commissioner's website (www.dpr.gov.uk/notify/4.html) can be completed by data processors, and will tell them whether they must register or not.

The notification includes a requirement to supply 'registrable particulars'. In relation to a data controller, these are:

(*a*) their name and address;

(*b*) if they have nominated a representative, the name and address of the representative;

(*c*) a description of the personal data being or to be processed and of the category(ies) of data subject to which they relate;

(*d*) a description of the purposes(s) for which the data are being or are to be processed;

(*e*) a description of any recipient(s) to whom the data controller intends or may wish to disclose the data;

(*f*) the name or a description of any countries or territories outside the European Economic Area to which the data controller transfers or intends or may wish to transfer the data; and

(*g*) where the personal data are of a type which is exempt from the prohibition against processing personal data without notification and where the notification does not extend to such data, a statement of that fact.

The Information Commissioner says in her Legal Guidance (October 2001):

> 'When a notification is made by a data controller he must also provide, in addition to the registrable particulars, a general description of the security measures taken to protect the personal data; this information will not appear on the register.'

Online notification 39.5

It is possible to register/notify online by completion of a form on the Commissioner's website. The form can currently be found at www.dpr.gov.uk/cgi-bin/dprproc?page=7.html.

Registration under DPA 1984 39.6

Many businesses are registered under *DPA 1984*. They are allowed to complete their earlier registration period before having to re-register, even if their registration expired after the first transitional period to 23 October 2001 (by the *Data Protection (Notification and Notification Fees) (Amendment) Regulations 2001* (*SI 2001/3214*) which altered the original law). However, they still have to comply with the rest of *DPA 1998*, including the Data Protection Principles, until they re-register under *DPA 1998* and thereafter. They are still obliged to notify the Commissioner of certain changes in processing.

Differences from DPA 1984 39.7

The principal differences between *DPA 1984* and notification under *DPA 1998* are as follows.

- Data processors do not need to notify under *DPA 1998*.
- Register entries will still contain a description of the processing of personal data. However, this description is in very general terms. The detailed coding system no longer exists.
- Businesses do not need to describe sources of personal data in the entry.

- Registration of disclosures are replaced by notification of recipients.
- Businesses only need to describe transfers of personal data outside the EEA.
- Businesses have to provide a statement about their security measures.
- There is now no need to provide an address for the receipt of subject access requests.
- *DPA 1998* provides some exemptions from notification.
- The notification period is one year.
- A data controller can only have one register entry.
- Headteachers and governing bodies of schools may notify in the name of the school (for many one notification rather than two registrations will be possible).

Fees 39.8

The notification fee is £35 (no VAT) for each year. The Data Protection Office does not send invoices but will acknowledge receipt of payments. Under *DPA 1984* a fee of £75 had to be paid every three years. Payment can be by direct debit, cheque or BACS.

The *Data Protection (Notification and Notification Fees) Regulations 2000* (*SI 2000/188*) include the provision for the £35 fee. The Regulations can be found at www.legislation.hmso.gov.uk/si/si2000/20000188.htm.

Notification by different groups 39.9

Notification by partnerships 39.10

Regulation 5 of the *Data Protection (Notification and Notification Fees) Regulations 2000* (*SI 2000/188*) provides that where a partnership is concerned the notification can be in the name of the firm.

Notification by schools 39.11

Regulation 6 of the *Data Protection (Notification and Notification Fees) Regulations 2000* (*SI 2000/188*) says that schools can register the name of the school on behalf of both the headteacher and the governing body. The name and address to be given is that of the school.

Frequently asked questions 39.12

The Information Commissioner has issued the following frequently asked questions with answers on notification.

Frequently Asked Questions

Q. What is notification?

A. The Commissioner maintains a public register of data controllers. Each register entry includes the name and address of the data controller and a general description of the processing of personal data by the data controller. Individuals can consult the register to find out what processing of personal data is being carried out by a particular data controller. Notification is the process by which a data controller's details are added to the register.

Q. Why do data controllers have to notify?

A. *DPA 1998* requires every data controller who is processing personal data to notify unless they are exempt.

Q. How can I find out if I am exempt?

A. The conditions required to be satisfied for each notification exemption are described in the publications 'Notification Handbook – A Complete Guide to Notification' and 'Notification Exemptions – A Self Assessment Guide', which can both be found at www.dpr.gov.uk

Q. Is there any link between notification and compliance?

A. No. The principal purpose of the notification process and the public register is openness. It is an important aspect of data protection legislation that the public should be able to find out who is carrying out the processing of personal data and other information about the processing, such as for what purposes the processing is carried out. However, notification does not equate to compliance with the Data Protection Principles.

The link between compliance and registration (or notification), which existed under *DPA 1984*, is no longer a feature of data protection legislation under *DPA 1998*. The Commissioner is able to enforce the Data Protection Principles against any data controller who is not otherwise exempt from compliance, regardless of their notification status, where she is satisfied that any of the Principles have been, or are being, contravened. It remains open to the Commissioner to investigate and prosecute those data controllers who are required to notify but who have not.

Notification offences 39.13

It is an offence to process personal data without notification unless:

- the personal data fall within either of the national security or domestic purposes exemptions;
- the personal data are exempt under the transitional exemptions;
- the personal data fall within the 'relevant filing system' or 'accessible record' or public register exceptions referred to above;
- the processing operation falls within the exemptions referred to in the *Data Protection (Notification and Notification Fees) Regulations 2000* (*SI 2000/188*), as amended by the *Data Protection (Notification and Notification Fees) (Amendment) Regulations 2001* (*SI 2001/3214*); or
- the processing is of a description which the Notification Regulations provide is exempt from the requirements to notify on the ground that it is unlikely to prejudice the rights and freedoms of data subjects. No such provision was included in the Regulations.

This is a strict liability offence, so even if the controller had no idea that *DPA 1998* existed, a prosecution could still follow.

Example 39.14

In the First Annual Report of the Information Commissioner (June 2001) one case study relating to failure to notify is discussed. An employee appropriated client data from his employer's database, then left that firm and established his own company. The appropriate data was retained on computer. He was convicted of unlawfully using the data for his own purposes and his new business was convicted of being an unregistered data user.

It is important to tell the Information Commissioner if a change occurs as otherwise an offence can be committed. The *Data Protection (Notification and Notification Fees) Regulations 2000* (*SI 2000/188*), as amended by the *Data Protection (Notification and Notification Fees)*

(Amendment) Regulations 2001 (*SI 2001/3214*), provided that such notification must be given as soon as is practicable, and in any event within a period of 28 days from the date upon which the entry becomes inaccurate or incomplete as a statement of the data controller's registrable particulars, or in respect of measures taken with regard to compliance with the Seventh Data Protection Principle. A defence is available to persons charged with such an offence if they can show that they exercised all due diligence to comply with the duty.

Further information 39.15

Further information on notification under *DPA 1998* can be found on the Commissioner's website www.dataprotection.gov.uk

The Commissioner has issued Notification Exemptions – A Self Assessment Guide, which contains questions to help data controllers to determine if notification is required.

Other documents in the notification field on the website of the Information Commissioner are:

Notification Handbook – A Complete Guide To Notification.

Form to alter or remove a register entry (see CHAPTER 23 FORMS).

Purpose form – to add a purpose to a register entry (see CHAPTER 23 FORMS)

Background information on the EU Data Protection Directive is on the Commission's web site at www.europa.eu.int/comm/ internal_ market/ en/dataprot/backinfo/info.htm [illegible] *independent* [illegible] *MIG* [illegible] [illegible] that the [illegible] [illegible] the [illegible] [illegible] in [illegible] should [illegible] [illegible] [illegible] [illegible] of the data controller [illegible] [illegible] the [illegible]

[illegible] [illegible] [illegible] [illegible] [illegible] [illegible] [illegible] [illegible]

[illegible] [illegible] [illegible] [illegible] [illegible] [illegible] [illegible] [illegible] [illegible] [illegible] [illegible] [illegible] [illegible]

[illegible] [illegible] [illegible] [illegible] [illegible] [illegible] [illegible] [illegible] [illegible] [illegible] [illegible] [illegible] [illegible] [illegible] [illegible] [illegible]

40 – Regulation of Investigatory Powers Act 2000

At a glance 40.1

- ✓ The *Regulation of Investigatory Powers Act 2000* (*RIPA 2000*) sets out legislation on interception of communications in the UK.
- ✓ *RIPA 2000* is supplemented by the *Telecommunications (Lawful Business Practice) (Interception of Communications) Regulations 2000* (*SI 2000/2699*).
- ✓ In September 2001 the Home Office issued three draft Codes of Practice under *RIPA 2000*.
- ✓ The *Anti-Terrorism, Crime and Security Bill*, published November 2001, included provisions for a code of practice under *RIPA 2000* which would require businesses to retain 'traffic data' about the use made of telecoms systems.

Introduction 40.2

RIPA 2000 governs the interception of communications in the UK. This chapter provides a summary of the Act and the latest developments under it. The *Telecommunications (Lawful Business Practice) (Interception of Communications) Regulations 2000* (*SI 2000/2699*) made under *RIPA 2000* were examined in CHAPTER 29 LAWFUL BUSINESS PRACTICE REGULATIONS. CHAPTER 38 RECORDING TELEPHONE CALLS AND E-MAILS contains information on recording telephone calls and e-mails, and includes Oftel's guidance to consumers on this topic.

Telecoms and e-mail monitoring is a growth area. The Privacy Foundation in the US has found that one in three of 40 million employees using e-mail or the Internet are monitored. and that 100 million workers on a worldwide basis are monitored by one means or another. The report is at www.sonic.net/~undoc/extent.htm

This area should be watched closely. An Anti-Terrorism, Crime and

Security Bill is likely to be enacted by December 2001, which will make further changes in this field.

Summary of RIPA 2000 — 40.3

The provisions of *RIPA 2000* are summarised at 40.4–40.7 below.

Part I: Interception and access to communications data — 40.4

Part I of *RIPA 2000* updates the previous interception law (the *Interception of Communications Act 1985*) to cover all communications service providers. This includes Internet Service Providers (ISPs). Interception must be personally authorised by the Secretary of State and is only allowed when the strict criteria laid down in *RIPA 2000* are met. The forms authorising such access are on the Home Office's website. Under *section 12* of *RIPA 2000* the Secretary of State may require *individual* communication service providers to maintain a reasonable intercept capability, by means of a notice. However, this must be subject to a consultation process involving industry and any draft notice must be approved by both Houses of Parliament. This part of the Act was very controversial, as many small ISPs felt they could not afford the cost of a compulsory scheme. The Government has announced that it will set aside £20m from April 2001 to 2004 to ease the introduction of the new arrangements.

RIPA 2000 also includes a provision to establish a Technical Advisory Board, which will be made up of both Government and industry members, to oversee the notices served on communications service providers requiring the maintenance of an intercept capability. The Government will be working in conjunction with industry on the proper composition of the Board.

Part I of *RIPA 2000* also introduces comprehensive statutory controls for the first time, governing access to communications data, such as billing information. Access must be properly authorised for specified purposes only, and is subject to independent oversight.

Part II: Surveillance and covert human intelligence sources — 40.5

Part II of *RIPA 2000* regulates techniques, such as the use of agents or informants, which have been used for many years by law enforcement, security and intelligence agencies, but which have up until now been authorised on a non-statutory basis. The *Human Rights Act 1998* requires there to be a statutory framework in place for authorising these activities. (See CHAPTER 26 HUMAN RIGHTS ACT 1998.) This part of *RIPA 2000* also provides a legal basis for the surveillance activities presently carried out by a wide range of Government departments in pursuance of their duties.

Part II of the Act was brought into force on 25 September 2000 to ensure that current surveillance operations were properly regulated and fully compliant with the *Human Rights Act 1998* for its commencement on 2 October 2000.

Part III: Encryption 40.6

Part III of *RIPA 2000* establishes a power to require any person served with an appropriate notice to disclose protected, that is encrypted, information in an intelligible form ('plain text'). The power is ancillary to all statutory and non-statutory powers and functions of public authorities. Its use requires proper and specific permission. A number of statutory requirements must be met before any such permission can be given to exercise the disclosure power. There are extra requirements where a decryption key – rather than plain text – is desired. *RIPA 2000* sets out statutory safeguards for the protection of all information obtained under the *Part III* power. In addition, there are associated offences.

This requirement has been heavily criticised as the Bill progressed through Parliament.

Part IV: Oversight and complaints 40.7

Part IV of *RIPA 2000* sets out the oversight and complaints mechanisms for the powers in the legislation. This includes:

- independent Commissioners (who must be judicial figures) with a statutory responsibility to oversee the exercise of the powers; and
- an independent Tribunal to hear complaints.

Part IV also deals with Codes of Practice, covering all parts of *RIPA 2000*, which will be admissible as evidence in criminal and civil proceedings. Three draft codes have now been issued (see 40.9 below).

Forms 40.8

The Home Office website, at www.homeoffice.gov.uk, provides full details of the forms which are used to authorise interceptions by public bodies such as the police. For example, the authorisation form provides for the grounds of interception to be stated, as set out below.

Grounds on which the action is **necessary**: (*delete as inapplicable*)
In the interests of national security.
For the purpose of preventing or detecting crime or of preventing disorder.
In the interests of the economic well-being of the United Kingdom.
In the interests of public safety.
For the purpose of protecting public health.
For the purpose of assessing or collecting any tax, duty, levy or other imposition, contribution or charge payable to a government department.

Codes of Practice 40.9

On 25 September 2000 the first three Codes of Practice governing the day-to-day operation of the law enforcement powers set out by *RIPA 2000* were published for consultation. They are:

- the Draft Code of Practice on the Use of Interception of Communications;
- the Draft Code of Practice on the Use of Covert Human Intelligence Sources; and
- the Draft Code of Practice on Covert Surveillance.

The Codes have been issued to:

- law enforcement and security agencies;
- public authorities;
- MPs; and
- key representatives from industry, telecommunications operators and ISPs.

A further code on traffic data is also proposed but not yet published.

Code of Practice for Communications Data and Anti-Terrorism, Crime and Security Bill 40.10

In August 2001 the Home Office issued a Draft Code of Practice on Accessing Communications Data for public consultation. The Code will govern the conduct of law enforcement and public bodies when obtaining information relating to the use of postal or telecommunication services, for example telephone billing information. The consultation period expired on 2 November 2001.

Data may only be sought by the police and others under *RIPA 2000* for certain stated purposes such as:

- in the interests of national security;
- for the purpose of preventing or detecting crime or preventing disorder; or
- in the interests of public safety.

Communications data **40.11**

Communications data, such as telephone billing information, is useful to the police. This type of data does not include the contents of the communication. *Chapter II, Part I* of *RIPA 2000* only deals with access to communications data. The Home Office say that, for example,

> 'a list of telephone numbers can be reasonably seen as just that and therefore is defined as communications data, it does not give any indication of what might have been said during a conversation'.

Communications content **40.12**

In contrast to what is stated at 40.11 above, what is said during the telephone call is communications content. The Government say that it remains strict policy that the content of communications can *only* be obtained under an interception warrant personally authorised by the Secretary of State.

Proposed legislation **40.13**

The Anti-Terrorism, Crime and Security Bill was published in November 2001, and is available at www.parliament.the-stationery-office.co.uk/pa/pabills.htm. On communications data, Part 11 contains provisions to allow communications service providers to retain data about their customers' communications for access by law enforcement agencies and for national security purposes, and to enable a code of practice to be drawn up in consultation with industry. The code of practice will allow communications service providers to retain data about their customers' communications for access by law enforcement agencies. Currently communications service providers are obliged to erase this data when they no longer need it for billing purposes. These provisions fall within

RIPA 2000 which sets out the limits on the purposes for which the law enforcement, security and intelligence agencies may request access to data relating to specific communications. There is also a reserve power to review the arrangements and issue directions if necessary. If still needed, it must be reviewed by an affirmative order every two years. As soon as the power is exercised, there is no need for further review.

In November 2001 the Information Commissioner issued a press release saying she was concerned about the privacy implications of the Bill, and would be commenting in detail on its provisions. She was particularly concerned about there being a code of practice in place rather than specific legislation.

Obligations imposed on the Secretary of State 40.14

Section 71 of *RIPA 2000* requires the Secretary of State to prepare, publish and consider any representations made to him on the content of the Codes before they are laid before Parliament for approval by affirmative resolution. The Codes of Practice are published on the official *RIPA 2000* website at www.homeoffice.gov.uk/ripa/ripact.htm. *Part I* of *RIPA 2000* updates the previous interception law (the *Interception of Communications Act 1985*) to encompass all communications service providers, including Internet Service Providers (ISPs). Interception must be personally authorised by the Secretary of State and only when the strict criteria laid down in *RIPA 2000* are met.

Powers given to the Secretary of State 40.15

Section 12 of *RIPA 2000* provides a power allowing the Secretary of State to impose obligations upon providers of publicly available communication services to maintain a reasonable intercept capability. The Secretary of State will do this through an order to be approved by both Houses of Parliament. This order will be subject to a consultation process involving industry before it is laid. It is envisaged that these provisions of the Act will be enacted by the end of 2001.

Interception requirements 40.16

Under *RIPA 2000* a small proportion of communication service providers (CSPs) may be required to maintain a reasonable intercept capability to assist investigations into serious crime and counterthreats to the nation's security or economic well-being. *RIPA 2000* will also establish a Technical Advisory Board, made up of an equal number of Government and CSP representatives under an independent chairman, to act as ombudsman and to advise the Home Secretary on matters concerning interception of communications via CSPs.

The Government has launched a consultation to hear CSPs' views on the form and detail of the interception requirements to ensure that they will be 'effective, technologically relevant and industry-friendly'. CSPs are also invited to nominate representatives for the Technical Advisory Board to ensure that the industry's interests are fully represented in these matters.

Section 12 40.17

Chapter I of *Part I* of *RIPA 2000* updates the previous interception law, the *Interception of Communications Act 1985*, to encompass all communications service providers, including ISPs. Its provisions were implemented on 2 October 2000 to coincide with the *Human Rights Act 1998*. However, implementing the interception provisions of *RIPA 2000* does not mean that UK communications service providers not currently required to have an intercept capability will immediately be required to install one.

Section 12 of *DPA 1998* provides a power enabling the Secretary of State to serve a notice requiring individual CSPs to maintain a reasonable intercept capability. This has led to much criticism, particularly about the cost of this. The notice will specify the services for which an interception capability is required, the steps and time-scale for meeting this requirement, and the division of costs between the government and CSPs. Before this can happen, an order must be approved by both Houses of Parliament.

RIPA 2000 specifies that interception warrants must be authorised personally by the Secretary of State, and may only be authorised where this is necessary as being in the interests of national security; for the purpose of preventing or detecting serious crime; or for the purpose of safeguarding the economic well-being of the United Kingdom.

Implementation timetable 40.18

The following is a general indication of the implementation timetable of the various parts of *RIPA 2000*. For further details refer to the *Regulation of Investigatory Powers Act 2000 (Commencement No. 1 and Transitional Provisions) Order 2000* (*SI 2000/2543*).

Part I Chapter I (Interception of Communications): With the exception of *section 1(3)*, this part of the Act came into force on 2 October 2000. *Section 1(3)* and the *Lawful Business Practice Regulations* (*SI 2000/2699*) referred to in *section 4(2)* came into force on

24 October 2000 (see the *Regulation of Investigatory Powers Act 2000 (Commencement No 1 and Transitional Provisions) Order 2000 (SI 2000/2543*).

Part I Chapter II (Access to Communications Data): The intention was for this part of the Act to be implemented during the second half of 2001.

Part II (Surveillance and Covert Human Intelligence Sources): This part of the Act was brought into force on 25 September 2000.

Part III (the investigation of electronic data protected by encryption): The intention was for this part of the Act to be implemented during the second half of 2001.

Part IV (Scrutiny etc of Investigatory Powers and of the functions of the Intelligence Services), Part V and the Schedules: Refer to the above commencement order to see which sections of this part have been enacted so far.

Discussion documents **40.19**

The following discussion documents are available on the Parliament website.

- *Draft Regulation of Investigatory Powers (British Broadcasting Corporation) Order 2001* and *Designation of Public Authorities for the Purposes of Intrusive Surveillance Order 2001* (First Standing Committee) House of Commons.
- *Regulation of Investigatory Powers (British Broadcasting Corporation) Order 2001 (SI 2001/1057)* and *Designation of Public Authorities for the Purposes of Intrusive Surveillance Order 2000* House of Lords, Hansard.
- First Standing Committee on Delegated Legislation – discussion of the *Regulation of Investigatory Powers (Notification of Authorisations etc) Order* (*SI 2000/2563*) and the *Investigatory Powers Tribunal Rules 2000* (*SI2000/2665*) on 30 October 2000.
- The *Regulation of Investigatory Powers (Notification of Authorisations etc) Order 2000* (*SI 2000/2563*) – House of Lords, Hansard, 27 October 2000.
- The *Investigatory Powers Tribunal Rules 2000* (*SI 2000/2665*) – House of Lords, Hansard, 27 October 2000.

Secondary legislation 40.20

The following Statutory Instruments are available on the HMSO website.

- The *Wireless Telegraphy (Interception and Disclosure of Messages)(Designation) Regulations 2000 (SI 2000/2409)*.
- The *Regulation of Investigatory Powers (Prescription of Offices, Ranks and Positions) Order 2000 (SI 2000/2417)*.
- The *Regulation of Investigatory Powers (Authorisations Extending to Scotland) Order 2000 (SI 2000/2418)*.
- The *Regulation of Investigatory Powers Act 2000 (Commencement No. 1 and Transitional Provisions) Order 2000 (SI 2000/2543)*.
- The *Regulation of Investigatory Powers (Notification of Authorisations etc.) Order 2000 (SI 2000/2563)*.
- The *Investigatory Powers Tribunal Rules 2000 (SI 2000/2665)*.
- The *Telecommunications (Lawful Business Practice) (Interception of Communications) Regulations 2000 (SI 2000/2699)*.
- The *Regulation of Investigatory Powers (Source Records) Regulations 2000 (SI 2000/2725)*.
- The *Regulation of Investigatory Powers (Juveniles) Order 2000 (SI 2000/2793)*.
- The *Regulation of Investigatory Powers (Cancellation of Authorisations) Regulations 2000 (SI 2000/2794)*.
- The *Regulation of Investigatory Powers (British Broadcasting Corporation) Order 2001 (SI 2001/1057)*.
- The *Regulation of Investigatory Powers (Designation of Public Authorities for the Purposes of Intrusive Surveillance) Order 2001 (SI 2001/1126)*.
- The *Regulation of Investigatory Powers Act 2000 (Commencement No. 2) Order 2001 (SI 2001/2727)*.

Case law 40.21

In the decision in the case of *PG and JH v United Kingdom (25 September 2001) (Times Law Reports 19 October 2001)* the European Court of Human Rights held that covert listening devices at police stations were a breach of *Articles 8* and *13* of the *European Convention on Human Rights*, which provide the right to respect for a private life (*Article 8*) and the right to an effective remedy (*Article 13*). However there was no *Article 6* breach of the right to a fair hearing.

The case arose from the armed robbery of a Securicor van in the UK about which the police had been tipped off, and so had set up surveillance. The Chief Constable had given authorisation for a listening device to be used to obtain more evidence. The two applicants in the case (known as 'P.G' and 'J.H.') were arrested in a stolen car in which there were two black balaclavas, five cable ties, two pairs of gloves and two army kit bags. Devices were placed in the cells of those arrested to hear what they said. Again, authorisation from the chief constable was obtained. In 1996 the accused were sentenced to 15 years in jail for armed robbery. Evidence derived from the surveillance was used in court. At the time the surveillance took place *RIPA 2000* was not in force.

Further information 40.22

The Home Office's website provides the fullest information on *RIPA 2000*. A useful page is www.homeoffice.gov.uk/ripa/ripact.htm

See also CHAPTER 3 CODES OF PRACTICE and CHAPTER 38 RECORDING TELEPHONE CALLS AND E-MAILS.

CHAPTER 15 E-MAILS and CHAPTER 16 EMPLOYMENT examine monitoring in relation to e-mail and employment respectively.

The Privacy Foundation of the US has a website at www.privacy foundation.org

Information on *RIPA 2000* can be obtained by post from the following address.

RIPA Implementation Team
Room 735
Home Office
50 Queen Anne's Gate
London
SW1H 9AT

Copies of the Draft Code of Practice on Accessing Communications Data is available from the Home Office website at www.homeoffice. gov.uk/ripa/ripact.htm. Hard copies are available from the Home Office Press Office on 020 7273 4545.

Explanatory notes on the Anti-Terrorism, Crime and Security Bill were published in November 2001 at www.parliament.the-stationery-office. co.uk/pa/cm200102/cmbills/049/en/02049x—.htm.

41 – 'Safe Harbor' Agreement

At a glance 41.1

- ✓ The Eighth Data Protection Principle prohibits the export of personal data from the European Economic Area (EEA) except where strict conditions are met.
- ✓ The EU and US agreed a Safe Harbor Agreement in July 2000 which would permit such exports where the US recipient has signed the Safe Harbor Agreement
- ✓ The agreement is not the only lawful manner in which personal data can be exported to the US. The Eighth Principle permits exports on other conditions such as when the EU model clauses for data export apply.
- ✓ The US has a safe harbor website on which information of relevance appears.

Introduction 41.2

The Eighth Data Protection Principle requires that personal data should not be exported without compliance with the requirements of that principle as set down in *DPA 1998*. On July 2000 the US agreed its 'Safe Harbor' agreement with the EU to permit exports of personal data to the US by those companies registering in the US as prepared to comply with the US Safe Harbor Agreement. Only those who register and meet the requirements can benefit from the Safe Harbor Agreement This is not the only lawful means of such data export, and often instead the EU Model Clauses can be used (see APPENDIX 3 and also the Frequently Asked Questions on the Model Clauses in APPENDIX 2) or other requirements of the Eighth Principle satisfied.

Coverage 41.3

The Model Clauses apply to e-commerce but not to financial services. They are intended to aid businesses shipping personal data between the

EEA and US. On 25 August 2000, the EU published its decision adopting the Safe Harbor Agreement (OJ L215/7) under the *EU Data Protection Directive* (*95/46/EC*). The US Government has said that failure to comply with data protection laws will be considered a deceptive business practice and a prosecutable offence. The US Commerce Department runs a register of industry self-regulators, and monitors those companies to ensure that they comply with privacy rules. Regulators are required to reapply for membership of the list each year. The Federal Trade Commission (FTC) and the US judicial system will be able to impose sanctions on companies that violate the rules.

The US safe harbor website is at www.export.gov/safeharbor/

How to comply with the rules 41.4

Companies are able to comply with the rules in four ways:

(*a*) by reporting to a data protection authority in Europe;

(*b*) by subjecting themselves to monitoring by US lawmakers;

(*c*) by joining a self-regulatory body, which will be monitored by the US FTC; or

(*d*) if a company is not online, by committing itself to obey a new European panel of data privacy officials.

Companies like Amazon.com, for example, will also be obliged to insert a link on their websites to their data privacy regulator in order to inform customers of the protection being provided.

What do the safe harbor principles require? 41.5

The US Department of Commerce summarise the requirements thus:

What do the safe harbor principles require?

Organisations must comply with the seven safe harbor principles. The principles require the following.

Notice: Organisations must notify individuals about the purposes for which they collect and use information about them. They must provide information about how individuals can contact the organisation with any inquiries or complaints, the types of third parties to which it discloses the information and the choices and means the organisation offers for limiting its use and disclosure.

Choice: Organisations must give individuals the opportunity to choose (opt-out) whether their personal information will be disclosed to a third party or used for a purpose incompatible with the purpose for which it was originally collected or subsequently authorised by the individual. For sensitive information, affirmative or explicit (opt-in) choice must be given if the information is to be disclosed to a third party or used for a purpose other than its original purpose, or the purpose authorised subsequently by the individual.

Onward Transfer (Transfers to Third Parties): To disclose information to a third party, organisations must apply the notice and choice principles. Where an organisation wishes to transfer information to a third party that is acting as an agent, it may do so if it makes sure that the third party subscribes to the safe harbor principles or is subject to the Directive or another adequacy finding. As an alternative, the organisation can enter into a written agreement with such third party requiring that the third party provide at least the same level of privacy protection as is required by the relevant principles.

Access: Individuals must have access to personal information about them that an organisation holds and be able to correct, amend, or delete that information where it is inaccurate, except where the burden or expense of providing access would be disproportionate to the risks to the individual's privacy in the case in question, or where the rights of persons other than the individual would be violated.

Security: Organisations must take reasonable precautions to protect personal information from loss, misuse and unauthorised access, disclosure, alteration and destruction.

Data integrity: Personal information must be relevant for the purposes for which it is to be used. An organisation should take reasonable steps to ensure that data is reliable for its intended use, accurate, complete, and current.

Enforcement: In order to ensure compliance with the safe harbor principles, there must be:

(*a*) readily available and affordable independent recourse mechanisms so that each individual's complaints and disputes can be investigated and resolved, and damages awarded where the applicable law or private sector initiatives so provide;

(*b*) procedures for verifying that the commitments companies make to adhere to the safe harbor principles have been implemented; and (*c*) obligations to remedy problems arising out of a failure to comply with the principles.

Sanctions must be sufficiently rigorous to ensure compliance by the organisation. Organisations that fail to provide annual self-certification letters will no longer appear in the list of participants and safe harbor benefits will no longer be assured.

To provide further guidance, the Department of Commerce has issued a set of frequently asked questions and answers (FAQs) that clarify and supplement the safe harbor principles.

Enforcement 41.6

Enforcement is expected to take place in the US under US law, and the Department of Commerce expects it to be largely private sector enforcement. 'The effect of these statutes is to give an organisation's safe harbor commitments the force of law *vis-a-vis* that organisation.'

The Department of Commerce states the following.

> **'Private Sector Enforcement:** As part of their safe harbor obligations, organizations are required to have in place a dispute resolution system that will investigate and resolve individual complaints and disputes and procedures for verifying compliance. They are also required to remedy problems arising out of a failure to comply with the principles. Sanctions that dispute resolution bodies can apply must be severe enough to ensure compliance by the organization; they must include publicity for findings of non-compliance and deletion of data in certain circumstances. They may also include suspension from membership in a privacy program (and thus effectively suspension from the safe harbor) and injunctive orders.
>
> The dispute resolution, verification, and remedy requirements can be satisfied in different ways. For example, an organization could comply with a private sector developed privacy seal program that incorporates and satisfies the safe harbor principles. If the seal program, however, only provides for dispute resolution and remedies but not verification, then the organization would have to satisfy the verification requirement in an alternative way.
>
> Organizations can also satisfy the dispute resolution and remedy requirements through compliance with government

supervisory authorities or by committing to co-operate with data protection authorities located in Europe.

Government Enforcement: Depending on the industry sector, the Federal Trade Commission, comparable US government agencies, and/or the states may provide overarching government enforcement of the safe harbor principles. Where a company relies in whole or in part on self-regulation in complying with the safe harbor principles, its failure to comply with such self-regulation must be actionable under federal or state law prohibiting unfair and deceptive acts or it is not eligible to join the safe harbor. At present, US organizations that are subject to the jurisdiction of the Federal Trade Commission or the Department of Transportation with respect to air carriers and ticket agents may participate in the safe harbor. The Federal Trade Commission and the Department of Transportation with respect to air carriers and ticket agents have both stated in letters to the European Commission that they will take enforcement action against organizations that state that they are in compliance with the safe harbor framework but then fail to live up to their statements.

Under the Federal Trade Commission Act, for example, a company's failure to abide by commitments to implement the safe harbor principles might be considered deceptive and actionable by the Federal Trade Commission. This is the case even where an organization adhering to the safe harbor principles relies entirely on self-regulation to provide the enforcement required by the safe harbor enforcement principle. The FTC has the power to rectify such misrepresentations by seeking administrative orders and civil penalties of up to $12,000 per day for violations.

Failure to Comply with the Safe Harbor Requirements: If an organization persistently fails to comply with the safe harbor requirements, it is no longer entitled to benefit from the safe harbor. Persistent failure to comply arises where an organization refuses to comply with a final determination by any self-regulatory or government body or where such a body determines that an organization frequently fails to comply with the requirements to the point where its claim to comply is no longer credible. In these cases, the organization must promptly notify the Department of Commerce of such facts. Failure to do so may be actionable under the False Statements Act (18 U.S.C. § 1001).

The Department of Commerce will indicate on the public list it maintains of organizations self certifying adherence to the safe harbor requirements any notification it receives of persistent failure to comply and will make clear which organizations are assured and which organizations are no longer assured of safe harbor benefits.

An organization applying to participate in a self-regulatory body for the purposes of re-qualifying for the safe harbor must provide that body with full information about its prior participation in the safe harbor.'

FAQs 41.7

The US Department of Commerce has issued some Frequently Asked Questions about safe harbor. These cover the following topics and are accessible under Documents on the safe harbor website at www.export.gov/safeharbor/sh_documents.html.

(*a*) Sensitive Data.

(*b*) Journalistic Exceptions.

(*c*) Secondary Liability.

(*d*) Investment Banking and Audits.

(*e*) The Role of Data Protection Authorities.

(*f*) Self-Certification.

(*g*) Verification.

(*h*) Access.

(*j*) Human Resources.

(*k*) Article 17 Contracts.

(*l*) Dispute Resolution and Enforcement.

(*m*) Choice – Timing of Opt-out.

(*n*) Travel Information.

(*o*) Pharmaceutical and Medical Products.

(*p*) Public Record and Publicly Available Information.

Further information 41.8

The US safe harbor website is at www.export.gov/safeharbor/.

Documents relating to safe harbor, including Frequently Asked Questions, are at www.export.gov/safeharbor/sh_documents.html.

The list of companies registered under safe harbor is at http://web.ita.doc.gov/safeharbor/shlist.nsf/webPages/safe+harbor+list.

The European Commission's Decision published August 2000 adopting the Safe Harbor Agreement is at http://europa.eu.int/ comm/ trade/pdf/safeharbour.pdf.

See CHAPTER 20 EXPORT OF DATA and CHAPTER 44 TRANSBORDER DATA FLOWS. For export of employee data see CHAPTER 16 EMPLOYMENT. CHAPTER 36 PRINCIPLES (THE EIGHT PRINCIPLES) also covers the Eighth Principle. APPENDICES 2 and 3 give the Commission's Frequently Asked Questions about the Model Clauses and the Model Clauses themselves respectively. For amendments to the Model Clauses see http://europa.eu.int/comm/internal_market/en/dataprot/news/annotateddecision.pdf

42 – Sensitive Personal Data

At a glance 42.1

- ✓ Handlers of sensitive personal data are subject to strict obligations under the *Data Protection Act 1998* (*DPA 1998*), as set out in *Schedule 3* to *DPA 1998*.
- ✓ Sensitive personal data includes data about race, political beliefs, union activities, sex life, commission of offences etc.
- ✓ Explicit consent must in many cases be obtained before such data is processed.
- ✓ The Commissioner's Legal Guidance and Draft Code of Practice on the Use of Personal Data in Employer/Employee Relationships provide useful guidance in this field.

Introduction 42.2

Sensitive personal data is subject to much stricter regulation under *DPA 1998* than ordinary personal data. The category of sensitive personal data includes information such as race, religion and sex life. *Schedule 3* to *DPA 1998* contains the requirements for the processing of data of this nature. In particular, sensitive personal data must not be processed unless:

- the data subject has given explicit consent;
- it is processed in performance of a legal right of employment law;
- it is a matter of life or death; or
- it comes under certain other categories.

What is sensitive personal data? 42.3

Section 2 of *DPA 1998* defines sensitive personal data as information as to:

(*a*) the racial or ethnic origin of the data subject;

(*b*) political opinions;

(*c*) religious beliefs or beliefs of a similar nature;

(*d*) membership of a trade union or non-membership;

(*e*) physical or mental health or condition;

(*f*) sexual life;

(*g*) the commission or alleged commission of any offence; or

(*h*) any proceedings for an offence committed or alleged to have been committed by him or her, the disposal of any such proceedings or the sentence of any court to such proceedings.

Examples 42.4

(*a*) A collection of which politicians are homosexual or which members of a royal family carry a defective gene would be sensitive personal data.

(*b*) An interesting issue is whether a name alone can be sensitive personal data. 'Seamus O'Hara' may appear to be of Celtic origin but may be from a Kenyan tribe.

(*c*) A photograph of someone may reveal sensitive personal data about them, such as whether they are clearly physically handicapped or their ethnic origin. That would appear to make photographs of individuals sensitive personal data, but the information is hardly confidential as every time that person walks down the street their ethnic origin is clear (to the extent that appearance does reveal such origin).

The law in this area is complex and advice should be sought.

Conditions for processing sensitive personal data 42.5

Schedule 3 to *DPA 1998* sets out the detailed conditions of the processing of sensitive personal data. This is addressed in depth in Chapter 3.1.3 of the Information Commissioner's Legal Guidance (October 2001). For employment and CCTV processing of personal data reference should be made to the Information Commissioner's Codes of Practice in those areas. Processing of sensitive personal data may take place where one of the conditions set out at 42.6–42.12 is satisfied.

Explicit consent **42.6**

The data subject gives their explicit consent to the process. The *EU Data Protection Directive (95/46/EC)*, implemented by *DPA 1998* in the UK, says that consent must be freely given and it should be a specific and informed indication of the data subject's wishes by which 'the data subject signifies his agreement to personal data relating to him being processed.'

> 'The consent must be "explicit" in the case of sensitive data. The use of the word "explicit" and the fact that the condition requires explicit consent "to the processing of the personal data" suggests that the consent of the data subject should be absolutely clear. In appropriate cases it should cover the specific detail of the processing, the particular type of data to be processed (or even the specific information), the purposes of the processing and any special aspects of the processing which may affect the individual, for example, disclosures which may be made of the data.'
>
> *Information Commissioner's Legal Guidance, October 2001*

Employment **42.7**

The processing of sensitive personal data is also allowed where the processing is necessary (not just desirable) in order to exercise or perform a function imposed by law on the data controller 'in connection with employment'. The Draft Code of Practice on the Use of Personal Data in Employer/Employee Relationships gives further information on this in the context of employment (see CHAPTER 16 EMPLOYMENT).

Vital interests **42.8**

Sensitive personal data may be processed where this is necessary to protect the vital interests of the data subject. However, this has been interpreted to mean where it is a matter of life or death.

Associations **42.9**

Processing of sensitive personal data is allowed where it is carried out by non-profit-making associations for political, philosophical, religious or trade union purposes with appropriate safeguards. It must only relate to members of or those with a contract with the body, and does not involve disclosure of the personal data to a third party without the third party's consent.

Data subject has made the information public 42.10

If the data subject has deliberately taken steps to make the sensitive personal data public then it can be processed. For example, if a famous person sells the stories of their extramarital gay affairs to the press, or if a well-known actor discloses that he is HIV positive.

Other exceptions 42.11

There are other exceptions in certain cases, such as where the processing of the sensitive personal data is necessary for legal advice or litigation, the administration of justice or for medical purposes.

Processing is also allowed where the data is gathered on race or ethnic origins to assess an equal opportunities policy.

Secondary legislation 42.12

The *Data Protection (Processing of Sensitive Personal) Data Order 2000* (*SI 2000/417*) includes rules on processing personal data, because *para 10* of *Schedule 3* to *DPA 1998* allows further categories to be laid down. These are not described here, but they include various law enforcement rights, rights to process for pensions and insurance matters, and rights for maintaining archives.

Commissioner's Legal Guidance 42.13

The issues addressed at 22.3 are also considered in detail in the Information Commissioner's Legal Guidance (October 2001). This gives an example of sensitive personal data, as well as describing in detail the rules considered above.

Example 42.14

> 'To illustrate this point, in a common scenario where negotiations are taking place between an individual and an insurance company with a view to entering into a contract of insurance, various disclosures have to be made which may include sensitive personal data about a third party to enable the insurer to assess the risk and calculate the premium. Examples could be a group

insurance policy for holiday insurance where medical details of individuals who are not party to the negotiations are disclosed, or car insurance where conviction details of named drivers would have to be revealed by the proposer. No contract exists at this stage and the insurance company may decide not to accept the risk and enter into a contract of insurance.

Reliance by the insurance company, as data controller, upon paragraph (c) of this condition as a basis for processing the sensitive personal data of a third party would not be acceptable to the Commissioner prior to the existence of the contract and the data controller would have to rely upon another condition for processing sensitive data in Schedule 3 or under the Sensitive Data Order unless, on a case by case analysis, the data controller has reasonable grounds for believing that an agency relationship exists between the individual with whom he is dealing and the data subject. (i.e. a relationship exists whereby one party, the "agent," has the authority or capacity to create legal relations between a person acting as "principal" and a third party).'

Conclusion 42.15

Many businesses process sensitive personal data, and these businesses need to ensure that they put in place adequate systems to cope with this. CHAPTER 37 PRIVACY POLICIES AND AUDITS provides guidance in this area.

Further information 42.16

Chapter 3 of the Commissioner's Legal Guidance deals with sensitive personal data. It can be found on the Commissioner's website at www.dataprotection.gov.uk.

For employee issues see CHAPTER 16 EMPLOYMENT and the Information Commissioner's Draft Code of Practice on the Use of Personal Data in Employer/Employee Relationships.

For information on CCTV see CHAPTER 2 CCTV.

43 – Subject Access Requests

At a glance 43.1

- ✓ *Section 7* of the *Data Protection Act 1998* (*DPA 1998*) gives individuals a right of access to much of the data held about them.
- ✓ The data controller must respond within 40 days to a subject access request, but may require the individual to provide further details in appropriate cases.
- ✓ A maximum charge of £10 can be imposed (£50 in cases of health records).
- ✓ There are a number of exemptions from subject access which need to be considered.
- ✓ Chapter 4.1 of the Commissioner's Legal Guidance examines subject access.
- ✓ Important security issues arise in ensuring that those seeking access are who they say they are.
- ✓ Those responding to subject access requests need to ensure they do not disclose third party data. The Commissioner has issued specific guidance on this aspect.
- ✓ Under the *Freedom of Information Act 2000* (*FIA 2000*) when fully in force similar rights will be given as against state bodies.

Introduction 43.2

Individuals are entitled to access to the personal data held about them by data controllers. This is known as subject access. *Section 7* of *DPA 1998* contains these rights. There are some exclusions to the rights of subject access (see CHAPTER 19 EXEMPTIONS). Employment issues are addressed in CHAPTER 16 EMPLOYMENT. Special rules in the health, education and social work sectors are covered in CHAPTER 25 HEALTH, EDUCATION AND SOCIAL WORK. It is important that those receiving subject access requests check that individuals making such a request are who they claim to be, as otherwise *DPA 1998* can be breached (see CHAPTER 5 COMPENSATION/DAMAGES).

Right of access to personal data 43.3

Individuals are entitled to be told by data controllers whether the controller is processing their data or not. If their data is being processed, then the data controller must give a description of the personal data, the purposes for which it is processed and the recipients to whom it is disclosed. Data subjects are entitled to have their personal data communicated to them in intelligible form.

Where processing of the data is by automated means to evaluate the individual's performance at work, creditworthiness, reliability, conduct or similar matters, and decisions will be made about the individual solely based on this information, then the individual is entitled to be informed by the data controller of 'the logic involved in that decision-taking' (see CHAPTER 1 AUTOMATED DECISION-TAKING).

An amendment to the entitlement to be informed of the logic behind a decision is to be brought in by *paragraph 1* of *Schedule 6* to *FIA 2000* (this is not yet in force – see CHAPTER 24 FREEDOM OF INFORMATION ACT 2000) which will provide that where a data controller:

(*a*) reasonably requires further information in order to satisfy himself as to the identity of the person making a subject access request and to locate the information which that person seeks; and

(*b*) has informed him of that requirement,

then the data controller is not obliged to comply with the request unless he is supplied with that further information.

The amendment does not address the situation where the data subject may have failed to provide the requisite fee. The Information Commissioner's Legal Guidance provides that unless a reasonable interval has elapsed between compliance with the previous request and the making of the current request, data controllers do not need to comply with a request where they have already complied with an identical or similar request by the same individual.

In defining a reasonable interval, the following factors should be considered:

- the nature of the data;
- the purpose for which the data are processed; and
- the frequency with which the data are altered.

The information given in response to a subject access request should be all that which is contained in the personal data at the time the request was received. The Commissioner says that:

> 'routine amendments and deletions of the data may continue between the date of the request and the date of the reply. To this extent, the information revealed to the data subject may differ from the data which were held at the time the request was received, even to the extent that data are no longer held. But, having received a request, the data controller must not make any special amendment or deletion which would not otherwise have been made. The information must not be tampered with in order to make it acceptable to the data subject.'

Guidance 43.4

The Commissioner has issued specific guidance on subject access as follows.

- Subject access – education records in England.
- Subject access and e-mails.
- Subject access and health records: fees for access.
- Subject access and health records.
- Subject access – local authority housing records.
- Subject access – medical records: Fees for access.
- Subject access to social services records.
- Subject access to social services records.
- Subject access and third party information.

Procedure and fee to obtain access 43.5

Data subjects wanting access to data held about them must apply in writing to the data controller. It is usually necessary to pay a fee. *Regulation 3* of the *Data Protection (Subject Access) (Fees and Miscellaneous Provisions) Regulations 2000* (*SI 2000/1910*) provide that the maximum subject access fee is £10. Requests must generally be complied with within 40 days of receipt of a request or, if later, within 40 days of receipt of both the fee and all the information required by the data controller to satisfy him or herself as to the identity of the person making the request, and to locate the information required by that person. For the health sector, reference should be made to CHAPTER 25

HEALTH, EDUCATION AND SOCIAL WORK, where the rules vary and a fee of £50 may be charged. For educational records there is a sliding scale in operation. There is a special period of seven working days for credit matters (see CHAPTER 7 CREDIT REFERENCES).

Further information on subject access is given in the Commissioner's Legal Guidance on the Commissioner's website (www.dataprotection.gov.uk).

Credit reference agencies 43.6

Where the data controller is a credit reference agency and the request has been limited to data about an individual's financial standing, then under specific regulations made under the *Consumer Credit Act 1974* applicable to the credit sector the maximum fee is £2, and requests must be complied with within seven working days.

Under *section 9* of *DPA 1998*, where the data controller is a credit reference agency and an individual makes a subject access request, this is taken to be limited to information about his financial standing, unless the request shows a contrary intention. Responding to such requests may also require a statement to be given under *section 159* of the *Consumer Credit Act 1974*. Credit issues are dealt with in CHAPTER 7 CREDIT REFERENCES.

Confidentiality and disclosure 43.7

Sometimes a subject access request might result in the disclosure of information about someone other than the data subject. In such cases, *DPA 1998* sets out only two circumstances when the data controller would then have to comply with the subject access request:

- where the other individual has consented; or
- where it is reasonable in all the circumstances to comply with the request without the consent of the individual.

Confidentiality issues are addressed in CHAPTER 6 CONFIDENTIALITY AND SECURITY: SEVENTH PRINCIPLE.

DPA 1998 provides that in considering when it is reasonable to comply with such a request, factors to be considered include:

- confidentiality owed to the other individual;
- steps the data controller has taken to obtain consent;
- whether the other individuals is capable of giving consent; and
- any express refusal of consent by the other individual.

Enforced subject access **43.8**

It is an offence under *DPA 1998* for someone to require another person to provide them with a copy of a relevant record, that is their personal data held by a data controller. In particular, the offence can be committed in connection with recruitment and employment, and where a person is providing goods or services to the public as a condition of their offering goods or services to that person. If a law imposes such a requirement or if it is in the public interest, then it is justified and allowed. *Section 56* of *DPA 1998* sets out the relevant law. Enforced subject access is also considered in CHAPTER 32 OFFENCES.

E-mails **43.9**

Separate guidance has been issued by the Information Commissioner on subject access and e-mails, and this is addressed in CHAPTER 15 E-MAILS.

Access to information held by the Commissioner and fees **43.10**

Separately, data subjects can ask the Commissioner who is registered under *DPA 1998*. This is free if it is searched for on the Internet at www.dpr.gov.uk. If instead a different form of request is made, then under the *Data Protection (Fees Under Section 19(7)) Regulations 2000* (*SI 2000/187*) a fee of £2 is paid for a duly certified copy of the data controller's entry on the register. This is not, of course, the personal data held by that controller. It is just the registered particulars of the controller himself.

Case law **43.11**

In *Norman Baker MP v Secretary of State for the Home Department (1 October 2001)*, under *DPA 1998* it was decided that the security service and Secretary of State were wrong to say that a blanket exemption (under *DPA 1998, s 28* national security exemption provisions) applied when a *section* 7 of *DPA 1998* subject access request was refused.

The security service had said that subject access requests would only be permitted in the categories of:

- staff administration;
- building security CCTV; and
- commercial agreements,

in which three categories in any event the security service held no data relating to the data subject, Mr Baker. This was held to be wrong in law by the Tribunal.

The Tribunal asked:

> 'When does national security take precedence over human rights?
>
> Where the context is national security, judges and tribunals should supervise with the lightest touch appropriate; there is no area (foreign affairs apart) where judges have traditionally deferred more to the executive view than that of national security; and for good and sufficient reason.'

They found, however, that there were no reasonable grounds for the Secretary of State to issue the certificate which he did. It was held that this led to the failure to disclose whether any information except in the three categories mentioned above.

Section 28 of *DPA 1998* provides an exemption from a number of provisions of *DPA 1998* if exemption from any such provision is required for the purpose of safeguarding national security. Such an exemption is, in effect, the Commissioner says, 'asserted by means of certificates, signed by a Minister of the Crown, certifying that exemption from all or any of the provisions is or was required for the requisite purpose. Such a certificate is conclusive evidence of that fact'. Any person directly affected by the issuing of such a certificate may appeal to the Data Protection Tribunal against the certificate.

The Tribunal is specially constituted to hear such appeals and is subject to different rules than in the case of appeals against enforcement and information notices (the *Data Protection Tribunal (National Security Appeals) Rules 2000* (*SI 2000/206*)). The first appeal to be heard by this Tribunal was the Baker case. As this was the first appeal, the parties consented to the proceedings taking place in public (subject to certain restrictions to protect the identity of some witnesses).

Third party data 43.12

It is crucial that those responding to subject access requests do not disclose third party data in the process. The Commissioner has issued separate guidance on subject access and third party data which is available on her website at www.dataprotection.gov.uk.

For third party data in the credit area see CHAPTER 7 CREDIT.

The Commissioner has also given guidance on subject access and e-mails which is considered in CHAPTER 15 E-MAILS. This also emphasises the point of not giving individuals access to third party data in responding to such requests.

Advice to data subjects 43.13

The Information Commissioner has issued some guidance to data subjects exercising their rights under *section* 7 of *DPA 1998* by way of Frequently Asked Questions as set out below

Frequently Asked Questions 43.14

Q. How can I find out what information is held about me?

A. A request for a copy of information held about you is known as a 'subject access request'. Requests must be made to the person or organisation ('data controller') who you think processes (for example, holds discloses and/or uses) the information to which you want access. Requests must be made in writing and must be accompanied by the appropriate fee (as to which see below).

You are entitled to be told if any personal data are held about you and, if so:

- to be given a description of the data;
- to be told for what purposes the data are processed; and
- to be told the recipients or the classes of recipients to whom the data may have been disclosed.

This information should include what sort of data are held, the purposes for which the data are processed and the type of organisation or people to whom the data may be disclosed.
You are also entitled:

- to be given a copy of the information with any unintelligible terms explained;
- to be given any information available to the controller about the source of the data; and
- to be given an explanation as to how any automated decisions taken about you have been made

Q. How much does it cost to gain access?

A. Data controllers may charge a fee of up to £10 for responding to a subject access request.

Unless you specifically ask to be given an explanation as to how any automated decisions about you have been made, the data controller is not obliged to provide such information. If you do specifically include a request for such information in your request then the data controller must provide it within the single £10 fee. If you do not, then the data controller is entitled to charge a separate fee of no more than £10 for the separate provision of such information. You should also be aware of the fact that data controllers may not be required to provide such information if, or to the extent that, the information amounts to a trade secret.

Different fee structures apply to some 'accessible records' such as health, education or social services files.

Q. What else do I need to do?

A. Data controllers may ask for the information they reasonably need to verify the identity of the person making the request and to locate the data. This means you may need to provide the data controller with proof of your identity and information such as whether you were a customer or employee of the data controller concerned.

Q. What is the timescale for gaining access to the information?

A. The 1998 Act requires data controllers to comply with subject access requests promptly and, in any event, within forty days from receipt of the request or, if later, forty days from the day on which the data controller has both the required fee and the necessary information to confirm your identity and to locate the data.

The Act requires the information to be provided promptly. This means a deliberate delay on the part of a data controller is not acceptable and the Commissioner might make an adverse assessment of a data controller where the data controller delayed requesting payment of any required fee, or the provision of any further details required to identify or locate the required information, where such delays resulted in the response to the subject access request being provided after forty days from receipt of the original subject access request.

There are different periods for requests for copies of credit files (seven days) and for school pupil records, which is fifteen school days.

If a data controller already has in place a system for the provision of information for one purpose (e.g. a data controller who provides information to a commercial organisation within a certain timescale) then the Commissioner would expect that data controller to be able to deal with a subject access request for the same or similar information promptly.

Q. What can I do if access is not given to me?

A. Although there are some limited circumstances in which access can be withheld, access should normally be provided to you. If you feel your request has not been complied with you may take further action, as follows.

1. Write back to the data controller setting out why you think that the information should have been provided to you. If you receive a response with which you are not satisfied, then the options available are as follows:

   (*a*) You may apply to the court alleging a failure to comply with the subject access provisions of the 1998 Act. The court may make an order requiring compliance with those provisions and may also award compensation for any damage you have suffered as a result and any associated distress.

   (*b*) You may write to the Information Commissioner. The Commissioner may do one of the following:

      (i) make an assessment as to whether it is likely or unlikely that the data controller in question has complied with the 1998 Act.

      (ii) issue enforcement proceedings if she is satisfied that the data controller has contravened one of the Data Protection Principles.

      (iii) recommend that you apply to court alleging a failure to comply with the subject access provisions of the 1998 Act.

Further information on individual rights is available, see paper entitled "Using the law to protect your information", which can be found at www.dataprotection.gov.uk under Guidance & other publications/Your rights. More specialist information on access to credit health social services, school pupils and local authority housing records is also available.

Q. How can I obtain a copy of my credit file?

A. Credit grantors exchange information with each other about their customers. They also have access to the electoral roll and to publicly available financial information, which will have a bearing on an individual's credit worthiness, including County Court Judgments and Scottish decrees. This information is held by credit reference agencies. In order to get a copy of the information which relates to your financial standing (i.e. your credit file), you should write to the two main credit reference agencies. These are:

Equifax Plc
Credit File Advice Service
PO Box 3001
Glasgow
G81 2DT

Experian Ltd
Consumer Help Service
PO Box 8000
Nottingham
NG1 5GX

You should send a fee of £2 and provide your full name and address, including postcode, and any other addresses you have lived at during the last 6 years and details of any other names you have used or been known by in that time. Unless the agencies require any further information to locate your file, they have 7 working days from the receipt of your letter in which to provide you with a copy of your file. For further information look at the paper 'No Credit' at www.dataprotection.gov.uk under Guidance & other publications/Your rights.

Freedom of Information Act 2000 — 43.15

FIA 2000 will give both individuals and companies rights of access to data held by Government bodies held about them when the Act is fully in force. The response period will be 20 working days. CHAPTER 24 FREEDOM OF INFORMATION ACT 2000 examines the Act.

Further information — 43.16

The following guidance on subject access is on the Information Commissioner's website.

- Subject access – education records in England
- Subject access & e-mails
- Subject access & health records: fees for access
- Subject access & health records
- Subject access – local authority housing records

- Subject access – medical records: Fees for access
- Subject access to social services records
- Subject access to social services records
- Subject access and third party information

The case *Norman Baker MP v Secretary of State for the Home Department (1 October 2001)* is not yet reported at the date of writing, but is available the full judgment on the Information Commissioner's website at www.dataprotection.gov under Tribunal Decisions.

Confidentiality issues are addressed in CHAPTER 6 CONFIDENTIALITY AND DATA SECURITY: SEVENTH PRINCIPLE.

CHAPTER 7 CREDIT REFERENCES AND ACCESS TO CREDIT FILES covers credit issues

CHAPTER 15 E-MAILS considers subject access requests relating to information in e-mails.

CHAPTER 19 EXEMPTIONS provides further information on the exemptions from subject access which are many and complicated.

CHAPTER 24 FREEDOM OF INFORMATION ACT 2000 examines *FIA 2000* which contains similar rights of access to data.

CHAPTER 32 OFFENCES, considered the offence of enforced subject access.

For employment issues see CHAPTER 16 EMPLOYMENT and the Commissioner's Draft Code of Practice on the Use of Personal Data in Employer/Employee Relationships.

Special rules in the health, education and social work sectors are covered in CHAPTER 25 HEALTH, EDUCATION AND SOCIAL WORK.

Automated decision taking is covered in CHAPTER 1 AUTOMATED DECISION-TAKING.

44 – Transborder Data Flows

At a glance 44.1

- ✓ Personal data under the *EU Data Protection Directive (95/46/EC)* may be exported from the European Economic Area (EEA) only where the conditions set out in the legislation are met.
- ✓ 'Transborder data flows' is the term used by the Commissioner relating to such exports.
- ✓ Two documents containing guidance have been issued by the Commissioner on transborder data flows and data export.
- ✓ Data may be exported either under the Model Clauses issued by the Commission to an approved country, under the US/EU Safe Harbor Agreement or otherwise in compliance with the Eighth Data Protection Principle.

Introduction 44.2

The export of personal data from the EEA requires careful consideration. The Eighth Data Protection Principle only allows such export where there are adequate levels of protection. In many cases the consent of the data subject can be obtained. In other cases the countries have been approved (see CHAPTER 20 EXPORT OF DATA). The US and EU have agreed a Safe Harbor Agreement, under which certain companies who are registered may export their data (see CHAPTER 41 SAFE HARBOR AGREEMENT). The Information Commissioner has issued two documents providing advice and guidance on the Eighth Principle:

- a lengthy *'The Eighth Data Protection Principle and Transborder Dataflows'* (available under Legal Guidance – International Transfers); and
- a shorter advice document on transborder data flows (available under Compliance – International Transfers Summary – Eighth Principle).

The Eighth Principle 44.3

The Eighth Data Protection Principle states:

> 'Personal data shall not be transferred to a country or territory outside the European Economic Area unless that country or territory ensures an adequate level of protection for the rights and freedoms of data subjects in relation to the processing of personal data'.

(Schedule 1 of the Data Protection Act 1998).

However, *DPA 1998* does allow the export of data outside the EEA where the transfer is necessary to perform a contract. In addition, a contract can include provisions protecting the data and thus the export may be permitted. There are detailed rules on this in the advice from the Commissioner in this field.

Schedule 1, paragraphs 13–15 44.4

Paragraphs 13–15 of *Schedule 1* to *DPA 1998* provide some guidance on the Eighth Data Protection Principle. These paragraphs state that an adequate level of protection is:

> 'one which is adequate in all the circumstances of the case, having regard in particular to:
>
> - the nature of the personal data;
> - the country or territory of origin of the information contained in the data;
> - the country or territory of the final destination of that information;
> - the purposes for which and period during which the data are intended to be processed;
> - the law in force in the country or territory in question;
> - the international obligations of that country or territory;
> - any relevant codes of conduct or other rules which are enforceable in that country or territory (whether generally or by arrangement in particular cases); and
> - any security measures taken in respect of the data in that country or territory.'

Paragraph 14 of *Schedule 1* to *DPA 1998* says that the Eighth Data Protection Principle does not apply to a transfer falling within *Schedule*

4 except where the Secretary of State provides. *Schedule 4* to *DPA 1998* is summarised at 44.7 below.

Paragraph 15 44.5

Paragraph 15 of *Schedule 1* to *DPA 1998* provides that where a 'community finding' has been made, then the question is determined in accordance with such finding. There are no such findings to date. Such a finding by paragraph 15(2) would be that a country outside the EEA does or does not ensure an adequate level of protection.

Examples 44.6

In her advice the Commissioner gives the following useful examples.

(*a*) The sporting achievements of well-known athletes are gathered from published material in the UK and put on a website. It is difficult to see that there could be a problem with adequacy. The personal data are already in the public domain, so there is no obvious reason why a data subject might object to their transfer and there is little if any scope for misuse.

(*b*) A customer list from company A in the UK is transferred to company B outside the UK to enable company A to send a mailing to customers of company B. If the data transferred are no more than names and addresses, there is nothing particularly sensitive about company A's line of business, the names and addresses are for one time use and must be returned or destroyed within a short time scale, company B is known to company A as reliable and there is a contract between them governing use of the data, the Commissioner is unlikely to call into question company A's decision that adequate protection exists. Other factors that might weigh in company A's decision include the nature of the country in which company B is located, whether company A and B are members of the same group, if so whether there is any group policy on data protection and the terms of such a policy or any contract that is in place.

(*c*) An employee travels abroad with a lap-top containing personal data connected with his/her employment. His/her employer in the UK remains the data controller. Provided the data remain in the possession of the employee and the employer has an effective procedure which addresses security and other risks posed by the use of lap-tops including the additional risks posed by international travel, a conclusion that there is adequate protection is likely to be reasonable.

(*d*) Company A, an insurer based in the UK, reinsures some of its business with company B in Jersey. In the course of this it transfers personal data to Jersey. Jersey has a data protection law that is similar to the UK Data Protection Act 1984. The main, relevant differences from the 1998 Act relate to international transfers and sensitive data. Provided the contract between companies A and B prevents any further international transfer of the personal data by B and either no sensitive data are transferred or consent to the transfer (which is likely to be required anyway to comply with Schedule 3) is obtained, a conclusion of adequacy is likely to be reasonable.

(*e*) A UK-based bank has a branch in India which collects personal data on local customers. The data are transferred to the UK where they are processed and then transferred from the UK back to India. The customers' expectations will be that their data are treated in accordance with Indian law. Given the source of the data and that the Bank has no reason to suppose the data will be misused after transfer, a conclusion of adequacy is reasonable."

Schedule 4 — 44.7

Schedule 4 to *DPA 1998* sets out the transfers to which the Eighth Data Protection Principle does not apply.

(*a*) The data subject has given their consent to the transfer. Paragraph 8.2 of the advice at Annex 1 gives some examples of the Commissioner's of what might and might not be a valid consent and model wording.

(*b*) The transfer is necessary:

- (i) for the performance of a contract between the data subject and the data controller; or
- (ii) for the taking of steps at the request of the data subject with a view to their entering into a contract with the data controller.

(*c*) The transfer is necessary:

- (i) for the conclusion of a contract between the data controller and a person other than the data subject which:

- is entered into at the request of the data subject;
- is in the interests of the data subject; or

(ii) for the performance of such a contract.

(*d*) The transfer is necessary for reasons of substantial public interest. The Secretary of State may by order specify the circumstances in which a transfer is taken to be necessary for reasons of substantial public interest. No such orders are in force to date.

(*e*) The transfer:

(i) is necessary for the purpose of, or in connection with, any legal proceedings (including prospective legal proceedings);

(ii) is necessary for the purpose of obtaining legal advice; or

(iii) is otherwise necessary for the purposes of establishing, exercising or defending legal rights.

(*f*) The transfer is necessary in order to protect the vital interests of the data subject.

(*g*) The transfer is part of the personal data on a public register, and any conditions, subject to which the register is open to inspection, are complied with by any person to whom the data are or may be disclosed after the transfer.

(*h*) The transfer is made on terms which are of a kind approved by the Commissioner as ensuring adequate safeguards for the rights and freedoms of data subjects.

(*j*) The transfer has been authorised by the Commissioner as being made in such a manner as to ensure adequate safeguards for the rights and freedoms of data subjects.

Consent 44.8

The Commissioner provides guidance in her advice as to what constitutes 'consent' for these purposes, in addition to her general guidance on consent in her Legal Guidance issued under *DPA 1998*.

> '**Consent**: Transfers can be made with the consent of the data subject. Consent must be freely given. It can be made a condition for the provision of a non-essential service but consent is unlikely to be valid if the data subject has no real choice but to give his/her consent. For example, if an existing employee is required to agree to the international transfer of personal data any consent given is

<table>
<tr><td colspan="2">unlikely to be valid if the penalty for not agreeing is dismissal. Consent must also be specific and informed. The data subject must know and have understood what he/she is agreeing to. The reasons for the transfer and as far as possible the countries involved should be specified. If the data controller is aware of any particular risks involved in the transfer it should bring these to the data subject's attention. Although all the circumstances of a particular case would need to be considered, it is possible to give some general examples.</td></tr>
<tr><td>'By signing below you accept that we can transfer any of the information we keep about you to any country when a business need arises.'</td><td>Unlikely to produce valid consent.</td></tr>
<tr><td>'By signing below you accept that we may pass details of your mortgage application to XYZ Ltd in Singapore who we have chosen to arrange mortgages on our behalf. You should be aware that Singapore does not have a data protection law.'</td><td>Likely to produce valid consent.</td></tr>
<tr><td>'By signing below you agree that we may pass relevant personnel records to our subsidiary companies in any country to which you are transferred. Your records will continue to be handled in accordance with our code of good practice although you might no longer have rights under data protection law.'</td><td>Likely to produce valid consent in the case of an employee of a multinational group who accepts a job involving international postings and where the multinational has a group-wide data protection code.</td></tr>
<tr><td>'By signing below you agree that we may pass information about you and your policy to other insurance companies with which we reinsure our business. These companies may be located in countries outside the UK that do not have laws to protect your information. Details of the companies and countries involved in your case will be provided on request.'</td><td>Likely to be acceptable where it is not practicable to list all the reinsurers and the countries in which they are located because the list is too long, because it changes regularly or because different reinsurers from the list are used in different cases.</td></tr>
</table>

Transit and transfer 44.9

When an e-mail is sent it will often be routed through 'servers' in a number of different countries before ending up in the place of destination. Does this constitute an export of data? The Commissioner says no. This is the difference between a transit and a transfer. Transfers are caught, but transits are not. What matters, therefore, is where the data came from and where it ended up.

For example, if an English company sends a list of prospective employees to another English company, there is no export of data even if the data went to France by e-mail en route. Conversely, if the English company sends the data to its US subsidiary then it would be caught.

In her advice at Annex 1, paragraph 4.3, the Commissioner says:

> 'Putting personal data on a website will almost certainly involve transfers to countries outside the UK. The transfers are to any countries from which the website is accessed.'

As there rarely, if ever, are technical means whereby a UK company can stop people accessing the site where they are outside the UK, all information on a website will therefore be 'exported'. It is possible that only those with user names and passwords can get on to the site, and that those would only be used to UK/EEA residents and thus any export prevented. This would be hard to achieve without checking the location of those users. In addition, many UK residents now take their laptops on holiday and would expect to be able to access the data whilst in a hotel in the US in any event. In such a case, it is not the individual taking their laptop to the US who is exporting the data (although they may be exporting data held generally on the laptop by so doing), but the company with the website, unless they were to say that their EEA authorised users must not, in the terms and conditions, use the site abroad. Even then they may be required to check that this did not occur.

It is therefore safest to assume that all data put on the website is exported.

The EEA 44.10

There are no restrictions on the export of personal data within the EEA. The EEA states are listed on the table below.

Countries to which data can be freely exported
Austria
Belgium
Denmark
Finland
France
Germany
Greece
Iceland
Ireland
Italy
Liechtenstein
Luxembourg
Netherlands
Norway
Portugal
Spain
Sweden

The list above is of those countries to which there is no restriction on export. They comprise the EEA and are all subject to the legal requirements of the EU Data Protection Directive. The Channel Islands and the Isle of Man are not part of the EEA, however, so those exporting data there need to take legal advice and may not be entitled to do so.

Designated territories 44.11

DPA 1998 does allow the Commissioner to designate certain foreign countries as having adequate measures for export of data in place. So far Hungary and Switzerland have been designated as such.

The advice document at Annex 1 on compliance lists the following countries as having full data protection laws in place and therefore likely to be so designated in future, although it must be stressed this is not yet the case.

Australia
Canada
Guernsey
Hong Kong
Hungary
Isle of Man
Israel
Japan
Jersey
New Zealand
Poland
Slovak Republic
Slovenia
Switzerland
Taiwan

The Commissioner intends to designate the adequate countries in due course on her website (www.dataprotection.gov.uk).

Model Clauses 44.12

In 2001 the European Commission issued standard clauses for the transfer of personal data to third countries. These are considered in CHAPTER 20 EXPORT OF DATA. The Model Clauses can be accessed from www.europa.eu.int/comm/internal_market/en/media/dataprot/news/callcom.htm and are in APPENDIX 3 of this book. In APPENDIX 2 the Commission's Frequently Asked Questions on the Clauses appear.

ICC clauses 44.13

In 2001 industry issued its own version of some standard clauses for data export and is seeking approval of them from the European Commission. The International Chamber of Commerce (ICC), which was involved in the process, says that its clauses, unlike those of the EU, would avoid imposing what it regards as excessive obligations on companies.

Seven associations submitted alternative model contract clauses to EC internal market

Business associations behind the move are: the ICC, the Federation of European Direct Marketing (FEDMA), the EU Committee of the American Chamber of Commerce in Belgium (Amcham), the Japan Business Council in Europe (JBCE), the Confederation of British Industry (CBI), the International Communications Round Table

(ICRT), and the European Information and Communications Technology Industry Association (EICTA).

The ICC says that the alternative clauses are intended to provide just as high a level of data protection as the Commission's clauses, but using more flexible mechanisms that reflect business realities. For example, the clauses provide an alternative to the 'joint and several liability' regime – or shared liability between exporters and importers – contained in the Commission's clauses (to which many companies have taken exception), and include a 'due diligence' responsibility on exporters in dealing with importers. A further safeguard allows exporters to carry out audits to check that the data supplied is not being misused. Further information is available on the ICC website at www.iccwbo.org/home/news_archives/2001/dataflow.asp

EU general guidance 44.14

The European Commission has issued Frequently Asked Questions (to be found at www.europa.eu.int/comm/internal_market/en/ dataprot/backinfo/info.htm) on data protection in general as it applies to transfer of data outside of the EEA. It has also issued FAQs on the Model Clauses for data export (see APPENDIX 2).

Further information 44.15

The Information Commissioner has issued two documents on this topic:

- the Eighth Data Protection Principle and Transborder Dataflows (under Legal Guidance – 'International Transfers' on her website); and
- a shorter advice document on transborder data flows (which is available under Compliance – 'International Transfers Summary – Eighth Data Protection Principle').

Information on Hungary and Switzerland is at http://europa. eu.int/eur-lex/en/oj/2000/l_21520000825en.html.
The ICC's alternative clauses are described at www.iccwbo.org/ home/news_archives/2001/dataflow.asp.

See also CHAPTER 20 EXPORT OF DATA and CHAPTER 41 SAFE HARBOR.
The Commission's Frequently Asked Questions on its new model clauses for data export are at www.europa.eu.int/comm/ internal_market/en/media/dataprot/news/clausesfaq.htm.

And see:http://europa.eu.int/comm/internal_market/ en/media/dataprot/wpdocs/wp40en.htm.

The US authorities have a safe harbor website which is at www.export.gov/safeharbor/.

The International Chamber of Commerce's information on data export is at www.iccwbo.org/home/news_archives/2001/dataflow.asp.

45 – Transitional Provisions (Timing)

At a glance 45.1

- ✓ The *Data Protection Act 1998* (*DPA 1998*) came into force on 1 March 2000.
- ✓ A first transitional period operated to 24 October 2001 for some of the provisions of *DPA 1998* in a very limited way (e.g. subject access requests for manual data being processed on 24 October 1998 became possible for such data from 24 October 2001).
- ✓ A second transitional period runs thereafter.

Introduction 45.2

DPA 1998 has applied from 1 March 2000. In areas where it changed the law radically, in many cases businesses were given an additional three years to bring their practices into line. This particularly applies in areas previously exempt such as manual data. This three year period ran from 24 October 1998 (when the *Data Protection Directive (EC/95/46)* should have been brought into force, not the 1 March 2000 implementation date). On 24 October 2001, for example, subject access requests for all manual data which falls within *DPA 1998* became possible (see CHAPTER 30 MANUAL DATA).

Transitional provisions 45.3

The transitional provisions under *DPA 1998* are extremely important, exempting certain areas relating to:

- manual data;
- processing otherwise than by reference to the data subject;
- payrolls and accounts;
- unincorporated members' clubs and mailing lists;

- back-up data;
- exemption for all eligible automated data from certain requirements; and
- historical research.

The Information Commissioner's *Legal Guidance* (Chapter 6) sets out a summary of the transitional provisions under *DPA 1998* to which reference should be made.

Processing 'underway' 45.4

Many of the transitional exemptions apply where processing of data was 'underway' on 24 October 1998. It is therefore crucial to know in relation to particular data whether this is the case or not. The Information Commissioner recognises that the meaning of this is not very clear. The questions that the Commissioner suggests can be asked include whether the processing is for a new purpose, whether the data being processed is in the same category, and if the recipients of the data remain the same.

For processing which was already under way on 24 October 1998, manual data (with some exceptions) was effectively exempt from all the provisions of *DPA 1998* until 24 October 2001. Following this date a further transitional period exists until 24 October 2007 during which some, but not all, of the provisions of *DPA 1998* will apply.

Examples 45.5

Examples given by the Information Commissioner include where:

- existing data is amended;
- additional personal data is added on existing data subjects;
- personal data is added on new data subjects;or
- essential program and software changes are carried out to enable existing operations to continue.

In such cases, unless these examples produce a different effect on the processing operation, 'it is unlikely that these things alone will mean that this is not processing already under way'.

Adding to manual systems 45.6

This means that data controllers can add names to, for example, a paper card index system without this being 'new data processing'. The effect would have been that such manual records would remain outside the provisions of *DPA 1998* until 24 October 2001.

Takeovers 45.7

Where there is a change in the legal entity which is the data controller, the Information Commissioner believes that as long as the processing is existing processing the change in legal entity will not mean the processing is not underway on the relevant date (DPR *Introduction* p28). However if the new entity takes on new functions then new processing takes place and *DPA 1998* would apply from 1 March 2000.

The first transitional period 45.8

The first transitional period ran to 23 October 2001. During this period, for example, credit reference agency records which came within *DPA 1998* for the first time under *DPA 1998*, would remain as under *DPA 1984* where the processing was already under way at 24 October 1998. The exemption was from the Data Protection Principles 1 – 8, *Part II* of the right – individual's rights in most cases and *Part III* of *DPA 1998* – notification.

Second transitional period 45.9

From 24 October 2001 to 23 October 2007 a very limited exception for manual data which was being processed at 24 October 1998 applies. This also covers credit reference agency records and accessible records. This does not apply where manual data are added on or after 24 October 1998. There are all sorts of caveats and exceptions to this which must be considered in practice. Legal advice should be sought.

Further information 45.10

For manual records and their transitional period see CHAPTER 30 MANUAL RECORDS.

The Commissioner's *Legal Guidance* (October 2001) covers the transitional provisions in some depth – see www.dataprotection.gov.uk.

[illegible]

[illegible] 45.7

[illegible]

The first transitional period 45.8

[illegible]

Second transitional period 45.9

[illegible]

Further information 45.10

[illegible]

[illegible]

Appendix 1 – CCTV Code of Practice

Foreword

Closed circuit television (CCTV) surveillance is an increasing feature of our daily lives. There is an ongoing debate over how effective CCTV is in reducing and preventing crime, but one thing is certain, its deployment is commonplace in a variety of areas to which members of the public have free access. We might be caught on camera while walking down the high street, visiting a shop or bank or travelling through a railway station or airport. The House of Lords Select Committee on Science and Technology expressed their view that if public confidence in CCTV systems was to be maintained there needed to be some tighter control over their deployment and use (Fifth Report – Digital Images as Evidence).

There was no statutory basis for systematic legal control of CCTV surveillance over public areas until 1 March 2000 when the Data Protection Act came into force. The definitions in this new Act are broader than those of the Data Protection Act 1984 and so more readily cover the processing of images of individuals caught by CCTV cameras than did the previous data protection legislation. The same legally enforceable information handling standards as have previously applied to those processing personal data on computer now cover CCTV. An important new feature of the recent legislation is a power for me to issue a Commissioner's Code of Practice (section 51(3)(b) of DPA 1998) setting out guidance for the following of good practice. In my 14th Annual Report to Parliament I signalled my intention to use this power to provide guidance on the operation of CCTV as soon as those new powers became available to me. This Code of Practice is the first Commissioner's Code to be issued under the Data Protection Act 1998.

This code deals with surveillance in areas to which the public have largely free and unrestricted access because, as the House of Lords Committee highlighted, there is particular concern about a lack of regulation and central guidance in this area. Although the Data Protection Act 1998 covers other uses of CCTV this Code addresses the area of widest concern. Many of its provisions will be relevant to other uses of CCTV and will be referred to as appropriate when we develop other guidance. There are some existing standards that have been developed by representatives of CCTV system operators and, more particularly, the British Standards Institute. While such standards are helpful, they are not legally enforceable. The changes in data protection legislation mean that for the first time legally enforceable standards will apply to the collection and processing of images relating to individuals.

This Code of Practice has the dual purpose of assisting operators of CCTV systems to understand their legal obligations while also reassuring the public about the safeguards that should be in place. It sets out the measures which must be adopted to comply with the Data Protection Act 1998, and goes on to set out guidance for the following of good data protection practice. The Code makes clear the standards which must be followed to ensure compliance with the Data Protection Act 1998 and then indicates those which are not a strict legal requirement but do represent the following of good practice.

Before issuing this Code I consulted representatives of relevant data controllers and data subjects, and published a draft copy of the Code on my website. I am grateful to all those consultees who responded and have taken account of their comments in producing this version.

Our experience of the Codes of Practice which were put forward under the 1984 Act was that they needed to remain relevant to the day to day activities of data controllers. They need to be 'living' documents, which are updated as practices, and understanding of the law develops.

This code will therefore be kept under review to ensure that it remains relevant in the context of changing technology, use and jurisprudence. In this context it is likely that the Human Rights Act 1998, which comes into force on 2 October 2000, and provides important legal safeguards for individuals, will lead to developments in legal interpretation which will require review of the Code.

It is my intention that this Code of Practice should help those operating CCTV schemes monitoring members of the public to do so in full compliance of the Data Protection Act 1998 and in adherence to high standards of good practice. There does seem to be public support for the widespread deployment of this surveillance technology, but public confidence has to be earned and maintained. Compliance with this Code will not only help CCTV scheme operators' process personal data in compliance with the law but also help to maintain that public confidence without which they cannot operate.

Elizabeth France

Data Protection Commissioner

July 2000

Introduction

This is a code of practice issued by the Data Protection Commissioner in accordance with her powers under section 51 (3)(b) of the Data Protection Act 1998 (the '1998 Act'). It is intended to provide guidance as to good practice for users of CCTV (closed circuit television) and similar surveillance equipment.

It is not intended that the contents of this Code should apply to:

- targeted and intrusive surveillance activities, which are covered by the provisions of the forthcoming Regulation of Investigatory Powers Act 2000;
- use of surveillance techniques by employers to monitor their employees' compliance with their contracts of employment[1];
- security equipment (including cameras) installed in homes by individuals for home security purposes[2];
- use of cameras and similar equipment by the broadcast media for the purposes of journalism, or for artistic or literary purposes.

This Code of Practice is drafted in two parts.

Part I

This sets out:

- the standards which must be met if the requirements of the 1998 Act are to be complied with. These are based on the Data Protection Principles which say that data must be
  - fairly and lawfully processed;
  - processed for limited purposes and not in any manner incompatible with those purposes;
  - adequate, relevant and not excessive;
  - accurate;
  - not kept for longer than is necessary;
  - processed in accordance with individuals' rights;
  - secure;
  - not transferred to countries without adequate protection;
  - guidance on good practice;
  - examples of how to implement the standards and good practice.

The Data Protection Commissioner has the power to issue Enforcement Notices where she considers that there has been a breach of one or more of the Data Protection Principles. An Enforcement Notice[3] would set out the remedial action that the Commissioner requires to ensure future compliance with the requirements of the Act. The Data Protection Commissioner will take into account the extent to which users of CCTV and similar surveillance equipment have complied with this Code of Practice when determining whether they have met their legal obligations when exercising her powers of enforcement.

Part II – Glossary

This sets out the interpretation of the 1998 Act on which Part I is based. Part I is cross-referenced to Part II to try to clarify the reasoning behind the standard or guidance.

It is intended that this Code of Practice will be revised on a regular basis in order to take account of developments in the interpretation of the provisions of the data protection legislation, developments in the technology involved in the recording of images, and developments in the use of such technologies, the use of sound recording, facial recognition techniques and the increased use of digital technology.

Please note that italicised text indicates good practice.

Initial Assessment Procedures

Before installing and using CCTV and similar surveillance equipment, users will need to establish the purpose or purposes for which they intend to use the equipment.[4] This equipment may be used for a number of different purposes – for example, prevention, investigation and detection of crime, apprehension and prosecution of offenders (including use of images as evidence in criminal proceedings), public and employee safety, monitoring security of premises etc.

Standards

1. Establish who is the person(s) or organisation(s) legally responsible for the proposed scheme.[5]
2. Assess the appropriateness of, and reasons for, using CCTV or similar surveillance equipment (First Data Protection Principle).
3. *Document this assessment process and the reasons for the installation of the scheme.*
4. Establish the purpose of the Scheme (First and Second Data Protection Principle).[6]

5. *Document the purpose of the scheme.*
6. Ensure that the notification lodged with the Office of the Data Protection Commissioner covers the purposes for which this equipment is used.[7]
7. *Establish and document the person(s) or organisation(s) who are responsible for ensuring the day-to-day compliance with the requirements of this Code of Practice (if different from above).*
8. *Establish and document security and disclosure policies.*

Siting the cameras

It is essential that the location of the equipment is carefully considered, because the way in which images are captured will need to comply with the First Data Protection Principle. Detailed guidance on the interpretation of the First Data Protection Principle is provided in Part II, but the standards to be met under this Code of Practice are set out below.

Standards

1. The equipment should be sited in such a way that it only monitors those spaces which are intended to be covered by the equipment (First and Third Data Protection Principles).
2. If domestic areas such as gardens or areas not intended to be covered by the scheme border those spaces which are intended to be covered by the equipment, then the user should consult with the owners of such spaces if images from those spaces might be recorded. In the case of back gardens, this would be the resident of the property overlooked (First and Third Data Protection Principles).
3. Operators must be aware of the purpose(s) for which the scheme has been established (Second and Seventh Data Protection Principles).
4. Operators must be aware that they are only able to use the equipment in order to achieve the purpose(s) for which it has been installed (First and Second Data Protection Principles).
5. If cameras are adjustable by the operators, this should be restricted so that operators cannot adjust or manipulate them

to overlook spaces which are not intended to be covered by the scheme (First and Third Data Protection Principles).

6. If it is not possible physically to restrict the equipment to avoid recording images from those spaces not intended to be covered by the scheme, then operators should be trained in recognising the privacy implications of such spaces being covered (First and Third Data Protection Principles).

   For example – individuals sunbathing in their back gardens may have a greater expectation of privacy than individuals mowing the lawn of their front garden.

   For example – it may be appropriate for the equipment to be used to protect the safety of individuals when using ATMs, but images of PIN numbers, balance enquiries etc should not be captured.

7. Signs should be placed so that the public are aware that they are entering a zone which is covered by surveillance equipment (First Data Protection Principle).

8. The signs should be clearly visible and legible to members of the public (First Data Protection Principle)

9. The size of signs will vary according to circumstances:

   ***For example** – a sign on the entrance door to a building society office may only need to be A4 size because it is at eye level of those entering the premises.*

   ***For example** – signs at the entrances of car parks alerting drivers to the fact that the car park is covered by such equipment will usually need to be large, for example, probably A3 size as they are likely to be viewed from further away, for example by a driver sitting in a car.*

10. e signs should contain the following information.

   (a) Identity of the person or organisation responsible for the scheme.

   (b) The purposes of the scheme.

   (c) Details of whom to contact regarding the scheme.

   (First Data Protection Principle)

   For example – Where an image of a camera is not used on a sign – the following wording is recommended:

'Images are being monitored for the purposes of crime prevention and public safety. This scheme is controlled by the Greentown Safety Partnership.

For further information contact 01234–567–890'

For example – Where an image of a camera is used on a sign – the following wording is recommended:

'This scheme is controlled by the Greentown Safety Partnership.

For further information contact 01234–567–890'

11. In exceptional and limited cases, if it is assessed that the use of signs would not be appropriate, the user of the scheme must ensure that they have:

- Identified specific criminal activity.
- Identified the need to use surveillance to obtain evidence of that criminal activity.
- Assessed whether the use of signs would prejudice success in obtaining such evidence.
- Assessed how long the covert monitoring should take place to ensure that it is not carried out for longer than is necessary.
- *Documented (a) to (d) above.*[8]

12. Information so obtained must only be obtained for prevention or detection of criminal activity, or the apprehension and prosecution of offenders.9 It should not be retained and used for any other purpose. If the equipment used has a sound recording facility, this should not be used to record conversations between members of the public (First and Third Data Protection Principles).

Quality of the images

It is important that the images produced by the equipment are as clear as possible in order that they are effective for the purpose(s) for which they are intended. This is why it is essential that the purpose of the scheme is clearly identified. For example if a system has been installed to prevent and detect crime, then it is essential that the images are adequate for that purpose. The Third, Fourth and Fifth Data Protection

Principles are concerned with the quality of personal data, and they are outlined in more detail in Part II. The standards to be met under this Code of Practice are set out below.

Standards

1. Upon installation an initial check should be undertaken to ensure that the equipment performs properly.
2. If tapes are used, it should be ensured that they are good quality tapes (Third and Fourth Data Protection Principles).
3. The medium on which the images are captured should be cleaned so that images are not recorded on top of images recorded previously (Third and Fourth Data Protection Principles).
4. The medium on which the images have been recorded should not be used when it has become apparent that the quality of images has deteriorated. (Third Data Protection Principle).
5. If the system records features such as the location of the camera and/or date and time reference, these should be accurate (Third and Fourth Data Protection Principles).
6. *If their system includes such features, users should ensure that they have a documented procedure for ensuring their accuracy.*
7. Cameras should be situated so that they will capture images relevant to the purpose for which the scheme has been established (Third Data Protection Principle)

   For example – if the purpose of the scheme is the prevention and detection of crime and/or apprehension and prosecution of offenders, the cameras should be sited so that images enabling identification of perpetrators are captured.

   For example – if the scheme has been established with a view to monitoring traffic flow, the cameras should be situated so that they do not capture the details of the vehicles or drivers.
8. If an automatic facial recognition system is used to match images captured against a database of images, then both sets of images should be clear enough to ensure an accurate match (Third and Fourth Data Protection Principles).
9. If an automatic facial recognition system is used, procedures should be set up to ensure that the match is also verified by a

human operator, who will assess the match and determine what action, if any, should be taken (First and Seventh Data Protection Principles).[10]

10. The result of the assessment by the human operator should be recorded whether or not they determine there is a match.

11. When installing cameras, consideration must be given to the physical conditions in which the cameras are located (Third and Fourth Data Protection Principles).

    For example – infrared equipment may need to be installed in poorly lit areas.

12. Users should assess whether it is necessary to carry out constant real time recording, or whether the activity or activities about which they are concerned occur at specific times (First and Third Data Protection Principles)

    For example – it may be that criminal activity only occurs at night, in which case constant recording of images might only be carried out for a limited period e.g. 10.00 pm to 7.00 am

13. Cameras should be properly maintained and serviced to ensure that clear images are recorded (Third and Fourth Data Protection Principles)

14. Cameras should be protected from vandalism in order to ensure that they remain in working order (Seventh Data Protection Principle)

15. A maintenance log should be kept.

16. If a camera is damaged, there should be clear procedures for:

    (*a*) Defining the person responsible for making arrangements for ensuring that the camera is fixed.

    (*b*) Ensuring that the camera is fixed within a specific time period (Third and Fourth Data Protection Principle).

    (*c*) Monitoring the quality of the maintenance work.

Processing the images

Images, which are not required for the purpose(s) for which the equipment is being used, should not be retained for longer than is necessary. While images are retained, it is essential that their integrity be maintained, whether it is to ensure their evidential value or to protect the rights of people whose images may have been recorded. It is therefore important that access to and security of the images is controlled in accordance with the requirements of the 1998 Act. The Seventh Data Protection Principle sets out the security requirements of the 1998 Data Protection Act. This is discussed in more depth at Part II. However, the standards required by this Code of Practice are set out below.

Standards

1. Images should not be retained for longer than is necessary (Fifth Data Protection Principle)

   For example – publicans may need to keep recorded images for no longer than seven days because they will soon be aware of any incident such as a fight occurring on their premises.

   For example – images recorded by equipment covering town centres and streets may not need to be retained for longer than 31 days unless they are required for evidential purposes in legal proceedings.

   For example – images recorded from equipment protecting individuals' safety at ATMs might need to be retained for a period of three months in order to resolve customer disputes about cash withdrawals. The retention period of three months is based on the interval at which individuals receive their account statements.

2. Once the retention period has expired, the images should be removed or erased (Fifth Data Protection Principle).

3. If the images are retained for evidential purposes, they should be retained in a secure place to which access is controlled (Fifth and Seventh Data Protection Principles).

4. On removing the medium on which the images have been recorded for the use in legal proceedings, the operator should ensure that they have documented:

   (*a*) The date on which the images were removed from the general system for use in legal proceedings.

   (*b*) The reason why they were removed from the system.

   (*c*) Any crime incident number to which the images may be relevant.

(*d*) The location of the images.

For example – if the images were handed to a police officer for retention, the name and station of that police officer.

(*e*) The signature of the collecting police officer, where appropriate (see below)(Third and Seventh Data Protection Principles).

5. Monitors displaying images from areas in which individuals would have an expectation of privacy should not be viewed by anyone other than authorised employees of the user of the equipment (Seventh Data Protection Principle).

6. Access to the recorded images should be restricted to a manager or designated member of staff who will decide whether to allow requests for access by third parties in accordance with the user's documented disclosure policies (Seventh Data Protection Principle).[11]

7. Viewing of the recorded images should take place in a restricted area, for example, in a manager's or designated member of staff's office. Other employees should not be allowed to have access to that area when a viewing is taking place (Seventh Data Protection Principle).

8. *Removal of the medium on which images are recorded, for viewing purposes, should be documented as follows:*

(a) The date and time of removal

(b) The name of the person removing the images

(c) The name(s) of the person(s) viewing the images. If this should include third parties, this include the organisation of that third party

(d) The reason for the viewing

(e) The outcome, if any, of the viewing

(f) The date and time the images were returned to the system or secure place, if they have been retained for evidential purposes

9. *All operators and employees with access to images should be aware of the procedure which need to be followed when accessing the recorded images (Seventh Data Protection Principle).*

10. *All operators should be trained in their responsibilities under this Code of Practice i.e. they should be aware of:*

    (*a*) The user's security policy e.g. procedures to have access to recorded images.

    (*b*) The user's disclosure policy.[12]

    (*c*) Rights of individuals in relation to their recorded images.[13]

(Seventh Data Protection Principle)

Access to and disclosure of images to third parties

It is important that access to, and disclosure of, the images recorded by CCTV and similar surveillance equipment is restricted and carefully controlled, not only to ensure that the rights of individuals are preserved, but also to ensure that the chain of evidence remains intact should the images be required for evidential purposes. Users of CCTV will also need to ensure that the reason(s) for which they may disclose copies of the images are compatible with the reason(s) or purpose(s) for which they originally obtained those images. These aspects of this Code are to be found in the Second and Seventh Data Protection Principles, which are discussed in more depth at Part II. However, the standards required by this Code are set out below.

Standards

All employees should be aware of the restrictions set out in this code of practice in relation to access to, and disclosure of, recorded images.

1. Access to recorded images should be restricted to those staff who need to have access in order to achieve the purpose(s) of using the equipment (Seventh Data Protection Principle).[14]

2. All access to the medium on which the images are recorded should be documented (Seventh Data Protection Principle).[15]

3. Disclosure of the recorded images to third parties should only made in limited and prescribed circumstances (Second and Seventh Data Protection Principles).

   For example – if the purpose of the system is the prevention and detection of crime, then disclosure to third parties should be limited to the following.

- Law enforcement agencies where the images recorded would assist in a specific criminal enquiry.
- Prosecution agencies.
- Relevant legal representatives.
- The media, where it is decided that the public's assistance is needed in order to assist in the identification of victim, witness or perpetrator in relation to a criminal incident. As part of that decision, the wishes of the victim of an incident should be taken into account.
- People whose images have been recorded and retained (unless disclosure to the individual would prejudice criminal enquiries or criminal proceedings).

4. All requests for access or for disclosure should be recorded. If access or disclosure is denied, the reason should be documented (Seventh Data Protection Principle)

5. If access to or disclosure of the images is allowed, then the following should be documented:

   (*a*) The date and time at which access was allowed or the date on which disclosure was made

   (*b*) The identification of any third party who was allowed access or to whom disclosure was made

   (*c*) The reason for allowing access or disclosure

   (*d*) The extent of the information to which access was allowed or which was disclosed.[16]

6. Recorded images should not be made more widely available – for example they should not be routinely made available to the media or placed on the Internet (Second, Seventh and Eighth Data Protection Principles).

7. If it is intended that images will be made more widely available, that decision should be made by the manager or designated member of staff. The reason for that decision should be documented (Seventh Data Protection Principle).

8. If it is decided that images will be disclosed to the media (other than in the circumstances outlined above), the images of

individuals will need to be disguised or blurred so that they are not readily identifiable (First, Second and Seventh Data Protection Principles).

9. *If the system does not have the facilities to carry out that type of editing, an editing company may need to be hired to carry it out.*

10. If an editing company is hired, then the manager or designated member of staff needs to ensure that:

(*a*) There is a contractual relationship between the data controller and the editing company.

(*b*) That the editing company has given appropriate guarantees regarding the security measures they take in relation to the images.

(*c*) The manager has checked to ensure that those guarantees are met

(*d*) The written contract makes it explicit that the editing company can only use the images in accordance with the instructions of the manager or designated member of staff.

(*e*) The written contract makes the security guarantees provided by the editing company explicit.

11. If the media organisation receiving the images undertakes to carry out the editing, then (a) to (e) will still apply.

(Seventh Data Protection Principle)

Access by data subjects

This is a right, which is provided by section 7 of the 1998 Act. A detailed explanation of the interpretation of this right is given in Part II. The standards of this Code of Practice are set out below.

Standards

1. All staff involved in operating the equipment must be able to recognise a request for access to recorded images by data subjects (Sixth and Seventh Data Protection Principles).

2. *Data subjects should be provided with a standard subject access request form which:*

(a) Indicates the information required in order to locate the images requested.

For example – an individual may have to provide dates and times of when they visited the premises of the user of the equipment.

(b) Indicates the information required in order to identify the person making the request.

For example –if the individual making the request is unknown to the user of the equipment, a photograph of the individual may be requested in order to locate the correct image.

(c) Indicates the fee that will be charged for carrying out the search for the images requested. A maximum of £10.00 may be charged for the search.

(d) Asks whether the individual would be satisfied with merely viewing the images recorded.

(e) Indicates that the response will be provided promptly and in any event within 40 days of receiving the required fee and information.

(f) Explains the rights provided by the 1998 Act.

3. *Individuals should also be provided with a leaflet which describes the types images which are recorded and retained, the purposes for which those images are recorded and retained, and information about the disclosure policy in relation to those images (Sixth Data Protection Principle).*[17]

4. *This should be provided at the time that the standard subject access request form is provided to an individual (Sixth Data Protection Principle).*[18]

5. All subject access requests should be dealt with by a manager or designated member of staff.

6. The manager or designated member of staff should locate the images requested.

7. *The manager or designated member of staff should determine whether disclosure to the individual would entail disclosing images of third parties (Sixth Data Protection Principle).*[19]

8. *The manager or designated member of staff will need to determine whether the images of third parties are held under a duty of confidence (First and Sixth Data Protection Principle).*[20]

For example – it may be that members of the public whose images have been recorded when they were in town centres or streets have less expectation that their images are held under a duty of confidence than individuals whose images have been recorded in more private space such as the waiting room of a doctor's surgery.

9. If third party images are not to be disclosed, the manager or designated member of staff shall arrange for the third party images to be disguised or blurred (Sixth Data Protection Principle).[21]

10. *If the system does not have the facilities to carry out that type of editing, a third party or company may be hired to carry it out.*

11. If a third party or company is hired, then the manager or designated member of staff needs to ensure that:

    (*a*) There is a contractual relationship between the data controller and the third party or company.

    (*b*) That the third party or company has given appropriate guarantees regarding the security measures they take in relation to the images.

    (*c*) The manager has checked to ensure that those guarantees are met.

    (*d*) The written contract makes it explicit that the third party or company can only use the images in accordance with the instructions of the manager or designated member of staff.

    (*e*) The written contract makes the security guarantees provided by the third party or company explicit

(Seventh Data Protection Principle)

12. If the manager or designated member of staff decides that a subject access request from an individual is not to be complied with, the following should be documented:

    (a) The identity of the individual making the request

    (b) The date of the request

    (c) The reason for refusing to supply the images requested

    (d) The name and signature of the manager or designated member of staff making the decision.[22]

13. All staff should be aware of individuals' rights under this section of the Code of Practice (Seventh Data Protection Principle)

Other rights

A detailed explanation of the other rights under Sections 10, 12 and 13 of the Act are provided in Part II of this Code. The standards of this Code are set out below.

Standards

1. All staff involved in operating the equipment must be able to recognise a request from an individual to:

   (*a*) Prevent processing likely to cause substantial and unwarranted damage to that individual.[23]

   (*b*) Prevent automated decision taking in relation to that individual.[24]

2. *All staff must be aware of the manager or designated member of staff who is responsible for responding to such requests.*

3. In relation to a request to prevent processing likely to cause substantial and unwarranted damage, the manager or designated officer's response should indicate whether he or she will comply with the request or not.[25]

4. The manager or designated member of staff must provide a written response to the individual within 21 days of receiving the request setting out their decision on the request.[26]

5. If the manager or designated member of staff decide that the request will not be complied with, they must set out their reasons in the response to the individual.[27]

6. *A copy of the request and response should be retained.*

7. If an automated decision is made about an individual, the manager or designated member of staff must notify the individual of that decision.[28]

8. If, within 21 days of that notification, the individual requires, in writing, the decision to be reconsidered, the manager or designated staff member shall reconsider the automated decision.[29]

9. On receipt of a request to reconsider the automated decision, the manager or designated member of staff shall respond within 21 days setting out the steps that they intend to take to comply with the individual's request.[30]

10. *The manager or designated member of staff shall document:*
    - *(a) The original decision.*
    - *(b) The request from the individual.*
    - *(c) Their response to the request from the individual.*

Monitoring compliance with this code of practice

Standards

1. The contact point indicated on the sign should be available to members of the public during office hours. Employees staffing that contact point should be aware of the policies and procedures governing the use of this equipment.
2. *Enquiries should be provided on request with one or more of the following:*
    - *(a) The leaflet which individuals receive when they make a subject access request as general information*
    - *(b) A copy of this code of practice*
    - *(c) A subject access request form if required or requested*
    - *(d) The complaints procedure to be followed if they have concerns about the use of the system*
    - *(e) The complaints procedure to be followed if they have concerns about non-compliance with the provisions of this Code of Practice*
3. *A complaints procedure should be clearly documented.*
4. *A record of the number and nature of complaints or enquiries received should be maintained together with an outline of the action taken.*
5. *A report on those numbers should be collected by the manager or designated member of staff in order to assess public reaction to and opinion of the use of the system.*
6. A manager or designated member of staff should undertake regular reviews of the documented procedures to ensure that the provisions of this Code are being complied with (Seventh Data Protection Principle).
7. *A report on those reviews should be provided to the data controller(s)*

in order that compliance with legal obligations and provisions with this Code of Practice can be monitored.

8. *An internal annual assessment should be undertaken which evaluates the effectiveness of the system.*
9. *The results of the report should be assessed against the stated purpose of the scheme. If the scheme is not achieving its purpose, it should be discontinued or modified.*
10. *The result of those reports should be made publicly available.*

Part II

Glossary

The Data Protection Act 1998

1. Definitions

There are several definitions in sections 1 and 2 of the 1998 Act which users of CCTV systems or similar surveillance equipment must consider in order to determine whether they need to comply with the requirements of the 1998 Act, and if so, to what extent the 1998 Act applies to them:

(a) Data Controller

> 'A person who (either alone or jointly or in common with other persons) determines the purposes for which and the manner in which any personal data are, or are to be, processed.'

For example: if a police force and local authority enter into a partnership to install CCTV in a town centre with a view to:

- preventing and detecting crime;
- apprehending and prosecuting offenders; and
- protecting public safety.

They will both be data controllers for the purpose of the scheme.

For example, if a police force, local authority and local retailers decide to install a CCTV scheme in a town centre or shopping centre, for the purposes of:

- prevention or detection crime;
- apprehending or prosecuting offenders; and
- protecting public safety.

All will be data controllers for the purposes of the scheme. It is the data controllers who should set out the purposes of the scheme (as outlined above) and who should set out the policies on the use of the images (as outlined in the Standards section of this Code of Practice).

The data controller(s) may devolve day-to-day running of the scheme to a manager, but that manager is not the data controller – he or she can only manage the scheme according to the instructions of the data controller(s), and according to the policies set out by the data controller(s).

If the manager of the scheme is an employee of one or more of the data controllers, then the manager will not have any personal data protection responsibilities as a data controller. However, the manager should be aware that if he or she acts outside the instructions of the data controller(s) in relation to obtaining or disclosing the images, they may commit a criminal offence contrary to section 55 of the 1998 Act, as well as breach their contract of employment.

If the manager is a third party such as a security company employed by the data controller to run the scheme, then the manager may be deemed a data processor. This is "any person (other than an employee of the data controller) who processes the personal data on behalf of the data controller. If the data controller(s) are considering using a data processor, they will need to consider their compliance with the Seventh Data Protection Principle in terms of this relationship.

(b) Personal Data

> 'Data which relate to a living individual who can be identified:
>
> - from those data, or
> - from those data and other information which is in the possession of, or is likely to come into the possession of, the data controller.'

The provisions of the 1998 Act are based on the requirements of a European Directive[31], which at, Article 2, defines, personal data as follows:

'Personal data' shall mean any information relating to an identified or identifiable natural person; an identifiable person is one who can be identified, directly or indirectly, in particular by reference to an identification number or to one or more factors specific to his physical, physiological, mental, economic, cultural or social identity.

The definition of personal data is not therefore limited to circumstances where a data controller can attribute a name to a particular image. If images of distinguishable individuals' features are processed and an individual can be identified from these images, they will amount to personal data.

(c) Sensitive Personal Data

Section 2 of the 1998 Act separates out distinct categories of personal data, which are deemed sensitive. The most significant of these categories for the purposes of this code of practice are information about:[32]

- the commission or alleged commission of any offences
- any proceedings for any offence committed, or alleged to have been committed, the disposal of such proceedings or the sentence of any court in such proceedings.

This latter bullet point will be particularly significant for those CCTV schemes which are established by retailers in conjunction with the local police force, which use other information to identify known and convicted shoplifters from images, with a view to reducing the amount of organised shoplifting in a retail centre.

It is essential that data controllers determine whether they are processing sensitive personal data because it has particular implications for their compliance with the First Data Protection Principle.

(d) Processing

Section 1 of the 1998 Act sets out the type of operations that can constitute processing:

> 'In relation to information or data, means obtaining, processing, recording or holding the information or data or carrying out any operation or set of operations on the information or data, including:
>
> - organisation, adaptation or alteration of the information or data,
> - retrieval, consultation or use of the information or data,
> - disclosure of the information or data by transmission, dissemination or otherwise making available, or

- alignment, combination, blocking, erasure or destruction of the information or data.'

The definition is wide enough to cover the simple recording and holding of images for a limited period of time, even if no further reference is made to those images. It is also wide enough to cover real-time transmission of the images. Thus if the images of individuals passing in front of a camera are shown in real time on a monitor, this constitutes "transmission, dissemination or otherwise making available. Thus even the least sophisticated capturing and use of images falls within the definition of processing in the 1998 Act.

2. Purposes for which personal data/images are processed

Before considering compliance with the Data Protection Principles, a user of CCTV or similar surveillance equipment, will need to determine two issues:

- What type of personal data are being processed i.e. are there any personal data which fall within the definition of sensitive personal data as defined by section 2 of the 1998 Act.
- For what purpose(s) are both personal data and sensitive personal data being processed?

Users of surveillance equipment should be clear about the purposes for which they intend to use the information/images captured by their equipment. The equipment may be used for a number of purposes:

- Prevention, investigation and/or detection of crime.
- Apprehension and/or prosecution of offenders (including images being entered as evidence in criminal proceedings).
- Public and employee safety.
- Staff discipline.
- Traffic flow monitoring.

Using information captured by a surveillance system will not always require the processing of personal data or the processing of sensitive personal data. For example, use of the system to monitor traffic flow in order to provide the public with up to date information about traffic jams, will not necessarily require the processing of personal data.

3. Data protection principles

First Data Protection Principle

This requires that

> 'Personal data shall be processed fairly and lawfully, and, in particular, shall not be processed unless:
>
> - at least one of the conditions in Schedule 2 is met, and
> - in the case of sensitive personal data, at least one of the conditions in Schedule 3 is also met.'

To assess compliance with this Principle, it is recommended that the data controller address the following questions:

(a) Are personal data and/or sensitive personal data processed?

The definition of sensitive personal data[33] has been discussed above and it is essential that the data controller has determined whether they are processing information/images, which fall into that category in order to assess which criteria to consider when deciding whether there is a legitimate basis for the processing of that information/images.

(b) Has a condition for processing been met?

The First Data Protection Principle requires that the *data controller* have a legitimate basis for processing. It is for the data controller to be clear about which grounds to rely on in this respect. These are set out in Schedules 2 and 3 to the Act.

Users of schemes which monitor spaces to which the public have access, such as town centres, may be able to rely on Paragraph 5 (d) of Schedule 2 because the processing is for the exercise of any other function of a public nature exercised in the public interest by any person. This could include purposes such as prevention and detection of crime, apprehension and prosecution of offenders or public/employee safety.

Users of schemes which monitor spaces in shops or retail centres to which the public have access may be able to rely on Paragraph 6(1) of Schedule 2 because the processing is necessary for the purposes of legitimate interests pursued by the data controller or the third party or third parties to whom the data are disclosed, except where the processing is unwarranted in any particular case by reason of prejudice to the rights and freedoms or legitimate interests of the data subject.

It should be noted that while this criterion may provide a general ground for processing, in an individual case, the interests of the data controller i.e. the user of the surveillance equipment might not outweigh the rights of an individual.

If the data controller has determined that he or she is processing sensitive personal data, then the data controller will also need to determine whether he or she has a legitimate basis for doing so under Schedule 3. It should be noted that Schedule 3 does not contain the grounds cited above in relation to Schedule 2.

Users of surveillance equipment in town centres, particularly where the local authority or police force (or a partnership of the two) are the data controllers may be able to rely on Paragraph 7(l)(b) of Schedule 3 because the processing is necessary for the exercise of any functions conferred on any person by or under an enactment. It may be that the use of such information/images by a public authority in order to meet the objectives of the Crime and Disorder Act 1998 would satisfy this criterion.

Users of information/images recorded in a shop or retail centre may be able to rely on one of the grounds contained in the Order made under Schedule 3(10) of the 1998 Act.[34]
For example-

'(1) The processing:

(*a*) is in the substantial public interest;

(*b*) is necessary for the purposes of the prevention and detection of any unlawful act; and

(*c*) must necessarily be carried out without the explicit consent of the data subject so as not to prejudice those purposes.'

It is for the data controller to be sure that he or she has legitimate grounds for their processing and therefore it is essential that the data controller has identified:

- what categories of data are processed, and
- why.

(c) Are the information/images processed lawfully?

The fact that the data controller has a legitimate basis for processing does not mean that this element of the First Data Protection Principle is automatically satisfied. The data controller will also need to consider whether the information/images processed are subject to any other legal duties or responsibilities such as the common law duty of confidentiality. Public sector bodies will need to consider their legal powers under administrative law in order to determine whether there are restrictions or prohibitions on their ability to process such data. They will also need to consider the implications of the Human Rights Act 1998.

(d) Are the information/images processed fairly?

The fact that a data controller has a legitimate basis for processing the information/images will not automatically mean that this element of the First Data Protection Principle is satisfied.

The interpretative provisions[35] of the Act set out what is required in order to process fairly. In order to process fairly, the following information, at least, must be provided to the individuals at the point of obtaining their images:

- the identity of the data controller
- the identity of a representative the data controller has nominated for the purposes of the Act
- the purpose or purposes for which the data are intended to be processed, and
- any information which is necessary, having regard to the specific circumstances in which the data are or are to be processed, to enable processing in respect of the individual to be fair.

(e) Circumstances in which the requirement for signs may be set aside

The Act does not make specific reference to the use of covert processing of (sensitive) personal data but it does provide a limited exemption from the requirement of fair processing. Because fair processing (as indicated above) requires that individuals are made aware that they are entering an area where their images may be captured, by the use of signs, it follows that the use of covert processing i.e. removal or failure to provide signs, is prima facie a breach of the fairness requirement of the First Data Protection Principle. However, a breach of this requirement will not arise if an exemption can be relied on. Such an exemption may be found at section 29(l) of the Act, which states that:

> 'Personal data processed for any of the following purposes:
>
> - prevention or detection of crime
> - apprehension or prosecution of offenders

> are exempt from the first data protection principle (except to the extent to which it requires compliance with the conditions in Schedules 2 and 3) … in any case to the extent to which the application of those provisions to the data would be likely to prejudice any of the matters mentioned … '

This means that if the data controller processes images for either or both of the purposes listed in the exemption, he or she may be able to obtain and process images without signs without breaching the fairness requirements of the First Data Protection Principle.

Second Data Protection Principle

This requires that:

> 'Personal data shall be obtained only for one or more specified and lawful purposes, and shall not be further processed in any manner incompatible with that purpose or those purposes.'

In order to ascertain whether the data controller can comply with this Data Protection Principle, it is essential that he or she is clear about the purpose(s) for which the images are processed.

Specified purposes may be those, which have been notified to the Commissioner or to the individuals.

There are a number of issues to be considered when determining lawfulness:

- Whether the data controller has a legitimate basis (see First Data Protection Principle) for the processing.
- Whether the images are processed in accordance with any other legal duties to which the data controller may be subject e.g. the common law duty of confidence, administrative law in relation to public sector powers etc.

It is quite clear from the interpretative provisions to the Principle that the requirement of compatibility is particularly significant when considering making a disclosure to a third party or developing a policy on disclosures to third parties. If the data controller intends to make a disclosure to a third party, regard must be had to the purpose(s) for which the third party may process the data.

This means, for example, that if the purpose(s) for which images are processed is:

- Prevention or detection of crime
- Apprehension or prosecution of offenders

The data controller may only disclose to third parties who intend processing the data for compatible purposes. Thus, for example, where there is an investigation into criminal activity, disclosure of footage relating to that criminal activity to the media in order to seek assistance from the public in identifying either the perpetrator, the victim or witnesses, may be appropriate. However, it would be an incompatible use if images from equipment installed to prevent or detect crime were disclosed to the media merely for entertainment purposes. For example, it might be appropriate to disclose to the media images of drunken individuals stumbling around a town centre on a Saturday night to show proper use of policing resources to combat anti-social behaviour. However, it would not be appropriate for the same images to be provided to a media company merely for inclusion in a 'humorous' video.

If it is determined that a particular disclosure is compatible with the purposes for which the data controller processes images, then the extent of disclosure will need to be considered. If the footage, which is to be disclosed contains images of unrelated third parties, the data controller will need to ensure that those images are disguised in such a way that they cannot be identified.

If the data controller does not have the facilities to carry out such editing, he or she may agree with the media organisation that it will ensure that those images are disguised. This will mean that the media organisation is carrying out processing, albeit of a limited nature on behalf of the data controller which is likely to render it a data processor. In which case the data controller will need to ensure that the relationship with the media organisation complies with the Seventh Data Protection Principle.

Third Data Protection Principle

This requires that:

> 'Personal data shall be adequate, relevant and not excessive in relation to the purpose or purposes for which they are processed.'

This means that consideration must be given to the situation of the cameras so that they do not record more information than is necessary for the purpose for which they were installed. For example cameras installed for the purpose of recording acts of vandalism in a car park should not overlook private residences. Furthermore, if the recorded images on the tapes are blurred or indistinct, it may well be that this will constitute inadequate data. For example, if the purpose of the system is to collect evidence of criminal activity, blurred or indistinct images from degraded tapes or poorly maintained equipment will not provide legally sound evidence, and may therefore be inadequate for its purpose.

Fourth Data Protection Principle

This requires that:

> 'Personal data shall be accurate and, where necessary, kept up to date.'

This principle requires that the personal information that is recorded and stored must be accurate. This is particularly important if the personal information taken from the system is to be used as evidence in cases of criminal conduct or in disciplinary disputes with employees. The Commissioner recommends that efforts are made to ensure the clarity of the images, such as using only good quality tapes in recording the information, cleaning the tapes prior to re-use and not simply recording over existing images, and replacing tapes on a regular basis to avoid degradation from over-use.

If the data controller's system uses features such as time references and even location references, then these should be accurate. This means having a documented procedure to ensure the accuracy of such features are checked and if necessary, amended or altered.

Care should be exercised when using digital-enhancement and compression technologies to produce stills for evidence from tapes because these technologies often contain pre-programmed presumptions as to the likely nature of sections of the image. Thus the user cannot be certain that the images taken from the tape are an accurate representation of the actual scene. This may create evidential difficulties if they are to be relied on either in court or an internal employee disciplinary hearing.

Fifth Data Protection Principle

This requires that:

> 'Personal data processed for any purpose or purposes shall not be kept for longer than is necessary for that purpose or those purposes.'

This principle requires that the information shall not be held for longer than is necessary for the purpose for which it is to be used. The tapes that have recorded the relevant activities should be retained until such time as the proceedings are completed and the possibility of any appeal has been exhausted. After that time, the tapes should be erased. Apart from those circumstances, stored or recorded images should not be kept for any undue length of time. A policy on periods for retention of the images should be developed which takes into account the nature of the information and the purpose for which it is being collected. For example where images are being recorded for the purposes of crime prevention in a shopping area, it may be that the only images that need to be retained are those relating to specific incidents of criminal activity; the rest could be erased after a very short period. The Commissioner understands that generally town centre schemes do not retain recorded images for more than 28 days unless the images are required for evidential purposes.

Sixth Data Protection Principle

This requires that:

> 'Personal data shall be processed in accordance with the rights of data subjects under this Act.'

The Act provides individuals with a number of rights in relation to the processing of their personal data. Contravening the following rights will amount to a contravention of the Sixth Data Protection Principle:

- The right to be provided, in appropriate cases, with a copy of the information constituting the personal data held about them – Section 7.[36]
- The right to prevent processing which is likely to cause damage or distress – Section 10.[37]
- Rights in relation to automated decision-taking – Section 12.[38]

Seventh Data Protection Principle[39]

This requires that:

> 'Appropriate technical and organisational measures shall be taken against unauthorised or unlawful processing of personal data and against accidental loss or destruction of, or damage to, personal data.'

In order to assess the level of security the data controller needs to take to ensure compliance with this Principle, he or she needs to assess:

- the harm that might result from unauthorised or unlawful processing or accidental loss, destruction or damage of the personal data.[40] While it is clear that breach of this Principle may have a detrimental effect on the purpose(s) of the scheme e.g. the evidence or images might not stand up in court, or the public may lose confidence in your use of surveillance equipment due to inappropriate disclosure, the harm test required by the Act also requires primarily the effect on the people recorded to be taken into account;

- the nature of the data to be protected must be considered. Sensitive personal data was defined at the beginning of this part of the Code, but there may be other aspects, which need to be considered. For example, a town centre scheme may coincidentally record the image of a couple kissing in a parked car, or a retailer's scheme may record images of people in changing rooms (in order to prevent items of clothing being stolen). Whilst these images may not fall within the sensitive categories as set in Section 2 (described above), it is clear that the people whose images have been captured will consider that information or personal data should be processed with greater care.

Eighth Data Protection Principle

This requires that:

> 'Personal data shall not be transferred to a country or territory outside the European Economic Area unless that country or territory ensures an adequate level of protection for the rights and freedoms of data subjects in relation to the processing of personal data.'

This Principle places limitations on the ability to transfer personal data to countries and territories outside of the EEA.[41] It is unlikely that the data controller would want, in general, to make such transfers of personal data overseas, but the data controller should refrain from putting the images on the Internet or on their website. In order to ensure that this Principle is not breached, the data controller should consider the provisions of Schedule 4 of the 1998 Act.

4. Right of subject access

Upon making a request in writing (which includes transmission by electronic means) and upon paying the fee to the data controller an individual is entitled:

- To be told by the data controller whether they or someone else on their behalf is processing that individual's personal data.

- If so, to be given a description of:

(*a*) the personal data,

(*b*) the purposes for which they are being processed, and

(*c*) those to whom they are or may be disclosed.

- To be told, in an intelligible manner, of:

  (*a*) all the information, which forms any such personal data. This information must be supplied in permanent form by way of a copy, except where the supply of such a copy is not possible or would involve disproportionate effort or the individual agrees otherwise. If any of the information in the copy is not intelligible without explanation, the individual should be given an explanation of that information, e.g. where the data controller holds the information in coded form which cannot be understood without the key to the code, and

  (*b*) any information as to the source of those data. However, in some instances the data controller is not obliged to disclose such information where the source of the data is, or can be identified as, an individual.

A data controller may charge a fee (subject to a maximum) for dealing with subject access. A data controller must comply with a subject access request promptly, and in any event within forty days of receipt of the request or, if later, within forty days of receipt of:

- the information required (i.e. to satisfy himself as to the identity of the person making the request and to locate the information which that person seeks); and
- the fee.

However, unless the data controller has received a request in writing, the prescribed fee and, if necessary, the said information the data controller need not comply with the request. If the data controller receives a request without the required fee and/or information, they should request whichever is outstanding as soon as possible in order that they can comply with the request promptly and in any event within 40 days. A data controller does not need to comply with a request where they have already complied with an identical or similar request by the same individual unless a reasonable interval has elapsed between compliance with the previous request and the making of the current request. In deciding what amounts to a reasonable interval, the following factors should be considered: the nature of the data, the purpose for which the data are processed and the frequency with which the data are altered.

The information given in response to a subject access request should be all that which is contained in the personal data at the time the request was received. However, routine amendments and deletions of the data may continue between the date of the request and the date of the reply. To this extent, the information revealed to the individual may differ from the personal data which were held at the time the request was received, even to the extent that data are no longer held. But, having received a request, the data controller must not make any special amendment or deletion which would not otherwise have been made. The information must not be tampered with in order to make it acceptable to the individual.

A particular problem arises for data controllers who may find that in complying with a subject access request they will disclose information relating to an individual other than the individual who has made the request, who can be identified from that information, including the situation where the information enables that other individual to be identified as the source of the information. The Act recognises this problem and sets out only two circumstances in which the data controller is obliged to comply with the subject access request in such circumstances, namely:

- where the other individual has consented to the disclosure of the information, or
- where it is reasonable in all the circumstances to comply with the request without the consent of the other individual.

The Act assists in interpreting whether it is reasonable in all the circumstances to comply with the request without the consent of the other individual concerned. In deciding this question regard shall be had, in particular, to:

- any duty of confidentiality owed to the other individual,
- any steps taken by the data controller with a view to seeking the consent of the other individual,
- whether the other individual is capable of giving consent, and
- any express refusal of consent by the other individual.

If a data controller is satisfied that the individual will not be able to identify the other individual from the information, taking into account any other information which, in the reasonable belief of the data controller, is likely to be in (or to come into) the possession of the individual, then the data controller must provide the information.

If an individual believes that a data controller has failed to comply with a subject access request in contravention of the Act they may apply to Court for an order that the data controller complies with the request. An order may be made if the Court is satisfied that the data controller has failed to comply with the request in contravention of the Act.

5. Exemptions to subject access rights

There are a limited number of exemptions to an individuals right of access. One of potential relevance to CCTV images is found at section 29 of the Act. This provides an exemption from the subject access rights, which is similar to that discussed in relation to the exemption to the fairness requirements of the First Data Protection Principle. This means that where personal data are held for the purposes of:

- prevention or detection of crime,
- apprehension or prosecution of offenders,

the data controller will be entitled to withhold personal data from an individual making a subject access request, where it has been adjudged that to disclose the personal data would be likely to prejudice one or both of the above purposes. Like the exemption to the fairness requirements of the First Data Protection Principle, this judgement must be made on a case-by-case basis, and in relation to each element of the personal data held about the individual. It is likely that this exemption may only be appropriately relied upon where the data controller has recorded personal data about an individual in accordance with guidance set out in relation to the fairness requirements of the First Data Protection Principle.[42]

6. Other rights

Right to prevent processing likely to cause damage or distress

Under section 10 of the Act, an individual is entitled to serve a notice on a data controller requiring the data controller not to begin, or to cease, processing personal data relating to that individual. Such a notice could only be served on the grounds that the processing in question is likely to cause substantial, unwarranted damage or distress to that individual or another person. There are certain limited situations where this right to serve a notice does not apply. These are where the individual has consented; the processing is in connection with performance of a contract with the data subject, or in compliance with a legal obligation on the data controller, or in order to protect the vital interests of the individual. If a data controller receives such a notice they must respond within 21 days indicating either compliance with the notice or why the notice is not justified.

Rights in relation to automated decision-taking

Under section 12 of the Act individuals also have certain rights to prevent automated decision taking where a decision, which significantly affects them is based solely on automated processing. The Act draws particular attention to decisions taken aimed at evaluating matters such as the individual's performance at work and their reliability or conduct. The Act does provide exemption for certain decisions reached by automated means and these cover decisions which have been taken in the course of contractual arrangements with the individual, where a decision is authorised or required by statute, where the decision is to grant a request of the individual or where steps have been taken to safeguard the legitimate interests of individuals. This latter point may include matters such as allowing them to make representations about a decision before it is implemented.

Where no notice has been served by an individual and a decision which significantly affects the individual based solely on automated processing will be made, then there is still an obligation on the data controller to notify the individual that the decision was taken on the basis of automated processing as soon as reasonably practicable. The individual may, within 21 days of receiving such a notification, request the data controller to reconsider the decision or take another decision on a new basis. Having received such a notice the data controller has 21 days in which to respond, specifying the steps that they intend to take to comply with the notice.

In the context of CCTV surveillance it may be the case that certain automated decision-making techniques are deployed, such as with automatic facial recognition. It is important therefore that any system takes account of an individual's rights in relation to automated decision taking. It should be noted that these rights are founded on decisions, which are taken solely on the basis of automated processing. If a decision whether to take particular action in relation to a particular identified individual is taken further to human intervention, then such a decision would not be based solely on automated processing.
The individual's rights to prevent processing in certain circumstances and in connection with automated decision taking are underpinned by an individual's right to seek a court order should any notice served by the individual not be complied with.

Compensation for failure to comply with certain requirements

Under section 13 of the Act, individuals who suffer unwarranted damage or damage and distress as a result of any contravention of the requirements of the Act are entitled to go to court to seek compensation in certain circumstances. This right to claim compensation for a breach of the Act is in addition to an individual's right to request the Data Protection Commissioner to make an assessment as to whether processing is likely or unlikely to comply with the Act.

1. It is intended that employers' use of personal data to monitor employee compliance with contracts of employment will be covered by the Data Protection Commissioner's forthcoming code of practice on use of employee personal data.
2. It is likely that the use of cameras by individuals to protect their own property is excluded from the provisions of the Act under the exemption at section 36 of the Act.
3. The Commissioner's powers to issue an Enforcement Notice may be found in section 40 of the Act.
4. The First Data Protection Principle requires data controllers to have a legitimate basis for processing personal data, in this case images of individuals. The Act sets out criteria for processing, one of which must be met in order to demonstrate that there is a legitimate basis for processing the images.
5. Section 4(4) of the Act places all data controllers under a duty to comply with the data protection principles in relation to all personal data with respect to which he is the data controller as defined by section 1(1) of the Act. See the section on definitions.
6. The First Data Protection Principle requires data controllers to have a legitimate basis for processing, one of which must be met in order to demonstrate that there is a legitimate basis for processing the images.
7. Section l7 of the Act prohibits the processing of personal data unless the data controller has notified the Data Protection Commissioner. The notification scheme requires that the purpose(s) of the processing be identified.
8. Section 29 of the Act sets out the circumstances in which the fair processing requirements of the First Data Protection Principle are set aside.
9. It may be that the particular problem identified is theft from cars in a car park. Following the appropriate assessment, surveillance equipment is installed but signs are not. If the equipment co-incidentally records images relating to other criminality for example a sexual assault, it will not be inappropriate for those images to be used in the detection of that crime or in order to apprehend and prosecute the offender. However, it might be inappropriate for images so obtained to be used in civil proceedings or disciplinary proceedings eg the car park attendant is recorded committing a minor disciplinary misdemeanour.
10. Users of such systems should be aware of the affect of section 12 of the 1998 Act regarding individuals' rights in relation to automated decision taking.
11. See the section on access to and disclosure of images to third parties.
12. See the section on access to and disclosure of images to third parties.
13. See the section on individual's rights.
14. See the section on the seventh data protection principle.
15. See the section on access to and disclosure of images to third parties.
16. See the section on access to and disclosure of images to third parties.
17. See the section on the right of subject access.
18. See the section on the right of subject access.
19. See the section on the right of subject access.
20. See the section on the right of subject access.
21. See the section on the right of subject access.
22. See the section on the right of subject access.

23. Section 10 of the Act provides individuals with the right to prevent processing likely to cause damage or distress. See the section on other rights.
24 Users of such a system should be aware of the effects of section 12 of the Act regarding individuals' rights in relation to automated decision taking.
25 Section 10 of the Act provides individuals with the right to prevent processing likely to cause substantial damage or distress. See the section on other rights.
26 Section 10 of the Act provides individuals with the right to prevent processing likely to cause substantial damage or distress. See the section on other rights.
27 Section 10 of the Act provides individuals with the right to prevent processing likely to cause substantial damage or distress. See the section on other rights.
28 Users of such systems should be aware of the effect of section 12 of the 1998 Act regarding individuals' rights in relation to automated decision taking.
29 Users of such systems should be aware of the effect of section 12 of the 1998 Act regarding individuals' rights in relation to automated decision taking.
30 Users of such systems should be aware of the effect of section 12 of the 1998 Act regarding individuals' rights in relation to automated decision taking.
31 European Directive 95/46/EC on the protection of individuals with regard to the processing of personal data and on the free movement of such data.
32 Section 2 of Act sets out the full list of categories of sensitive personal data. This part of the Code only refers to some of the categories, which may have particular relevance for users of CCTV. For a full list, please see the relevant section of the Act.
33 Section 2 of Act sets out the full list of categories of sensitive personal data. This part of the Code only refers to some of the categories, which may have particular relevance for users of CCTV. For a full list, please see the relevant section of the Act.
34 The Data Protection (Processing of Sensitive Personal Data) Order 2000 (SI 2000/417).
35 Schedule l Part II Sections 1–4 of the Act.
36 See the section on the right of subject access.
37 Section 2 of the Act sets out the full list of categories of sensitive personal data. This part of the Code only refers to some of the categories, which may have particular relevance for users of CCTV. For a full list, please see the relevant section of the Act.
38 Users of such systems should be aware of the effect of section 12 of the 1998 Act regarding individuals' rights in relation to automated decision taking.
39 British Standard Institute – BS 7958:1991 'Closed Circuit Television (CCTV) – Management and Operation Code of Practice' provides guidance on issues of security, tape management etc.
40 Schedule 1, Part II, Paragraph 9 of the Act.
41 Schedule 1, Part II, Paragraphs 13–15 of the Act.
42 See the subsection on circumstances in which the requirements for signs may be set aside.

Appendix 2 – European Commission Frequently Asked Questions on Model Clauses for Data Export

Commission decision on standard contractual clauses for the transfer of personal data to third countries (2001/497/EC)

Frequently asked questions

1. Are the standard contractual clauses compulsory for companies interested in transferring data outside the EU?
2. Do these clauses set a minimum standard for individual contracts or future model contracts?
3. Can companies still rely on different contracts approved at national level?
4. Will the Commission consider issuing in future other standard contractual clauses?
5. When using the standard contractual clauses do companies still need a national authorisation to proceed with the transfer?
6. Is the deposit of the contract before the Member States compulsory? And can the transfer take place before the deposit?
7. How can companies protect their confidential information if they have to deposit a copy of these clauses with the Supervisory Authorities and provide the data subject with a copy on request?
8. Can Member States block or suspend data transfers using the standard contractual clauses?
9. What is meant by 'restrictions necessary in a democratic society' in Article 3 (a)?
10. What is covered by the term 'legislation' in Clause 5 (a)? And what specific action should the Data Importer take to ascertain that he is not prevented from fulfilling his obligations under the contract?

11. Can companies implement the standard contractual clauses in a wider contract and add specific clauses?

12. Does joint and several liability mean that the liability of the parties is strict?

13. Does joint and several liability mean that the Data Importer can be sued for the Data Exporters' violation before the transfer has taken place?

14. Does joint and several liability mean that the Data Importer will never be sued?

15. Does joint and several liability mean that the Data Exporter is responsible in relation to the individual for breach of contract by the Data Importer?

16. Does joint and several liability mean that the Data Exporter has to pay for any damages caused to individuals as a consequence of the violations committed by the Data Importer in a third country?

17. Does compliance with the "Mandatory Data Protection Principles" mean compliance with the provisions of the Directive 95/46/EC?

18. The model contract allow the Data Subject the right of access to his or her personal information. Is the right of access absolute and does it apply to both the Data Exporter and the Data Importer?

19. Can Data Importers be exempted from the application of the mandatory principles to fulfil their obligations under national law?

20. Are the parties liable for damages caused to individuals in such cases?

21. Can US based organisations that have joined the Safe Harbor use the standard contractual clauses to receive data from the EU?

22. Can U.S. based companies that have not joined the Safe Harbor use the relevant Safe Harbor rules under the contract?

23. What is an onward transfer?

24. Do the restrictions on onward transfers apply to onward transfers to recipients that have been found to provide for adequate protection?

These Frequently Asked Questions are very different from the FAQs of the Safe Harbor Decision. The FAQs of the Safe Harbor were part of Safe Harbor system issued by the U.S. Department of Commerce and therefore were part of the Commission Decision approved by the European Commission. These FAQs on the standard contractual clauses, on the contrary, do not form part of the draft Commission decision, have not been approved by the European Commission and do not have any legal value.

They are aimed at providing additional information to companies and individuals about the draft decision the Commission is likely to approve before the summer break, and they summarise those questions the Commission's services have been receiving from interested parties during the last months (see also letters received and replies from the Commission) and, in particular, in the meetings hold with representatives of business associations. These FAQs will be improved or updated if and when the need arises.

Directive 95/46/EC on the protection of individuals with regard to the processing of personal data and on the free movement of such data, requires Member States to permit transfers of personal data only to third countries where there is adequate protection for such data, unless one of a limited number of specific exemptions applies. Where this is not the case, the transfer must not be allowed.[1]

Without such rules, the high standards of data protection established by the Directive would quickly be undermined, given the ease with which data can be moved around on international networks.

Article 26 (4) allows the Commission, with the support of a Management Committee composed of Member States representatives, to issue standard contractual clauses for the purpose of fulfilling the requirements set down by the directive when transferring data to third countries.

The present FAQs summarise the main issues of the draft Commission decision and provide information to individuals and companies on how to best make use of the standard contractual clauses. They are not part of the Commission decision, have not gone through a consultative process either with the Article 29 Working Party or the Management Committee and do not have a legal status of their own.

1. Are the standard contractual clauses compulsory for companies interested in transferring data outside the EU?

   No. The standard contractual clauses are neither compulsory for businesses nor are they the only way of lawfully transferring data to third countries.

   First of all, organisations do not need contractual clauses if they want to transfer personal data to recipients in countries which have been recognised as adequate by the Commission. This is the case of transfers to Switzerland,[2] Hungary[3] or US based companies adhering to the Safe Harbor Privacy Principles issued by the US Department of Commerce.[4]

Secondly, even if the country of destination does not offer an adequate level of protection, data may be transferred in specific circumstances. These are listed in Article 26 (1) and include cases where:

1. the data subject has given his consent unambiguously to the proposed transfer; or
2. the transfer is necessary for the performance of a contract between the data subject and the controller or the implementation of pre-contractual measures taken in response to the data subject's request; or
3. the transfer is necessary for the conclusion or performance of a contract concluded in the interest of the data subject between the controller and a third party; or
4. the transfer is necessary or legally required on important p public interest grounds, or for the establishment, exercise or defence of legal claims; or
5. the transfer is necessary in order to protect the vital interests of the data subject; or
6. The transfer is made from a register which according to laws or regulations is intended to provide information to the public and which is open to consultation either by the public in general or by any person who can demonstrate legitimate interest, to the extent that the conditions laid down in law for consultation are fulfilled in the particular case.

Finally, under Article 26 (2) national authorities may authorise on a case by case basis specific transfers to a country not as offering an adequate protection where the exporter in the EU adduces adequate safeguards with respect to the protection of privacy by fundamental rights and freedoms of individuals and as regards the exercise of the corresponding rights.. This could be done for example by contractual arrangements between the exporter and the importer of data, subject to the prior approval of national authorities.

2. Do these clauses set a minimum standard for individual contracts or future model contracts?

   No. The standard contractual clauses do not have any effect on individual contracts or future model contractual clauses.

   Once adopted this decision will simply oblige Member States to recognise the contractual clauses annexed to the decision as providing adequate safeguards and fulfilling the requirements set down in Articles 26 of the directive for data transfers to non-EU countries that do not provide for an adequate level of protection for personal data.

3. Can companies still rely on different contracts approved at national level?

   Yes. The standard contractual clauses do not prejudice past or future contractual arrangements authorised by national Data Protection Authorities pursuant to national legislation.

   Authorisations at national level may be granted if Data Protection Authorities consider that the safeguards adduced by Data Exporters to protect the individuals privacy are sufficient in relation to the specific contract.[5] The content of these national contracts may be different from the Commission's standard contractual clauses. These contracts need to be notified to the Commission and the other Member States.

4. Will the Commission consider issuing in future other standard contractual clauses?

   Yes. The Commission intends to start work on other standard contractual clauses, in particular to deal with low risk transfers that may allow for a lighter approach to be followed. A first decision is likely to concern the transfer of data to a subcontractor for the mere processing, a category of transfers excluded from the scope of the draft Decision (see recital 9). We welcome input from businesses, in particular the submission of drafts from Industry Associations and encourage them to signal their needs in this respect.

5. When using the standard contractual clauses do companies still need a national authorisation to proceed with the transfer?

   Member States are obliged to recognise the standard contractual clauses as fulfilling the requirements set down by the directive for the export of data and consequently may not refuse the transfer. In most cases there is no need for a prior national authorisation to proceed with the transfer but some Member States maintain a license system. In this case however, the authorisation is automatically given and its requirement can in no way delay or hinder the performance of the contract.

6. Is the deposit of the contract before the Member States compulsory? And can the transfer take place before the deposit?

   The answer may vary from one Member State to another, as this is an option under the standard contractual clauses. Some Member States have already announced that they will request the deposit of the contract. Others may request the presentation of the contract or decide that no deposit or presentation will be necessary. Should the deposit or presentation of the contract be requested at national level, Member States will determine the procedure dealing with this question.

The deposit of the contract is only a formality to facilitate the work of the national data protection authorities and should not unduly delay the performance of the contract.

7. How can companies protect their confidential information if they have to deposit a copy of these clauses with the Supervisory Authorities and provide the data subject with a copy on request?

   In the case of standard contractual clauses, the clauses relating to the individual's data are those already in the public domain, and published in annex to the decision. All other clauses relating to the company's business can remain confidential. Moreover, data protection authorities and the European Commission are bound by a duty of confidentiality when exercising their duties.

8. Can Member States block or suspend data transfers using the standard contractual clauses?

   Yes, but only in the exceptional circumstances referred to in Article 3 of the Commission Decision. These include cases where:

   (*a*) It is established that the law to which the Data Importer is subject imposes upon him to derogate from the relevant data protection rules beyond the restrictions necessary in a democratic society as provided for in Article 13 of Directive 95/46/EC where those derogations are likely to have a substantial adverse effect on the guarantees provided by the standard contractual clauses, or

(*b*) A competent authority has established that the Data Importer has not respected the contractual clauses, or

(*c*) There is a substantial likelihood that the standard contractual clauses in the annex are not being or will not be complied with and the continuing transfer would create an imminent risk of grave harm to the Data Subjects

It is expected that this safeguard clause will be very rarely used as it caters for exceptional cases only. As provided for in Article 3 (3) of the draft decision, the European Commission will be informed of any use made by the Member States of this safeguard clause and will forward the information received to other Member States. The Commission may take appropriate measures in accordance with the procedure laid down in Article 31 (2) of Directive 95/46/EC

It is also important to highlight the fact that prior to the transfer it is the national law implementing the directive that apply and not the standard contractual clauses. In other words, transfers outside the EU can be lawfully made only if the data have been collected and further processed in accordance with the national laws applicable by the data controller established in the EU.

Therefore, companies interested in using the standard contractual clauses would still need to comply with the conditions for the lawfulness of the disclosure of the personal data in the Member State where the data exporter is established. Where a disclosure of data to a third party recipient inside a Member State would not be lawful, the mere circumstance that the recipient may be situated in a third country does not change this legal evaluation.

9. What is meant by "restrictions necessary in a democratic society" in Article 3 (a)?

Exceptions to the basic data protection principles must be limited to those which are necessary for the protection of fundamental values in a democratic society. These criteria cannot be laid down for all countries and all times but should be considered in the light of the given situation in the country in question. The interests protected are listed in article 13 of the directive and include all such measures that are necessary to safeguard:

(*a*) national security;

(*b*) defence;

(*c*) public security;

(*d*) the prevention, investigation, detection and prosecution of criminal offences, or of breaches of ethics for regulated professions;

(*e*) an important economic or financial interest of the State including monetary, budgetary and taxation matters;

(*f*) a monitoring, inspection or regulatory function connected, even occasionally, with the exercise of official authority in cases referred to in (c), (d) and (e);

(*g*) the protection of the data subject or of the rights and freedoms of others.

The condition "necessary in a democratic society" derives from Articles 8–11 of the European Convention of Human Rights and extensive case law has been developed by the Commission of Human Rights on this issue. The same principle also occurs in the Council of Europe Convention 108.

10. What is covered by the term "legislation" in Clause 5 (a)? And what specific action should the Data Importer take to ascertain that he is not prevented from fulfilling his obligations under the contract?

    The term "legislation" in Clause 5 (a) also covers case law, rule or regulation that may impede on the performance of the contract. The Data Importer should take reasonable care to determine if there are any such rules that might prevent him from fulfilling his obligation.

11. Can companies implement the standard contractual clauses in a wider contract and add specific clauses ?

    Yes. Parties are free to agree to add other clauses as long as they do not contradict, directly or indirectly, the standard contractual clauses approved by the Commission or prejudice fundamental rights or freedoms of the data subjects. It is possible, for example, to include additional guarantees or procedural safeguards for the individuals (e.g. on-line procedures or relevant provisions contained in a privacy policy, etc.). All these other clauses that parties may decide to add would not be covered by the third party beneficiary rights and would benefit from confidentiality rights where appropriate.

    Member States may also further specify or complete the Appendix annexed to the contract.

    In all cases, the standard clauses have to be fully respected if they are to deploy the legal effect of providing for an adequate safeguard for the transfer of personal data as required by the EU directive.

    Recital 10 of the Draft decision states that Member States retain the power to particularise the information the parties are required to provide in the Appendix. What does it mean?

    The Appendix to the contract contains the minimum information that should be included in the contract. This said, it may be necessary to add additional requirements laid down in national law and necessary to make the transfer from a specific Member State lawful (see FAQ 6). For this reason Member States retain the power to add such specifications, relating for example to If a Member State decides to particularise the Appendix to the contract , it is that modified Appendix that must be used when data is transferred from that Member State.

The Commission recognises that it may be useful, in future and on the basis of experience, to amend the Appendix in order to ensure that the information requirements are as similar as possible throughout the Union.

12. Does joint and several liability mean that the liability of the parties is strict?

    No. A party can be exempted from liability if it proofs that it is not responsible for the event causing the damage. It does not need to prove that the other party is responsible for the damage but at the same time it cannot be exempted from liability simply by alleging that the other party is responsible for the event causing the damage. In other words, exemption from liability is possible, for instance, in cases of force majeur or to the extent that there is a participation of the data subject in the event causing the damage.

13. Does joint and several liability mean that the Data Importer can be sued for the Data Exporters' violation before the transfer has taken place?

    No. This case is excluded from the third party beneficiary's rights (Clause 3). Data subjects can however exercise their rights in the European Union against the Data Exporter for unlawful processing in the European Community.

14. Does joint and several liability mean that the Data Importer will never be sued?

    Not necessarily. The data subjects may decide to sue the Data Exporter, the Data Importer or both. Although an action against the Data Exporter before a European court seems the preferable way for an individual to obtain compensation, he or she may decide to take action against the Data Importer, if, for example the Data Exporter has disappeared or filed for bankruptcy. In these cases, the Data Importer may be sued before the Data Exporter's Courts (clause 7) or before the Courts of his own country if so permitted under private international law.

15. Does joint and several liability mean that the Data Exporter is responsible in relation to the individual for breach of contract by the Data Importer?

    No. Data Exporters are jointly and severally liable vis-à-vis the data subjects only for damages caused to individuals resulting from the violation of those provisions covered by third party beneficiary's rights (Clause 3). In the cases where the violation of the clauses does not result in damages for individuals, every party is solely responsible vis-à-vis the data subjects.

16. Does joint and several liability mean that the Data Exporter has to pay for any damages caused to individuals as a consequence of the violations committed by the Data Importer in a third country?

    Yes, but only to the extent that the provision violated is covered by the third party beneficiary's rights (clause 3). Subsequently the Data Exporter has a right to recover any cost, charge, damage, expenses or loss from the Data Importer, to the extent that the latter is liable (see clause 6 (3)[6]).

    Indemnification has been considerably eased by some of the provisions contained in the standard contractual clauses. In fact, the Data Importer agrees and warrants to deal promptly and properly with all inquires from the Data Subjects, the Data Exporter or the Supervisory Authority (Clause 5, letter c) and to submit its data processing facilities for audit at the request of the Data Exporter (clause 5, letter d).

    It is therefore expected as a practical way to proceed that Data Exporters in the case of data subjects' complaints for damages caused by Data Importers' violations of the clauses will be able to convince their contractual counterparts to provide any necessary compensations himself in the first place and therefore to avoid subsequent indemnification. As it was already explained before, parties are free to include any additional clauses on mutual assistance or indemnification they consider pertinent.

    In conclusion, "joint and several liability does not need to leave one party paying for the damages resulting from the unlawful processing of the other party because clause 6 (3) provides for mutual indemnification" (see recital 18).

17. Does compliance with the "Mandatory Data Protection Principles" mean compliance with the provisions of the Directive 95/46/EC?

    No. The mandatory data protection principles reflect a set of substantive data protection principles that guarantees an adequate, not an equivalent level of protection. They have been construed on the basis of the Working Party's opinion 12/98.[7]

18. The model contract allow the Data Subject the right of access to his or her personal information. Is the right of access absolute and does it apply to both the Data Exporter and the Data Importer?

    Both the Data Exporter and the Data Importer agree and warrant to respond properly and reasonably to inquiries from the Data Subjects about the processing of the data transferred. As indicated in Clause 4 c), the Data Exporter will respond to the extent reasonably possible as the questions posed by the Data Subjects would relate to the processing of personal data carried out by the Data Importer.

Clause 5 c) stipulates that the Data Importer warrants to deal promptly and properly with all reasonable inquiries from the Data Exporter. Therefore, if a Data Exporter receives an access request from a Data Subject concerning processing operations carried out by the Data Importer, the Data Exporter is expected to enforce clause 5 c) against the Data Importer, if necessary, to give satisfaction to the access request posed by the Data Subject.

19. Can Data Importers be exempted from the application of the mandatory principles to fulfil their obligations under national law?

Yes, as provided for in the closing paragraph of the mandatory principles they may do so as long as they are not confronted with mandatory requirements that go beyond what is necessary in a democratic society, namely because they constitute a necessary measure to safeguard national security, defence, public security, the prevention, investigation, detection and prosecution of criminal offences or of breaches of ethics for the regulated professions; an important economic or financial interest of the State or the protection of the Data Subjects or the rights and freedoms of others.

20. Are the parties liable for damages caused to individuals in such cases?

No, the exemption from the Mandatory Principles is complete.

The Data Importer (and the Data Exporter via application of Clause 6), however, would be liable for damages caused to individuals in case of compliance with mandatory requirements of national legislation that go beyond what is necessary in a democratic society on the basis of one of the interests mentioned above. In fact, at the signature of the contract, the Data Importer warrants that he has no reason to believe the legislation applicable to him prevents him from fulfilling his obligations under the contract and he undertakes to notify the Data Exporter and the Data Protection Authority of any change of this situation.

21. Can US based organisations that have joined the Safe harbor use the standard contractual clauses to receive data from the EU?

As a general rule, standard contractual clauses are not necessary if the data recipient is covered by a system providing adequate data protection such as the Safe Harbor. However, if the transfer concerns data that is not covered by their Safe Harbor commitments, use of the standard contract clauses is one way of providing the necessary safeguards.

22. Can U.S. based companies that have not joined the Safe Harbor use the relevant Safe Harbor rules under the contract?

    Yes, provided that they also apply the three mandatory data protection principles in the Annex (applicable to all countries of destination): the purpose limitation, restrictions on onward transfers and the right of access, rectification, deletion and objection.

23. What is an onward transfer

    There is an onward transfer every time personal data is transferred from the Data Importer to another natural or legal person that autonomously determines the purpose and means of processing.

    Processing means any operation which is performed on personal data, such as collection, recording, organisation, storage, adaptation or alteration, retrieval, consultation, use disclosure, dissemination, alignment or combination, blocking, erasure or destruction.

24. Do the restrictions on onward transfers apply to onward transfers to recipients that have been found to provide for adequate protection?

    No, the restrictions on onward transfers apply only to those cases where the recipient does not benefit from an adequacy finding. So far transfers to Switzerland, Hungary and US based organisations that have adhered to the Safe Harbor benefit from an adequacy finding.

    The restrictions on onward transfers also do not apply when the recipient is established in a Member State of the EU or in an EEA Member State (Norway, Iceland and Liechtenstein).

1 See Articles 25 and 26
2 Commission decision 2000/518/EC (OJ L 215 of 25.08.2000, p. 1–3)
3 Commission decision 2000/519/EC (OJ L 215 of 25.08.2000, p. 4–6)
4 Commission decision 2000/520/EC (OJ L 215 of 25.08.2000, p. 7–47)
5 See Article 26 (2) of Directive 95/46/EC.
6 The parties agree that if one party is held liable for a violation by the other party of any of the provisions referred to in Clause 3, the second party will indemnify the first party from any cost, charge, damages, expenses or loss incurred by the first party to the extent to which the second party is liable
7 WP12: Transfers of personal data to third countries : Applying Articles 25 and 26 of the EU data protection directive, adopted by the Working Party on 24 July 1998, available in the web site "europa.eu.int/comm/internal_markt/en/media.dataprot/wpdocs/wp12/en" hosted by the European Commission.

Appendix 3 – Model Clauses for Data Export

COMMISSION DECISION

of 15 June 2001

on Standard Contractual Clauses for the transfer of personal data to third countries under Directive 95/46/EC

(notified under document number C(2001) 1539)

(Text with EEA relevance)

(2001/497/EC)

THE COMMISSION OF THE EUROPEAN COMMUNITIES,

Having regard to the Treaty establishing the European Community,

Having regard to Directive 95/46/EC of the European Parliament and of the Council of 24 October 1995 on the protection of individuals with regard to the processing of personal data and on the free movement of such data[1], and in particular Article 26(4) thereof,

Whereas:

1. Pursuant to Directive 95/46/EC, Member States are required to provide that a transfer of personal data to a third country may only take place if the third country in question ensures an adequate level of data protection and the Member States' laws, which comply with the other provisions of the Directive, are respected prior to the transfer.

2. However, Article 26(2) of Directive 95/46/EC provides that Member States may authorise, subject to certain safeguards, a transfer or a set of transfers of personal data to third countries which do not ensure an adequate level of protection. Such safeguards may in particular result from appropriate contractual clauses.

3. Pursuant to Directive 95/46/EC, the level of data protection should be assessed in the light of all the circumstances surrounding

the data transfer operation or set of data transfer operations. The Working Party on Protection of Individuals with regard to the Processing of Personal Data established under that Directive[2] has issued guidelines to aid with the assessment[3].

4. Article 26(2) of Directive 95/46/EC, which provides flexibility for an organisation wishing to transfer data to third countries, and Article 26(4), which provides for standard contractual clauses, are essential for maintaining the necessary flow of personal data between the Community and third countries without unnecessary burdens for economic operators. Those articles are particularly important in view of the fact that the Commission is unlikely to adopt adequacy findings under Article 25(6) for more than a limited number of countries in the short or even medium term.

5. The standard contractual clauses are only one of several possibilities under Directive 95/46/EC, together with Article 25 and Article 26(1) and (2), for lawfully transferring personal data to a third country. It will be easier for organisations to transfer personal data to third countries by incorporating the standard contractual clauses in a contract. The standard contractual clauses relate only to data protection. The data exporter and the data importer are free to include any other clauses on business related issues, such as clauses on mutual assistance in cases of disputes with a data subject or a supervisory authority, which they consider as being pertinent for the contract as long as they do not contradict the standard contractual clauses.

6. This Decision should be without prejudice to national authorisations. Member States may grant in accordance with national provisions implementing Article 26(2) of Directive 95/46/EC. The circumstances of specific transfers may require that data controllers provide different safeguards within the meaning of Article 26(2). In any case, this Decision only has the effect of requiring the Member States not to refuse to recognise as providing adequate safeguards the contractual clauses described in it and does not therefore have any effect on other contractual clauses.

7. The scope of this Decision is limited to establishing that the clauses in the Annex may be used by a controller established in the Community in order to adduce sufficient safeguards within the meaning of Article 26(2) of Directive 95/46/EC. The transfer of personal data to third countries is a processing operation in a Member State, the lawfulness of which is subject to national law. The Data Protection Supervisory Authorities of the Member States, in the exercise of their functions and powers under Article

28 of Directive 95/46/EC, should remain competent to assess whether the Data Exporter has complied with national legislation implementing the provisions of Directive 95/46/EC and, in particular, any specific rules as regards the obligation of providing information under that Directive.

8. This Decision does not cover the transfer of personal data by controllers established in the Community to recipients established outside the territory of the Community who act only as processors. Those transfers do not require the same safeguards because the processor acts exclusively on behalf of the controller. The Commission intends to address that type of transfer in a subsequent decision.

9. It is appropriate to lay down the minimum information that the parties must specify in the contract dealing with the transfer. Member States should retain the power to particularise the information the parties are required to provide. The operation of this Decision should be reviewed in the light of experience.

10. The Commission will also consider in the future whether standard contractual clauses submitted by business organisations or other interested parties offer adequate safeguards in accordance with Directive 95/46/EC.

11. While the parties should be free to agree on the substantive data protection rules to be complied with by the Data Importer, there are certain data protection principles which should apply in any event.

12. Data should be processed and subsequently used or further communicated only for specified purposes and should not be kept longer than necessary.

13. In accordance with Article 12 of Directive 95/46/EC, the Data Subject should have the right of access to all data relating to him and as appropriate to rectification, erasure or blocking of certain data.

14. Further transfers of personal data to another controller established in a third country should be permitted only subject to certain conditions, in particular to ensure that data subjects are given proper information and have the opportunity to object, or in certain cases to withhold their consent.

15. In addition to assessing whether transfers to third countries are in accordance with national law, Supervisory Authorities should play a key role in this contractual mechanism in ensuring that personal data are adequately protected after the transfer. In

specific circumstances, the Supervisory Authorities of the Member States should retain the power to prohibit or suspend a data transfer or a set of transfers based on the standard contractual clauses in those exceptional cases where it is established that a transfer on contractual basis is likely to have a substantial adverse effect on the guarantees providing adequate protection to the data subject.

16. The standard contractual clauses should be enforceable not only by the organisations which are parties to the contract, but also by the Data Subjects, in particular, where the Data Subjects suffer damage as a consequence of a breach of the contract.

17. The governing law of the contract should be the law of the Member State in which the Data Exporter is established, enabling a third-party beneficiary to enforce a contract. Data Subjects should be allowed to be represented by associations or other bodies if they so wish and if authorised by national law.

18. To reduce practical difficulties which Data Subjects could experience when trying to enforce their rights under the standard contractual clauses, the Data Exporter and the Data Importer should be jointly and severally liable for damages resulting from any violation of those provisions which are covered by the third-party beneficiary clause.

19. The Data Subject is entitled to take action and receive compensation from the Data Exporter, the Data Importer or from both for any damage resulting from any act incompatible with the obligations contained in the standard contractual clauses. Both parties may be exempted from that liability if they prove that neither of them was responsible.

20. Joint and several liability does not extend to those provisions not covered by the third-party beneficiary clause and does not need to leave one party paying for the damage resulting from the unlawful processing of the other party. Although mutual indemnification between the parties is not a requirement for the adequacy of the protection for the Data Subjects and may therefore be deleted, it is included in the standard contractual clauses for the sake of clarification and to avoid the need for the parties to negotiate indemnification clauses individually.

21. In the event of a dispute between the Parties and the Data Subject which is not amicably resolved and where the Data Subject invokes the third-party beneficiary clause, the parties agree to provide the Data Subject with the choice between mediation, arbitration or litigation. The extent to which the Data Subject will

have an effective choice will depend on the availability of reliable and recognised systems of mediation and arbitration. Mediation by the Supervisory Authorities of a Member State should be an option where they provide such a service.

22. The Working Party on the Protection of Individuals with regard to the processing of Personal Data established under Article 29 of Directive 95/46/EC has delivered an Opinion on the level of protection provided under the standard contractual clauses annexed to this Decision, which has been taken into account in the preparation of this Decision[4].

23. The measures provided for in this Decision are in accordance with the opinion of the Committee established under Article 31 of Directive 95/46/EC,

HAS ADOPTED THIS DECISION:

Article 1

The standard contractual clauses set out in the Annex are considered as offering adequate safeguards with respect to the protection of the privacy and fundamental rights and freedoms of individuals and as regards the exercise of the corresponding rights as required by Article 26(2) of Directive 95/46/EC.

Article 2

This Decision concerns only the adequacy of protection provided by the standard contractual clauses for the transfer of personal data set out in the Annex. It does not affect the application of other national provisions implementing Directive 95/46/EC that pertain to the processing of personal data within the Member States.

This Decision shall not apply to the transfer of personal data by controllers established in the Community to recipients established outside the territory of the Community who act only as processors.

Article 3

For the purposes of this Decision:

(a) the definitions in Directive 95/46/EC shall apply;

(b) 'special categories of data' means the data referred to in Article 8 of that Directive;

(c) 'supervisory authority' means the authority referred to in Article 28 of that Directive;

(d) 'data exporter' means the controller who transfers the personal data;

(e) 'data importer' means the controller who agrees to receive from the data exporter personal data for further processing in accordance with the terms of this Decision.

Article 4

1. Without prejudice to their powers to take action to ensure compliance with national provisions adopted pursuant to chapters II, III, V and VI of Directive 95/46/EC, the competent authorities in the Member States may exercise their existing powers to prohibit or suspend data flows to third countries in order to protect individuals with regard to the processing of their personal data in cases where:

   (a) it is established that the law to which the data importer is subject imposes upon him requirements to derogate from the relevant data protection rules which go beyond the restrictions necessary in a democratic society as provided for in Article 13 of Directive 95/46/EC where those requirements are likely to have a substantial adverse effect on the guarantees provided by the standard contractual clauses; or

   (b) a competent authority has established that the data importer has not respected the contractual clauses; or

   (c) there is a substantial likelihood that the standard contractual clauses in the Annex are not being or will not be complied with and the continuation of transfer would create an imminent risk of grave harm to the data subjects.

2. The prohibition or suspension pursuant to paragraph 1 shall be lifted as soon as the reasons for the prohibition or suspension no longer exist.

3. When Member States adopt measures pursuant to paragraphs 1 and 2, they shall without delay inform the Commission which will forward the information to the other Member States.

Article 5

The Commission shall evaluate the operation of this Decision on the basis of available information three years after its notification to the Member States. It shall submit a report on the findings to the Committee established under Article 31 of Directive 95/46/EC. It shall include any evidence that could affect the evaluation concerning the adequacy of the standard contractual clauses in the Annex and any evidence that this Decision is being applied in a discriminatory way.

Article 6

This Decision shall apply from 3 September 2001.

Article 7

This Decision is addressed to the Member States.

Done at Brussels,

For the Commission

Frederik BOLKESTEIN

Member of the Commission

ANNEX

Standard Contractual Clauses

for the purposes of Article 26(2) of Directive 95/46/EC for the transfer of personal data to third countries which do not ensure an adequate level of protection

Name of the data exporting organisation...

....

Address...

Tel....................; ***Fax***.......................; ***e-mail:*** ....

Other information needed to identify the organisation...............................

('the data **exporter**')

and

Name of the data exporting organisation...

....

Address...

Tel....................; ***Fax***.......................; ***e-mail:*** ....

Other information needed to identify the organisation...............................

('the data **importer**')

HAVE AGREED on the following contractual clauses ('the **Clauses**') in order to adduce adequate safeguards with respect to the protection of privacy and fundamental rights and freedoms of individuals for the transfer by the Data Exporter to the Data Importer of the personal data specified in Appendix 1.

Clause 1

Definitions

For the purposes of the Clauses:

(a) ***'personal data'***, ***'special categories of data'***, ***'process/processing'***, ***'controller'***, ***'processor'***, ***'Data Subject'*** and ***'Supervisory Authority'*** shall have the same meaning as in Directive 95/46/EC of 24 October 1995 on the protection of individuals with regard to the processing of personal data and on the free movement of such data ('the Directive');

(b) 'the ***Data Exporter***' shall mean the Controller who transfers the Personal Data;

(c) 'the ***Data Importer***' shall mean the Controller who agrees to receive from the Data Exporter personal data for further processing in accordance with the terms of these Clauses and who is not subject to a third country's system ensuring adequate protection.

Clause 2

Details of the transfer

The details of the transfer, and in particular the categories of personal data and the purposes for which they are transferred, are specified in Appendix 1 which forms an integral part of the Clauses.

Clause 3

Third-party beneficiary clause

The Data Subjects can enforce this Clause, Clause 4 (b), (c) and (d), Clause 5 (a), (b), (c) and (e), Clause 6 (1) and (2), and Clauses 7, 9 and 11 as third-party beneficiaries. The parties do not object to the Data Subjects being represented by an association or other bodies if they so wish and if permitted by national law.

Clause 4

Obligations of the data exporter

The Data Exporter agrees and warrants:

(a) that the processing, including the transfer itself, of the personal data by him has been and, up to the moment of the transfer, will continue to be carried out in accordance with all the relevant provisions of the Member State in which the Data Exporter is established (and where applicable has been notified to the relevant Authorities of that State) and does not violate the relevant provisions of that State;

(b) that if the transfer involves special categories of Data the Data Subject has been informed or will be informed before the transfer that his data could be transmitted to a third country not providing adequate protection;

(c) to make available to the Data Subjects upon request a copy of the Clauses; and

(d) to respond in a reasonable time and to the extent reasonably possible to enquiries from the Supervisory Authority on the processing of the relevant Personal Data by the Data Importer and to any enquiries from the Data Subject concerning the processing of his Personal Data by the Data Importer.

Clause 5

Obligations of the data importer

The Data Importer agrees and warrants:

(a) that he has no reason to believe that the legislation applicable to him prevents him from fulfilling his obligations under the contract and that in the event of a change in that legislation which is likely to have a substantial adverse effect on the guarantees provided by the Clauses, he will notify the change to the Data Exporter and to the Supervisory Authority where the Data Exporter is established, in which case the Data Exporter is entitled to suspend the transfer of data and/or terminate the contract;

(b) to process the Personal Data in accordance with the Mandatory Data Protection Principles set out in Appendix 2;

or, if explicitly agreed by the parties by ticking below and subject to compliance with the Mandatory Data Protection Principles set out in Appendix 3, to process in all other respects the data in accordance with:

- the relevant provisions of national law (attached to these Clauses) protecting the fundamental rights and freedoms of natural persons, and in particular their right to privacy with respect to the processing of personal data applicable to a Data Controller in the country in which the Data Exporter is established, or,

- the relevant provisions of any Commission decision under Article 25(6) of Directive 95/46/EC finding that a third country provides adequate protection in certain sectors of activity only, if the Data Importer is based in that third country and is not covered by those provisions, in so far those provisions are of a nature which makes them applicable in the sector of the transfer;

(c) to deal promptly and properly with all reasonable inquiries from the Data Exporter or the Data Subject relating to his processing of the Personal Data subject to the transfer and to cooperate with the competent Supervisory Authority in the course of all its inquiries and abide by the advice of the Supervisory Authority with regard to the processing of the data transferred;

(d) at the request of the Data Exporter to submit its data processing facilities for audit which shall be carried out by the Data Exporter or an inspection body composed of independent members and in possession of the required professional qualifications, selected by the Data Exporter, where applicable, in agreement with the Supervisory Authority;

(e) to make available to the Data Subject upon request a copy of the Clauses and indicate the office which handles complaints.

Clause 6

Liability

1. The Parties agree that a Data Subject who has suffered damage as a result of any violation of the provisions referred to in Clause 3 is entitled to receive compensation from the parties for the damage suffered. The Parties agree that they may be exempted from this liability only if they prove that neither of them is responsible for the violation of those provisions.

2. The Data Exporter and the Data Importer agree that they will be jointly and severally liable for damage to the Data Subject resulting from any violation referred to in paragraph 1. In the event of such a violation, the Data Subject may bring an action before a court against either the Data Exporter or the Data Importer or both.

3. The parties agree that if one party is held liable for a violation referred to in paragraph 1 by the other party, the latter will, to the extent to which it is liable, indemnify the first party for any cost, charge, damages, expenses or loss it has incurred*.

[* paragraph 3 is optional]

Clause 7

Mediation and jurisdiction

1. The parties agree that if there is a dispute between a Data Subject and either party which is not amicably resolved and the Data Subject invokes the third-party beneficiary provision in Clause 3, they accept the decision of the Data Subject:

(a) to refer the dispute to mediation by an independent person or, where applicable, by the Supervisory Authority;

(b) to refer the dispute to the courts in the Member State in which the Data Exporter is established.

2. The Parties agree that by agreement between a Data Subject and the relevant party a dispute can be referred to an arbitration body, if that party is established in a country which has ratified the New York Convention on enforcement of arbitration awards.

3. The parties agree that paragraphs 1 and 2 apply without prejudice to the Data Subject's substantive or procedural rights to seek remedies in accordance with other provisions of national or international law.

Clause 8

Cooperation with supervisory authorities

The parties agree to deposit a copy of this contract with the Supervisory Authority if it so requests or if such deposit is required under national law.

Clause 9

Termination of the clauses

The parties agree that the termination of the Clauses at any time, in any circumstances and for whatever reason does not exempt them from the obligations and/or conditions under the Clauses as regards the processing of the data transferred.

Clause 10

Governing law

The Clauses shall be governed by the law of the Member State in which the Data Exporter is established, namely..

Clause 11

Variation of the contract

The parties undertake not to vary or modify the terms of the Clauses.

On behalf of the Data Exporter:

Name (written out in full):..

Position:..

Address:..

Other information necessary in order for the contract to be binding (if any):...

Signature...

(stamp of organisation)

On behalf of the Data Importer:

Name (written out in full):...

Position:...

Address:...

Other information necessary in order for the contract to be binding (if any):...

Signature...

(stamp of organisation)

APPENDIX 1 to the Standard Contractual Clauses

This Appendix forms part of the Clauses and must be completed and signed by the parties

(*The Member States may complete or specify, according to their national procedures, any additional necessary information to be contained in this Appendix)

Data exporter

The data exporter is (please specify briefly your activities relevant to the transfer):

....

....

....

Data importer

The data importer is (please specify briefly your activities relevant to the transfer):

....

....

....

Data subjects

The personal data transferred concern the following categories of data subjects (please specify):

....

....

....

Purposes of the transfer

The transfer is necessary for the following purposes (please specify):

....

....

....

Categories of data

The personal data transferred fall within the following categories of data (please specify):

....

....

....

Sensitive data (if appropriate)

The personal data transferred fall within the following categories of sensitive data (please specify):

....

....

....

Recipients

The personal data transferred may be disclosed only to the following recipients or categories of recipients (please specify):

....

....

....

Storage limit

The personal data transferred may be stored for no more than (please indicate):.........(months/years)

Data exporter	Data importer
Name..	....
Authorised Signature..	....

APPENDIX 2 to the Standard Contractual Clauses

Mandatory Data Protection Principles referred to in the first paragraph of Clause 5(b).

These data protection principles should be read and interpreted in the light of the provisions (principles and relevant exceptions) of Directive 95/46/EC[5].

They shall apply subject to the mandatory requirements of the national legislation applicable to the Data Importer which do not go beyond what is necessary in a democratic society on the basis of one of the interests listed in Article 13(1) of Directive 95/46/EC, that is, if they constitute a necessary measure to safeguard national security, defence, public security, the prevention, investigation, detection and prosecution of criminal offences or of breaches of ethics for the regulated professions, an important economic or financial interest of the State or the protection of the Data Subject or the rights and freedoms of others.

(1) *Purpose limitation:* data must be processed and subsequently used or further communicated only for the specific purposes in Appendix 1 to the Clauses. Data must not be kept longer than necessary for the purposes for which they are transferred.

(2) *Data quality and proportionality:* data must be accurate and, where necessary, kept up to date. The data must be adequate, relevant and not excessive in relation to the purposes for which they are transferred and further processed.

(3) *Transparency:* data subjects must be provided with information as to the purposes of the processing and the identity of the data controller in the third country, and other information insofar as this is necessary to ensure fair processing, unless such information has already been given by the data exporter.

(4) *Security and confidentiality:* technical and organisational security measures must be taken by the data controller that are appropriate to the risks, such as unauthorised access, presented by the processing. Any person acting under the authority of the data controller, including a processor, must not process the data except on instructions from the controller.

(5) *Rights of access, rectification, erasure and blocking of data:* as provided for in Article 12 of Directive 95/46/EC, the Data Subject must have a right of access to all data relating to him that are processed and, as appropriate, the right to the rectification, erasure or blocking of data the processing of which does not comply with the principles set out in this Appendix, in particular because the data are incomplete or inaccurate. He should also be able to object to the

processing of the data relating to him on compelling legitimate grounds relating to his particular situation.

(6) *Restrictions on onward transfers:* Further transfers of personal data from the Data Importer to another controller established in a third country not providing adequate protection or not covered by a Decision adopted by the Commission pursuant to Article 25(6) of Directive 95/46/EC (onward transfer) may take place only if either:

(a) Data Subjects have, in the case of special categories of data, given their unambiguous consent to the onward transfer or, in other cases, have been given the opportunity to object.

The minimum information to be provided to Data Subjects must contain in a language understandable to them:

- the purposes of the onward transfer,
- the identification of the Data Exporter established in the Community,
- the categories of further recipients of the data and the countries of destination, and
- an explanation that, after the onward transfer, the data may be processed by a controller established in a country where there is not an adequate level of protection of the privacy of individuals;

or

(b) the Data Exporter and the Data Importer agree to the adherence to the Clauses of another controller which thereby becomes a party to the Clauses and assumes the same obligations as the Data Importer.

(7) *Special categories of data:* where data revealing racial or ethnic origin, political opinions, religious or philosophical beliefs or trade union memberships and data concerning health or sex life and data relating to offences, criminal convictions or security measures are processed, additional safeguards should be in place within the meaning of Directive 95/46/EC, in particular, appropriate security measures such as strong encryption for transmission or such as keeping a record of access to sensitive data.

(8) *Direct marketing:* where data are processed for the purposes of direct marketing, effective procedures should exist allowing the data subject at any time to 'opt-out' from having his data used for such purposes.

(9) *Automated individual decisions:* data subjects are entitled not to be subject to a decision which is based solely on automated processing of data, unless other measures are taken to safeguard the individual's legitimate interests as provided for in Article 15(2) of Directive 95/46/EC. Where the purpose of the transfer is the taking of an automated decision as referred to in Article 15 of Directive 95/46/EC, which produces legal effects concerning the individual or significantly affects him and which is based solely on automated processing of data intended to evaluate certain personal aspects relating to him, such as his performance at work, creditworthiness, reliability, conduct, etc., the individual should have the right to know the reasoning for this Decision.

Appendix 3 *to the Standard Contractual Clauses*

Mandatory Data Protection Principles referred to in the second paragraph of Clause 5(b).

(1) *Purpose limitation:* data must be processed and subsequently used or further communicated only for the specific purposes in Appendix 1 to the Clauses. Data must not be kept longer than necessary for the purposes for which they are transferred.

(2) *Rights of access, rectification, erasure and blocking of data:* As provided for in Article 12 of Directive 95/46/EC, the Data Subject must have a right of access to all data relating to him that are processed and, as appropriate, the right to the rectification, erasure or blocking of data the processing of which does not comply with the principles set out in this Appendix, in particular because the data is incomplete or inaccurate. He should also be able to object to the processing of the data relating to him on compelling legitimate grounds relating to his particular situation.

(3) *Restrictions on onward transfers:* Further transfers of personal data from the Data Importer to another controller established in a third country not providing adequate protection or not covered by a Decision adopted by the Commission pursuant to Article 25(6) of Directive 95/46/EC (onward transfer) may take place only if either:

(a) Data subjects have, in the case of if special categories of data, given their unambiguous consent to the onward transfer, or, in other cases, have been given the opportunity to object.

The minimum information to be provided to Data Subjects must contain in a language understandable to them:

- the purposes of the onward transfer,
- the identification of the Data Exporter established in the Community,
- the categories of further recipients of the data and the countries of destination, and,
- an explanation that, after the onward transfer, the data may be processed by a controller established in a country where there is not an adequate level of protection of the privacy of individuals;

or

(b) the Data Exporter and the Data Importer agree to the adherence to the Clauses of another controller which thereby becomes a party to the Clauses and assumes the same obligations as the Data Importer.

1. OJ L 281, 23.11.1995, p. 31.
2. The web address of the Working Party is: http://www.europa.eu.int/comm/internal_market/en/media/dataprot/wpdocs/index.htm.
3. WP 4 (5020/97) 'First orientations on Transfers of Personal Data to Third Countries – Possible Ways Forward in Assessing Adequacy', a discussion document adopted by the Working Party on 26 June 1997;

   WP 7 (5057/97) Working document: 'Judging industry self-regulation: when does it make a meaningful contribution to the level of data protection in a third country?', adopted by the Working Party on 14 January 1998;

   WP 9 (5005/98) Working Document: 'Preliminary views on the use of contractual provisions in the context of transfers of personal data to third countries', adopted by the Working Party on 22 April 1998;

   WP 12: Transfers of personal data to third countries: Applying Articles 25 and 26 of the EU data protection directive, adopted by the Working Party on 24 July 1998, available in the web site 'europa.eu.int/comm/internal_markt/en/media.dataprot/wpdocs/wp12/en' hosted by the European Commission.
4. Opinion No 1/2001 adopted by the Working Party on 26 January 2001 (DG MARKT 5102/00 WP 38), available in the web site 'Europa' hosted by the European Commission.
5. Directive 95/46/EC of the European Parliament and of the Council of 24 of October 1995 on the protection of individuals with regard to the processing of personal data and on the free movement of such data, *Official Journal of the European Communities*, L 281, 23.11.1995, p. 31.

Table of Cases

Table of Statutes

2001	**Health and Social Care Act**	3.6, 25.9
	s 60	3.6, 25.9
	(2)(a)	25.9
	(8)	25.10
	(9)	25.10
	s 61	25.9
	Part 5	25.9
2001	**Social Security Fraud Act**	3.6

Table of Statutory Instruments

Table of European Material

1999	**Consumer Guarantees Directive** (99/44/EC)	14.19
2000	**Electronic Commerce Directive** (2000/31/EC)	15.1, 15.5
	Art 2(f)	15.6
	Art 5	15.8
	Art 6	15.5, 15.8, 15.13
	Art 7	15.6, 15.8
	Art 7(1)	15.13
	Art 8	15.6
	Art 16	15.8
	Art 21(2)	15.10

Index

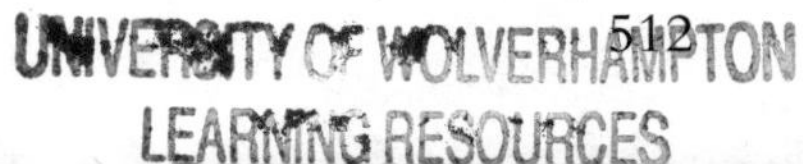